Vivian F~

Advance Praise for

FROM LE

(our parents were left) became a _st_

PETRO-STATE

"Dale Eisler thinks he has written a book about Saskatchewan politics. In fact, he has written a profound meditation on the complex relationship between political leadership, ideology (which only matters to the cognoscenti) and the yearning of voters for representatives who care about what they care about. The 'experts' long thought Saskatchewan was 'on the left,' but left and right don't signify for most people. Those who think Canada is 'progressive,' Alberta 'conservative,' or Quebec 'left wing' just don't get it. Eisler has written a field manual for transformational politics that should be read anywhere insurgents struggle against entrenched and seemingly unassailable electoral machines." —**BRIAN LEE CROWLEY**, Managing Director, Macdonald-Laurier Institute

"As a former journalist and daily columnist in Saskatchewan, Eisler...has written a very clear and important book....It will gain a wide readership and spark a lot of debate." —**KEN RASMUSSEN**, Director of Johnson-Shoyama Graduate School of Public Policy, University of Regina

"In 1944, Saskatchewan unleashed a political revolution that spilled beyond its borders. Today, the counter-revolution. Only Dale Eisler can chronicle the twists and turns that got us here." —**ED GREENSPON**, President and CEO of Public Policy Forum

"Dale shows us how narratives turned into myths, making it perilous for politicians facing new realities to dare make necessary changes and very tempting for populists to keep pandering to old grievances. A very instructive read for all Canadians." —**LOUIS LÉVESQUE**, former Federal Deputy Minister

"Eisler has authored several of Saskatchewan's must-read books about its history and roots—and has contributed another with *From Left to Right*. Here he asks one of the most important questions facing modern democracies. Why have voters—in this case, Saskatchewan voters—set aside long progressive traditions and embraced angry right-wing populism, often against their own economic and social best interests? That history is well told here. What remains to be seen is how permanent the grip of the right on Saskatchewan will be. As Eisler knows well, nothing in politics is permanent." —**BRIAN TOPP**, Max Bell School of Public Policy, McGill University

"Rarely does a hinge in history occur at a single event. But Dale Eisler's book takes the reader through an arc of events, international, national, and provincial, that comprehensively explains a political sea change in Saskatchewan." —**GARY G. MAR**, QC, President and CEO of Canada West Foundation

"Weaving together the interplay of regional, national, and global issues, Dale Eisler has produced an insightful and compelling analysis of Saskatchewan's transformation." —**THE RIGHT HONOURABLE PAUL MARTIN**

"A very important book on the process of political change. It is history looking for answers in all the right places. A must read for Canadians struggling to understand the evolution of political leadership and influence on our lives." —**KEVIN PAGE**, President of the Institute of Fiscal Studies and Democracy, University of Ottawa, and former Parliamentary Budget Officer of Canada

"Dale Eisler just writes one damn good book after another." —**DYLAN JONES**, President, Pacific Economic Development Canada

"Truly excellent studies of Canadian politics and public policy are rare in Canada. Dale Eisler's *From Left to Right* is one of the most insightful and informative examinations of provincial politics in years. The book focuses on the province that is, at once, among the most innovative and often ignored in the country. Eisler pulls off the near impossible, producing an examination that reveals deep understanding of provincial culture and politics, an astute analysis of changing political and economic priorities in a truly misunderstood province, and a non-partisan insider's appreciation for the nuances of public policy and policy-making. Saskatchewan continues to outperform national expectations, despite a profound political transformation that saw the province shift from the birthplace of social democracy to the heartland of small "c" conservatism and libertarianism in Canada. The province is fortunate to have found such talented, well-informed and insightful analyst!" —KEN COATES, Canada Research Chair in Regional Innovation, University of Saskatchewan

"*From Left to Right* provides a unique perspective on how the intersection of global trends, provincial events, national policies and strong personalities have shaped (and indeed reshaped) the evolution of politics in Saskatchewan, and also informs our understanding of political developments elsewhere in Canada." —THE HONOURABLE KEVIN LYNCH, PC, OC, PhD, LLD

"Dale Eisler's conclusions are sobering to those of us who seek balance at Saskatchewan's political centre." —LORNE CALVERT, former premier of Saskatchewan

"Dale Eisler has done it again! In *False Expectations: Politics & Pursuit of the Saskatchewan Myth* he wove economics, politics, policy and history, each often alleged to be dull subjects, into a page turner. In *From Left to Right*, Eisler updates the story, focusing on the dramatic shift in natural governing. The story is important and interesting from the perspective of Saskatchewan, but Eisler's insights present a much broader canvas with lessons for other jurisdictions, other political parties and policy makers everywhere. It pays to study Saskatchewan as the province has often led the rest of Canada on important policies such as Medicare and fiscal consolidation. Eisler's analysis...serves up a master class in politics that should be studied by all. But what sets him apart as a compelling storyteller is his ability to draw out how the residents of the province were feeling about and shaping events. Economists and historians be warned, Eisler has again raised the bar on how to communicate your subjects." —DON DRUMMOND, former senior official Finance Canada, former Chief Economist and SVP at TD Bank, currently Stauffer-Dunning Fellow Queen's University and Adjunct Professor McGill University

From
LEFT *to*
RIGHT

SASKATCHEWAN'S POLITICAL
AND ECONOMIC TRANSFORMATION

DALE EISLER

University of Regina Press

Printed and bound in Canada at Imprimerie Gauvin. The text of this book is printed on 100% post-consumer recycled paper with earth-friendly vegetable-based inks.

Cover art: Ripe ears of wheat bunch isolated on white background by Prostock-studio / AdobeStock
Cover design: Duncan Campbell, University of Regina Press
Interior layout design: John van der Woude, JVDW Designs
Copy editor: Alison Jacques
Proofreader: Alison Strobel
Indexer: Lisa Fedorak

Library and Archives Canada Cataloguing in Publication

Title: From left to right : Saskatchewan's political and economic transformation / Dale Eisler.

Names: Eisler, Dale, author.

Description: Includes bibliographical references and index.

Identifiers: Canadiana (print) 20210393750 | Canadiana (ebook) 20210393831 | ISBN 9780889778641 (softcover) | ISBN 9780889778672 (hardcover) | ISBN 9780889778658 (PDF) | ISBN 9780889778665 (EPUB)

Subjects: LCSH: Right and left (Political science)—Saskatchewan. | LCSH: Saskatchewan—Politics and government—20th century. | LCSH: Saskatchewan—Politics and government—21st century. | LCSH: Saskatchewan—Economic conditions—20th century. | LCSH: Saskatchewan—Economic conditions—21st century.

Classification: LCC FC3528.2 .E47 2022 | DDC 971.24/03—dc23

10 9 8 7 6 5 4 3 2 1

University of Regina Press, University of Regina
Regina, Saskatchewan, Canada, S4S 0A2
tel: (306) 585-4758 fax: (306) 585-4699
web: www.uofrpress.ca

We acknowledge the support of the Canada Council for the Arts for our publishing program. We acknowledge the financial support of the Government of Canada. / Nous reconnaissons l'appui financier du gouvernement du Canada. This publication was made possible with support from Creative Saskatchewan's Book Publishing Production Grant Program.

To Madeline and Genevieve

Contents

Acknowledgements

When it comes to writing of a book of this nature, it is always somewhat risky to identify individuals who you believe deserve to be acknowledged and thanked for their comments, perspectives, and advice. A person does not want to implicate or insinuate others as being in agreement with something that does not necessarily reflect their views. It is especially true in this case. What you are about to read is an interpretation and recitation of moments in time, from both a personal perspective and experience over several decades, that help me understand the political and economic transformation of Saskatchewan. Others will have their own opinions. So the following people are acknowledged not because they agree with my views, as I'm certain they will disagree in whole or in part with this treatment of and perspective on Saskatchewan's political economy. But each was kind enough to view sections or all of the draft manuscript and offer frank advice and criticism, which I took into consideration. So, the final product is on me, not them.

With that caveat, I'd like to thank Dr. Ken Rasmussen and Jim Marshall, my colleagues at the Johnson Shoyama Graduate School of Public Policy, for their thoughts and considerations. Ken is one of Canada's outstanding public policy and public administration minds, a respected author whose clear-eyed understanding of policy and politics is widely recognized across academic and media circles. Jim is a former senior economist with the Saskatchewan Finance Department who combines the unique ability to understand economics, particularly its relationship and application to the design of public policy, and to write about it with skill and clarity.

I also want to thank Dr. Kathy McNutt, Vice-President (Research) at the University of Regina. Kathy read an early draft of the manuscript and encouraged me along the way. Her background as a political scientist allowed her to provide invaluable advice and insights on the contours of Saskatchewan's political history.

I'd also like to thank Karen Clark and Kelly Laycock at the University of Regina Press for their advice and help, along with others at URP, in arriving at a final manuscript. Finally, I want to express my appreciation and thanks to Alison Jacques, whose expert copyediting of the manuscript was superb.

Introduction

It is common to look at periods of history in specific blocks of time, for example, by the decade, or by a specific era defined by a governing party. It is a tidy way to compartmentalize events, as if they have specific beginnings and ends. Of course, they do not. There is no beginning and end to history. It is a continuum, or as historian Arnold Toynbee once said, "History is just one damned thing after another." But the aggregation of exact and often conflicting events can still form discernible patterns because so much of what happens is linked to cause and effect, which allows for an understanding of why things unfolded the way they did.

For Saskatchewan there are several such defining episodes. One was the early years of immigration and settlement, when the social and economic fabric of the province was established. Another era that had a powerful influence on the psychology and politics of the province was the Great Depression and drought of the 1930s. A third era was the post–Second World War years, when Saskatchewan entered a period of relative economic stability and modest growth. Those episodes in the life and development of the province certainly were all interconnected, but each in its own discrete way had specific identifiable characteristics that were unique to its precise era.

I believe another such period can be identified as the years from the late 1960s to the late 1990s. Although not precisely aligned—nothing ever is in the seamless unfolding of history—one can point to two provincial elections, one in 1971 and the other in 1999, as political bookends that provide a framework for understanding the Saskatchewan of today. It is that particular stretch of time when major issues confronting the province were grappled with and addressed. The result was that effectively a new province emerged at the dawn of a new century.

The Saskatchewan of today is far different from the province that was once seen as something of an outlier in terms of taking a different political and economic approach than others. At one time, Saskatchewan had the reputation as a place with a distinctive and somewhat unique collectivist culture. It was evident in the co-operative movement: the rise of farm organizations that sought to gather farmers in groups that enhanced their market power. Politically it became expressed in the Co-operative Commonwealth Federation (CCF), which later became the New Democratic Party (NDP). Together they formed what was seen as the "natural governing party" of the province for decades.

The primary example of that political culture, of course, was Saskatchewan as the pioneer of publicly funded, universally accessible health care. The implementation of a groundbreaking provincial system of Medicare in 1962 became a defining moment for the province in that it, more than anything else, shaped others' perceptions of Saskatchewan. To this day, sixty years later, Medicare remains for some an important symbol that is seen to reflect the province's character. But it is also true that the lingering effect of that moment in time is dissipating as a different Saskatchewan has emerged.

In large part, external perceptions of Saskatchewan as having its own distinctive political culture came from comparisons with Alberta. Both provinces entered Confederation on the same day in 1905. And while each has experienced the rise of prairie populism, their politics and economies have diverged. Alberta's modern economy emerged with the development of its rich oil and gas sector that was fuelled by private investment. Meanwhile, Saskatchewan's economy remained much more agrarian and collectivist in terms of its agricultural institutions. When the latter province's more diverse natural resource sector began to develop, government ownership played a much bigger role than it did in Alberta. For a time, government ownership in Saskatchewan was a significant tool used to exploit resource development, a public policy approach that was seen to reflect the history and political culture of the province. But what the two provinces share is a history shaped by alienation from the centres of political and economic power in central Canada and the prairie populist politics that spawned as a result.

The three-decade period that ended with the turning of the page to a new century had within it powerful and momentous issues at the global, national, and provincial levels that altered the province in profound ways. But what unfolded in those years was not isolated to that period. The events were also a reaction to what took place before, during, and after. So, for the purposes of trying to make sense of history, the period can be identified as having a beginning and an end, even though it didn't then and doesn't today.

There can be little doubt that Saskatchewan has undergone a political and economic transformation in recent decades. It is most evident politically. The Saskatchewan Party, which emerged in the late 1990s as an alternative to challenge the political dominance of the NDP, has become the natural governing party of the province. It has created a hegemony that includes not only complete dominance of rural Saskatchewan but also strength in urban areas exceeding that of the NDP, which has been forced to the margins of electoral politics. The degradation of the NDP to the point that today it is no longer a seriously competitive electoral factor in much of the province, let alone the dominant force it once represented, is the greatest evidence of the province's transformation. In the October 2020 election, the Saskatchewan Party won its fourth consecutive majority term—only the second party in the province's history to achieve such an electoral feat. The other was the CCF, which won five consecutive majorities with Tommy Douglas as its leader.

The rapid rise to power of the Saskatchewan Party in 2007 motivated others to address the political transformation of the province as seen through the lens of political ideology. In his introduction to *Saskatchewan Politics: Crowding the Centre*, a 2009 book he edited and contributed a chapter to, political scientist Howard Leeson "concluded that the reality of the global economy and a dominant ideology of corporatism would serve to create a new Saskatchewan." He added, "In my opinion that process is largely complete." Leeson then noted that "this volume demonstrates not just continued change, but a massive convergence in political attitudes that would have been unthinkable even 20 years ago."[1] Given the political and economic reality of today in Saskatchewan, those words of thirteen years ago seem extraordinarily prophetic.

Two facts make the Saskatchewan Party's emergence truly unique.

One is the scope of its political ascendancy. The margins of victories, including the most recent in 2020, have been so large that the Saskatchewan Party appears immune to what are traditionally considered inevitable electoral trends, namely the growing erosion of public trust the longer a party is in power. With it comes the onset of a "mood for change," which ultimately determines the course of politics and government. And the scale of Saskatchewan Party's victories far exceeds those of the CCF when that party ruled the province for twenty uninterrupted years. This ability of the Saskatchewan Party to resist the normal currents of politics comes in spite of a record as government that by objective measures has been far from flawless, particularly when it comes to fiscal management. The budgetary management record of the Saskatchewan Party government—much of it during a period of strong growth, powered by a commodity "super-cycle" linked to global economic factors that were beyond the influence of a provincial government—has been less than stellar. So too has the Saskatchewan Party government been tainted by allegations of corruption during its time in power. More recently, the wrenching social and economic effects of the COVID-19 pandemic have taken their toll on public sentiment toward the government. But that is a reality shared by governments around the world. At this point there is no definitive evidence that those factors have seriously weakened the Saskatchewan Party's political hold on the province.

The other fact has been the corresponding decline and fall of the NDP, which emerged from the CCF in 1961. The NDP has been relegated to the margins of politics in the very province of its birth. Indeed, the NDP nationally has for generations looked to Saskatchewan as a place from which to take political inspiration, a province where the NDP was long considered the natural governing party and the source of ideas that helped shape the party. Instead, one could argue that Saskatchewan has gone from birthplace of the NDP to its possible deathbed.

The question is, how, and why, did this happen?

In many respects it is one of the more interesting and, I would argue, least explored questions in Canadian politics. It goes beyond just Saskatchewan for the very reason that the province has been the foundation, a kind of centre of gravity, for the NDP nationally. A perennial third, or even fourth, party federally, the NDP could always look to Saskatchewan as its homeland, a kind of lifeboat as it struggled for relevance nationally or in other provinces. Those days appear to have vanished, taking with them a big part of what was Saskatchewan's economic and political identity.

This book is the story that considers the events that not only allowed this to happen but, more precisely, made it happen. As it covers much of my adult life, it contains personal biases and recollections of events, some of which I witnessed and were part of as a journalist and others that I remember as milestones significant enough that they remain touchpoints in memory. As someone who came of age in the late 1960s, the tumultuous events nationally and globally of that time very much shaped my formative ideas about society, the economy, and politics.

What you are about to read does not profess, nor attempt to be, historically comprehensive. That is not the point of the book. Rather, it is to track and understand the political and economic transformation of Saskatchewan through the prism of unfolding events and trends that reshaped public priorities, opinions, and expectations. In the process it attempts to reflect how ideology became an impediment in adapting to change.

Nor is it an academic treatment of the moments in time that it touches upon. It includes personal reflections and interpretations of events and resulting conclusions with which, no doubt, some will disagree. What it seeks to do is put Saskatchewan's political and economic transformation in the context of people and events that I believe have changed Saskatchewan in fundamental and, some might argue, profound ways over time. In so doing, it questions whether the traditional left-right, progressive-conservative ideological perspective has been the proper lens through which to view Saskatchewan's political history and culture. Perhaps there are other, more profound characteristics and currents, many of which have unfolded far beyond the borders of Saskatchewan, that better explain the province.

It is the accumulation of those often distant and forgotten events and factors that have shaped Saskatchewan's political and economic transformation. The question today is whether there remains enough of the old Saskatchewan for the province to reclaim its identity as a place that made a difference for Canada.

The telling of this story begins with a pivotal event in 1982 that marked what was regarded as a stunning election result. To fully appreciate its significance, one needs to understand what came before and after. It is a story that includes the deeply embedded populism in Saskatchewan's sense of itself and the issues that created the conditions for 1982 to happen. What unfolds in terms of other moments that shaped Saskatchewan's transformation begins in 1969.

A Before and After Moment

IT WAS FIFTEEN MINUTES AFTER THE POLLS CLOSED ON Monday, April 26, 1982. New Democratic Party workers and supporters had gathered at their election night headquarters at the Four Seasons Palace in Regina. Premier Allan Blakeney was at home watching the early returns and would join the others shortly for what many thought would be the celebration of a fourth majority NDP government.

One of the first polls to report from the hundreds across the province was from Saskatoon Westmount. A few minutes later came the first poll results from Saskatoon Riversdale. In both cases the Progressive Conservative (PC) candidates were leading. Valorie Preston, an advisor to Blakeney, looked at the numbers from the first two polls. "It's a Conservative landslide," she said. Others watched grimly and said nothing.[1]

The reason that two early polls could trigger the conclusion of the rout about to unfold was simple. Both were considered NDP strongholds. There had never been a poll in Westmount or Riversdale that showed a result anything close to what was on the screen. It was the first tremor of the political earthquake that was under way, and the aftershocks would be felt for decades. It was an election that became a division point in Saskatchewan politics and the economy. So significant would be the consequences of the election that, going forward, understanding Saskatchewan could be segregated into periods of "Before Devine" and "After Devine."

By the end of the night, the ruling NDP had been literally decimated by the Progressive Conservatives. For thirty-one of the previous thirty-eight years, the New Democratic Party, and its forerunner, the Co-operative Common-wealth Federation, was the dominant political force in the province. The CCF had been created in Saskatchewan as what was thought to be the expression of the province's political, social, and economic culture. It had deep political grassroots that were evident in the rural co-op movement, credit unions, the Saskatchewan Wheat Pool, the family farm, and the preservation of rural life. It had an exceptionally strong and seemingly resilient rural base, both on the farms and in small towns. In urban Saskatchewan, the NDP had a formal alliance with the trade union movement and was on good terms with the public service, teachers, and the university community. In practical terms, the Blakeney government owned a record of fiscal responsibility and sound administration. Blakeney himself had developed a national profile as a strong defender of Saskatchewan and western interests, while being a voice for national unity during a perilous time for the nation.[2]

That the NDP could be defeated was certainly not unthinkable. It had happened before, in 1964, when Ross Thatcher ended twenty years of CCF-NDP rule by leading the Liberals to power. But that it could be defeated in such a humiliating landslide was certainly beyond accepted political wisdom.

Going into the election, the eleven-year-old Blakeney government held a comfortable majority of twenty-nine seats in the sixty-four-member Legislative Assembly of Saskatchewan. The final tally for what became known as the "Monday Night Massacre" was PC 55, NDP 9.[3] The Conservatives gained forty seats; the New Democrats lost thirty-five. No one, not even victorious PC leader Grant Devine, had anticipated the scale of the victory. The party's internal polling, done by Allan Gregg of Decima Research, had indicated a possible path to victory for Devine and the PCs. But their optimism was a cautious one because they were going against the vaunted NDP election machine and a well-respected Blakeney. "I expected somewhere between 35 and 40 seats," Devine said at his election night victory party in his constituency of Estevan. "But this is incredible."[4]

Reasons for the result were many and stretched back years. Perhaps the most significant was a national economy that was being ravaged by inflation, high interest rates, and unemployment. It fuelled a mood for change, the kind that inevitably settles into an electorate. The Blakeney government, after three successive majority mandates, was not immune to the tides of politics and a fickle electorate. But a mood for change by itself is not enough; it needs something or someone to make change seem attractive. To ignite the spark of prairie populism that had always lurked as an undercurrent in Saskatchewan politics required someone with a match. That was what Grant Devine brought to the campaign.

He certainly was a "fresh" face who embodied change. In fact, Devine did not even have a seat in the legislature, having first lost as a candidate in the 1978 election and then again as newly installed party leader in a by-election two years later. The by-election had come after one of the party's MLAs resigned to open what was considered a "safe" seat for the new leader. For a brief time, the by-election defeat in 1980 prompted the NDP to bestow on Devine the moniker of "Mr. Invisible." The first time he would take his seat in the legislative chamber would be as premier—the first such political neophyte in Saskatchewan history.

But Devine was young, well educated, and nothing if not optimistic and energetic. He exploited a vein of prairie populism that had remained largely dormant in Saskatchewan politics ever since Tommy Douglas had left for federal politics more than two decades earlier, to lead the newly named New Democratic Party. Using language on the campaign trail that was informal and very much reflective of rural Saskatchewan, Devine urged voters that "there's so much more we can be."[5] His message was less about government and more about instilling in people the confidence that they could do better.

He tapped into deep currents of anxiety during a period of repressive interest rates and a sluggish economy. A core part of Devine's message was that the government had grown out of touch with Saskatchewan people. He argued the NDP measured success by the government's achievements, rather than dealing with the harsh reality that people faced in their daily lives. The PC platform offered mortgage interest relief, cancellation of the provincial gas tax, elimination of the sales tax on clothing and utility bills, a freeze on utility rates, and support for farmers during a period of low wheat prices and high interest rates.[6]

The NDP response to the PC platform was a mixture of alarm and incredulity. As a government, the NDP had consistently delivered balanced budgets, sound administration, a focus on social programming, and a commitment to public ownership of resources through the Crown corporation sector. The NDP campaign had focused more on the instruments of government as a means to appeal to people. The contrast with the Conservatives' campaign could not have been more stark. Blakeney and the NDP accused the PCs of making financially irresponsible commitments. This was during the conservative era of what the NDP considered the failed politics of the Ronald Reagan presidency in the United States, and they painted the Devine Conservatives with a similar brush. "Conservatives won't learn from experience; but they want to experiment with you. They're determined to repeat the mistakes made elsewhere," the NDP platform stated.[7] The styles of the two opposing campaigns, both in messaging and at the level of the leaders, were a study in divergence.

A key behind-the-scenes figure in the Devine campaign was the young pollster Allan Gregg, president of Decima Research in Toronto and Ottawa. With shoulder-length hair and a propensity for leather jackets and jeans, Gregg did not exactly fit the buttoned-down image of the Progressive Conservatives. But he had already established a reputation as a brilliant public opinion research mind and political strategist. Thinking back to those years in Canadian politics, Gregg remembers it as a period when the public lost faith in governments:

The 1981–82 period was a seminal time for politics and indeed the entire socio-political culture of the country. The country was in deep recession and Canadians were more anxious about the future than any time since [the] Second World War. Rather than view the problems they and the country were facing as permanent, however, they saw them as aberrations, caused largely by governments which were either uninterested or unable to solve them. This then was the beginning of what has been a four-decade-long erosion of trust in traditional leaders. It also meant that if you were an incumbent government, you were extremely vulnerable to defeat.[8]

There had been a leading indicator that something politically was afoot in Saskatchewan in the months leading up to the election. Proud of the record of its Crown corporation sector, the Blakeney government had commissioned video ads in support of what it labelled Saskatchewan's "family of Crown corporations." The advocacy advertising touched on the success of the Potash Corporation of Saskatchewan, the Saskatchewan Mining Development Corporation, and SaskOil, among other government-owned enterprises. The so-called Crowns had established a record of profitability, paying annual dividends to the government's general revenue fund. The Crown corporation revenues and assets themselves made up a $1 billion Heritage Fund that had been established in 1978, with resource revenues flowing into the fund and from it into the government's operating expenditure account. The NDP platform had a section that outlined the benefits paid by the Crown corporations to reduce taxes and support programs.[9]

These ads extolling the virtues of the "family of Crown corporations" played on television and often in cinemas before the feature movie began. Funded by government, they were designed as if they were non-partisan. There was no mention of the NDP, only that the message was brought to viewers by the Government of Saskatchewan. But if the political subtext was not explicit, it was obvious; the ads were about the merits and virtues of government ownership in key sectors of Saskatchewan's economy. The issue of activist government as a means of public enterprise was a partisan dividing line that the government-funded ads were trying to exploit.

Invariably, they were greeted with boos and murmurs of discontent from moviegoers. Response to the ads served as a barometer of public opinion that exposed the government's vulnerability. On the campaign trail, Devine said the ads were evidence of how far out of touch the NDP government had become. He would tell his audiences that his interest was in helping "real Saskatchewan families" to meet their mortgage payments and reduce their cost of living, not the family of Crown corporations. With bank mortgage interest rates at an unconscionable level of 18 percent or more at the time, the PC promise to subsidize the rate "down" to 13.25 percent for the first $50,000 of a home mortgage was a powerful incentive for voters struggling to keep their financial heads above water. An NDP campaign slogan was that it delivered a government that was "tried and trusted." The PC response was that the Blakeney government was "rusted and busted."

Initially the NDP thought the defining issue, particularly in rural Saskatchewan, would be the party's defence of the Crow's Nest Pass freight rate—known as the Crow Rate, or simply the Crow—which was considered a cornerstone of the prairie wheat economy. Established in 1897, the Crow Rate guaranteed by federal statute a set rate of half-a-cent per ton-mile for the cost to farmers of shipping their grain by rail to export positions in Thunder Bay or Vancouver. By 1982 it represented a tiny fraction of what it cost railways to transport the grain. At the time, it seemed to be the perfect ballot issue, one that pitted the interests of Saskatchewan farmers against the highly unpopular federal Liberal government of Pierre Trudeau and the railways.

On February 8, 1982, federal transport minister Jean-Luc Pepin had announced plans to abolish the Crow Rate. He appointed University of Manitoba economist Clay Gilson to "identify and enhance" a consensus on a new freight rate to be negotiated by farmers, consumers, railways, and government.[10] The Trudeau government made it clear that farmers would be paying more to ship their grain by rail but in return would get a service guarantee from the railways. The proposal to end the Crow was part of the federal government's sweeping economic development strategy to offset a weakening economy and crushingly high interest rates.

Saskatchewan farm organizations, specifically the Saskatchewan Wheat Pool and the provincial wing of the National Farmers Union (NFU), vehemently opposed the initiative. In the weeks leading up to the Saskatchewan election campaign, the NFU organized a "Crow Train" to Ottawa carrying 200 farmers protesting the so-called Pepin Plan. At an NFU rally in the town of Delisle, 1,300 gathered to express their opposition to the federal government's plan to end the Crow.[11] Completely aligned with the NFU and the then 70,000-member Saskatchewan Wheat Pool in opposition to the federal plan was the NDP government of Saskatchewan. In fact, to demonstrate its defence of the Crow and heighten the political focus on the issue, the Blakeney government called for a "Grain Summit," inviting other western provinces, the Canadian Wheat Board, and the federal government. Not surprisingly, when the federal government refused the invitation and the Wheat Board withdrew, the summit idea died. Instead, the NDP government launched a "Save the Crow" campaign, sending out cabinet ministers around the province to mobilize opposition to the Pepin Plan.[12]

Days before Blakeney called the election for April 26, the NDP government attempted to build momentum in the legislature behind the Crow issue. An emergency debate was held on a motion that read as follows: "This Assembly, recognizing the grave social and economic implications of the federal government's attack on the Crow Rate, rejects the federal government's plan to abolish the statutory Crow Rate and replace it with a law designed to protect the railroads, and affirms the commitment of this legislature to the Crow Rate with its fundamental principles of a fixed rate for producers and equal rates for equal distance."[13] Through the course of the debate, the federal initiative was framed as an issue "that strikes at very heart of Saskatchewan's way of life," with the NDP accusing the Tory Opposition of being weak and secretly supportive of an end to the Crow.

As a tactical move, it was a failure. As a partisan weapon to motivate voters, it fizzled. The problem was that the Devine PCs did not take the bait. At the outset of the campaign they immediately said they agreed with the NDP's position on the Crow, effectively rendering it a non-issue. The NDP had characterized the Crow initiative as a frontal assault on Saskatchewan farmers and the rural economy. Clearly not everyone saw it in such cataclysmic terms. If it truly was that critical an issue, it would have been much more of a defining issue in the campaign. The fact that it was so easily sidelined in terms of what drove the campaign issues and debate was an early signal of a weakening in the farm consensus that for decades had shaped and fuelled Saskatchewan politics. It was a sign too of how the ground was shifting under the NDP as the party attempted to defend "a way of life" created many decades earlier that was becoming less viable in the changing economic circumstances that were beginning to unfold by the early 1980s. Another key factor was Devine's own background. Holding a PhD as an agricultural economist, Devine had been a faculty member of the College of Agriculture at the University of Saskatchewan. Prior to entering politics, he had spent time travelling the province as part of the college's agriculture extension program, which allowed him to develop a profile with many farmers and farm groups as an expert in agriculture, someone who espoused a more market-based approach to the sector.

As political tools, the party platforms themselves were stark contrasts in effective campaign messaging. The NDP platform was thirty-one pages, covered nineteen subject areas, and was detailed, comprehensive, and defensive. It sought to counter the positions taken by the Conservatives and to offer a record of sound government.[14] Clearly, however, the Devine Tories were setting the agenda. The PC platform was two pages. It focused on eight ideas, the key ones being mortgage interest relief, elimination of the gas tax, protecting farm ownership, freezing utility rates, and improving rural health care. The Conservative platform was clear and easy to grasp. The NDP's was diffuse and bureaucratic and, in effect, underscored the notion that the NDP indeed had lost touch with Saskatchewan voters.

The message from Devine in the platform captured what the election was about. It might have been laden with what amounted to empty rhetoric, but

it framed the choice in language that many found evocative. As with all elections, the fundamental question was about the role and nature of government
on offer. "Quite simply, the critical decision in this election is whether we are
to become servants of the government in the next decade or whether we enter
a new era where our government becomes the servant of our people," Devine
said. "I believe that with careful management of our vast resources, and a government determined to serve our people, Saskatchewan will rise to the great-
ness we all know awaits us. There really is so much more we can be."[15] It was
an aspiration that perfectly reflected the founding myth of Saskatchewan as a
"promised land" with a boundless future and limitless possibilities. All politicians, before 1982 and since, have played to the Saskatchewan myth as a way
to motivate voters.

This notion of a greater Saskatchewan—one that can be more prosperous,
more just, and offering greater opportunity—is the fuel of politics. It is certainly not unique, nor is it harmful in and of itself. Far from it. Politics is the
means by which to motivate citizens, to inspire them to act together through
government to achieve their individual and collective aspirational goals. Every
election is about that very thing.

Much of the NDP response was that the PCs were being irresponsible, that
what they were offering was unrealistic and unaffordable. The centrepiece of
the critique was the PC promise to eliminate the provincial tax on gasoline,
which in budget year 1982–83 was expected to generate approximately $138
million in revenue.[16] It perfectly reflected Blakeney's image as a sound admin-
istrator with an eye for detail and responsible fiscal management. The fact that
what the NDP said was true didn't matter. It was a message that essentially
denied the myth, and Blakeney delivered it time and again on the campaign
trail. "So, what's the difference between the Tories and the New Democrats?
Well, I'll tell you what the difference is in one word—responsibility. People
have been asking the Tories, where are you going to get the money? It's pretty
clear the Tories haven't thought much about that," Blakeney warned. "The
hard, cold facts are that there is simply no way you can find a billion dollars
or anything resembling that sort of money except by imposing new taxes or

slashing health care to the very bone."[17] Devine's glib response was he would
not buy Norcanair, a private air service that the Blakeney government had
speculated it might purchase. In a fundamental way the April 26, 1982, election in Saskatchewan was about whether the Saskatchewan myth as defined
by Devine and the Conservatives was legitimate and politically worth pursuing. The NDP said it was not.

So, after eleven years in power, the NDP government was swept aside amid
a mood for change that was seized upon and magnified by Devine and the
Progressive Conservatives. It was a populist response to what had been a government that eventually was perceived to be focused more on itself and the
machinery of government—whether program delivery or public ownership—
than on the day-to-day lives of people. This, at least, was what the political
choice in the election hinged on. Blakeney defended his government's record
as a proxy for the public interest, and Devine spoke more in the language
of the needs of individuals. He contrasted the interests of government with
those of people—"a government as good as its people" was the way Devine
put it on the campaign trail. When the counting was complete, the PCs had
collected 54 percent of the vote to 38 percent for the New Democrats.[18] At
the time, in terms of seats it represented the largest election landslide in
Saskatchewan's history.

One of the most remarkable dimensions of the result was the breadth of
the NDP defeat. Much of the party's rural electoral base, a cornerstone of the
party going back to the early days of Tommy Douglas and the CCF, simply
disappeared that night. One after another, rural ridings considered to be bedrock in the NDP base fell to PC candidates. What made it all the more noteworthy was that agriculture issues were front and centre in the NDP platform.
The problem for the NDP was that the Crow Rate was not on the minds of
voters as the party had planned for and believed.

In rural Saskatchewan, the focus turned to Devine's promise of one-time
loans of up to $350,000 at government-subsidized low interest rates as part of a
pledge to "protect and preserve the family farm." The promise was positioned
as an alternative to the NDP's Land Bank, which was a centrepiece of the NDP

government's agriculture policy. The Land Bank was an instrument wherein the government purchased land from farmers and leased it back to others as a mechanism to help intergenerational transfer of land. What resulted was that the Land Bank accumulated a million acres and made government the largest farmland owner in the province. The dramatic electoral outcome on the farms and in small towns was the first clear evidence of the NDP's vulnerability that had been growing for years.

The stage had been set during the 1970s. It was a decade that would come to be identified as an era of big government in Saskatchewan. In a period of crippling interest rates, the political landscape was ripe for a spasm of prairie populism. It erupted the night of April 26, 1982.

To understand the dynamics and consequences of that time, a few framing questions need to be asked and answered. How did it come to this in Saskatchewan? What set the stage for the populist emergence of the Devine government? How significant was the Monday Night Massacre in terms of the transformation of Saskatchewan and its politics? Was it inconsistent with the fundamental nature of Saskatchewan society and opinion? Did it represent a turning point in Saskatchewan political and economic history? Or was it a point-in-time aberration, merely a reflection of a particular convergence of transitory events and circumstance? To answer those questions and understand the Saskatchewan of today, the moment has to be put in the context of what came before, and after, the Monday Night Massacre. No single election outcome can be considered in isolation, but instead must be seen as a part of multiple evolving circumstances.

It begins with understanding the psychology of the province's people, the society they have created, and how it has changed such that Saskatchewan in 2022 is a much different place than it once was.

CHAPTER 1

Onward Christian Soldiers

I T IS A DELICATE SUBJECT, AND FOR GOOD REASON. THE LABEL at times can be applied to virtually any political party or movement, and often is. It is seen to reflect the so-called popular will, the *vox populi*, which in a democracy is the pathway to power.

Not limited by ideology, it can be the force for progressive or conservative movements, a source of unity or division—sometimes both at the same time. At its core it is fuelled by emotions, both negative and positive. The sentiments can range from anger and alienation to compassion and empathy for the less fortunate; from disenchantment, distrust, and nativism to social and economic justice, equality, and charity. In all its expressions, it purports to represent the "average" or "common" people, who unite against a shared adversary seen as the "elites." It seeks more power for the people and less power for the established economic and political classes.

It's called populism.

The term itself elicits different reactions. Depending on its application it can be dangerous and divisive, an odious force that leads to illiberal authoritarianism, the very antithesis of the democracy that it purports to represent. Canadians have witnessed in recent times an example in real time, next door in the United States, of where an aberrant strain of populism can lead. The rise of Donald Trump, his appeal to racists, his overt efforts to divide Americans, undermine the institutions of democracy, and sow hatred, have been chilling to watch.

At the core of populism is opposition to an established and privileged power structure that reflects dominant ideas and values. Populism of the left sees the "people" in socioeconomic terms as a working class exploited by the wealthy elite. Right-wing populism often sees the "people" in ethnonational terms where ethnicity determines membership in the group. In both cases, the assumed unity of the group creates antagonistic relationships with those seen as wielding power.[1]

Saskatchewan has at times been fertile ground for populism. Indeed, populism has been a recurring impulse through periods of the province's history, shaping the province politically and economically, and at other times emerging only for brief episodes around specific issues or events. The good news is that populism has, for the most part, been a positive force in the public life of the province. The Saskatchewan variant has been largely contained to charismatic leadership that used the power of populism with measured discretion. In those cases, populist appeal has targeted what are considered to be the core communitarian values of Saskatchewan society, including hard work, individual initiative, perseverance, and commitment to community. In that context, populism can be a useful lens through which to understand Saskatchewan society and its politics.

As history demonstrates, and as many have documented, populism was woven into the fabric of Saskatchewan before it was even a province. It was reflected in a deeply felt sense of economic vulnerability and grievance, in large measure a backlash against national policy that engineered a tariff-protected economy to the benefit of the Ontario and Quebec manufacturing sectors at the expense of settlers to the Prairies.

Small farmers believed they were at the mercy of distant, powerful economic and political forces—large grain companies, the railways, banks, and a federal government captive of central Canadian interests. The alienation they felt created a grassroots sense of the need to organize into collectives that would give them more market power and political clout. This was expressed in many economic forms, including the Territorial Grain Growers' Association, the Saskatchewan Co-operative Elevator Company, Saskatchewan Co-operative Wheat Producers, and ultimately the Saskatchewan Wheat Pool, or Sask Pool. Politically it was voiced for a time in the Progressive Party and later in the CCF. Populism became the vehicle to achieve economic, social, and political objectives.

As historian Richard Allen noted, "The agrarian revolt in the West, like its predecessors and successors, had obvious political, social and economic roots. Politically, farmers had been underrepresented in Parliament. The West had been the stepping stone of nation-building, and stood on the sidelines of the federal power structure."[2] So, to understand the nature and cycles of politics in Saskatchewan, it is impossible to ignore the power of populism that moulded the province. While the Saskatchewan of today is far different from what it was a century or even fifty years ago, it still carries the imprint of those days. Recognizing the role of prairie populism, rooted in an agrarian society as a motivating force for political purposes, is key to understanding the evolution of the province's values, economy, and political culture.

Trying to actually define populism is not easy. As a fuel for revolutions, some argue that because it can be applied so broadly to the rise of fascism, communism, and other forms of authoritarianism the label itself has been rendered meaningless. The imprecision of populism's meaning, and the scope of its application in contemporary times, was aptly addressed in 2016 in the pages of the *Economist*:

Donald Trump, the populist American president-elect, wants to deport undocumented immigrants. Podemos, the populist Spanish party, wants to give immigrants voting rights. Geert Wilders, the populist Dutch politician, wants to eliminate hate-speech laws. Jaroslaw Kaczynski, the populist Polish politician, pushed for a law making it illegal to use the phrase "Polish death camps." Evo Morales, Bolivia's populist president, has expanded indigenous farmers' rights to grow coca. Rodrigo Duterte, the Philippines' populist president, has ordered his police to execute suspected drug dealers. Populists may be militarists, pacifists, admirers of Che Guevara or of Ayn Rand; they may be tree-hugging pipeline opponents or drill-baby-drill climate-change deniers. What makes them all "populists," and does the word actually mean anything?[3]

In his essay "Why Populism," Rogers Brubaker, a sociologist at the University of California, Los Angeles, calls the term a "contested concept." It can mean almost anything to anyone and is found on the left and the right and sometimes as part of hybrid movements. "They may be economically statist, protectionist, welfarist, and/or redistributionist, but they may also be neoliberal," says Brubaker, who points to what has occurred in Latin America and more recently in parts of Europe.[4] "If populism is everywhere—as it appears to be in broad and inclusive accounts that focus on the claim to speak in the name of the people—then it is nowhere in particular."[5]

Brubaker argues that the term "the people" is itself evidence of the ambiguity of populism.

It can refer to the common or ordinary people, and to culturally or ethnically distinct people, the people as nation or ethnos. To speak in the name of the "little people" against "those on top" would seem to imply a politics of redistribution. To speak in the name of the sovereign people against ruling elites would seem to imply a politics of re-democratization. And to speak in the name of a bounded and distinct people against threatening outside groups or forces would seem to imply a politics of cultural or ethnic nationalism. The problem of disparateness thus remains: what could be gained by subsuming these very different forms of politics under the label "populism"?[6]

Another, more contemporary view of populism is expressed by British journalist David Goodhart. In his book *The Road to Somewhere: The Populist*

Revolt and the Future of Politics, Goodhart sees the politics of culture and identity challenging the traditional left-right axis of politics.[7] His thesis is that British politics is split into what he terms "two rival values blocks." The political division is between two groups he terms the "anywheres" and the "somewheres." Goodhart says one reason for the rise of populism in current times is that the more educated, mobile, and often political class—the any-wheres—lacks the group attachment to place of the somewheres, who are more rooted, value group attachments, place, and stability, and are uneasy with rapid change. Goodhart's provocative view on the rise of populism is based in part on the belief that mass immigration has eroded the social cohe-sion fashioned by the welfare state. "I blame the masses, but not in the way the London School of Economics left-wing professors blame the masses," he says. "I blame mass immigration and mass higher education for the current instability in politics."[8]

Back in the mid-1980s—when he was travelling across western Canada, particularly Alberta and Saskatchewan, as putative leader of what would become the upstart western Canada–based Reform Party—Preston Manning saw himself as leader of a nascent populist movement. He came by his ambi-tions honestly, as Manning's political beliefs were very much shaped by Alberta populism. He was the son of former Alberta premier Ernest Manning, who had succeeded William Aberhart, the founder of the Alberta Social Credit Party, a populist movement spawned during the economic calamity of the 1930s. When the younger Manning spoke to the media as part of his grass-roots organizational efforts, he would often refer to "the common sense of the common people."[9] It is probably as good a description of populism as any, at least in a benignly positive way.

The role of populism in the politics of Saskatchewan, at least as a clearly discernible factor, has varied significantly through the years. Its zenith was during the early decades of the province when the activist farm movement was the dominant force in public life. Indeed, it found its most resonant political expression in the 1930s with the formation of the CCF, a political party that, like the Social Credit in Alberta, grew from rural populism in Saskatchewan during the Great Depression. It reflected the grim economic reality of that era, when people felt both vulnerable and powerless. Other than brief outbreaks in recent decades, populism has been a more latent force lurking below the surface of a province that often sees itself as trying to overcome odds stacked against itself. It's a psychology deeply embedded in Saskatchewan's self-identity and remains fertile ground for politicians to exploit.

The roots of the alienation that spawns populism was well described by Columbia University professor Robert Lynd in the introduction to *Agrarian Socialism*, Seymour Martin Lipset's seminal work on the rise of the CCF in Saskatchewan:

> Farmers, especially those in the one-crop economy of the Great Plains, embody in an extreme form the modern anachronism of the independent enterpriser bereft of control over his market, a stranger in the ruling institutional world of organized urban big business. And yet the farmer retains, better than the urban man, sources of resistance to the mass tendency: he produces a product that men indubitably need, and he accordingly respects his crop, the land that produces it, and his own labor. He and his family, especially in regions remote from large cities, know the value of cooperative social living, and they are relatively less distracted by the impersonal substitute activities that accompany competitive urban getting and spending. Here is a stance from which a man may still believe in the democratic right to stand and fight.[10]

The power of populism as a vehicle for ideology is what makes it such a constant part of all politics. Aside from the unifying force of alienation, in a democracy the ability of an individual or party to define what is considered the general will can provide the legitimacy necessary to attain power and implement what is considered a "populist" agenda. But given that anger is often a subset of alienation, as a motivational ingredient in politics, populism can be a force for good or ill. It depends on the objectives of the motivators. Politicians are the ones who recognize the opportunity to mobilize voters in certain ways and use that knowledge to capitalize on the prevailing instincts of voters to achieve their partisan ends. It is why public opinion research is such an important tool for political parties. Before you can mobilize people, you first need to know the issues, ideas, and incentives that will engage them in the political process.

When considered in this sense—namely, when people feel left out or have lost control of their destiny, in economic and/or cultural terms—the power of populism in the hands of politicians can be immense. It can become even more potent when it is blended with religion. The language of religious faith as part of a populist message, sometimes imbued with biblical references, often adds to its persuasive power for people who feel victimized. For populism to ignite, two things are needed: something or someone for people to focus their anger and alienation on, and somebody who articulates their emotions in compelling and emotional language.

One way to understand the power of populism is through the lens of agrarian politics. In that context we can see how the rise of collective impulses and socialist parties took root on the farms of the Great Plains of North America, first in the United States and later in Canada, and specifically Saskatchewan. Many find it confounding that socialism would emerge among those who were considered conservative, fiercely independent, private-land-owning farmers. It is a subject that Lipset identifies in his study on the rise of the CCF in Saskatchewan. He attributes it to the economic reality they faced. "It is significant that the first electorally successful North American socialist movement, the Co-operative Commonwealth Federation, came to power in the almost completely rural province of Saskatchewan in 1944," Lipset writes. "It is impossible to understand why an avowedly socialist party should have won a majority vote among supposedly conservative farmers unless one recognizes how often the social and economic position of the American wheat-belt farmers, in the U.S. and Canada, has made him the American radical."[11]

Some have argued that use of the term "socialism" in the context of the Saskatchewan CCF does not accurately reflect the reality of those days, suggesting the label was always an uncomfortable fit in the province. The late

University of Saskatchewan political scientist Duff Spafford noted the contradiction at the heart of the CCF: "The Saskatchewan CCF originally declared
itself to be socialist, but quickly found the socialist label to be a political liability and played it down. Its original program called for the nationalization
of all natural resources, which came to include land as a by-product of 'use-
lease' land tenure for farmers. The land tenure policy was dropped when it too
proved to be a liability, and support for the traditional family farm became
the party's policy."[12]

In Saskatchewan, the figure who became the clearest example of prairie
populism was T.C. (Tommy) Douglas, the former CCF premier. He was a prairie populist with the personal attributes necessary to lead an agrarian-based
democratic-socialist movement and party. Douglas was a Baptist minister, an
inspirational orator who frequently spoke in religious terms that "common"
people could relate to and appreciate. His political message was rooted in the
social gospel, a Protestant movement that applied Christian ethics to address
social and economic issues—in other words, the belief that politics guided
by Christianity can change people and societies, creating what Douglas often
referred to as the "new Jerusalem." Shortly before he died in 1986, Douglas
expressed his lifelong belief in the power of religion to play an incrementally
progressive role in creating a better society. "You're never going to step out
of the front door into the kingdom of God," he said. "What you're going to
do is slowly and painfully change society until it has more of the values that
emanate from the teachings of Jesus or from other great religious leaders."[13]

It was little wonder that Douglas's social gospel message would resonate
in Saskatchewan, a province with deep religious roots and church influences.
As an immigrant society, the people who came, especially those from eastern
Europe, often were fleeing religious persecution. They settled in communities
that frequently had a primary, if not exclusive, religious denomination, where
churches were the focal point for the community and its people. Even the
Saskatchewan Wheat Pool was described as "a religious, social, educational,
political and commercial organization all in one, and in the truest and deep-
est meaning of these several terms."[14]

In subsequent years, Saskatchewan has undoubtedly become more secular. But the importance and influence of religion in modern-day Saskatchewan society is often underestimated, particularly by those who do not adhere to a specific religion or are atheist. In 2011, when Statistics Canada surveyed religious beliefs in the province, it found that 72 percent of respondents identified themselves as Christian, with the next largest group associating themselves with Indigenous spirituality. Meanwhile, 24 percent had no religious affiliation.[15] Among those who attached themselves to a specific religion, the number who were regular churchgoers was much smaller. But the less religious, in terms of church attendance, does not mean that faith-based values are not important to their personal priorities, which often get expressed politically. The leader who expresses political aspirations in a manner aligned with ethics that derive from what are often common religious roots can become recognized as a populist figure.

For Douglas, becoming politically active was a logical extension of his religious beliefs. In the early years of the 1930s, as a Baptist Church minister in Weyburn, Douglas witnessed the effects of the Depression on his congregation and beyond. "I felt that the church could not divorce itself from social and economic, and consequently political involvement, and that just as I ought to be active in relief, in helping the unemployed, helping distribute milk or active in any mental health association, so I ought to belong to a political party and try to do something about these economic conditions," Douglas said in 1932.[16]

The social gospel as a political force can be traced to Walter Rauschenbusch, an American Christian theologian and Baptist pastor who died in 1918. For Rauschenbusch, the social gospel was the path to a better world. He wrote, "The influence of Christianity in taming selfishness and stimulating the sympathetic affections, in creating a resolute sense of duty, a staunch love of liberty and independence, an irrepressible hunger for justice and a belief in the rights of the poor, has been so subtle and penetrating that no one can possibly trace its effects....And yet human society has not been reconstituted in accordance with the principles of Jesus Christ."[17] Taking inspiration from the

social gospel and the likes of Rauschenbusch, Douglas was an agrarian populist who, during his more than seventeen years as premier of a CCF government, appealed in evocative terms to the alienation that farm people felt. As
Lipset noted in his writings on the rise of the CCF to power in Saskatchewan,
the primary ingredient that led to the party's election and twenty-year period
in government was its grassroots, populist, and protest nature.

Douglas's brand of religious populism was shaped in part by his experience while studying at the University of Chicago during the depths of the
Depression. It was there that he became familiar with the writings and teachings of Protestant theologian Reinhold Niebuhr, who professed a more pragmatic and less certain social gospel theology than Rauschenbusch.[18] Douglas
embraced Niebuhr's pragmatism, termed by many as Christian realism, as
part of his political outlook. Witnessing the widespread unemployment in
Chicago, and its toll of suffering, deeply affected Douglas.

> As I went among them (the unemployed), this was the first time that I
> began to feel a challenge to the whole way of life which I was a part. Here I
> was working with these people all day and then get up early the next morn-
> ing to go and worship in the beautiful cathedral built by the Rockefeller
> money on the Chicago campus. And here was a $60 million cathedral and
> I was going out all day handing out a dime, if I had one, to some fellow so
> he could get something to eat. And I thought, there is something wrong
> here. Here is the richest country in the world and 20 million people walk-
> ing the streets. People starving, when up in Canada, where I come from,
> we can't get rid of wheat. And in British Columbia farms can't get rid of
> their apples. There is something crazy about a system like this, it's not only
> economic, it's insane and unChristian. That made me think first of all.[19]

A splendid example of Douglas's agrarian populist style was a story entitled "The Cream Separator" that he used to enthrall and motivate his audiences. He told it throughout his political career, including his time as leader
of the national NDP, but it was most effective in the small towns and farm

homes of rural Saskatchewan. He introduced it by saying that when he visited farm families, often everyone would be busy doing chores and he would offer to help. But, not being a farmer, all they would trust him to do was to turn the handle on the cream separator.

"I got to be pretty good at it," Douglas would say.

I got to the place where I could tell you how many verses of "Onward Christian Soldiers" it takes to put a pan of milk through the separator. As I was turning the handle I could see the cream coming out of one spout and milk out of the other. One day it finally penetrated my thick Scot's head. This cream separator is exactly like our economic system.

Here are the primary producers, the farmers, the fishermen and the loggers, they're pouring in the milk. And here are the workers, whether they work on the railroad, or down in the mines, sail ships, work in a store, or bank, teach school or work in a hospital, they're the people whose services make the economy go round, and they're turning the handle. Primary producers put in the milk, people who work with their hands and brains turn the handle.

And there's another fellow, who owns the cream separator and he's sitting on a stool with the cream separator spout in his mouth. The primary producer and the worker they take turns on the skim milk spout. They don't like skim milk, nobody likes skim milk, and they blame it on each other. The worker says if those farmers and fishermen work a little harder, I wouldn't be drinking the skim milk. And the fishermen and farmers say if those workers didn't demand a 40-hour week and such high wages, I wouldn't have to live on this skim milk. But you know they're both wrong. The farmers and the fishermen produce so much that we don't know what to do with it. We've got surpluses of food and the workers produce so well that today nearly a half million of them are unemployed.

Douglas would end his story by talking about the cream going to the "corporate elite." The problem, he said, was in who controls the cream separator.

"What the democratic socialist party has been saying for a long time is that the time has come in this land of ours for the worker and the primary producer to get their hands on the regulator of the machine so that it begins to produce homogenized milk, in which everyone will get a little cream."[20]

In retelling the story today, it might sound rather facile and simplistic. But in populist terms, that was what made it so effective. For the populist, speaking in the language of the people was the way to connect at a human level. Douglas understood it was something that "ordinary" farm folk could relate to; it reflected their lives and experiences. It appealed to the underdog identity of Saskatchewan, where people often believed the odds were stacked against them and they were victims of an unjust system that ignored their needs.

Beyond the power of his populist oratory, there was little doubt that Douglas's use of religious imagery inspired and motivated voters. It was evident to the very end of his political career. In 1971 at the federal NDP leadership convention to choose his successor, Douglas ended his final speech as leader by harking back to the very early days of the CCF, in the darkest days of the Depression. "May we be the children of that brighter and better day, which even now is beginning to dawn," he said. "May we not impede, but rather co-operate with those spiritual forces which we believe are impelling the world upwards and onward. For our supreme task is to make our dreams come true, to transform our city into the Holy City and to make this land in reality, God's own country."[21]

True to its inherent ambiguity, populism in Saskatchewan politics has presented itself in different forms. While Douglas is held out as the standard against which others are measured, there is a dark side to Saskatchewan populism. The starkest example came in the late 1920s when the Ku Klux Klan briefly rose to prominence in the province, fuelled by nativism, bigotry, and xenophobia.

An imported version of the U.S. Klan, the Saskatchewan form was a grassroots backlash against Roman Catholics and non-English-speaking immigrants, whether Ukrainian, German, or Polish, who had immigrated to the province in increasing numbers as part of farm settlement. The Klan's objective was to preserve the British character of the province. In his book *Keeping Canada British: The Ku Klux Klan in 1920s Saskatchewan*, James Pitsula says the Klan found fertile ground in Saskatchewan. Pitsula dismisses the idea of the hatred and prejudice espoused by the Klan as being an aberration; rather, he argues it was part of a mainstream British nationalism that was "a somewhat more extreme version of what most people thought."[22] The Klan emerged as an important political factor in a 1928 by-election that the Liberals lost to the Conservatives. At its height, some claimed the Klan had fifty thousand members in the province, making Saskatchewan at the time a hotbed for the Klan in Canada.

One voice that confronted the rise of the Klan and the bigotry it espoused was that of Jimmy Gardiner. As Liberal premier of the province first from 1926 to 1929 and then again briefly from 1934 to 1935, followed by twenty-two years as a powerful cabinet minister in the federal Liberal government, Gardiner was a politician who deeply understood the power of populism in Saskatchewan politics. A pugnacious partisan, he lacked the common-man touch or oratorical flourish of Douglas. But what made Gardiner unique was his effort to manage the populist nature of Saskatchewan politics by using a take-no-prisoners approach. He blended his unwavering commitment to the Liberal Party, both provincially and federally, with his understanding of the fundamental nature of Saskatchewan. The force of his personality and beliefs made him one of the most influential figures in Saskatchewan's political history, someone his biographers have called "stubborn, resilient, relentless and combative."[23] In some ways it made Gardiner a larger-than-life figure, with a force of personality that created loyalty among his followers.

An impoverished background, coupled with a doctrinaire education in religion and liberalism at Manitoba College, a Presbyterian school in Winnipeg, gave Gardiner a deep and powerful belief in individual initiative and small but focused government. At the same time, his own hardscrabble upbringing instilled in him a fervent sense of the power of determination, the importance of hard work, and an intensely competitive spirit. Those are the very attributes at the core of the Saskatchewan psyche. There was also a religious dimension to Gardiner's fervour. "I like to think as far as possible God speaks to me as He spoke to Moses," Gardiner once told the audience at a church event.[24]

While not one to invoke the social gospel, Gardiner was motivated by the challenges that rural Saskatchewan farm families experienced, particularly during his long tenure as federal minister of agriculture. In policy terms, his greatest achievement as agriculture minister—a position he held from 1935 to 1957—was as the driving force behind the establishment of the Prairie Farm Rehabilitation Administration (PFRA). Based in Regina, the PFRA oversaw the recovery of rural Saskatchewan after the devastation of the drought and Depression of the 1930s. The PFRA was eventually disbanded in 2011 as part of federal cutbacks.

But perhaps more important was Gardiner's unwavering voice against the racist strain of populism that emerged in the late 1920s. Arguably his finest moment as premier was in 1928 when, with an election approaching, the Ku Klux Klan emerged in Saskatchewan. Gardiner saw the Klan as a racist money-making racket from the United States that stirred the nativist emotions of English-speaking residents and recruited heavily from the Orange Lodge, the anti-Catholic British and Protestant fraternal organization with branches across Saskatchewan. In a 1927 letter to Prime Minister Mackenzie King, Gardiner warned of the Klan's emergence in the province. He noted that "all the leading Orange Conservatives are spreading propaganda to the effect that the Catholic Church is controlling activities of both the federal and provincial governments....I do not know that this propaganda will do us any harm politically...as it seems to be rallying to its cause those who have been very rabid against us and at the same time the bitterness with which they attack the Roman Catholic Church will, in all probability, compel a great many to vote Liberal who would not do so other wise."[25]

In typical fashion, Gardiner was relentless in his attack on the Klan and its activities. It culminated in June 1928 when he agreed to debate Klan leader J.H. Hawkins in the town of Balcarres.[26] Before a packed community hall, including many Klan supporters, Gardiner did not hold back in his denunciation of the organization. "If the Ku Klux Klan is allowed to run its course, it will do to Canada what it has done to the United States. Now is the time to strike them, and I'm proud to do it," he said. "Today a time of blackflies from another country presume to trespass our holy ground by raising their filthy hands to hold the Holy Bible and the Union Jack. It's necessary for the people of this province to repudiate the Ku Klux Klan."[27] A few months later in 1929, James Anderson became premier when Gardiner and the provincial Liberals were defeated by an alliance of Conservatives and Progressives. The populist discontent and anger stirred by the KKK and Gardiner's intent opposition to the anti-immigrant sentiment was widely considered a factor in his defeat.[28]

A third figure who understood the power of populism and exploited it to mobilize not only Saskatchewan people but Canadians was John Diefenbaker. Throughout his career, Diefenbaker carried with him the persona of an outsider who reflected his Prairie roots. As a provincial politician and leader of the provincial Conservative Party, Diefenbaker had little success. But there was no mistaking his populist instincts. In the 1938 provincial election, Diefenbaker advocated for a publicly funded system of universal health care. In its platform the Conservative Party called for the establishment of "state medicine, and hospitalization" and pledged to "fully investigate the various forms thereof and to bring in legislation in accordance with the result of such investigation."[29]

Even as prime minister, "Dief" was an anti-establishment figure, never fully accepted by the federal Progressive Conservative Party business-class elites of Ontario. It was what endeared him to the Saskatchewan people. They saw Dief as someone who shared their sense of alienation from those at the centre of power in far-off Ottawa and the power brokers of central Canada. In many ways, Diefenbaker personified how populism was unbounded by ideology and defined more by whether one was considered part of the ruling elite. Although conservative and avowedly committed to free enterprise, Diefenbaker had a successful career in federal politics, winning the support of people in Saskatchewan who voted for the CCF-NDP in provincial elections.

Perhaps the most definitive examination of Diefenbaker's rise to power and time in office is Peter C. Newman's book *Renegade in Power: The Diefenbaker*

Years. Newman writes of Diefenbaker that "he reached out and stirred in the voters a feeling of trust. His magnificent campaigns turned the nation into one vast constituency." Ultimately, though, Diefenbaker, who overshadowed his party, became divisive rather than a unifying figure in the party. According to Newman, "He could not rid himself of the distrust he felt for the nation's economic, social and cultural establishment, and he never even tried to comprehend the aspirations of contemporary French Canada."[30] It is an observation that, aside from exposing a character flaw in Diefenbaker, reflects a truth about prairie populism that explains it as a regional phenomenon that is not transferable to the application of federal power.

In his eulogy at Diefenbaker's funeral, then prime minister Joe Clark, a fellow westerner and political outsider, spoke of Diefenbaker in terms of his ability to connect with the common man or woman. "He was the great populist of Canadian politics," Clark said. "John Diefenbaker opened the politics of our country to those to whom it had always been closed. He gave politics a lively reality to those to whom it had seemed remote. He brought daylight to a process too long obscured in shadow and mystery."[31] Perhaps Diefenbaker's greatest achievement was the 1960 Canadian Bill of Rights, which sought to defend the rights, privileges, and civil liberties of all Canadians, regardless of their ethnic background.[32]

The power of populism went beyond partisan politics. Aaron Sapiro was not a politician, at least not in the formal sense. Nor was he even Canadian. But for a brief period in the 1920s this California lawyer was a powerful populist voice helping to shape the political culture and identity of Saskatchewan. He was invited to the province in 1923 to conduct a speaking tour at a particularly turbulent time in farm politics. The federal government had ended the first incarnation of the Wheat Board in 1920, which had emerged from government control of wheat during the First World War. The end of the Wheat Board, which was popular with farmers, created an angry backlash but no consensus as to the way forward. Sapiro's work helping to organize American wheat farmers and California citrus fruit growers into marketing pools was well known in western Canada.

Sapiro quickly became recognized as a charismatic and compelling figure. His 1923 speaking tour on the merits of pooling by farmers rapidly took on the characteristics of a religious crusade. Barnstorming the province, he attracted overflow crowds who jammed arenas, theatres, and even fairgrounds to what seemed the equivalent of religious tent-revival gatherings. Sapiro was described as "perhaps the most compelling stump orator to ever reach the West" and compared to "a meteor flaring through the sky."[33] Ian MacPherson wrote, "He built on the accumulated frustrations of the previous few years and a tradition of agrarian radicalism that reached back into the 1880s. He made another tour in 1924, a tour that was even more successful than the first. For years afterward, the Sapiro tours were remembered with awe and affection."[34] Pat Waldron, a journalist who covered Sapiro at the time, was captivated by what he saw and heard from the American advocate for pooling. "He was the most inspiring, invigorating speaker I've ever heard," Waldron recalled. "He moved, he played on that audience like an artist. He controlled their emotions, they yelled and cheered. He could do anything with them. I never saw anything to equal what Sapiro could do on a platform."[35]

Sapiro's message was one of farmers taking control of their destiny and not being divided into differing organizations, all struggling for control. He had developed an approach, known as the California Method, that had successfully organized farm producers in his home state. "Leaders were not created by God to exploit you. They were created, if for anything, either to bring you the light or get out of your way to let you see the light," Sapiro told his audiences.

This is a problem where the Saskatchewan business man, the Saskatchewan banker, the Saskatchewan press, the Saskatchewan minister, the Saskatchewan lawyer, the Saskatchewan doctor and the Saskatchewan farm organizations ought to be walking alongside to solve the problem. You have enough brains in Saskatchewan to solve any question under the sun, you have enough money, enough weight, enough farmers, enough organization here, what you need is unity. You cannot get unity by having one group swallow up another group; you must rise above your groups. Your chief

need today is co-operative marketing; but even behind that your real need
is such a spirit of harmony, such a spirit of bigness, that you will all start in
to work together to solve the problem that cannot be solved unless you do
work together. I ask you to approach it in that spirit.[36]

The blend of political populism with religion in Saskatchewan was very
much part of a regional reality. Concurrent with the rise of the CCF in
Saskatchewan was the emergence of Social Credit in Alberta. The parallels
are quite striking. The Social Credit movement was led by William Aberhart,
who, like Douglas, was a Baptist minister and powerful orator. Aberhart too
professed a version of the social gospel and had the influential vehicle of a
weekly radio broadcast to reach hundreds of thousands of Albertans. With
the Depression taking a devastating toll, Aberhart embraced the social credit
theories of Major Clifford Hugh Douglas as a means to empower people
against the control of banks and other powerful elites. Social Credit would
disperse economic and political power to individuals by government granting
people the buying power through what amounted to an annual income that
would give them the financial capacity to acquire their basic needs. For a time,
Douglas flirted with the ideas of social credit and even considered becoming
part of a similar movement in Saskatchewan.

Years earlier in the United States, in the early 1890s, the Populist Party
grew out of left-wing agrarian populism. For a time, the Populist Party was
a growing force in American politics, even nominating William Jennings
Bryan as its candidate in the 1896 presidential election. The northern plains
states that border the Canadian Prairie provinces were a hotbed of rural populism. This culture of agrarian populism was not constrained by borders and
became very much part of the rural psychology in Saskatchewan, a province
that felt the same grievance as its American neighbours.

The important historical figures of Douglas and, to a lesser degree,
Gardiner and Diefenbaker reflect varying forms and styles that blended prai-
rie populism and religion as integral currents through Saskatchewan's history.
But beyond the political figures themselves is the sentiment that politicians

identify and seize upon as a vehicle for partisan political expression. In that regard, it is difficult, if not impossible, to overstate how deeply embedded the sentiment of grievance is in the province's psyche.

The populist influence at the leadership level on Saskatchewan politics was greatly diminished when Douglas left in 1961 to lead the newly formed federal NDP. From that point, the NDP as a populist vehicle has been steadily diminished, for several reasons. One is that the party has never been able to find a leader who had the qualities and charisma of a Douglas. Another is that in recent decades the party has come more and more to be seen as an urban-based party, dominated by a combination of identity politics, special interests, and policy technocrats, which has weakened its ability to create a unifying message that resonates with a broad cross-section of the population. At the same time, the NDP has itself become secularized, abandoning its social gospel roots and, with them, the language of inspiration that once made it such a powerful political movement in the best sense of populism.

But there is also another view of populism. It states that grassroots democratic organizations inevitably lead to the rule of the governed by elites, becoming, in other words, the antithesis of populism. This was expressed by German-Italian sociologist Robert Michels, who famously coined the term "the iron law of oligarchy." Simply put, all complex organizations, whether political parties or governments, ultimately are run by a leadership class. In Michels's words, "reduced to its most concise expression, the fundamental sociological law of political parties may be formulated in the following terms: 'It is organization that gives birth to the domination of the elected over the electors, of the mandataries over the mandators, of the delegates over the delegators. Who says organization, says oligarchy.'"[37] The result is that what starts out as grassroots direct democracy, the central feature of populist organizations and politics, becomes controlled by a group that wields power. In political terms, what emerges from populism becomes the domain of government, its bureaucracy, and the elites within it, a kind of bureaucratic aristocracy, which centralizes power.

Oligarchy is the inevitable outcome of organizations and becomes particularly acute in government. The daily decisions of government cannot be made through large numbers of disorganized people but only by those who control the decision-making process. In her article "The Iron Law of *What* Again?" sociologist Darcy K. Leach writes, "Though a dedicated socialist at the time, Michels nevertheless concluded that in modern society, socialism and democracy were both structurally impossible—that the very principle of organization made oligarchy the inevitable result of any organized collective endeavor."[38] Leach distills Michels's theory into three principles: bureaucracy happens; if bureaucracy happens, power rises; and, if power rises, power corrupts.

It is an important perspective to keep in mind when considering the arc of Saskatchewan politics. With populism an essential ingredient in the founding political culture of the province, Michels's "iron law of oligarchy" takes on particular significance. If true, it becomes a critical factor in the fate of governments that came to power as the democratic expression of what they considered to be the popular will, only to become the reason for a renewed expression of populism.

CHAPTER 2

What's in an Era?

IN CONSIDERING SASKATCHEWAN'S TRANSFORMATION, CON-
text matters. So, in addition to the impact and role of populism, matters
of substance need to be identified. It begins by recognizing and understanding the major global trends and how they shaped political and economic
reality during the past fifty years. Too often overlooked when judging decisions and events at the provincial level is how they result from much bigger
factors that influence the way people see both the world and their place in
it. Therefore, it is important to draw back and take a much broader perspective. Saskatchewan is not an island with a political culture that is so unique or
resilient that it is impervious to much greater forces.

Trying to identify a specific era with a beginning and an end is often difficult, if not impossible, as history is a continuum of interconnected occurrences. But by looking back it is possible to identify a series of events and policy decisions largely confined to a particular time frame that, collectively, was
pivotal in shaping the Saskatchewan of today. For the purposes of this attempt
to understand the transformation of Saskatchewan's political economy, the

years from the late 1960s to the late 1990s form an era that provides a road map in understanding how and why Saskatchewan changed.

Surprisingly perhaps, none of these events and decisions was specifically concerned with Saskatchewan. They all happened externally as part of much bigger issues, often, but not always, at the international level. Yet each had significant and lasting effects on the province. The province merely reacted in a way that most, if not all, would say was rational.

The era unfolded in stages, beginning in the late 1960s and stretching through much of the next three decades. Together the events, which often seemed isolated and disconnected, formed a period when the world, and forces beyond the province's borders, began to intervene in ways that could not be ignored or avoided. Trade barriers slowly started to dissolve, the Cold War ended, the migration of people accelerated, and the global economy truly began to emerge like never before. It is virtually impossible to overstate the political and economic impacts this period had on the world. People can debate whether the consequences have been good or bad, but what cannot be denied is the seismic effects that have been felt. In its own small way, the Saskatchewan of today is an example of how fundamental the changes have been.

Having said that, it's not as if the emergence of international trade, the expansion of global commerce, and the movement of people were anything new. They certainly were not. In fact, the nineteenth century was an era when global trade began to flourish, dominated by the British Empire and its client colonial nations that supplied the cheap raw goods and commodities to support the British economy. With its economic dominance entrenched, the United Kingdom in 1846 officially adopted a policy of free trade and abolished its Corn Laws, which had imposed tariffs on imports.[1]

World trade subsequently expanded and retracted through the decades. It went through periods of significant disruption in the first half of the twentieth century, particularly in the wake of the First World War with the emergence of Soviet communism and strident nationalisms in Europe. The ultimate blow to world commerce was the destruction and ruination across Europe from the Second World War. Then, with the peace came the Bretton Woods

Agreement and the creation of international bodies, such as the International Monetary Fund (IMF), the International Bank for Reconstruction and Development, and the General Agreement on Tariffs and Trade (GATT)—now the World Trade Organization (WTO)—to give some rules-based order to the international system.

While world trade steadily grew after the war, it was not until four decades later, with the collapse of the Soviet Union and the ascendancy of liberal democracies, that globalization took hold as the prevailing economic paradigm. Although it came ten years before the end of the century, in some ways the collapse of communism as a credible governing and economic concept marked the end of the twentieth century. The Soviet communist experiment emerged in the early years of the century and shaped world economic and political affairs for much of it. So its demise was a truly heady time—a point when Francis Fukuyama was famously declaring "the end of history," which was a history that for much of the twentieth century had been defined by the struggle between liberal democracy and communism, between the market and the state.

Many specific events give shape to the argument that the world changed significantly during the period from the late 1960s to the mid-1990s. Some, if not many, might seem insignificant, and taken individually that is very likely true. But as with all of history it is never one event that creates real change but many. Even though Saskatchewan was not an actor of any notable consequence, the events that unfolded during this period had a powerful effect on transforming the province's economy, society, and politics. For Saskatchewan the political effect during this period of change ranged from resistance to acceptance to adaptation. The common feature in each case was the opening of people's minds to the world. In effect, perceptions, along with economic and political assumptions, changed because of events beyond the province's borders. Saskatchewan people became sensitized to the world in a way they had not been before.

As someone who came of age in the late 1960s, I have vivid memories of that time. They are not Saskatchewan memories as such but recollections of events elsewhere that affected how people saw the world. Much of them were rooted in the turbulence of the 1960s in the United States, during a period when we witnessed the assassinations first of President John F. Kennedy and then, five years later, of Martin Luther King Jr. and Bobby Kennedy, followed by race riots in American cities and the anti–Vietnam War protest movement. Then came the Kent State massacre. Television cameras captured the scene as unarmed university students, demonstrating against the war, were shot and killed by members of the U.S. National Guard on the Ohio campus.

As the United States was experiencing spasms of violence and unrest, Canada too was entering a period of change—less turbulent, perhaps, but an equally significant transition. It unfolded in multiple forms and on many fronts, but together the result was to connect Canada to the world and help people understand their integration into a much broader global reality.

IMMIGRATION

For much of Canada's history, immigration was a critical social and economic policy in the country's development. The early years of the twentieth century were a period of massive immigration, as Canada sought to solidify its national economy. The single largest year for immigration in Canada was 1913, when more than 400,000 people immigrated to Canada, many of them settling in Saskatchewan. The flow dropped dramatically during the First World War, the high unemployment period of the Great Depression, and throughout the Second World War, before rebounding with the high growth of the 1950s. In 1957–58 there was a spike in immigration, in part to accommodate refugees fleeing the Hungarian revolution.[2]

Historically, Canadian immigration policy was essentially race based. This was evident in the *Chinese Immigration Act* of 1885, which imposed a duty on every Chinese immigrant, and again in the *Immigration Act* of 1906 and its subsequent amendments in 1910. In both cases, restrictions were tightened by not only expanding the list of prohibited immigrants but also giving government greater discretion to determine the admissibility and deportation of immigrants. Those deemed to be "unsuited to the climate or requirements of Canada" were prohibited. So too were those seeking to enter Canada who were sponsored by religious institutions.[3]

It wasn't until 1962 that overt racial restrictions on immigration and the focus on country of origin were eased. Federal regulations were changed to allow for skills to be considered, with an Order-in-Council that revoked the special status treatment that for decades was given to immigrants from Britain, France, and the United States and ended the limitations on immigrants from Asian countries.[4] A 1966 White Paper on Immigration became the basis for changes the following year when skills and ability, not race or country of origin, became the key factors in determining admissibility to Canada.[5]

The points system for immigration established in 1967 created an objective measurement for determining who would be granted entry. It was based on education, age, language, and factors such as occupational skills and employment prospects that were deemed beneficial in terms of the individual being a productive member of society. Implementing the points system also limited the discretionary power of immigration officers by setting out an explicit set of guidelines. The stage was being set for Canada to become a nation that would attract people from all regions and nations of the world.

The final piece came in October 1971 when then prime minister Pierre Trudeau announced in the House of Commons that multiculturalism was to be an official position of the Government of Canada. The policy, which would become law in the *Multiculturalism Act*, stated that multiculturalism is

> the most suitable means of assuring the cultural freedom of all Canadians. Such a policy should help to break down discriminatory attitudes and cultural jealousies. National unity, if it is to mean anything in the deeply personal sense, must be founded on confidence in one's own individual identity; out of this can grow respect for that of others, and a willingness to share ideas, attitudes and assumptions....The Government will support and encourage the various cultural and ethnic groups that give structure and vitality to our society. They will be encouraged to share

their cultural expression and values with other Canadians and so contribute to a richer life for all.[6]

In his book on the history of immigration in Canada, Reg Whitaker identifies 1967 as a turning point:

> Although many have argued that this [points-based] system was not free of biases which were indirectly racial (it may have stacked the deck against poor immigrants from Third World Countries), it did establish at the level of formal principle that Canadian immigration policy is "colour blind." This principle represented an historic watershed. The trend of the 1950s toward southern European immigration was maintained in the 1960s, but after 1967 the pattern of immigration to Canada showed a reversal, away from Europe, toward Asia, and to other Third World areas. By the mid-1970s there were more immigrants arriving from the Third World than from the developed world.[7]

In the years since, annual immigration rates have fluctuated largely based on prevailing economic conditions. During periods of slow growth and rising unemployment the flow is restricted to protect the existing domestic labour market; then, during times of stronger growth and declining unemployment rates, it is expanded. But overall, since 1967 and the later adoption of official multiculturalism, Canada's immigration rate has exceeded that of previous decades, other than in the first two decades of the twentieth century.

THE RE-EMERGENCE OF CHINA

In the late 1960s, the arrival of Pierre Trudeau and "Trudeaumania" injected passion, both positive and negative, into Canadian politics. These were events that helped sensitize people to international events and help set the stage for what was to come in the decades ahead. Trudeau came to power with an unorthodox reputation in traditional Canadian terms. He was a writer best known for his contributions to the Quebec literary and political journal *Cité Libre*. He was seen as an academic, a world traveller, and, to some, "a philosopher king." Certainly, Trudeau's profile was one of someone with a broader world view. In 1950 he had travelled to China to interview Mao Tse Tung, the leader of the Chinese Communist Revolution, who had taken power a year earlier. The experience clearly influenced Trudeau and his view of geopolitics and the world.[8]

In late 1970, after two years in office as prime minister, Trudeau achieved what had been his top foreign policy priority: official recognition of and formal diplomatic relations with China.[9] It was a move that cemented what had been the cordial, if unofficial, state-to-state relationship between the two nations. A key reason why Canada and Communist China had friendly, if unofficial, relations was the positive reputation of Norman Bethune, a surgeon from Gravenhurst, Ontario, who became a legend in China for serving on the front lines as a doctor for the revolutionary forces led by Mao. Bethune was buried with other "martyrs" who died as part of the revolution. Then in 1962, in an initiative led by federal agriculture minister Alvin Hamilton, who was from Saskatchewan, the Canadian Wheat Board made its first major wheat sale to China. It was an important breakthrough that helped set the stage for Trudeau to later establish formal diplomatic relations and a new era in Sino-Canadian relations.[10]

The greater significance of Trudeau's China policy was that it was a precursor to the broader opening of relations with China by other western nations. The most significant came in 1972, when U.S. President Richard Nixon shocked many by visiting China for eight days to begin the process of establishing formal state-to-state diplomatic ties with the Communist nation. Nixon's visit ended a twenty-five-year period when there was no communication between the two countries.

Nixon's initiative was both economic and political. The United States recognized the trade and commercial potential of a Chinese market that could not remain isolated from the global market and hope to develop a modern economy. But it was also part of Cold War strategic policy to prevent a Communist bloc from solidifying. The U.S. outreach would help drive a wedge between China and the Soviet Union, which had been involved in skirmishes along contested parts of their shared border. The significance of Nixon's China initiative, and to a lesser extent Trudeau's outreach, was to signal that China, the world's most populous nation, was making a very early move in joining the global economy. It was clear in the early 1970s that the Chinese economy was in a dire condition and needed to begin reforming itself. As Robert Sutter notes in his essay "Why Does China Matter?," at the time of Nixon's visit, "China was actually in a weak state with a stagnating economy and an obsolete military enmeshed in a wrenching leadership struggle."[11]

THE OCTOBER CRISIS

It was a moment in time that lingers to this day. The effects of the terrorist acts that unfolded in Montreal in the fall of 1970 challenged Canada and its founding principles of "peace, order and good government." The October crisis was a three-month period when radical and violent Quebec nationalism shocked Canadians and forced Canada to confront its own identity as a democratic society. It also forced the issue of Quebec's relationship with the rest of Canada emphatically onto the national agenda, as a subject that would dominate domestic politics for more than the next two decades. Deeply engaged in the subsequent constitutional negotiations through its eleven years in office was the Allan Blakeney government of Saskatchewan.

The impact of the October crisis—when the Front de libération du Québec (FLQ), a paramilitary cell of Quebec separatists, kidnapped and murdered Quebec labour minister Pierre Laporte and kidnapped British trade commissioner James Cross—was vividly recalled in 1990 on its twentieth anniversary. Barbara Frum, host of the CBC national newsmagazine *The Journal*, prefaced a retrospective documentary on that turbulent time in a way that captured the raw emotion of the events: "At the time, it seemed unreal, unbelievable. In orderly, peaceful Canada a diplomat kidnapped, a prominent politician murdered, troops and armour were patrolling the streets of Montreal and guarding the national institutions in Ottawa. There were revolutions in the air, civil rights suspended, almost 500 people arrested and detained. It was more like Chile than Canada. That time has become known as the October crisis."[12]

With the military already patrolling the streets of Montreal and Ottawa, journalist Tim Ralfe on the steps of Parliament's Centre Block expressed concern to Trudeau about the heavy military presence. "Yes, well, there are a lot of bleeding hearts around who just don't like to see people with helmets and guns," Trudeau said. "All I can say is, go on and bleed, but it is more important to keep law and order in a society than to be worried about weak-kneed people." When Ralfe asked Trudeau how far he would go in crushing the violent separatists, Trudeau famously replied, "Just watch me." Three days later the federal government suspended civil rights and imposed the *War Measures Act* to quell what was termed an "apprehended insurrection." In his address to the nation explaining the decision, Trudeau said, "I am speaking to you at a moment of grave crisis, when violent and fanatical men are attempting to destroy the unity and the freedom of Canada. One aspect of that crisis is the threat which has been made on the lives of two innocent men. These are matters of the utmost gravity and I want to tell you what the Government is doing to deal with them."[13] A day after the imposition of the *War Measures Act*, Laporte's strangled body was found in the trunk of a car.[14]

The suspension of civil liberties stirred critics of the action taken by Trudeau, with federal NDP leader Tommy Douglas voting against the action in Parliament, saying Trudeau had "used a sledgehammer to crack a peanut." Trudeau's response was dismissive: "Peanuts don't make bombs, don't take hostages, and don't assassinate prisoners. As for the sledgehammer, it was the only tool at our disposal."[15]

For Trudeau, who had spent much of his adult life opposing ethnic Quebec nationalism, the October crisis became a defining moment. The raw emotion of the time and the need to address Quebec nationalism within a renewed Canadian federation became the genesis for long, arduous, and complex constitutional negotiations that would dominate much of the federal-provincial agenda for years to come. As the process unfolded, it would steadily consume more and more time and energy of federal and provincial governments in the effort to address the very nature of the Canadian federation. At the forefront of those negotiations was Saskatchewan's NDP government. Everything, from control of natural resources to a *Charter of Rights and Freedoms* to jurisdiction over language policy to the status of Quebec as a distinct society and what special privileges that would entail, would become dominant themes in the language of Canadian politics.

OIL AS A GEOPOLITICAL WEAPON

In October 1973, the Yom Kippur War briefly raged in the Middle East. It involved Egypt and Syria, which had attacked Israel in an effort to reclaim territory that had been lost to the Israelis six years earlier. The Israelis quickly began pushing back the advancing Egyptian and Syrian troops, who received reinforcements from Iraq, Jordan, and Saudi Arabia. But even with the involvement of other Arab nations, it was to no avail. Within days the Israeli army was occupying large swaths of Egyptian and Syrian territory. After only ten days, the attack had been repulsed and Israeli troops were well within striking distance of Cairo and Damascus. It was at that point the Arabs decided to fight back with a new weapon: oil. It would be a move that would send economic shock waves around the globe, including in Canada and Saskatchewan, for years to come.[16]

What would become the OPEC oil crisis began with the announcement by the Arab member nations that controlled the Organization of the Petroleum Exporting Countries (OPEC) that it would begin reducing its oil production by 5 percent a month and would continue "until the Israeli forces are fully withdrawn from all Arab territories occupied during the June 1967 War, and the legitimate rights of the Palestinian people are restored."[17] The effect was immediate. The price of oil increased by 70 percent. Less than two months later, OPEC raised the price another 130 percent and also imposed a total oil embargo on the United States because of its support for Israel. By today's standards the oil price climb from $3 to $12 a barrel over a six-month period might seem inconsequential. But in the early 1970s it played havoc with the world economy.

The reaction, particularly in the United States, verged on panic. Just how deeply it affected perceptions is described by Michael Ross in a retrospective piece on the OPEC crisis for *Foreign Affairs Magazine* some forty years later. "For oil-importing countries, the 1973 oil shock triggered years of inflation and stagnant growth. It also fostered a widespread belief that the world was running out of oil. In the space of just a few years, Americans went from believing that oil would remain cheap forever to believing it would soon run out."[18] Ross continues:

> The U.S. government's response was bipartisan and far-reaching. Nixon pushed emergency conservation measures through Congress, including a nationwide 55-mile-per-hour speed limit. President Gerald Ford signed legislation that established mandatory fuel economy standards.
>
> Shortly after President Jimmy Carter took office, he delivered a televised national address on the energy crisis, which he described as "a problem unprecedented in our history." "With the exception of preventing war," he continued, "this is the greatest challenge our country will face during our lifetimes." Drawing on Central Intelligence Agency estimates, Carter warned that oil wells "were drying up all over the world." His secretary of energy, James Schlesinger, predicted "a major economic and political crisis in the 1980s as the world's oil wells start to run dry." To curb oil imports, Carter pushed for both conservation and price deregulation and greater reliance on solar energy, coal, and "synthetic" fuels made from coal and shale. Even one of President Ronald Reagan's market-oriented policies made a difference: removing price and allocation controls in 1981 promoted conservation and fuel-switching, although the global collapse in oil prices later nullified these effects.[19]

In Canada, the reaction was not dissimilar. In December 1973 the federal government announced the creation of Petro-Canada, a federal Crown

corporation with a mandate to develop Canadian oil reserves, including the
Alberta oil sands and those in the Far North. The policy objective in part was
energy security for the nation through public ownership. But it went beyond
that. The federal government also sought to exert greater control over natural
resources, and oil in particular, which were under the constitutional jurisdiction of the provinces. When Ottawa became concerned about the large shipments of Canadian oil going to the United States, raising fears of an oil shortage in Canada, it froze the domestic price and imposed an export tax. The
rationale was to ensure what it considered to be fair returns on oil that would
be used to subsidize Canadians in central and eastern Canada who were
dependent on imported oil. Not surprisingly, the oil-producing provinces of
Alberta and Saskatchewan saw the federal intrusion as a frontal assault on
provincial control of natural resources, as explicitly stated in section 92 of the
British North America (BNA) Act. It triggered what would be almost a decade-
long fight over control of resources.

STAGFLATION, AN ECONOMIC CONUNDRUM

To this day, Canada has never again experienced the economic malaise that
struck the economy in the 1970s and persisted through to the early 1980s.
It was a period when stagflation stalked the land. The word is derived from
two economic conditions: stagnation and inflation. Until the 1970s, it was
believed that the two could not occur at the same time, being that they are
mirror opposites. Economists were of the view that low or no growth, high
unemployment, and inflation were simultaneously incompatible. But in
Canada they coexisted for a decade.

There is no overarching consensus among economists about the causes of
stagflation, but it is widely believed that a key reason in this case was the economic shock created by the OPEC crisis. It came in two waves of rapid oil
prices increases, the first in 1972–73 and a second in 1979–80. The result was
a supply shock as the economy faced a rapid rise in oil prices, increasing the
costs of production, and rising inflation and interest rates, resulting in falling

demand, all leading to rising unemployment and slow economic growth. Measured in terms of domestic currency, the price of oil rose by US$32.64 in Canada during the period from 1973 to 1982, and by US$29.58 in the United States.[20] The problem is also attributed to other factors, including unsustainable government spending in the 1960s and monetary policy that kept interest rates low to support employment, which led to rising inflation.

The point is, no matter the cause, stagflation was seen largely as a result of international events that had serious negative effects on the global economy. As an oil-producing province, the Saskatchewan government found its revenues increasing because of rising oil prices but its population suffering from high interest rates and sluggish growth. The impact is evident in economic growth rates during the decade compared with those in the years before (specifically the 1960s) and after (beginning in the early 1980s). In that context, the economic decline of the 1970s was stark.

In Canada from 1962 to 1973 real gross domestic product (GDP) per capita grew by an annual average rate of 3.80 percent. During the period from 1973 to 1982, GDP increased by a meagre annual average of 0.84 percent, and from 1982 to 1987, by 1.2 percent. An even more startling number is the unemployment rate. Through the 1960s, specifically from 1962 to 1973, the Canadian unemployment rate averaged 4.4 percent. From 1973 to 1982 it averaged 7.5 percent, and in the period from 1982 to 1985 it reached an average of 11.2 percent before decreasing slightly to just under 10 percent from 1985 to 1987. The story was similar in the United States, except the duration of the stagnant growth period there was not as extended as in Canada. In the United States, the average annual GDP growth rate was 0.55 percent from 1973 to 1982, but it rebounded more quickly than in Canada, with the U.S. economy growing at an average pace of 2.8 percent from 1982 to 1987. As well, the U.S. unemployment rate never reached the levels in Canada during the comparable periods.[21]

The economy during those years was trapped in a cost-price squeeze. In other words, inflation seemed to feed on itself. The reality was that people believed the prices of goods would keep rising, so they bought more in the belief that those goods would be more expensive in the future. The result was an upward spiral. Higher demand drove up prices, which in turn created demand for higher wages, which in turn pushed prices even higher. In that kind of an economic environment, labour contracts sought automatic cost-of-living adjustments, which in an era of high inflation and interest rates in the double digits led to huge wage increases, which fuelled the crippling economic cycle.[22] In 1975, shortly after being re-elected with a majority government, in part by campaigning against wage-and-price controls as a tool to quell inflation, Trudeau announced mandatory wage-and-price controls. To appreciate how the economy was being devoured by inflation at the time, it needs to be considered in the context of today's low interest rate environment. The *Anti-Inflation Act* of 1975 limited pay increases for federal public employees and those in companies with more than five hundred employees to 10 percent the first year, 8 percent the next, and 6 percent thereafter.[23]

THE FALL OF SOVIET COMMUNISM

It is possible to identify two crucial events that served as bookends to the pivotal decade of the 1980s. The first came in 1979 with the election of Margaret Thatcher as British prime minister. Few national elections in the last half of the twentieth century had the resulting impact of Thatcher's time in power. She had an undeniable influence on economic thought and the course of international politics, including the collapse of the Soviet Union. One can debate the policies of Thatcherism, as many do to this day, but no one can deny the effect she and her government had far beyond Britain itself. Indeed, "Thatcherism" found its way directly into major decisions of the Saskatchewan government in the 1980s.

The second came in 1989, a decade after Thatcher won power. The Soviet Union began imploding under the weight of its own economic, social, democratic, and human rights contradictions. The unravelling of Soviet communism was a long and insidious process. It was delayed only by the totalitarian nature of the regime that for decades had brutally suppressed dissent and by the communist apologists in other nations who ignored reality. But the process of internal economic and political decay accelerated during the 1980s, sped along in part by Thatcher, the "Iron Lady" of Britain. It went beyond Thatcher's avowedly anti-communist beliefs, which she expressed often and emphatically. She also had a political message for domestic consumption that echoed in political debates of other western democratic nations.

"Socialists cry 'power to the people' and raise the clenched fist as they say it," Thatcher said. "We all know what they really mean—power over people, power to the state."[24] The statement captured Thatcher's political target in the United Kingdom, which was social democracy. It is a point explained by Andrew Gamble, a professor at Cambridge University, who sees Thatcherism as having a clear strategic purpose. "Thatcherism has appeared most clearly as a radical force through its challenges to many features of the existing state," Gamble writes. "Its main target has been social democracy. During the 1970s it [social democracy] came under strong attack in many countries, both as a form of government and as a governing doctrine….As the balance of forces between classes and nations shifted, so too a new politics began to emerge, giving opportunities for both left and right. Old orthodoxies were swept away."[25]

In terms of economic effect, Thatcher's focus was on reducing the power of the British state. To do that she embarked on an aggressive agenda of privatization of nationalized industries, believing she could revitalize a stagnant British economy through market-based reforms. The force of Thatcher's personality, and her determination to see her agenda achieved in the face of often strident opposition, made her the darling of the political right in many western nations. Before long, her acolytes became advocates for an agenda of privatization that eventually reached as far as Saskatchewan.

WESTERN ALIENATION

As what might be termed a pathology in Canadian politics, western alienation is certainly nothing new. It has a long and important history that for generations has shaped attitudes and political outcomes in the West, including Saskatchewan. But there was a brief period following the defeat of the federal

Liberal government in 1984 and election of the Progressive Conservative government led by Brian Mulroney when a sense emerged that the voice of western anger against Ottawa had been heard. It was as if the West had finally become a full partner engaged in the destiny—and, more importantly, the decisions—of the nation.

Many regarded the election result in 1984 as a vindication that the grievances of the West, largely rooted in federal incursions to control the development of natural resources, had been recognized. The single biggest symbol of that tension had been the Trudeau government's National Energy Program (NEP), which was seen as transferring a huge amount of wealth, primarily from Alberta, to central Canada. What the NEP did was set a domestic price for Alberta oil below that of the world price and impose a federal tax on the export of oil. Beyond the economic and federal-provincial implications, the NEP was recognized too as an example of how the interests of Ontario and Quebec dominated the decisions and interests of the federal government.

Mulroney's landslide victory was regarded as a seismic geographic shift in Canadian politics. The Progressive Conservative majority government swallowed much of western Canada, including a sweep of all Alberta seats and nine of fourteen seats in Saskatchewan, where the Liberals failed to elect a single member.[26] The Mulroney cabinet was shaped to recognize the need for strong western representation, with many of the key portfolios going to western MPs—Joe Clark, Don Mazankowski, Erik Nielsen, Bill McKnight, Harvie Andre, Charlie Mayer, and Pat Carney, among others. But the honeymoon between Ottawa and the West was not to last long. By 1986 the first signs were emerging of a new kind of populist western discontent, this one directed squarely at the Mulroney government itself. A major impetus was federal government's decision to award a major contract for the construction of CF-18 aircraft to a Quebec company instead of to Bristol Aerospace in Winnipeg, which many believed had made the best case to win the contract. For many in the West, including Saskatchewan, it was yet another example of how federal politics and decision-making were fully in the control of central Canada, and too often weighted toward Quebec.

Another factor was the Mulroney Tories' continuation of the ongoing deficit budgets that had become the norm under the Trudeau Liberals. A current of "fiscal responsibility" in the form of balanced budgets—long considered a cornerstone of good governance, especially among farmers on the Prairies—became a growing public concern in Saskatchewan and Alberta. In part it reflected a sentiment toward "smaller government" as a virtue to be pursued. Both the PCs and Liberals had made deficit reduction a central theme of their 1984 campaigns. The Mulroney government had promised upon taking office that deficit reduction would come from expenditure cuts, not tax increases. When they failed to rein in the deficit, however, public discontent with the Mulroney government on the Prairies slowly but steadily emerged.[27] The cleavage between East and West had not disappeared with the rise of the Progressive Conservatives into a truly national government of 211 seats, with the Liberals reduced to 40 and the New Democrats to 30 seats. Instead, it was only temporarily in abeyance, as if waiting to see if things had really changed. Many soon believed they had not.

By the second half of the 1980s the Reform Party, a western-based right-wing populist party, had emerged in opposition to the Mulroney government's continuing deficit budgets and a perception of bias to Quebec. It sought to assert the region's role in federalism, running on the slogan of "The West Wants In."

THE URUGUAY ROUND

From the beginning, when a new round of the General Agreement on Tariffs and Trade talks started in 1986 at Punta del Este, Uruguay, agriculture was the key subject in the declaration that started what would become seven years of negotiations. The objective was to find solutions to the challenges confronting agriculture through greater market access. Implicit in the initiative was to find trade remedies by addressing domestic agriculture policies. The crux of the challenge was the ability of nations to control export subsidies in agricultural markets and the distortions that resulted in terms of process and market access.

The fact that negotiations dragged on for years was an indication of the difficulty in reaching agreement on how to reduce subsidies—both domestic and export related—as well as agriculture sector tariffs and non-tariff barriers. The United States and the European Union were the primary players in the negotiations. In both cases, domestic politics was a huge limiting factor, as agriculture policy was driven and designed unapologetically to protect farm interests. In the United States, the primary agriculture and farm policy tool of the federal government is the Farm Bill, which is renewed every five years. The EU equivalent was its Common Agricultural Policy (CAP), which dates back to 1962 and explicitly recognizes "a partnership between agriculture and society, and between Europe and its farmers," and seeks to "safeguard European Union farmers to make a reasonable living," while preserving the rural landscape and the farming way of life.[28]

The progress made in opening agricultural markets during the Uruguay Round was not insignificant, but it did not create anything close to the liberalized trade in other sectors. To appreciate how marginal the progress really was, all a person needs to know is that the conversion of non-tariff barriers to tariffs was considered major progress.[29] Even though the tariffs were set at a higher level than the non-tariff equivalent and would continue to protect domestic markets, the fact the tariffs had become explicit and transparent would make them easier to identify and remove in subsequent bilateral or multilateral trade negotiations. There was a sense that agriculture had finally been brought into the mainstream of trade diplomacy.

In its analysis of the Uruguay Round, the International Trade Consortium in 1994 had faint praise for the progress truly made: "The Agreement embodied in the final Act of the Uruguay Round breaks new ground for agriculture, and takes a big step toward placing this sector of world trade under rules more consistent with those in operation in other areas. However, the degree of liberalization of markets is modest, and much remains to be done in future rounds of negotiations."[30]

Canada had two primary and arguably conflicting objectives in the negotiations. On the one hand, it sought to gain greater access to global grain markets through the elimination of export subsidies in the United States and European Union. On the other hand, it aimed to protect its system of supply management, which effectively shut out imports in domestic dairy, poultry, and egg markets. The conclusion of the International Trade Consortium was that the outcome was a "qualified success" for Canada. That is, Canada made some progress on limiting grain export subsidies and successfully protected its supply-managed sector by implementing tariffs at such high levels that its domestic market was not threatened.[31]

But arguably the most important outcome of the Uruguay Round was to place greater access to agriculture markets, which means a much more market-oriented policy framework, on the international trade agenda. It added to growing opinion that trade liberalization and the emergence of a global economy were now the accepted paradigm. The only questions were how fast and far the world would move in that direction, and how it would shape the political debate and public opinion. Time would soon tell.

CANADA-U.S. FREE TRADE

In November 1982 the Canadian economy was in recession, contracting at an annual rate of 3.2 percent.[32] Inflation and crushingly high interest rates were strangling the economy. The prime bank mortgage rate hovered at approximately 14 percent. A year earlier it had peaked at 20 percent.[33] In response, Prime Minister Trudeau announced the creation of a royal commission with a mandate to set out an economic strategy for Canada to finally emerge from its struggling economy. The Royal Commission on the Economic Union and Development Prospects for Canada was headed by former Liberal finance minister Donald Macdonald and completed its final report three years later. By that time Trudeau had retired from politics and the Liberals, under new leader John Turner, had been routed by Mulroney and the Progressive Conservatives. The Macdonald Commission report that was delivered to Prime Minister Mulroney called for a more market-based and flexible approach to economic growth, with its key recommendation the negotiation

of a free trade agreement with the United States. The report was unequivocal about trade liberalization. "Central to the Commissioners' policy recommendations is a rejection of protectionism and of a dirigiste centrally planned
industrial strategy behind tariff and other barriers," the report stated.[34] By
coincidence, U.S. President Reagan had reached out to Mulroney shortly after
the PC leader had taken power and the two held bilateral talks in Washington
in the fall of 1984. Reagan had come to power in 1981 espousing smaller government, lower taxes, balanced budgets, and a greater emphasis on a market
economy. Among the president's priorities was to establish a free trade zone
between the United States and Canada.[35] The idea of reducing trade barriers and creating a Canada-U.S. free trade zone that would eventually include
Mexico reflected a growing consensus regarding trade liberalization as a
mechanism to stimulate growth. It was a period when market liberalization was ascendant, reflected in the election of Conservative Prime Minister
Thatcher in Britain and Republican President Reagan in the United States.

The incremental success of the GATT in reducing tariffs and trade barriers
in the two decades following the Second World War had stalled by the 1970s.
The economic recessions in the 1970s and early 1980s led governments to
employ non-tariff barriers and other forms of protection. For example, high
unemployment and factory closures in western Europe and North America
drove governments to seek bilateral market-sharing arrangements with competitors and, most significantly for Saskatchewan, to depend on subsidies to
maintain their grip on agricultural trade.

As a result, GATT's credibility and effectiveness were weakened as a
forum for trade liberalization. According to GATT's successor, the World
Trade Organization, "The reality was that world trade had become far more
complex and important than 40 years before: the globalization of the world
economy was underway, trade in services—not covered by GATT rules—was
of major interest to more and more countries, and international investment
had expanded. The expansion of services trade was also closely tied to further
increases in world merchandise trade."[36] GATT had been found particularly
wanting in agriculture, where attempts to open up farm markets had achieved

little success in multilateral negotiations during the Uruguay Round. These and other factors convinced GATT members that a new effort to reinforce and extend the multilateral system should be attempted. That effort resulted in a new round of negotiations that began with a meeting in Uruguay, which eventually led to the creation of the WTO as a late-twentieth-century modernization of the GATT.

In retrospect, the period beginning in the 1970s and extending into the 1980s was one in which the dominant economic view of globalization and free trade was clearly taking hold. There was a growing consensus that an end to stagflation and a return to economic growth required the elimination of trade barriers and greater access to global markets. If there was any doubt that liberal democracy, open markets, and more constrained government intervention in the economy was dominant, it vanished in November 1989 with the fall of the Berlin Wall. In a span of a few months the world witnessed the utter collapse and dismemberment of the Soviet Union and its governing paradigm of state ownership and control.

Beyond the elimination of tariffs, a less obvious but equally pivotal outcome of the free trade agreement was its psychological effect on Canadian business. Key components of the Canadian business sector matured as a result of free trade. With all but a few of the last vestiges of national policy and its protectionist measures gone, Canadian business realized that given a relatively level playing field it could compete, succeed, and prosper in an integrated Canada-U.S. market. That realization would be the first step toward the far more global perspective by Canadian business that would unfold as world markets began to open.

THE BURDEN OF DEBT

Growing government debt was a consequence of recessionary times. Governments around the world acted rationally and used their fiscal capacity to support struggling economies. They followed the Keynesian model, which maintains that aggregate demand in an economy during a recession when the private sector is withdrawing from the economy needs to be buoyed by government spending. To put it simply, you cannot foster growth in stagnant or recessionary times through austerity. That assertion might seem self-evident. But in the context of political debate, the notion of government austerity can become a powerful weapon. It is particularly nonsensical during periods of slow or stagnant growth when the private sector is cutting back and withdrawing from the economy. In spite of that, there is the inevitable chorus of "fiscal conservatives" who call for cuts in government spending to reduce public debt levels. So, instead of an increase in spending to stimulate the economy when the private sector is cutting back, they suggest the opposite—for government to also cut its spending. In other words, government should add to the economic misery by withdrawing from the economy like the private sector.

Why such a view can resonate with the public rests with the fiscal decisions that politicians consistently make. The problem in many instances is that the deficit financing that governments use to deal with a recession or a slow-growing economy becomes permanent, even in periods of higher growth. Some refer to it as "bastardized Keynesianism," because the economist John Maynard Keynes himself called for governments to balance their budgets over the business cycle and not run continuous structural deficits. The inevitable result of the political dilemma is that increasing spending is much easier than reducing the funding for what the public has come to expect. Thus, the annual deficits became structural, each adding to the total debt. Coupled with an extended period of inflation and high interest rates, the interest payments on the growing debt increasingly consume more and more of government revenues, leaving less and less to support social programs and other priorities.

In terms of the Government of Canada, beginning in the mid-1970s federal deficits became structural. In thirteen of the sixteen years prior to 1990, the federal government's cyclically adjusted budget—in other words, after accounting for spending increases and revenue reductions brought about because GDP was short of its full-employment value—was in deficit.[37] In an essay entitled "The Path to Fiscal Crisis," economist Livio Di Matteo explains,

The federal government ran an overall deficit every year from 1970–1 to 1996–7—at 27 years it was the longest string of deficits in the country's history. Even the Great Depression and the demands of the war years had not extracted such a toll of continuous deficits. As a share of GDP, the deficit peaked following the recession of the early 1980s, hitting eight percent in 1984–5. Meanwhile, from the early 1970s to 1995–6, the net federal debt rose from $20 billion to nearly $600 billion, while the federal debt's ratio to GDP rose from 20 percent in 1973–4 to its peak of 72 percent in 1995–6.[38]

At its peak, in 1997, servicing the federal debt consumed 36 cents of every tax dollar in government revenues.

The pressure to rein in government spending and return to balanced budgets had been growing for years, both domestically in Canada and internationally. The Organisation for Economic Co-operation and Development had been warning for years that a debt reckoning was coming for governments. In its 1987–88 survey of Canada, the OECD rang alarm bells about the country's fiscal situation. It noted that the general government deficit was high by international standards, with only Italy among larger countries having a larger deficit (as a share of GDP). Even smaller European countries had smaller deficits in aggregate than Canada.[39]

In its 1992–93 report on Canada, the OECD did not mince words.

The source of Canada's persistent fiscal problem is the emergence of a structural imbalance between government spending and revenues in the decade following the first oil shock. In combination with rising interest rates, this led to a very rapid growth in public debt in the first half of the 1980s. In the subsequent years, fiscal restraint and strong economic expansion brought down budget deficits considerably, slowing debt accumulation. However, with hindsight, it is clear that consolidation efforts made during the cyclical upswing were not sufficient to restore control over the fiscal situation. With weak economic activity since 1990, the public-sector deficit has widened markedly again, despite corrective fiscal action. As a result, the public debt-to-GDP ratio has grown sharply, and now exceeds the OECD average by a wide margin.[40]

In Canada by the early 1990s the political pressure was mounting, and consensus building, that governments needed to get their fiscal houses in order. The first to act were provincial governments, led by Saskatchewan and closely followed by Alberta. With the federal government facing a debt burden that was consuming a third of its annual revenue to service, the issue could no longer be ignored. The government debt issue had slowly grown over the years, reaching the point by the early 1990s of becoming a political albatross. Eventually politicians and the public came to the conclusion that dealing with deficit spending was a greater priority than continuing on the path of growing debt. In a national survey by the Angus Reid polling company days before the release of the 1995 federal budget, 48 percent of respondents listed public deficit and debt as the most important issue facing the country.[41]

The 1995 federal budget became a watershed moment. Its language was brutally frank: "This budget will fundamentally reform what the federal government does and how it does it. That reform is structural—i.e. it will change permanently the way government operates. The objective is to get government right so that it can fulfil its social and economic mandates more effectively and sustainably. This will include deep cuts in the level of federal program spending—not simply lower spending growth, but a substantial reduction in actual dollars spent."[42]

There were certainly other issues that helped shape the period, including public attitudes and the inevitable economic and political outcomes. But with the benefit of hindsight, it was clear that a new world was emerging between the late 1960s and the 1990s. What is also clear is that not everyone in Saskatchewan fully recognized the magnitude of what was unfolding, its consequences, and what to do about it.

CHAPTER 3

1969

"Why Should I Sell Your Wheat?"

MAJOR SOCIETAL CHANGE IS NEVER EASY AND SELDOM sudden. It tends to happen gradually and slowly, the product of people and events that can appear incidental or insignificant at the time. That's not to say there are not moments that seem, and truly are, momentous when they occur, ones that become recognized as turning points that change the course of history. But when it comes to societies and their politics, the tides of change tend to ebb and flow. Such moments are more often incremental and barely discernible, made up of small moments in time, even forgettable incidents that become part of the constantly changing and evolving nature of society. Inherent in change is a transformation in the way people think. Perhaps the clearest description comes from Albert Einstein, who said, "The world as we have created it is a process of our thinking. It cannot be changed without changing our thinking." He then took it one step further: "the measure of intelligence is the ability to change."

Recognizing how Saskatchewan has changed is not difficult. It is self-evident, in its politics and on the farms and in the small towns and cities. The pattern of life in rural Saskatchewan today is far different from what it was thirty or forty years ago. In a sense, the most visible indicators are the things that have disappeared or are disappearing. Gone are the wooden grain elevators that stood as sentinels to a farm economy created many decades earlier. Just as they were symbols of a pattern of rural life, their disappearance is a reflection of a different rural society and economy. Gone are many small communities that either have died or exist now as remnants of a gone-by era. The evidence in human terms is the dwindling rural population. In 1971, out of a population of 926,000, there were 435,610 people living in rural Saskatchewan, representing 47 percent of the total population; 233,330, or one-quarter of the province's residents, lived on farms.[1] In 2018, less than 16 percent of the province's population of 1.1 million lived in rural Saskatchewan, defined as villages and rural municipalities.[2]

The challenge in attempting to map the process of political change is in understanding how and why it happened. In the case of Saskatchewan it comes by identifying the events large and small—the broad strokes of which are outlined in the previous chapter—that together altered the way people think. That's because when people think differently so too will they act differently. People everywhere think differently today than they did as recently as in the 1990s. It has been a remarkable transformation. The question for Saskatchewan is twofold: Why, and how, did it happen? There is no one answer. Rather, the change is the product of a continuum that, at any point along it, has no single determining factor. It is the combination and accumulation of many events, some more relevant than others, that creates not only the progression leading to change but also the realization that it has happened. So it is with Saskatchewan.

The challenge in trying to trace the unfolding of history is deciding what events matter, and to what extent. Individually, certain incidents might seem hardly relevant, mere glimpses of a particular moment, but together they form a pattern that begins to make sense. One small event in particular is worth considering, even if it is shrouded in a lack of clarity. Simply identifying it and putting it in context is not easy, though; obscured in the mists of time is a firm understanding of not only why it happened but even where. Still, it remains a moment that has become a part of political history. It occurred in 1969.

On a visit to western Canada in July, only one year into his first term as prime minister, Pierre Trudeau travelled to Regina, Saskatoon, and Winnipeg to meet prairie farmers. He was venturing into hostile territory, as the farm community was unhappy with the consequences of an oversupplied wheat market, the result of which was low wheat prices and growing financial insecurity in rural Saskatchewan. In an attempt to use its influence to manipulate the market and raise prices, the Canadian Wheat Board, along with the United States, Argentina, and other wheat-exporting nations, withheld grain from the global market.[3] The unsold wheat clogged farm granaries, some even rotting in piles on the ground.

Outside a downtown Regina hotel where Trudeau was meeting with the Saskatchewan Farmers Union (SFU), hundreds of farmers had gathered to express their anger. In the July heat they dumped a mound of decomposing, foul-smelling wheat on the street and sidewalk as an expression of their disgust. Some carried signs that read "Hustle grain, not women" and "P.E.T. is a PIG." As Trudeau stood clutching a bullhorn on the back of a truck to speak to the farmers, some pelted him with handfuls of wheat. A furious Trudeau was widely reported as saying to the farmers, "Why should I sell your wheat?" A day later in Saskatoon, the prime minister met a similar, if less obnoxious, group of farmers. He complimented them for not carrying abusive signs. "I didn't get into politics to be insulted," Trudeau said.[4]

Unlikely as it sounds given the heated nature of the moment in Regina, some have maintained over the years that Trudeau's words were a rhetorical question taken out of context and that, in fact, he answered his own question. If he did, it was not amid the loud and raucous scene in Regina, where a rational, let alone respective, exchange was not possible. More likely, the answer was delivered in a private meeting with farmers in Winnipeg on the same western trip. "The Canadian farmer is entitled to as much protection from the Canadian government as other producers in other countries with whom he has to be in competition," Trudeau said. "But basically, unless you take the view that the government should step in and own the farms and hire the farmers, I think we all share responsibility and we will all have to do the best we can all together."[5]

In terms of the trajectory of Saskatchewan's politics and economy, Trudeau's response to his own question proved irrelevant. What mattered was the question, which survived the decades: "Why should I sell your wheat?" These words—which were to shape the perception of Trudeau among a majority of prairie farmers—were interpreted as evidence that the prime minister didn't care about Saskatchewan farmers or understand them. The alienation felt in the West from the federal Liberal government, which has persisted for decades, can at least partially be traced to those July 1969 events. For that matter, his son Prime Minister Justin Trudeau today still carries the burden of his father's legacy from those days.

Looking back on that moment more than fifty years later amplifies its significance, but not in the manner one would expect. Rather than merely a callous comment, as it was perceived by some, Trudeau's question actually cut to the heart of a critical question relating to the prairie farm economy and the political culture of Saskatchewan at the time. To be precise, his words touched on the idea of the Canadian Wheat Board itself and whether it was the proper vehicle for the marketing of wheat in a global market. There is no way of knowing if that was Trudeau's intent, but that was the effect, which explains the angry backlash. Fully appreciating the significance of the moment begins with understanding Saskatchewan's economic and political culture that had emerged over the decades.

There was good reason for the anger. The Wheat Board represented the dominant view of Saskatchewan farmers at the time, a position deeply rooted in history and experience. From the earliest days of settlement, Saskatchewan farmers had been exposed to forces that created a profoundly felt sense of vulnerability. Small, individual-family farm units were at the mercy of large institutional economic players such as railways, banks, and tariff-protected central Canadian manufacturers. A national policy to serve the needs of central Canadian industry made prairie farmers pawns in a larger agenda that served the corporate needs of Ontario and Quebec. To this day, as people talk of alienation on the Prairies, its roots can be traced to that formative period of Canada.

To defend themselves and their interests in the early years of the twentieth century, farmers began taking matters into their own hands. An entire rural culture emerged built on collectivist ideals. They formed collaborative mechanisms to give them greater control of their economic destiny—co-operative enterprises such as the Saskatchewan Grain Growers' Association in 1906, the Saskatchewan Co-operative Elevator Company in 1911, and ultimately the Saskatchewan Wheat Pool in 1924. At the same time, local credit unions and retail co-ops were formed to provide alternatives to the central Canadian banking and manufacturing sector. In 1949, the Saskatchewan arm of the United Farmers of Canada was reconstituted as the Saskatchewan Farmers Union, which twenty years later was absorbed in the creation of the National Farmers Union. The SFU's first president was Joe Phelps, a firebrand former CCF member of the Saskatchewan Legislature, which reflected the political alignment between the CCF and the dominant opinion in rural Saskatchewan at the time.[6]

A critical tool in furthering the prairie farm agenda was the *Western Producer*, a widely read and respected weekly farm newspaper owned by the Saskatchewan Wheat Pool. The *Producer*, as it is commonly known, began publishing in 1924 under the ownership of Modern Press in Saskatoon. The press and the newspaper were formerly acquired by the Wheat Pool in 1930 with the explicit objective to promote pooling by farmers.

Another crucial factor that shaped Saskatchewan farm culture was the Crow's Nest Pass freight rate. A public policy set in federal statute in 1897, for generations the Crow Rate was considered an absolute cornerstone of the prairie farm economy. The Crow Rate set in perpetuity maximum amounts railways could charge farmers for hauling prairie grain to export positions. The rate to ship a bushel of grain east to the Lakehead was less than the cost of mailing a letter. Other than when it was suspended during the First World War and then reinstated at a slightly higher level, the Crow Rate remained static over the decades.[7]

The symbolism of the Crow Rate in the psychology of Saskatchewan farm politics was immensely powerful. It was established as a counterweight to a federal grant of more than $3 million that Canadian Pacific Railway (CPR) received to construct a rail line through the Crowsnest Pass to Nelson, BC, where coalfields were being developed. As compensation to prairie grain farmers, freight rates for grain shipment east to the Lakehead and west to Vancouver were frozen by federal law. Captive to the railway duopoly— namely, the privately owned CPR and eventually the state-owned Canadian National Railway (CNR)—farmers felt a deep sense of grievance regarding the unequal relationship that left them no choice other than be at the mercy of the railways to get their grain to market. With prairie farmers landlocked many hundred (and in some cases even more than a thousand) kilometres from export ports, the Crow Rate was seen as part of the Confederation bargain where the commercial power of railways was offset by the imposition of low grain freight rates.[8]

It was the same collective impulse to offset forces elsewhere in the grain trade that led to the creation of the Canadian Wheat Board in 1935 by an act of Parliament. During the First World War, the federal government used its emergency powers to create a stable grain market that resulted in attractive prices for farmers. The Wheat Board, which replaced private grain merchants operating on the Winnipeg Grain Exchange, was given the monopoly for the sale of Canadian prairie wheat, oats, and barley. The concept was based on orderly marketing that would maximize the market power of prairie grain in a global market dominated by state buyers. As a single-desk seller, the Wheat Board served as the farmers' marketing arm, pooling their grain and dispensing to farmers the revenue from sales minus the costs of administration based on the average price it received over the course of the crop year.[9]

It is virtually impossible to overstate the importance of the political and economic culture that emerged from the experience of farmers in those early years. At its peak in the mid-1940s, there were more than 125,000 individual farm units in the province.[10] Many of them were on acreages of one or two quarter sections—160 to 320 acres—very much at the mercy of larger corporate interests like railways, banks, and grain companies that controlled their economic destiny. For example, in 1961 almost 51,000 farms in Saskatchewan, representing more than 54 percent of the 93,924 farms in the province, were less than 560 acres.[11]

It was only logical that the farm culture would eventually be expressed in partisan political terms. In the depths of the Great Depression and drought of the 1930s, the collectivist culture crystallized politically in the formation of the Co-operative Commonwealth Federation, a national political party deeply rooted in Saskatchewan's rural society. Given the toll the Depression took on farmers and unemployed wage earners in cities across Canada, what emerged was a sense of shared interests between farmers and labour to overcome the economic consequences of the period.

The dominant political mood at the time was clearly expressed in the Regina Manifesto, the 1933 philosophical framing document for the creation of the CCF. The Manifesto was heavily influenced by left-wing academics from Toronto and Montreal and clearly reflected a Marxist class perspective on the economic and social challenges of the time. Its preamble stated, "We aim to replace the present capitalist system, with its inherent injustice and inhumanity, by a social order from which the domination and exploitation of one class by another will be eliminated, in which economic planning will supersede unregulated private enterprise and competition, and in which genuine democratic self-government, based upon economic equality will be possible." Specifically, in terms of agriculture, the Manifesto made clear the control of markets and farm prices was key. It did so by referring to "the substitution for the present system of foreign trade, of a system of import boards to improve the efficiency of overseas marketing, to control prices, and to integrate the foreign trade policy with the requirements of the national economic plan." The CCF founding document closed with words that resonated for decades, though seldom to the political benefit of the party itself: "No C.C.F.

Government will rest content until it has eradicated capitalism and put into operation the full programme of socialized planning which will lead to the establishment in Canada of the Cooperative Commonwealth."[12]

Darrin Qualman, former staff writer and researcher for the NFU and a self-described "long-term thinker and civilization critic," perhaps explains it as well or better than anyone. "In Saskatchewan's recent history you had an interlocking network of progressive institutions, that in a way even included the Co-operative Commonwealth Federation (CCF), but most important were the co-operatives at the local levels," says Qualman. "Also, there was the National Farmers Union, focused on policy and education, also workers unions that supported the farmer co-operatives and also an expanding network of credit unions much more locally oriented than big corporate banks. Really this was an interlocking set of political, economic and material entities that to a very significant extent developed our society in Saskatchewan." As for "the echoes of this history today," he explains, "a great part of the economy, the infrastructure and the identity in Saskatchewan was constructed through this co-operative history."[13]

This kind of left-wing prairie populism was common also in the U.S. Midwest. One of the earliest examples of a formal farmer-labour coalition occurred in the United States at the advent of the First World War. The impact of the war, which had the effect of raising prices and depressing wages, led to the union of farmer and labour interests and the creation in 1918 of the Minnesota Farmer-Labor Party.[14] Next door in North Dakota, the same farmer-labour activism was expressed in the creation of the Nonpartisan League, a movement that united progressives, reformers, and left-wing radicals in support of policies that ranged from improved state services and full suffrage for women to state ownership of banks, mills and elevators, and insurance companies.[15] In many ways, the progressive populist current in U.S. politics of that era was a precursor of what happened years later in Saskatchewan with the creation of the CCF and, before that, the rise of the United Farmers and Progressive Party of the 1920s. Clearly the deeply ingrained sense of vulnerability in the farming population and the need for collective action in defence of their interests was not limited by international borders; rather, it was shared by circumstance.

So, the significance of Trudeau's words in the context of the evolution of Saskatchewan's political culture is less about the anger directed at him and more about the inference of what he said. Support for the Canadian Wheat Board remained solid among a significant majority of Saskatchewan farmers in 1969. As an agency of the federal government the Wheat Board was not a co-operative, but it was a democratic farmer-controlled organization in that its directors were elected from active farmers who were Wheat Board permit-book holders. But it would also be a mistake not to recognize that the farmers' anger reflected more than just their dislike of Trudeau and the lack of attention in Ottawa to their needs. It also was evidence of the fraying edges around the existing consensus on how the farm economy was structured and organized. Farmers at the time felt they were again victims in a system that failed to adequately protect their interests.

There was good reason for their anger. It was apparent in the oversupplied global wheat market, its impact on seeded acreage in Saskatchewan, and the knock-on effects on farm income. For example, in 1967 there were 28.4 million seeded acres of spring wheat in Canada, and in 1971 there were slightly more than 9 million acres.[16] Of those totals, the vast majority was in Saskatchewan. In 1970 the total of seeded wheat acreage in Saskatchewan was 8 million acres, down from 19 million just two years earlier.[17] It was not hard to see who was bearing the brunt of the chaos in the global wheat market. It was only a matter of time before the anger would manifest itself, and when it did it was in a way that challenged the accepted wisdom of the Saskatchewan farm economy.

In December 1969, five months after Trudeau's infamous visit to the province, a farmer from Pense, Saskatchewan, named John Wood drove fifty kilometres from his home to the town of Avonlea. He walked into the John Deere dealership to speak with owner Wally Nelson. It was a difficult moment. Wood was there to tell Nelson that he could not pay his bill at the dealership. He had no money. Nelson understood and said not to worry. Wood then went to the nearby town of Drinkwater to tell Nelson's friend and seed dealer Bob Ferguson that he had no money to pay his seed bill.[18]

Ironically, like most Saskatchewan farmers at the time, Wood's grain bins were full. But he was unable to sell his grain because of a world wheat glut that had driven down prices. It had been caused in large measure by the Soviet Union's withdrawal from the market. In an effort to raise prices, Canada, the United States, Europe, Australia, and Argentina colluded to limit supply by withholding grain from the world market. The Wheat Board had imposed a three-bushel-per-acre delivery quota, creating a cash crunch on Saskatchewan farms in spite of their large wheat inventories. The result was a billion-bushel carryover, equalling almost a three-year supply of Canadian grain.[19] True to form and to Saskatchewan's political and economic culture, farmers again felt like pawns in a much larger power play. The difference this time was that, for many, the anger was directed not at the usual suspects—namely, the private grain trade—but at the farmers' own sales agent and creation of the federal government, the Canadian Wheat Board.

At the same time, the federal Liberal government's response was to put in place a program known as Lower Inventory for Tomorrow (LIFT). Implemented by Otto Lang, the member of Parliament from Saskatoon and minister responsible for the Wheat Board, LIFT required farmers to reduce their seeded acreage by 50 percent. Farmers were paid $6 an acre for unseeded acreage to a maximum of $6,000.[20] The situation was what appeared to be a market failure of immense proportions, with the government's Wheat Board withholding Canadian wheat from the market, while the government paid farmers not to grow wheat. Total wheat receipts in Saskatchewan in 1970 were $353 million, down from $553 million in 1968 and $642 million in 1967. The bottom fell out of total net farm income in 1970, plummeting to $195 million from $462 million two years earlier.[21]

For Wally Nelson, the situation was unacceptable. He, Wood, and Ferguson talked about the circumstances and saw the problem as a lack of market competition. They bristled under the Wheat Board's monopoly, the collusion with other wheat-exporting nations, and the inability of individual farmers to market their grain as they saw fit. It was consistent with the decades-old sentiment that farmers lacked control over their lives.

Angered by the fact they had harvested a bumper crop but had a quota of only three bushels an acre, in the fall of 1969 Nelson, Wood, and Ferguson decided to call a group of farmers together to discuss the situation. A total of thirteen showed up, all frustrated by the inability to sell their wheat. "The first thing that became apparent to us was that there was a defeatist attitude prevailing in the marketing end of the business, which seemed to accept a lack of sales as the fate of the best wheat in the world," recalled Art Thompson, one of the original thirteen. "The Saskatchewan group refused to accept the premise emanating from some quarters that a market for unsold Canadian wheat was non-existent." They decided to travel to Winnipeg to meet with Wheat Board officials, the Canadian Grain Commission, and the Winnipeg Commodity Exchange and then travelled to Ottawa to meet with federal politicians. They were told that if they wanted changes, they should form an organization that speaks for their interests. So they did. In April 1970 the Palliser Triangle Wheat Growers Association was officially formed.[22]

Created as a free-market-oriented group, the Palliser Wheat Growers exposed the inherent contradiction in prairie grain farming. Farmers are, in many respects, the ultimate in private entrepreneurs, landowners, and risk takers. They are driven by market incentives. But from the earliest days of settlement in Saskatchewan, and with farm units that, in many cases, were a mere quarter section (160 acres), they were engaged as much in subsistence farming to support their families as in commercial enterprises. It was that foundation for the farming economy that provided the collectivist counter-balance to the free enterprise instincts of farmers and formed the tension in the farming community.

But gradually, as mechanization increased farm productivity and econom-ics drove consolidation of farms, farmers themselves became operators of larger business enterprises. It was an inexorable evolution that slowly under-mined the collectivist and co-operative traditions integral to Saskatchewan agriculture. The emergence of the Palliser Wheat Growers, as a voice that counterbalanced the dominant position expressed by the Saskatchewan Wheat Pool, was an early signal of the shift under way in rural Saskatchewan.

In more modern Saskatchewan terms, the clearest political expression of that strain was the ongoing struggle within the NDP to balance the needs of farmers as private sector entrepreneurs with the urban-based organized labour movement. From the outset, when the former prairie-based CCF joined with the Canadian Labour Congress to form the New Democratic Party in 1961, it was a tactical marriage of convenience intended to build a broad coalition of what were considered like-minded progressive interests. But in one important way it never made sense because the economic needs of farmers and urban-based organized labour were often misaligned. What kept the newly formed party more or less intact was the collectivist and survival impulse of farmers who, in the days of small family farm units, could see the benefit in organizing together for market power to maximize their profit and incomes. It created at least a notional brotherhood with the similarly inspired labour movement. But when labour work stoppages directly affected the farm economy—whether at ports, preventing the loading of grain, or in the movement of railways—the self-interests of farmers and labour inevitably collided.

Underlying the political reality was a sociological fact of a population that steadily became more ethnically diverse as immigration increased. By the late nineteenth century, immigration to Saskatchewan was dominated by people who were Canadian by birth, largely with a British national origin. Virtually erased, both literally and figuratively, by the wave of settlement were the province's Indigenous people. They became economically and socially marginalized, relegated to reserves where they were excluded from the emerging mainstream of the province. As settlement rapidly increased in the first three decades of the twentieth century, many, if not most of, the immigrants were from eastern Europe.[23] A majority were Ukrainian, Austro-Hungarian, Polish, Russian, and German, many fleeing the oppressive policies of forced collectivization and religious persecution they suffered under the rise of Bolshevism. They had learned from experience that state power in the pursuit of the general welfare was something that needed to be used carefully.

It was no coincidence that the key figures who helped establish and lead the CCF were of British origin. They included J.S. Woodsworth, M.J. Coldwell, F.R. Scott, Percy Wright, David Lewis, Lorne Ingle, Carl Hamilton, and T.C. Douglas. Many were born in Britain, or had studied there, and were inculcated by the labour movement and the rise of the class-conscious British Labour party of the 1920s.[24] It was a knowledge far removed from the reality and experience of rural Saskatchewan. The lack of a diverse ethnic leadership in the CCF-NDP would be a factor for decades. Its successive leaders were Coldwell, Douglas, Woodrow Lloyd, and Allan Blakeney, none of whom had a farm background.

In his analysis of prairie politics, political scientist Nelson Wiseman argues that those with roots in British politics, or what he terms "labour-socialists," were the dominant group shaping Saskatchewan's political culture. "Without the new British impact, the CCF never would have attained the stature it did," Wiseman states. The other groups, particularly the non–Anglo Saxons from continental Europe who settled mostly in rural areas, deferred to the British in terms of political leadership.[25] As Wiseman notes, "It seemed both fitting and telling that Saskatchewan's premier in this labour-socialist tradition (Tommy Douglas) was British born and grew up and was politically socialized in Winnipeg's new British labour-socialist environment."[26]

The contradiction inherent in the marriage of the CCF, an agrarian-based populist party, with organized labour dominated by central Canada was always self-evident. The decision by Douglas to leave Saskatchewan to lead the newly created federal New Democratic Party marked a turning point in Saskatchewan politics—it just didn't become apparent until many years later. Not until Roy Romanow, the son of Ukrainian immigrants, became leader in 1987 did the ethnic dominance of leaders of British heritage in the CCF-NDP end.

Ironically, Romanow would often tell the story of how growing up in the Ukrainian neighbourhood on the west side of Saskatoon he saw that his parents and others in the Ukrainian community looked warily on the CCF-NDP. To be a supporter was seen by many to border on heresy. The party was seen to share too many of the collectivist beliefs and instincts that count-less thousands of eastern European immigrants had fled when they came to Saskatchewan. For those people, many of whom farmed or lived in the small towns of rural Saskatchewan, believing in the co-operative movement was one thing. Socialism was something else entirely.

CHAPTER 4

1971

A New Deal

THERE ARE ENDLESS QUOTES ABOUT HISTORY REPEATING itself. One of the more popular is ascribed to Mark Twain. "History doesn't repeat itself, but it often rhymes," he is quoted as saying. As aphorisms go, it's probably as good as any about the cycles of history. In the lead-up to the 1971 election in Saskatchewan, echoes of the past could certainly be heard in the ranks of the Saskatchewan New Democratic Party.

The party had a new leader, Allan Blakeney, selected at a 1970 leadership convention to replace Woodrow Lloyd, who had resigned. The dynamics around Lloyd's resignation were part of other drama playing out within the Saskatchewan and federal NDP at the time. It was a period of considerable tension and ideological strife within the party. In many ways, the NDP was engaged in an existential struggle for its soul. At stake was policy, the party's direction, and, more importantly, its very identity. It had been triggered by the rise of the "Waffle," a fervent wing of the party that issued a manifesto espousing an "independent socialist Canada." The Waffle was driven by a

group of largely Ontario-based academics who advocated a hard-leftward ideological shift for the party where it would proudly embrace the socialist label.
Lloyd was among those who believed the party needed new ideas and was supportive of the Waffle Manifesto. His position created tension and anger for
many in the Saskatchewan party, who saw the Waffle as anathema to the more
pragmatic political culture of Saskatchewan.

It is important to recognize the context of the times. The Saskatchewan
NDP, with Lloyd as leader, had lost power to Ross Thatcher and the Liberals
in 1964, ending twenty uninterrupted years of CCF-NDP rule. The defeat
was particularly galling for the New Democrats as Thatcher, a one-time CCF
MP, had become an ardent and forceful right-wing critic of his former party
and its socialist beliefs. Moreover, the late 1960s were a period of growing
social and political unrest in the United States, much of it focused on anti–
Vietnam War sentiment and the racial divide that stained American society.
Intensifying the unrest were the assassinations of Martin Luther King Jr. and
Robert Kennedy. Canada was not immune to what was happening south of
the border. The same kind of activism was reflected particularly on university
campuses; one hotbed of student radicalism was the Regina campus of the
University of Saskatchewan.[1] As a party of the left, the NDP faced the inevita-
ble pressure to embrace the idealism that was animating debate in the United
States, but from a perspective of overt Canadian nationalism.

The struggle within the Saskatchewan NDP was more than intense. It was
also pivotal. The choice was whether to remain faithful to its populist, agrarian, and more pragmatic Saskatchewan roots, which had been a hallmark of
the party for almost forty years, or to become a much more ideologically socialist party.[2] In many ways the internal pressure of the time was an echo—or a
rhyme, as Twain would describe it—of what took place decades earlier with the
creation of the CCF. Ontario-based labour activists and academics insisted the
Regina Manifesto conclude with the declaration that "no C.C.F. Government
will rest content until it has eradicated capitalism." These were unambiguous words that haunted the party and made many in the Saskatchewan CCF
uncomfortable, especially among the farm population. It wasn't surprising.

As private landowners, many of the people who settled Saskatchewan had come escaping the collectivism and government control of eastern Europe. They sought the promise of owning their own land and the opportunity to build a better life. In some respects, one can argue that those who came to Saskatchewan were pursuing the American dream of "life, liberty and the pursuit of happiness." They were choosing the "New World" of North America, and as farmland became occupied and unavailable in the United States, the option became Canada. The choice was less between Canada and the United States than for the freedom and opportunity that came with a new life in the new world. These shared values and ideals are often overlooked but were at the heart of the rural societies created on both sides of the border. What made the Saskatchewan experiment unique was that, unlike in the Great Plains states of the United States, a democratic socialist party won government in the province. In the United States, the rise of populist socialist sentiment waned and essentially disappeared, other than the remnants of rural co-operative enterprises.

In 1956, the CCF issued its "Winnipeg Declaration," which sought to soften if not erase the Regina Manifesto's commitment to a post-capitalist future. It committed the CCF to what could best be described as Keynesian welfare capitalism, where the state would intervene to mitigate negative economic and social effects. In so doing, it abandoned the Regina Manifesto's call for the nationalization of the finance sector and major industry.[3] The Waffle movement of the late 1960s was a counterforce to that initiative. It was strongly nationalistic, calling explicitly for an independent socialist Canada and even supporting self-determination for Quebec. The Waffle Manifesto opened with the following words: "Our aim as democratic socialists is to build an independent socialist Canada. Our aim as supporters of the New Democratic Party is to make it a truly socialist party."

So, in a very real sense it was déjà vu for the Saskatchewan NDP. The Regina Manifesto, which hung heavily over the Saskatchewan CCF for decades, was a product of Toronto intellectuals who were part of a group known as the League for Social Reconstruction. The primary authors were Frank Underhill from the University of Toronto and Frank Scott of McGill. The Waffle Manifesto carried similar fingerprints. It was a document that, in Saskatchewan political terms, framed the struggle between socialist ideology and the agrarian social democratic pragmatism espoused by Douglas. What unfolded almost forty years after the Regina Manifesto was the same internal conflict over the Waffle and its manifesto, which was also largely the work of Toronto academics, namely James Laxer, Mel Watkins, and Gerry Caplan.[4] Ultimately, in a Saskatchewan context, the more moderate social democrats prevailed, but not without concessions to the left. It played out in the most visible terms in the 1970 leadership race to replace Lloyd. Blakeney won narrowly over Romanow. Both were seen as moderates, with the thirtysomething Romanow considered even more centrist in the NDP spectrum than the more left-leaning Blakeney. The declared Waffle candidate Don Mitchell might have finished third, but the Waffle influence on the party could not be ignored.

One of the first orders of business after Blakeney won the leadership was to begin preparing for a provincial election that was expected within a year. For the Saskatchewan NDP it became a process of accommodating the emergence of the new left sentiment reflected in the Waffle, while not abandoning the pragmatic prairie populism that had been a defining feature of the CCF under Douglas. It was to be an awkward fit, in terms of substance and style. Gone was the populism that had been the lifeblood of Douglas and the CCF, replaced by the politics of policy, deliberation, and the influence of the state. The belief was that the popular appeal of the NDP under Blakeney could be voiced through the channels of government policy.

Blakeney was the first to admit that he was not a populist politician. As someone who grew up in Nova Scotia and came to Saskatchewan early in his working career, Blakeney did not have deep roots in the province. Nor was he fully comfortable with its agrarian culture. This was most evident when he was out in rural Saskatchewan, in town halls, on coffee row, or making small talk with farmers. A Rhodes scholar, lawyer, and government bureaucrat before turning to elected politics, Blakeney's strength was his mind for detail and policy. As Dennis Gruending notes in his political biography of Blakeney,

Promises to Keep, the new NDP leader was "perceived as competent, straight and rather square."⁵ Like many committed socialists who came to Saskatchewan to work for the Douglas government, Blakeney too was attracted by the possibility of joining North America's first and only socialist government.

As a politician, Blakeney realized his style could not compete with the likes of a fiery, blunt-talking Thatcher. "Nor was I ever going to be a tribune of the people like Tommy Douglas, who could encapsulate their hopes and fears in a phrase," Blakeney said of himself. "I was always going to be a quasi-scholar or the re-tread public servant who would analyze the problems and say, this is what we ought to do."⁶ It was an honest self-assessment that conceded he was not in the tradition of a prairie populist. Blakeney's appeal was to reason, not to the passion and emotion at the core of populism. Instead of the hopes and aspirations of people being articulated and embodied in an individual, it would be the government that was to be the vehicle of populist expression. Or so the NDP believed. In retrospect, decades later, this time marked a turning point for the party in Saskatchewan.

Within days of taking over as leader, Blakeney appointed a policy committee to begin work on an election platform. The idea of a government "land bank," which had been generated by the Waffle, became a point of heated debate. The core issue was land tenure. The land bank would purchase land and rent it ostensibly to young farmers who did not have the capital to buy it. The question was whether the land bank would be a means to maintain the transfer of private ownership of land or a mechanism to accumulate privately held land into government control. Blakeney and others recognized the importance of private farm ownership as a founding principle of the province and the political danger of government overreach. He successfully insisted that an option-to-purchase the land had to be included to ensure that land purchase by government could be sold back into private hands.⁷ Even with Blakeney's intervention, it was a policy with huge political implications that went to the heart of the foundations of rural Saskatchewan.

What Blakeney sought was to position the Saskatchewan Land Bank program as a vehicle to assist in the intergenerational transfer of farmland, not an attempt by government to take ever-increasing ownership of privately held farms in the province. The government would be a facilitator, to help bridge the transfer of private land from one generation to the next. Ideally any land acquired by the Land Bank would be held only temporarily in government hands until it could be purchased by a farmer who had acquired the capital necessary for purchase.

When the Blakeney government implemented the Saskatchewan Land Bank Commission in 1972, Agriculture Minister Jack Messer, himself a farmer, explained it this way:

> A great many farmers in Saskatchewan are beyond retirement age, but due to the poor economics of farming they have not been able to sell other than at fire-sale prices. They haven't been able to transfer land to their sons because their sons, or daughter are were [sic] not in the position to guarantee them the kinds of money from that farming unit that would allow them to retire with dignity and security and also provide them with a living farming that land....I think they'll see the Land Bank as a real attractive means of being able to sell their land to the commission, thereby providing them with the kinds of money they need to retire and also transfer the land to their sons through the commission giving their sons or daughters an opportunity to establish a farming enterprise.[8]

The reaction of the Opposition Liberals was explicit and telling, reflecting how the Land Bank was at odds with the core founding principle of Saskatchewan—specifically, the opportunity for immigrants to settle on the Prairies and own their own plot of land. The Liberals said they did not oppose government assisting in the transfer of farmland from one farmer to another but emphatically and categorically rejected the transfer of private land to state ownership. "It will result in the Saskatchewan farmer becoming nothing but a tenant and a sharecropper," said Liberal MLA Cy MacDonald. "We violently oppose state ownership and state control of the agricultural soil of Saskatchewan."[9]

In the months leading to the June 1971 provincial election, the NDP put together a detailed and far-reaching platform it called the "New Deal for People." It was a document with the explicit intent of establishing an agenda where government would play a major role in the economy. The contrast from the private enterprise model and largely non-interventionist government of Ross Thatcher could hardly have been more pronounced.[10] The NDP's "New Deal" represented a seismic shift in the politics and role of government in Saskatchewan. It was, in no small measure, a result of the Waffle influence within the party.[11]

The twenty-one-page New Deal for People set out more than one hundred specific promises and actions. Chief among an exhaustive and exhausting list was what the party saw as the degradation of agriculture and decline of small communities. The rural strategy was nothing if not comprehensive. In response to the perceived rural challenge, the NDP promised to exercise greater control over what it saw as the socially destructive efforts to achieve economic efficiency through the development of large, corporately managed farms, as part of a strategy to arrest the depopulation of rural Saskatchewan.[12]

The objective was to stabilize farming by intervening against market forces. For years the evidence had been mounting that rural Saskatchewan was inexorably changing, as reflected primarily in the growth of individual farm units. By 1971, the average farm size in the province was 845 acres, compared with 686 acres a decade earlier. During the same period the number of farms had declined by almost 20 percent, from 93,924 to 76,970.[13] The NDP believed something had to be done to halt the change.

The foundation for the strategy was to maintain the rural economy and society that had been the backbone of the NDP's political strength during the Douglas years. Maximizing the number of viable family farms, which would help maintain vibrant small communities, was key. The proposal was, in a very explicit sense, inherently conservative. Government was to serve as a bulwark to preserve the fabric of rural Saskatchewan against the economic forces of change. As a result, the agriculture plan called for a restriction on corporate ownership of family farms and co-operatives, in part by keeping farm ownership in Canadian hands. The proposed Land Bank Commission would assist in the intergenerational transfer of land, and a government lending agency would provide capital credit to farmers. There would even be a farmers' bill of rights, a hog marketing board to prevent the growth of large-scale corporate hog operations, and a commitment that small hospitals would remain open, coupled with small-town housing projects. In total, the "New Deal" included thirty-seven rural and farm-specific commitments. Underlying it all was the NDP's absolute belief in the sanctity of the Crow Rate as a non-negotiable cornerstone of the Saskatchewan farm economy.

The platform went much further. In response to the private control and development of resources under the Thatcher government, the NDP promised that Saskatchewan's people would develop their own resources as a means to maximize benefits for the province. A Saskatchewan Development Corporation would mobilize capital for public investment in economic development and prevent the further sale of resources to private interests by giving first priority to public ownership through Crown corporations. It would also support co-operative ownership and partnerships between government and co-operatives/private developers; scrutinize and, if necessary, renegotiate royalty and other arrangements; renew renewable resources and conserve non-renewable resources; require business and industry to adhere strictly to environmental policies; and support small business. Additional specific commitments were made in fourteen other policy areas, including labour, small business, taxation, education, health, social security and welfare, pollution, and Indian and Métis programs.[14]

When voters went to the polls on June 23, 1971, the choice between the NDP and the governing Thatcher Liberals could not have been clearer or more stark. But aside from the parties' different visions for the role of government in the province, a powerful factor in the election was the negative public sentiment against Pierre Trudeau's federal Liberal government. Trudeau's words—"Why should I sell your wheat?"—still echoed as Saskatchewan farmers continued to struggle under an oversupplied global wheat market, weak export sales, and low prices hovering around $1.70 a bushel, below what it was five years earlier.[15] But there were early signs that the worst of the previous three years, when wheat export sales plummeted, was over. By 1970, sales had reached 410 million bushels—91 million bushels more than the year before and well above the low point of 281 million bushels in 1968.[16]

The NDP campaign was designed to link the anti–federal Liberal sentiment in the province to Thatcher and the provincial Liberals. It mattered little that Thatcher and Trudeau could hardly have been more different in style and ideology and often clashed over policy, with Thatcher disagreeing with much of the federal agenda. "A Liberal is a Liberal is a Liberal," Blakeney would say at virtually every campaign stop. To drive home the point, the NDP used a federal government task force report issued in 1969, called *Canadian Agriculture in the Seventies*, as a weapon to attack both the provincial and federal Liberals. The report played perfectly to the NDP's "New Deal" agriculture policy, which sought to protect and maintain the status quo on farms and across rural Saskatchewan. Not surprisingly, the federal task force found widespread dissatisfaction with low farm incomes, uncertain markets and prices, overproduction, small non-viable farms, and diminishing export markets. Today, the report reads like a window on the reality of Saskatchewan in 2022. It recommended that government reduce its direct involvement in agriculture. Specifically, it called for the phase-out of subsidies and price supports and for a reduction in the farm population and recommended that younger low-income farmers should leave farming, while older non-viable farmers should be assisted to achieve a better standard of living. The report also predicted that wheat surpluses would continue in the 1970s and suggested that farmers should begin diversifying into other crops.[17]

The influence of federal politics, particularly the prevailing negative attitudes toward the federal Liberal government and the NDP strategy to exploit that reality, was reflected in media reports on the campaign. Bill Cameron, a CBC reporter in Regina covering the campaign, made a point of focusing on it in his report to a national radio audience ten days before the election. "The NDP has been trying very hard, and with some success I think, to link the federal and provincial Liberals all in the same bag. The

Liberals are hoping an improved situation for grain markets, wheat sales to Russia and China, the $100 million acreage payout that's pending from the federal government, that these will create a better atmosphere and take some of the heat off them," Cameron said.[18]

It was not to be for the Liberals. The NDP won a large majority, collecting forty-five seats to the Liberals' fifteen. At 55 percent, the NDP share of the popular vote rose by almost 11 percent from what it had been in 1967, while the Liberal share of the vote dropped by 2.75 percent to slightly less than 43 percent.

. A curious and relevant outcome was the surprising resilience of the Liberal vote. It held amazingly firm for an election where the mood for change was evident. The total Liberal vote in 1971 was 193,864, only seven votes fewer than the 193,871 the party had received to win a majority in 1967. The most significant result, at least in terms of effect on the outcome, was the steep drop in support for the provincial Progressive Conservative Party. Although in a perpetual weakened state for decades, often without representation in the legislature, the PCs saw their vote fall by more than 7 percent. The party was able to run only sixteen candidates, in part owing to Thatcher's effort in polarizing the vote on a left-right basis to create a head-to-head Liberal-NDP battle. It was a tactic that failed on two levels. It did not grasp the depth of the anti-Liberal mood amongst the electorate, much of it focused on Trudeau and the federal Liberal government. Nor did it adequately recognize that a significant portion of NDP voters in provincial elections supported the PCs federally. It was a transfer of loyalties that worked both ways, with a large portion of the provincial PC vote transferable to the Saskatchewan NDP.

What happened was that the PC vote essentially collapsed, with a majority going to the NDP. This was evidence of two interrelated factors. One was the deeply rooted anti–federal Liberal sentiment in the province whereby many traditional PC supporters could not bring themselves to vote for a party under the Liberal banner yet could comfortably vote for the NDP. It was an opportunity to send a message to Ottawa. The other factor was the effectiveness of the NDP's campaign in tying the Thatcher and Trudeau Liberals together. The migration of voters to the NDP was also consistent with the crossover PC voters who had supported Diefenbaker federally and the CCF-NDP provincially. They saw it as consistent with their populist instincts.

On election night, a jubilant Blakeney was clearly happy and surprised by the scope of the NDP victory. He had predicted the NDP would win thirty-seven seats. They won forty-five. "We thumped them. We will put the province once again in the hands of the people," Blakeney said. He attributed the success largely to a "straight repudiation of federal agriculture policies."[19] It was an explanation consistent with the strain of prairie populist protest that had long been the driving force of the economic alienation that animated Saskatchewan politics.

Not surprisingly, the NDP interpreted the result to be a strong endorsement of its New Deal for People platform. The victory was taken as consent for sweeping action, and the Blakeney government eagerly acted on its mandate. A new era was dawning for the NDP—one it thought would be consistent with its own populist past. However, it wasn't and wouldn't be.

CHAPTER 5

1974

A Federal Invasion

WHEN FINANCE MINISTER JOHN TURNER ROSE IN THE House of Commons to deliver the Trudeau government's budget on November 18, 1974, it was for the second time in six months. To say the repeat was anticlimactic would be an understatement. More accurate would be to argue that for some, particularly the governments of Saskatchewan and Alberta, the federal budget was like salt rubbed into the open wound created by the previous budget on May 6. What it did was further complicate a conflict over natural resource control that was beginning to consume the Blakeney government's attention and energy, and would for years to come.

The November budget was largely an echo of what Turner had presented in May, which had been a budget that led to the defeat of the minority Liberal government when the federal NDP abandoned its support of the Liberals and voted with the Progress Conservatives to defeat the government. The PCs believed the budget did not properly address the inflation that was ravaging the economy at a crippling rate of 11.5 percent. The NDP argued that the Liberals had ignored its wishes and the party could no longer prop up the Trudeau government.

For the eighteen months of the Liberal minority that resulted from the 1972 federal election, the NDP wielded the balance of power and used it to take credit for measures that the Trudeau government implemented. The list included the creation of the Crown-owned Petro-Canada, increased pensions and family allowances, cuts in personal income tax, subsidies to offset higher bread and milk prices, greater controls on foreign investment, an export tax on oil, and controls on election spending.[1] It was obviously a calculated political risk for the NDP to defeat the government—one that the party and its leader, David Lewis, who was defeated in the subsequent July 8 election, would live to regret.

"The government brought it down upon itself," Lewis said minutes after the budget was defeated. "It produced a budget that was unacceptable to anyone with any sensitivity about the needs of the Canadian people, the cost of living. To ask us to support a budget that gave the ordinary workers 96 cents a week in a tax cut is just irresponsible and the prime minister was responsible for it and the government had to come down. I think they were becoming paralytic almost, and the people of Canada will have the opportunity to say whether the kind of budget they presented was right or wrong."[2] For his part, PC leader Robert Stanfield had staked his economic message on the need for federally imposed wage-and-price controls to tame the inflationary pressures ravaging the economy. Trudeau opposed any such heavy-handed intervention in the economy—a position that he would take in the subsequent election campaign and then abruptly reverse shortly after regaining a majority government.

Two key dimensions in the May budget set the stage for years of federal-provincial struggle over the control of natural resources, and oil in particular. One was treatment of provincial royalties and taxes for federal tax purposes, and the other was levels of federal tax on the production of natural resources. The words of the May budget echoed throughout the subsequent election campaign and its aftermath. "Revenues derived by provincial governments in respect of production from a petroleum or mineral resource should no longer be deductible in computing the income of the operator of the resource," Turner said when delivering that budget. "I propose that with regard to the taxation of mineral resource profits, none of these payments to provinces be recognized as deductible in determining corporate tax. I point out, moreover, that this bears not only on the federal corporation tax but also on the provincial corporation tax for those provinces for whom we collect this tax."[3] The Trudeau government took it one step further. It cut federal tax incentives, including depletion allowances, and scaled back the Canadian exploration and development expenditures that had been an immediate deductible expense.

Emboldened by the Liberals' majority government win in the July election, Turner's subsequent budget do-over in November further asserted the government's determination to exercise greater control over natural resources. In his speech, Turner reiterated verbatim the five principles that he had outlined in his previous budget. There were two key ones. In Turner's own words, "it is essential to ensure that all the people of Canada derive a fair share of the substantially increased revenues that flow from the higher value placed by the world on these resources," and "the federal government must ensure that provincial royalties, provincial mining taxes and other arrangements having similar effects do not unreasonably erode the corporate income tax base."[4] They were words that could have been taken out of the Saskatchewan government's handbook as expressed in its New Deal for People platform. The crucial difference was the order of government that had control and ownership of natural resources. A conflict with provinces, which had constitutional jurisdiction over natural resources, was inevitable.

It didn't take long. Ten days after the November budget, the Blakeney government delivered its Throne Speech to open a new sitting of the Saskatchewan Legislature. The speech led off with ominous language about the federal intrusion into provincial jurisdiction over resources. It argued that the budget "invades the right of a province to control the development of natural resources within its boundaries. By undermining the relationships which have existed between Federal and Provincial Governments for many decades, it has set government against government, and region against region and in so doing has weakened the fabric of Confederation."[5]

The clash between federal and provincial interests had been building for months. In the wake of the OPEC oil crisis a year earlier and the rapid escalation in oil prices that fanned the flames of inflation, the Trudeau government had been seeking measures that would give it greater access to the revenue from high oil prices. First, in September 1973 it froze the wellhead price of Alberta and Saskatchewan oil at $3.80 a barrel to protect central Canadian consumers from having to shoulder higher gasoline prices. The freeze was supposed to be temporary, for five months, at which point the price would return to world levels; however, when there was a rapid increase in the world price in the ensuing months, the freeze remained to protect Canadian consumers.[6] Next, the Trudeau government imposed a 375 percent increase in the federal export tax, from 40 cents to $1.90 a barrel, in November 1973 as part of measures to limit exports and protect Canadian energy self-sufficiency.[7]

In response to rising oil prices and the federal intrusion, the Blakeney government passed *The Saskatchewan Oil and Gas Corporation Act*. It served three purposes. By creating SaskOil, a Crown corporation engaged in the exploration and production of oil, the government was shielded from federal taxation. The BNA Act unequivocally states that one order of government cannot impose a tax on another. As a provincial Crown corporation owned by the province, SaskOil would thus be exempt from federal taxes. It also allowed government to determine the level of oil profits that would flow to the provincial treasury as dividends. SaskOil also gave the government a "window" into the operations of an oil company to better judge appropriate oil sector royalty rates, corporate tax levels, and regulatory measures.

A case study by Robert Sexty for the Institute of Public Administration of Canada identified several policy considerations that were part of the decision to create SaskOil. They included social concerns, "including sensitive issues such as the OPEC oil boycott, increasing petroleum prices, and the need to preserve petroleum resources for Saskatchewan residents."[8] The government also wanted to stimulate more oil production at a time when interest and investment were bypassing Saskatchewan and flowing to Alberta. According to Sexty, the belief was that being an active player in the oil industry would give the government the insight it needed to shape policy in the best interests of Saskatchewan. Yet it was not entirely clear how creating a government-owned oil company was going to encourage greater investment in the sector.

The mounting tension between Ottawa and the provinces, particularly Alberta and Saskatchewan, led to the First Ministers' Conference on Energy held in January 1974. In his opening statement, Trudeau plainly stated the federal government's priority due to rapid oil price increases resulting from the actions of OPEC to cut its production in response to the Yom Kippur War. "It is because the consequences of this sudden crisis are so great that this conference must not be solely about oil or even about energy. It must also concern the nature of our Canadian community, and the purposes which join us in our Confederation," he said. "While the federal government recognizes the legitimate interests of both provincial governments and private companies, we are determined to safeguard the interests of the consumers of Canada."[9] The federal government had watched as Saskatchewan and Alberta moved quickly to capture the economic rent from windfall profits created by the OPEC-induced rise in oil prices. Ottawa clearly wanted to get its hands on some of that revenue.

For the Blakeney government, the federal intrusion was another complication among a growing number of headaches over control of resources in the province. The NDP had come to power promising in its New Deal for People platform to ensure that Saskatchewan reaped the full benefits of its resources. In the wake of the OPEC crisis, the Blakeney government acted in the fall and winter of 1973–74 by aggressively moving to scoop the windfall profits flowing to oil companies as a result of the escalating price.[10] Bill 42, *The Oil and Gas Conservation, Stabilization and Development Act*, imposed what was termed a "mineral income tax" of 100 percent of the difference between the price at the wellhead and the "basic well-head price," which was a statutory amount that was the same as the per barrel price received by producers prior to the energy crisis.[11]

Shortly after the legislation took effect, Canadian Industrial Gas & Oil Ltd. (CIGOL) filed a constitutional challenge, arguing that the new royalties and taxes were unconstitutional under section 92 of the *BNA Act*. CIGOL's claim rested on two points: first, that the new mineral tax and royalty surcharge amounted to an indirect tax, which was beyond the constitutional powers of the province; and second, that the tax constrained interprovincial trade and commerce, which also exceeded provincial jurisdiction. It opened a new front in the struggle between the Blakeney government and resource sector companies.

The conflict over resources was not limited to oil. From the moment the NDP took power, it had been engaged in back-and-forth wrangling with potash-mining companies over a system of prorationing that the Thatcher government had imposed on the industry. In 1969, during a period of over-production, the price of potash plummeted to $10 a ton—far from a high of $26 a ton in 1964.[12] In response, the government implemented the Potash Conservation Regulations, which gave the government control of production by requiring potash producers to obtain a producing licence from the minister responsible. Giving the province control of production effectively gave it control over the price. Facing what was clearly a textbook example of market failure, there was no outcry from the potash companies at the time.

As the official opposition, Blakeney and the NDP had opposed the prorationing scheme, promising instead to use other means to ensure Saskatchewan people got a "fair return" on the province's resources. As Blakeney told the 1972 annual NDP convention, "The public interest—not private gain—must be the basis for an alternative strategy."[13] Once in power, however, Blakeney realized that until the potash market and price recovered, the Thatcher regulations should remain in place. To make good on its election promise to extract more revenue from resource development for taxpayers, the NDP government initially moved by implementing a prorationing fee of 60 cents a ton, while maintaining control over production. What unfolded was escalating tension and unfolding legal drama between the government and the potash industry, as the government sought to capture higher rents as potash prices recovered.[14]

One company, Central Canada Potash, launched a court action in December 1972 that the prorationing regulations be declared beyond the province's legal power and authority. At issue was the prorationing and price stabilization scheme that would reduce the amount Central Canada Potash could produce. The company refused to be bound by the new scheme, arguing that it was being prevented from meeting the signed supply contracts that it had with customers. In a subsequent letter, the deputy minister responsible demanded that the company comply with the scheme and warned that if it didn't its licence to produce potash would be revoked. The company then sought a court order requiring the minister to issue a more favourable producing licence. The application was dismissed and two appeals were likewise dismissed. Before the issue reached the Supreme Court of Canada, Central Canada Potash filed a case challenging the constitutionality of the legislation. The Attorney General of Canada intervened and joined with the company as a plaintiff in the action, further souring relations between Saskatchewan and Ottawa.[15]

Ultimately, in a unanimous decision, the Supreme Court ruled in favour of Central Canada Potash. Its decision hinged on the fact that potash produced in Saskatchewan is destined for international markets and interprovincial and international trade was the exclusive jurisdiction of the federal government. The Supreme Court overturned the decision of the Saskatchewan Court of Appeal, which had found the legislation valid because it sought to control the production and sale of potash, to determine fair prices, and to prorate production when advisable.[16] In other words, the Saskatchewan court believed the legislation allowed the province to manage its natural resources as it saw fit as part of its constitutional jurisdiction established under *The Natural Resources Transfer Act* of 1930.

Meanwhile, the provincial NDP government and the potash industry were also about to clash on a second legal front. In April 1974, mere weeks before Turner's first budget, the Blakeney government met with the industry to explain a series of policy changes, including the introduction of a potash reserve tax that would be based on the assessed value of potash deposits. According to a study of Saskatchewan resource taxation by David Anderson, a professor of business administration at the University of Regina, the reserve tax was "as much a non-tax instrument as a revenue generator." He said it could be more accurately described as a "disguised profits tax."[17] The levy was forecast to raise $60 million annually in new revenue. But it required the co-operation of potash companies that included the release of their financial statements as part of the assessment process. When the Trudeau government subsequently announced that taxes and royalties paid by resource companies to provincial governments would be non-deductible for federal income tax purposes, the Blakeney government's reserve tax became untenable from the perspective of the companies.

The government waited for a response from the potash industry to its reserve tax initiative. "We waited in vain," Blakeney said later. "The companies did not put forward any counter proposals for the tax regime. They did not provide us with any financial statements. And they went one step further; they began to withhold information on how much potash they were in fact mining, so that we had no way to calculate royalties on the old basis. This was wholly unacceptable. No company can remove a public resource and decline to pay for it."[18] Then, in June 1975, just nine days after the Blakeney government had won re-election with another majority, the potash companies launched a court challenge against the reserve tax. It was a reaction to an October 1974 potash policy announcement that actually reduced the original reserve tax applied on production but, because of strengthening potash prices, would still increase revenue to the province. The conflict with the potash sector was quickly escalating into a direct challenge to the Blakeney government's stated political objectives in both the 1971 New Deal for People platform and a second version of the New Deal on which it campaigned and won in the 1975 election.

Faced with battles on two fronts—the intransigence and growing legal challenges from the potash industry, and the federal intrusion into provincial royalties and resource taxation—the Blakeney government made a critical decision. In February 1975, four months prior to the provincial election, the government created a new Crown corporation called the Potash Corporation of Saskatchewan (PCS). According to John Burton, a close associate of Blakeney who was intimately involved in developing potash policy during the period, PCS would "provide an instrument to manage any participation in the industry that might flow from the October 1974 policy."[19] Burton's book *Potash: An Inside Account of Saskatchewan's Pink Gold* offers an excellent, comprehensive, and detailed perspective and analysis of the policy, strategy, and execution on the potash issue during the Blakeney government years.

The conflict over resources had a profound effect on the economy and political climate of Saskatchewan. In many respects the agenda was imposed on the government by external factors, from the OPEC crisis and its economic consequences to the federal government's policy decisions to assert greater control and derive more revenue from the increased value of oil production. Not only did it dominate the NDP government's first term; more broadly, it further entrenched the long-held sense of regional alienation from federal power in Ottawa. In that regard, it was a period consistent with the province's political history. What was different was the government-to-government and constitutional nature of the conflict. The two levels of government were at odds over fundamental issues of constitutional jurisdiction including control of resources and international trade—important, even critical, issues, but seen as arcane by many people simply trying to survive the effects that stagflation was having on their lives.

But NDP ideology was also a determining factor in the federal-provincial conflict. The Blakeney government had come to power with an expansive and ambitious agenda, one where the instruments and institutions of government would be used to take greater control of the economy. It was a philosophy grounded in the socialist principles that government could intervene through tax policy and public ownership in a way that would shape the market and capture a greater share of the economic rent from the development of resources, maximizing the benefit to the government and, therefore, to the people of the province. It was fundamentally about what the NDP saw as economic and social justice through redistribution using the levers of power. The agenda had not changed during Blakeney's first term, only the speed of its application owing to world events and the response of other governments, particularly the Government of Canada.

There had certainly been federal-provincial tensions in the past. The previous Thatcher government was often at odds with the government in Ottawa, but never to the depth experienced during the first term of the Blakeney government. The stage was much bigger, with the Saskatchewan and federal governments meeting in court to determine the limits of power in the context of Canada's constitution, the BNA Act. It was very much about governments and their jurisdiction in the exercise of power. The struggle over control of resources, much of it imposed on Saskatchewan by federal government policy, steadily began to consume the attention, focus, and energy of the Blakeney government. It was a major distraction that, in retrospect, eroded the sitting government's political instincts as well.

While all this was unfolding, the political ground in the province was shifting. Largely unnoticed, the long moribund provincial Progressive Conservative Party—a perennially marginalized third-place party since the rise of the CCF in the 1930s—was stirring to life. The NDP's defeat of the Liberal government in 1971 had in large measure resulted from the provincial PC vote collapsing and going to the NDP as an expression of anger against the federal Liberal government of Pierre Trudeau. In 1973, a political neophyte and one-time Saskatoon mayoral candidate named Richard Collver became leader of the provincial Tories, infusing the party with energy at a time when many on the right in Saskatchewan politics believed the Liberals lacked what was needed to defeat the NDP. They also felt the Liberal Party had not renewed itself following the loss of government, most evident in the elevation of Dave Steuart as leader following Thatcher's sudden death in 1971. Steuart was closely associated with Thatcher, seen as his lieutenant, and became a symbol of the party's failure to regenerate itself. The fact too that Trudeau had won a second majority in 1974 and remained persona non grata for many in the West further weakened the provincial Liberals' standing.

In the 1975 provincial election campaign, the NDP ran on an updated version of its New Deal for People. A central ingredient in its campaign rhetoric was the Blakeney government's defence of Saskatchewan's resources by standing up to the attempted incursions by the federal Liberal government. The NDP campaign was built on leadership, strong and effective resource management, and an expansion of the welfare state. The NDP was asking voters to give it a mandate to negotiate taxation issues that were at the heart of relations with the federal government.[20] It was a message that resonated.

There were two primary objectives to the Liberal campaign, both linked to reducing government power. One was to open the province to more private investment, which would generate more corporate tax revenue. The other was to put an end to the Saskatchewan Land Bank. It would be phased out, with a Liberal government offering financial support to farmers wishing to buy the land they were leasing from the government-owned Land Bank. Rhetorically, Steuart described the Land Bank and other NDP policies as designed to "take over" agriculture. He claimed it was part of a government policy strategy to, first, buy the land; second, create marketing boards to control how farmers can market their product; third, restrict foreign ownership of land; and fourth, implement succession duties and tax legislation that would impede the generational transfer of land.[21]

As the NDP and Liberals went at each other, left out of the fray were Collver and the Conservatives who, for the first time in several elections, ran a full slate of candidates. With virtually no significant expectations going into the campaign, it was a no-lose situation for the Tories. Collver was a mercurial character, a compelling speaker with a populist flair, and a superb and tireless organizer. Long-time party member and one-time mayor of Prince Albert Dick Spencer talked about there being a "good" Collver and a "bad" Collver. Spencer said the good Collver was "sympathetic, upbeat and waggish," while the bad Collver was "impatient, explosive and sullen."[22] Good or bad, it was just the combination of traits that a party trying to escape from the margins of provincial politics needed from its leader. Collver would chastise the New Democrats and Liberals as they attacked each other on the campaign trail and call for more civility in politics. "Mud thrown is ground lost," he would often say.

The 1975 election results were, on the surface, a comfortable victory for the NDP. The Blakeney government returned with a majority, winning thirty-nine seats in the sixty-one-seat legislature, representing a decline of six seats. The Liberals won fifteen seats, the same number they held going into the election. Beyond the NDP's re-election, the most noteworthy outcome was the rise of Collver and the PCs. Going into the campaign they had no representation in the legislature. By the end of election night they held seven seats. But even more telling was the popular vote. The NDP share of the vote fell 15 percentage points from where it was in 1971, to 40 percent; the Liberals plummeted 12 points, from 43 to 31 percent; and the Progressive Conservatives shot up 26 points, from 2 percent in 1971 to 28 percent. Do the math. It indicated that NDP and Liberal voters had deserted their parties to vote for the PCs, with slightly more New Democrats than Liberals voting for Collver and the PCs. Something was afoot.

The political tremors of the moment across Saskatchewan the night of June 11, 1975, seemed minor, with attention focused on the NDP's comfortable, if reduced, majority. It would be several years before the magnitude of the shift under way would become apparent and the aftershocks fully felt.

CHAPTER 6

1975

A New Year's Eve Party

A SMALL GROUP OF PEOPLE GATHERED TO WELCOME THE arrival of the new year at the Regina home of a couple who were ardent lifelong supporters of the New Democratic Party. The invited guests included mostly NDP supporters and one couple from the neighbourhood. The hosts' daughter was babysitting for the next-door couple so they could join the celebration. Among the guests was Premier Allan Blakeney.

It was an entirely pleasant evening of conversation that was spiced with political banter and good cheer. One of the many conversations was about the looming advent of cable television to Saskatchewan and its potential effects on attitudes and the very political culture of the province. In the borderline region near the Saskatchewan-U.S. boundary, some Saskatchewan homes had for several years been able to get local programming over the air from small American local TV stations, such as in Williston, North Dakota. But the situation was changing as the process to bring cable television to Saskatchewan was well under way. On offer would be the prime U.S. networks—CBS, NBC,

ABC—from major cities like Detroit, bringing into Saskatchewan homes wall-to-wall American news and programming. The Blakeney government was in the midst of protracted negotiations with what was then called the Canadian Radio and Television Commission (CRTC) over control of the delivery hardware for cable TV and the multitude of programming choices that would be on offer to Saskatchewan residents.

In the course of the informal conversations that night, Blakeney talked briefly and thoughtfully about the arrival of cable TV and what it would mean for Saskatchewan. He put it in the traditional context of Canadian nationalism. The influence of the United States, economically, culturally, and politically, had long been an issue of concern in Canada, particularly among members of the left. Only a few years earlier, the NDP had gone through a wrenching debate, driven by the emergence of the Waffle within its ranks. The Waffle Manifesto of 1969 focused largely on the influence of America on Canada. It spoke of creating "an independent socialist Canada" and asserted that "the major threat to Canadian survival today is American control of the Canadian economy. The major issue of our times is not national unity but national survival, and the fundamental threat is external, not internal." Its objective was to end U.S. dominance of Canada, economically and culturally, noting that "the American empire is the central reality for Canadians."[1]

Specifically, Blakeney talked of the need for the provincial government to ensure, as best it could, the opportunity for local and Canadian programming to also flourish with the arrival of cable TV so as to counterbalance the cultural effects of the arrival of unfiltered American TV. But speaking with a friendly gathering of partisans, the premier also put it into blunt political terms. He conceded that his government's agenda was already constrained by the existing political influence of the U.S. giant to the south. He lamented that the arrival of cable television would make it increasingly difficult for his government to advance a more activist socialist agenda, which he clearly would prefer to do. Heads were nodding in agreement as the premier expressed reservations about the growing cultural and political impact of U.S. television on Saskatchewan and Canada.[2]

Those were the very early days of the telecommunications revolution that was to unfold and that continues to this day. A great deal has been written about the effects on Canadian culture and attitudes in a world where borders dissolve as global mass communications expand. In one analysis, George Barnett and Thomas McPhail suggest that with the importation of a "foreign" culture through the mass media, the possibility grows that people will adopt norms and expectations appropriate to the external culture but considered inappropriate to the local (Canadian) culture. They ask, how much American socialization is taking place in Canada? They answer their own question by suggesting two hypotheses: the greater the exposure to U.S. television, the more a Canadian will perceive of him or herself as an American; and, by extension, with increased exposure to U.S. television, the less a Canadian will perceive of him or herself as a Canadian.[3]

In the context of today's world of instantaneous and ubiquitous digital communications, which are completely impervious to national borders, the concern in 1975 over the arrival of three U.S. network channels seems almost quaint. But as we know now, the advent of cable TV marked the leading edge of a communications revolution that was to unfold over the following decades, creating the completely interconnected and culturally borderless world of today. The consequences of what is now an utterly interconnected world, down to the level of the individual, have been utterly transformative in terms of social, political, and economic outcomes. Like all societies, Saskatchewan has felt the effects as it has become integrated into a global consciousness that has empowered individuals, exposing them to ideas and influences that can stir populist passions and impulses.

The arrival of cable television in the mid-1970s was the very earliest evidence of the transformation in communications beginning to emerge that has fundamentally reshaped the world of today. In retrospect, trying to quantify in any objective measurable way the effect of people's exposure to the arrival of U.S. television in their living rooms is virtually impossible. The factors that shape attitudes, cultures, and societies are almost limitless in number. But it is certainly true that, over time, dominant cultures weaken the values that serve to create the social cohesion of the societies that the dominant culture encounters.

There are those who argue that Canada's policy of official multicultural-ism is itself a factor that weakens the fabric of the nation. Encouraging people to retain their cultural differences and identities, they would say, results in a population defined by what makes each group distinct, rather than a common national identity that is greater than simply a recognition of diversity.[4]

Barnett and McPhail say that defining one's self requires an understanding of the conceptual environment that forms personal identity. In their study, they defined the self in terms of the United States, Canada, and media con-cepts, and they saw a direct correlation between exposure to American TV and identity. "The measured distances of the self from Canada and the United States gives an indication of the strength of Canadian identity. The results indicate the segment of the sample that watches more U.S. TV perceives of themselves further from Canada or less Canadian and closer to the United States or more American, than the group that watches little U.S. television. This group could be expected to hold more American than Canadian values," they concluded.[5]

In another study of TV viewers in borderland Canadian cities that had access to over-the-air U.S. programming, the results also indicate significant effects. In the city of Windsor, for example, authors Stuart Surlin and Barry Berlin found a "consistent pattern of response" in that those who view a higher percentage of U.S. television programming exhibit a more favourable attitude toward U.S. programming. Compared with other viewers, they also believe that Canada is culturally less unique, consider Canadian culture to be less worth preserving, and are less conscious of television's potential to under-mine culture and interpersonal relations.[6] The political implications of those effects are obvious.

This was exactly the point that Blakeney feared about the incursion of cable TV and American programming into Saskatchewan. The problem for his government was the issue of control. As was so often the case in mat-ters of natural resources, it came down to jurisdiction and who had the legal authority to act. When it came to cable TV, the federal government had clear and unequivocal authority over telecommunications and programming in Canada. The provincial government was limited to the ownership of hardware for the distribution of programming. The licenses for cable TV operators would be determined and awarded by the CRTC. Prior to the arrival of cable TV, the CRTC limited the American programming carried by the two Canadian networks—CBC and CTV—to entertainment such as variety shows and comedy. That American programming was also wildly popular among Canadian audiences. According to Ray Peters, a former president of the Canadian Association of Broadcasters, "American programming has been used by Canadian TV stations since the start of Canadian television because that was what Canadian TV audiences wanted to watch."[7]

Unable to insulate Saskatchewan from the effects of cable TV by controlling or limiting the amount of U.S. programming coming into the province, the Blakeney government's only tool to try to offset the influence was to encourage local co-operative enterprises to seek licences and provide locally produced community programming. The government planned to eventually have a provincial cable network that would connect all of the locally owned community groups together. But in the end, the NDP government's attempt to mitigate the coming wave of American programming and influence would falter. The CRTC allowed only two co-operatives, one in Regina and the other in North Battleford, to provide cable television service in Saskatchewan, with private companies serving the remainder of the province.[8] The world and its forces beyond the provincial boundaries were yet again imposing themselves on Saskatchewan.

With politics being inherently the public expression of culture and values, as those values evolve so too does politics. For generations Canada had been able to shield itself from excessive influence by American culture. The Canadian Broadcasting Corporation was established as a Crown corporation in 1936 with the explicit mandate that the broadcasting system "should be Canadian in content and character."[9] For decades, the barriers of distance and technology kept the American media influence mostly at arm's length in Canada. That began to rapidly change in the 1970s.

Trying to understand and explain the cultural divide between Canada and the United States has long been a subject for Canadian social scientists. Ironically, the one who perhaps has done the most incisive and compelling analysis is American academic Seymour Martin Lipset. His analysis began, as previously noted, with his study of the origins and rise of the socialist Co-operative Commonwealth Federation, which explored the reasons why an agrarian populist party could rise to become government in Saskatchewan, the first socialist party in North America to do so. Maintaining his interest in the unique characteristics defining Canada and the United States, Lipset later wrote *Continental Divide: The Values and Institutions of the United States and Canada.*

Relative to the United States, Lipset saw Canadian society and its institutions as rooted in Canada's counter-revolutionary origins as a nation that remained loyal to Britain while the United States engaged in its revolutionary War of Independence. He identified the counter-revolutionary society of Canada as more elitist, class based, law abiding, statist, collectivity oriented, and particularistic, meaning each political group has a right to promote its own interests. He talked of a "Tory fragment" in Canada, with "Tory" referring to someone who subscribes to the British version of traditionalism and conservatism. In Canadian historical terms, it included the loyalists who fled to Canada during the American Revolution, becoming a paternalistic, exclusive, Tory fragment of British society consolidated in North America. Lipset said it resulted in a hierarchical, corporate entity composed of estates and classes, not merely an agglomeration of individuals pursing self-interest as emerged in U.S. society. The elitism of the Tory fragment, Lipset argued, created more deference for authority, a more law-abiding citizenry, and less crime.[10]

A similar view is expressed by University of Toronto sociologist Metta Spencer, who studied under Lipset at the University of California, Berkeley. In a review of Lipset's work she writes, "The United States was organized around the populist ideology expressed in the Declaration of Independence. Even today, to become American is an ideological—he [Lipset] even calls it a religious act....Americanism involves patriotism, religiosity, populism, anti-elitism, and a belief in meritocracy. Canadian national identity, on the other hand, offers only one ideological certainty: that Canadians are not Americans."[11]

It is interesting that Lipset concluded Canada need not worry greatly about the cultural influence of the United States weakening Canadian culture. "In spite of the foreign [largely American] domination of popular culture in Canada, the vitality of the creative arts north of the border is striking. The country is producing world class novelists, playwrights, dancers, painters and other artists in numbers never before witnessed," he wrote.[12] Angering many on the left in Canada, Lipset maintained Canadians should not be overly concerned about closer ties to the United States. Writing in 1990 and acknowledging the "end of ideology" where welfare states were integrated into capitalist societies, Lipset said, "If in the 1950s we were all socialists, as we approach the last decade of the 20th Century we are all free marketers and libertarians."[13]

Seeking to determine the effects of American television on Canadian, and in this case Saskatchewan, culture is as difficult as defining the word itself. Beyond saying that culture is a set of socially acquired values, it defies any precise meaning. Judging and specifically identifying what influences and shapes those values is no less challenging. The factors range across all of human experience, of which television-viewing habits is only one. But it seems safe to assume that, at a minimum, exposure to other cultures, values, and lifestyles different from one's own will make one more aware of how societies differ and at least potentially change how individuals see themselves.

One of the most internationally famous figures in analyzing the media and its effects was Canadian academic Marshall McLuhan. His oft-cited quote that "the medium is the message" was a lens to see how different media cover the same news in different ways, all with differing effects on the person consuming the news. For example, television presents the news in a much different manner than print media. As a visual medium, TV can also evoke a much different response from the viewer because it presents video footage with narration. One only needs to think of television as witness to major events— including President Kennedy's assassination in 1963, the Vietnam War, the 1969 moon landing, the FLQ October crisis of 1970, the 1971 Canada-USSR summit hockey series—to appreciate the impact it can have on an individual's sense of self and a nation's sense of its identity. A more recent example of the power of visual media came in the weeks leading to the 2015 federal election. A photograph of the lifeless body of three-year-old Alan Kurdi, washed up on the coast of Turkey as his desperate family sought to join relatives who immigrated to Canada, was widely broadcast on TV and printed in newspapers at a time when Justin Trudeau was contrasting his priority to bring in 25,000 Syrian refugees against a more restrictive policy of the Harper government.[14]

A 2001 Statistics Canada survey of television-viewing habits in Saskatchewan showed that 69.1 percent of respondents watched "foreign" programs, while just 30.9 percent reported watching Canadian programs. The same survey also found that when it came to news and public affairs, Canadian news coverage dominated: 16.1 percent of respondents watched Canadian productions and 6 percent watched non-Canadian news programming. In terms of non-news programs, the largest non-Canadian viewing share was drama, which attracted 23.6 percent of viewers. Only 3.4 percent reported watched Canadian drama.[15]

What's clear is that concern about the influence of American media on Canadian society in the mid-1970s was a significant issue, and had been for years. It was reflected in policy debates about both print and television media and in ongoing efforts by the federal government to enforce Canadian-content provisions for Canadian-produced TV and radio. One example was the subject of the Canadian edition of the U.S. weekly magazine *Time*. Established in 1923, *Time* became the dominant newsmagazine that at its peak had global weekly circulation of more than twenty million.[16] In 1943 it established a Canadian version, which was essentially the U.S. edition with a Canadian news section produced by Canadian journalists, and it had a weekly circulation in Canada of 444,000. In 1961, a royal commission found that *Time* and *Reader's Digest* dominated the general interest magazine market in Canada, accounting for 75 percent of sales. In its conclusion the report stated that it did not intend to dictate editorial content or impinge in any way on freedom of the press, but rather to ensure that foreign publications were not simply vehicles solely to attract Canadian advertising. "The only aim was to preserve for Canada publications essential to her existence as a distinctive entity," the commission stated.[17]

The impact of American TV beginning with the advent of cable in the mid-1970s came in the wake of the 1970 Davey Commission report, which looked at the concentration of ownership of the mass media. In 1975, CBC president Laurent Picard said that the invasion of American programming through cable TV represented "the gravest threat to a (Canadian) television organization that has ever existed."[18] It was a view echoed by Peter C. Newman, editor of *Maclean's*, who saw that publication as a guardian of Canadian nationalism. "Our quarter-century-old admiration of all things American exhausted itself in the blazing villages of Vietnam, the dark labyrinth of Watergate, and the long overdue realization that the United States was crowding out not just our industries, but our way of life," he said in 1975. "By the very act of confronting our problems of domination from without, Canadians may be able to rework the miracle of their existence."[19]

There could be little doubt that the growing exposure of Canadians, and more particularly, people in Saskatchewan, to U.S. television would have an effect on people's perceptions of North American society and their place in it. For decades, Saskatchewan had been able to carve out something of a unique identity. As Lipset noted, the election of the CCF in 1944, giving Saskatchewan North America's only socialist government, was an exceptional moment in time. Other similar agrarian societies in the U.S. Midwest had flirted with socialism but never been able to replicate what happened in Saskatchewan.

In some ways, one could say Saskatchewan was something of a political enclave. But by the mid-1970s, the question was whether that could continue when the influence of American society, values, and politics was about to enter the living rooms of the province.

CHAPTER 7

1976

The Politics of Identity

I T IS WIDELY ACCEPTED THAT A DEFINING POLITICAL MOMENT in the history of Saskatchewan, and for the New Democratic Party, came on July 1, 1962, when *The Saskatchewan Medical Care Insurance Act* came into force. Simultaneously, in an act of defiance and protest, doctors in the province staged a work stoppage. The walkout ended twenty-three days later when the Saskatoon Agreement was reached on the implementation of North America's first publicly funded, universal system of Medicare.

The end to the bitter standoff came with something of a whimper. The strident militancy of the doctors, many of whom vowed never to work under the "conscription" of government, dissolved when the government made simple concessions. First, doctors could opt out of the plan if they wished, but few of them did. Also, doctors could keep their existing practice of sending invoices for their services to private insurers, who would simply forward the bills to the government's Medical Care Insurance Commission, which would then reimburse the insurers. So, what the doctors had claimed as a matter of great principle ended up being merely one of process.

Medicare is considered a defining moment for many reasons. A primary one is its impact. It became an international story beyond the province's and even Canada's borders. No other government in North America had created such a comprehensive system of medical care, a process that had begun in 1947 with publicly funded insurance to cover patients' hospital expenses. With Medicare, insurance coverage was extended to cover patients' costs of seeing a doctor. What elevated the moment and magnified its effect was the protest by doctors. The so-called doctors' strike created international media interest, with Saskatchewan for a few short weeks attracting journalists from across Canada, the United States, and other parts of the world.

Both the emotion and tension of the moment are difficult to overstate. The role of Woodrow Lloyd—who had taken over as premier less than a year earlier, when Tommy Douglas left to lead the federal NDP—in managing the crisis is often overlooked. Lloyd faced the withdrawal of services by almost seven hundred doctors and the dangers that created for health care in the province. He stared the doctors down. "It is no longer a matter of medical care," Lloyd said, "but an outright challenge to the procedure of constitutional government."[1] The bitterness was evident in the ranks of physicians as well. In one case, Dr. Gerhard Beck, a doctor from Jacksonville, Florida, came to Saskatchewan to help out by working as a hospital intern in the town of Leader. He said that he was harassed constantly during the ten days he worked at the hospital and left under pressure from the College of Physicians and Surgeons, claiming he was "run out" and told that U.S. doctors had no place meddling in the Medicare dispute. "I came to help. I didn't come to fight," Beck said.[2]

Five years later in 1967, when the Saskatchewan Medicare model was embraced and implemented as a national program, the magnitude of what Saskatchewan had pioneered became entrenched as a defining moment not just for the province but for the nation. To this day, Canada's system of universal, publicly funded Medicare remains an integral symbol of what sets Canada apart from the United States. Given the economic and cultural dominance of the United States, it is no small thing for the nation next door to have something as significant as publicly funded universal health care to define the difference—an identity that was created in Saskatchewan.

Applying a similar measurement—that is, impact, international media interest, and groundbreaking provincial public policy—another defining moment for the NDP came in 1976. It arrived with the Blakeney government's implementation of its agenda to take control of the potash industry in the province through public ownership. After almost five years of legal and taxation struggles with the private companies that controlled potash development in the province, the Blakeney government acted.

It signalled its intent in the Speech from the Throne that opened a new session of the legislature on November 12, 1975, five months after the NDP government had been re-elected to a second majority term. It was an election that clearly indicated a shift was under way on the political right in Saskatchewan. The Liberals were in advanced stages of decline and the long marginalized Saskatchewan Progressive Conservative Party was on the rise under its new leader, Dick Collver. The Throne Speech repeated the NDP's long-stated overarching position on resource development: "The cornerstone of that policy is the right of the people of Saskatchewan to receive their fair share of benefits from the development of their resources." It went on to say the government had attempted to work with companies, which—through regulation, taxation, and participation in their future expansion—would guarantee increased production capacity, an assured fair return to the provincial government, and a greater ownership role for the people of Saskatchewan. The efforts failed. "Government has been frustrated in these attempts," the speech stated, and legislation would be introduced to create the Potash Corporation of Saskatchewan, a government-owned enterprise.[3]

The idea of public ownership was certainly nothing new for Saskatchewan. Before the province had been officially formed, the Territorial Hail Insurance Company was created in 1901 to provide coverage for farmers. In the 1940s and '50s, the previous CCF-NDP governments had blazed something of a trail, often unsuccessfully, when it came to the creation of commercial

Crown corporations. There had been the major public utilities—Saskatchewan Power Corporation, Saskatchewan Government Telephones, the Saskatchewan Government Insurance Office, Saskatchewan Transportation
Company—but also failed commercial enterprises such as the Prince Albert
Box Factory, Saskatchewan Industries Ltd. (which included a wood products
division and leather tannery), and Estevan Clay Products.

So, the fact that the Blakeney government was embarking on a new commercial venture was not in itself a break from tradition. The difference in the
case of the PCS was the scale and intent of the initiative. It was not, strictly
speaking, "public enterprise," because the enterprise had been undertaken
by private investment. This would instead be "public ownership," with the
government "taking over" existing private mining operations in the province, with an objective of securing 50 percent ownership of total production. And the targets were not small companies but multinationals like the
Potash Company of America, which was the first to begin potash mining
in Saskatchewan in 1958; Texas-based Pennzoil's Duval Mining; and others
including the Canadian giant Noranda, Hudson Bay Mining and Smelting,
Central Canada Potash, and the German company Alwinsal Potash.[4] It was
cast by many as nationalization by expropriation, and the government was
determined enough to use its powers of expropriation, if necessary, to gain
control of the industry. But its stated intent was to negotiate the "fair-market
value" purchase of mining operations. Still, the potential for expropriation,
in effect a hostile takeover of industry by the government, was what gave the
policy its impact, drawing national and international attention.

A month after the PCS announcement, the U.S. government sent an *aide-
mémoire* to the federal government in Ottawa expressing its "disquiet" about
the potash takeover. It warned of "major potential damage to United States
interests and to United States-Canada relations." It also suggested that the
move could have negative effects on other U.S. companies engaged in the
Saskatchewan resource sector. A resolution in the U.S. Senate was passed
expressing concern with what the Blakeney government had done.[5] In the
midst of the growing tension, the U.S. Justice Department filed criminal

charges against eight American companies for price-fixing dating back to the prorationing scheme of the Thatcher government seven years earlier. Also charged were several individuals, including former New Mexico governor David Cargo. Named as an unindicted co-conspirator was Liberal Opposition leader Dave Steuart, who was provincial treasurer in the Thatcher government at the time the prorationing policy was devised and implemented.

Steuart, in his typically feisty style, did not pull punches in his response to the U.S. action. "It is a piece of arrogant stupidity on the part of the Government of the United States to try to interfere in what has happened and is happening in Canada and the province of Saskatchewan," Steuart said. Moreover, he argued that what the government had done was perfectly legal. "Of course it was price-fixing. We set the price—we had every right to do it." He said the policy to stabilize the price was no different from what is done by marketing boards in other sectors of the Canadian economy.[6]

The potash nationalization effort by the Blakeney government was such that it drew the ongoing attention of the *New York Times*. A September 1976 lead article in its business section, headlined "Potash debate in Canada heightens," said the government's efforts to "nationalize partially" the potash industry was "drawing sharp criticism on both sides of the border." It reported that the industry in 1975 had earnings of $374 million, with the province expected to receive $100 million in taxes and royalties. As well, the report said the reduction in American and foreign capital that results from the nationalization was "a favorite theme" of what it called the "mildly leftist" NDP government.[7]

The story was timed to coincide with the Blakeney government's purchase, for US$128.5 million, of the Duval mine from Pennzoil. It noted that 70 percent of the potash produced in Saskatchewan was sold to U.S. farmers, raising concerns about security of supply with the Saskatchewan government takeover. The story also made passing reference to the domestic federal-provincial taxation issue, noting taxes "traditionally collected by the Canadian Government in Ottawa, which would be lost to Canada through nationalization." When asked why the government did not simply take control of the entire industry, Elwood Cowley, the cabinet minister in charge of the potash initiative, had a ready answer: "We just want enough ownership to be a power in the market, and 50 percent is enough to accomplish that objective."[8] That indeed was exactly the policy's intent—to take a major ownership position in order to maximize resource royalty returns to the province, shield the revenues from federal corporate taxation, and be positioned to manage the market from a position of ownership, as well as a regulator.

In terms of its defining effect for a party and government, the creation of PCS was pivotal. It might not have been on the scale of Medicare some fourteen years earlier, which impacted the entire population and led to a cascading effect that shaped national policy. Admittedly, public ownership was not new in Saskatchewan, or Canada for that matter. But its significance should not be minimized, because its implications can be measured on several levels. At its core, the issue brought into clear focus the issue of provincial ownership and control of natural resources. It pitted the interests of the provincial government against both the Government of Canada, which was seeking to capture more of the economic rent from rising resource prices, and private potash companies wanting to maximize their profits.

All governments strive to have an issue or collection of issues that, in political and philosophical terms, define them and separate them from their political opponents. It becomes their public identity. What the creation of the Potash Corporation of Saskatchewan did was give the Blakeney government a signature policy event, one that perfectly reflected its belief in public ownership as a means of economic control and maximizing returns to the provincial treasury. The political division created by PCS was expressed in explicitly political terms. Ted Malone, a member of the Liberal Opposition who would take over from Steuart as leader of the Liberal Party, captured it well. "The Premier is kidding nobody when he disclaims the principles of socialism on which his party is based. There is one reason and one reason only that the government is taking over the potash companies and that is because they believe in socialism. They believe that the means of production should be controlled by the state," Malone said in the initial days of debate over the PCS legislation.[9]

For Blakeney and New Democrats, the argument was more nuanced. Rather than casting it as a move entirely driven by socialist ideology, the government explained its position in terms of ensuring that Saskatchewan realized a "fair return" for its ownership of natural resources. With that as its baseline objective, the argument went, it had no other choice given two crucial factors. One was the intransigence of the private potash companies. They refused to pay their taxes or provide the government with their corporate financial details and instead launched court action against the government. The other was the federal Trudeau government's incursion into provincial jurisdiction over natural resources. It was a policy response in large measure driven by the OPEC oil crisis and the federal government's intention to seize a greater share of the windfall revenues of escalating oil prices, and natural resources more generally. Adding to the tension was Ottawa's decision to join with both CIGOL and Central Canada Potash in their constitutional challenges to the province's taxes and control over natural resource production.

But to suggest that ideology and a commitment to public ownership as a critical tool of economic policy was not the most crucial factor would be disingenuous. Blakeney made that explicit during the budget speech debate of 1972. "At the outset let me make clear that this Government will encourage the continued operation and expansion of Crown corporations....We will develop our resources for the benefit of Saskatchewan people and where appropriate, this will be done through crown corporations," Blakeney said.[10] As with any policy decision taken by a government, application of the words "where appropriate" provides all the subjective justification necessary to defend a position. For that matter, the Blakeney NDP government saw itself carrying on the tradition of the previous Douglas government, which for a time had greatly expanded public enterprise, before retreating to more pragmatic economic policy approaches.

However, in one key area, there was an important qualitative difference from the Douglas years when the government engaged in actual "public enterprise" by starting new businesses to create new wealth. In other words, government used its financial resources to generate new enterprises that expanded economic activity. In terms of potash, the Blakeney government was engaged in "public ownership" rather than "public enterprise," where it was purchasing existing enterprises and assets that others created through private enterprise and investment. Its objective was less about enterprise and more about providing access to revenue that government could deploy as part of its broader social and economic agenda.

The importance of PCS in particular, and Crown corporations generally, to the messaging of the NDP government became apparent in the second reading debate of Bill 2, *The Potash Corporation of Saskatchewan Act*. Responsibility for shepherding the bill through the legislature belonged to Roy Romanow, the attorney general and deputy premier. While Cowley was in charge of putting together the actual organization, administration, and financing capacity of PCS, Romanow was in charge of selling the initiative to the public. As a skilled debater and eloquent communicator, Romanow was to provide the political and economic rationale for the initiative, both in the legislature and beyond.

The communications strategy was built on the foundation of Crown corporations and the history of public enterprise stretching back decades. In his defence of the legislation, Romanow noted that the critics of the government's decision to form PCS were engaged in a "direct or indirect attack on the principle of a Crown Corporation."[11] To deal with it, Romanow gave a detailed history, going back to the earliest days of the province, and recited the many examples of public enterprise by all stripes of Saskatchewan governments. He noted that twenty-eight Crown corporations had been created over the years and that, while some smaller ones had failed financially, the total accumulated profit since 1944 was $350 million, over and above the employment of seven thousand people and the $700 million paid in wages and benefits.[12] In his speech, Romanow introduced and then mentioned several times the "family of Crown corporations." At the time they were words that carried no particular significance beyond a simple turn of phrase. Yet in a few short years "the family of Crown corporations" was to become a political label that the NDP would come to regret.

By October 1976, with the negotiated purchase of the Duval Potash Mine from Houston-based Pennzoil, the Potash Corporation of Saskatchewan was directly engaged as an owner-operator of a producing mine. Quickly, industry resistance began to fade as the private companies saw the potential for making a deal to sell at a price that made sense for their shareholders. Within two years, PCS had spent $520 million to purchase three more mines and a portion of a fourth, totalling 40 percent of potash production in the province.[13]

Prior to potash nationalization, the reality of the natural resource sector in Saskatchewan had fundamentally changed over the course of four years, with government emerging as a major player in the oil and gas and mining sectors. The impetus was a review of mineral resource policy shortly after the NDP took power in 1971. It began taking shape in 1973 with the creation of Crown-owned SaskOil, a policy decision designed as a vehicle that would give the government greater access to oil revenues and also shield it from federal intrusion. Another important motivating factor in SaskOil's creation was the decision by private sector oil refiners to shut down their refining capacity in Saskatchewan and Manitoba, while consolidating and expanding it in Alberta. By creating SaskOil, the government believed it could retain refining capacity in the province.[14] But in ideological terms, the fact that the oil sector in Saskatchewan was controlled by foreign, or out-of-province, companies was seen as unacceptable to many in the Blakeney government. The remaining members of the Waffle movement who were still in the party, and in particular Saskatoon MLA John Richards, began pressuring Blakeney after the NDP took power to establish public ownership of the oil sector. The lobbying paid off a year later, when SaskOil was created, but it was a move that did not go nearly far enough for those who wanted government to assume majority ownership of the oil sector.[15]

The other incursion by government into the resource sector came in 1974 with the creation of the Saskatchewan Mining Development Corporation (SMDC). It was actually a responsive, rather than proactive, move. The Blakeney government was approached by Inexco, a mining company from Alberta that was seeking a buyer for its share of a uranium property with its exploration partner Uranerz, a Germany-based company. With Inexco unable to find a private sector company willing to make a deal, the Blakeney government agreed to take part ownership.[16] It was an example of true "public enterprise" that paid big dividends. A year later the government-Uranerz partnership discovered the first of two rich uranium finds at Key Lake, Saskatchewan, that were among the richest ore bodies in the world. Unlike PCS, where the government bought production outright, SMDC followed the joint venture model with other private sector partners.

In a defence of Crown corporations after the defeat of the Blakeney government, published by the Law Society of Saskatchewan, Romanow conceded that ideology was a determining factor that drove the decision-making in the 1970s, but it was within a much broader context. He wrote, "Ideological considerations were not the only reason for a return of a period of maximizing the role of Crown corporations. National and international developments surrounding oil and natural gas resources also provided a major impetus to the growth of public enterprise in the 1970s."[17] He also noted that the 1973 OPEC oil crisis was a key factor, as Canadians became concerned about skyrocketing prices and supply uncertainty. As a result, all governments reassessed their mineral policies as part of dealing with the impact of international events. To find the evidence, all a person had to do was look west to neighbouring Alberta.

It was a period when the Blakeney NDP government of Saskatchewan and Peter Lougheed's Progressive Conservative government of Alberta became allied in defence of provincial control over natural resources. Despite their ideological differences, both shared the goal of not only defending provincial jurisdiction but maximizing financial returns for their provinces. The key point of departure was how best to achieve that goal. In Lougheed's case, private investment was seen as the primary means to generate economic development. He believed the public interest could best be realized not through public ownership but by using the right application of royalties, taxation, and regulation to private enterprise.

One of Lougheed's first acts as premier of Alberta in 1971 was to implement a royalty review to increase provincial revenues from the oil and gas sector, which had been a central position of his election campaign. Lougheed believed the increased revenues from high royalty rates would generate the financial capacity for a "remaking of the province, including a program of economic diversification that would wean Alberta off of its dependence on the oil industry."[18]

In their book *Prairie Capitalism: Power and Influence in the New West*, John Richards and Larry Pratt identify four objectives of Lougheed's policies: gaining control over the Alberta economy, encouraging capital accumulation, reducing the province's dependence on external political and economic forces, and diversifying the economy away from overreliance on oil and gas. Lougheed felt it was his role to create initiatives and a policy environment that fostered co-operation between government and business leaders that didn't raise "conservative anxieties in a community where property rights and a hatred of socialism are virtually a secular religion."[19] They were goals, if not methods, that closely paralleled the objectives of the Blakeney government.

The reality was that when faced with the difficult issues of price, supply, and management, all Canadian governments felt compelled to take a hard look at their respective mineral policies and devise measures that would offset the negative effects of international resource decisions. One response was to establish Crown resource corporations.

In his Law Society defence of Crown corporations, Romanow noted that the result was a proliferation of Crown resource corporations. By the early 1980s, fifty-six state corporations were operating in the resource sector in Canada: seventeen federally and thirty-nine at the provincial level. They were active in all aspects of exploration, development, and marketing.[20] Between 1973 and 1975, with the creation of three new, major resource corporations— SaskOil, PCS, and the Saskatchewan Mining Development Corporation— Saskatchewan simply reflected what was happening nationally.

So in that context, the actions of the Saskatchewan government were hardly radical in a political or public policy sense. Given the issues and challenges facing the Blakeney government, the policies made perfect sense. At least that was the belief within the NDP and the government. But the growth of public ownership, and the role of government more generally during the period, had other effects. As noted earlier, sociologist Robert Michels talked of the "the iron law of oligarchy," an inevitable process that unfolded over time in all organizations and governments. They might begin, and see themselves, as expressions of populism and democracy. But in large complex organizations, decision-making becomes controlled by a ruling class within the organization, a managerial class of professional bureaucrats who wield influence and become a class where power is centralized. So what might have been spawned by populism, or popular will, evolves into organizational structures that become detached from the grassroots sentiments that inspired it.

Michels's "iron law" embedded itself within the Blakeney government, which took great pride in its record as an effective and efficient government. It became apparent in the eventual realization that, far removed from the intrigue of policy debates and constitutional wrangling over resources, something was going on in the lives of people—something to do with trying to make ends meet and surviving financially. Emerging politically were two solitudes, each based in its own reality: on one side was a government that saw its record as one of achievement; on the other was a population that felt its reality did not match the one government saw for itself. The cleavage was to be a critical factor in the months and years ahead.

CHAPTER 8

1978

Selling Furniture

H E ENDED UP BEING PRETTY MUCH A SASKATCHEWAN footnote. The kind of politician who came, went, and was quickly forgotten. Sometimes, though, footnotes can tell you a lot. As the writer and political philosopher George Santayana once said, there are times when footnotes can be more interesting than the actual text.

In the case of this footnote, for six years as leader of the Saskatchewan Progressive Conservative Party, Dick Collver played a pivotal role in the political transformation of Saskatchewan. There was even a brief period in the months leading to the 1978 provincial election when the idea that he might become premier was not entirely far-fetched. In fact, the NDP government of Allan Blakeney was feeling the heat of growing PC momentum.

As bizarre as it might seem, to understand Collver's approach to politics you needed to hear him talk about the days in his early twenties spent as a furniture salesman in Alberta. Collver considered himself something of an expert when it came to selling furniture. It was all about psychology and tactics. He said that you needed to get people excited about buying furniture. Make it an experience. Engage with them, have a funny story, offer advice, even encourage them to do comparison shopping at other stores. "That was a clincher. Telling them they should look around at what else was on offer by competitors was always a great tactic," Collver would say. "They would trust you and believe you had quality furniture at the best price if you were telling them to compare it with other stores. They figured you must be pretty confident that they would come back. Lots of times they'd leave the store, sit in their car for a few minutes, and come back in and make a purchase. You just knew they talked it over and figured there was no need to go look anywhere else."[1]

As far as Collver was concerned, politics was just one big furniture showroom and politicians were the salespeople. When it came to sales, Collver was a natural.

He was doggedly determined, full of energy, and a skilled orator who showed flashes of passion and charisma. Like with most things in politics, the most crucial ingredient was timing. In 1973 what the Saskatchewan Progressive Conservatives desperately needed was a leader who could breathe life into the moribund party, which for decades had been relegated to the margins of Saskatchewan politics and held no seats in the sixty-one-seat provincial legislature. Collver brought an organizational zeal and a dedication to doing the grassroots work at the constituency level to attract candidates and drive memberships. He also arrived on the scene when the Liberal Party was in decline after having lost power in 1971. In the wake of defeat and the sudden death of former premier Ross Thatcher, the Liberals' decision to turn to Dave Steuart, who was seen as Thatcher's right-hand man, was a tactical and strategic mistake. The elevation of Steuart signalled that the party was stagnating rather than undergoing a serious renewal after its defeat. The door was open for the PCs to begin positioning themselves as a new, right-wing alternative to the NDP.

In the early days of his leadership, Collver expressed a simple rationale to capture the notion that political realignment in favour of an ascendant PC party was possible. "How can anyone have negative feelings about a party that hasn't been in government for 40 years?" he would ask rhetorically. It was a good question, the sort that one answered just by asking it. For Collver, the PCs were a blank slate that he could shape as he wished, which he proceeded to do.

By the 1975 election in Saskatchewan, Collver and the PCs had become a rising force, and the party won seven seats and 28 percent of the popular vote. Even though the Liberals were able to hold Opposition status by winning fifteen seats, the same number they had going into the election, the shift was clearly on in terms of right-wing politics in the province. For the NDP, the split in the right-wing vote between the Liberals and the Conservatives was the perfect outcome. Blakeney and the NDP were re-elected to a second majority term with thirty-nine seats, but the party's share of the popular vote fell to 40 percent, from 55 percent in the previous election in 1971.[2] You didn't need a pocket calculator to tell you that if the right-wing, conservative vote in the province coalesced behind one party, the NDP would lose, badly.

The most telling outcome in the 1975 election was where the PCs drew their votes. In 1971, the PCs had 2 percent of the vote—a figure that in 1975 rose by a stunning 26 percentage points. As noted previously, the Liberals' share of the vote fell 11 percent and the NDP vote was down 15 percent. In other words, the gain in votes for Collver and the PCs in the 1975 election came more from those who had previously voted NDP than it did from those who had voted Liberal. Essentially, the PC vote that had gone to the New Democrats in the 1971 election to defeat the Thatcher Liberal government flooded back to the Collver-led PCs in 1975. It was more evidence of how Saskatchewan voters would often shift between the PCs and the NDP, a fact that was particularly evident in the days of the Douglas CCF and the Diefenbaker PCs, when many Saskatchewan people who voted CCF provincially also supported Diefenbaker and the Conservatives federally. The key ingredient was not ideology, but populism. Both Douglas and Diefenbaker were seen as prairie populists who would stand up against the political and business establishment of central Canada, which represented the political base of the federal Liberals.

It was a point that years later, in 1986—long after he had left Saskatchewan and politics to live in Phoenix, Arizona—Collver used to explain his take on Saskatchewan politics. He claimed that there were essentially two groups of voters in the province: the Liberals and the anti-Liberals. His explanation was simple: "Look, for the first three decades in provincial politics there were two parties—the Liberals and the Conservatives. Then in the 1930s it became the Liberals and the CCF. It's not hard to tell where the CCF came from."[3] Blakeney himself recognized the NDP-PC organic reality of Saskatchewan politics. In the weeks leading to the 1978 election Blakeney realized that Collver was appealing to both NDP and Liberal voters and that the NDP needed to attract as many Conservatives as possible. "We were trying to say if you were an NDP in the past, but really wanted to vote Conservative, we're not that far away from you," Blakeney said of the campaign to stem Collver's rise.[4]

This non-ideological trait of Saskatchewan politics that defies the traditional left-versus-right divide in favour of a populist analysis is reflected in electoral outcomes. Over the years prior to the early 2000s, there was a bifurcation of political opinion drawn on federal-provincial lines, particularly, but not exclusively, in rural Saskatchewan. The simplest way to express it is that many Saskatchewan people voted PC in federal elections and NDP provincially. The late 1950s through the 1960s provide the starkest examples in numerical seat terms. In the 1958 federal election, the Progressive Conservatives won sixteen seats in the province and the then CCF only one. In the 1960 provincial election, the CCF won thirty-seven seats, the Liberals seventeen, and the PCs none. In the 1962 federal election the PCs again won sixteen seats and the newly named NDP one seat. A year later in the 1963 federal election the Conservatives won all seventeen seats in the province.

The headline result in the 1975 provincial election of a second NDP majority papered over the underlying shift happening in Saskatchewan politics. The question was, how long would the political transformation take?

Recognizing the looming threat on the horizon, the Blakeney NDP decided not to govern for a full four-year mandate and called an election for October 1978. The primary reason, at least for public consumption, was that an early election was necessary to avoid a clash with an anticipated 1979 federal campaign. Prime Minister Trudeau's Liberal government was trailing in federal polls, which led Trudeau to indicate that an expected 1978 federal election would not be held until the Liberals reached the limit of their five-year mandate, in 1979. But there were multiple other considerations as to why the Blakeney government decided on going to the voters in October 1978, only three-and-a-half years into their mandate. One was to stage the election at a time when the Trudeau Liberals were still in office federally, and were widely disliked in Saskatchewan, providing a useful point of attack for the NDP in the campaign. Another reason was to not give Collver and the PCs more time to organize, recruit candidates, and prepare for the election. There was great unease in NDP ranks that the Collver Conservatives were posing a very serious threat. The third and most pivotal reason was that the New Democrats, recognizing the rising danger that Collver posed politically, believed they had extrapolitical factors at their disposal to engage in an attack on Collver himself. And it worked.

There was nothing fabricated or contrived by the NDP campaign in 1978 to discredit Collver by calling into question his business ethics and character. The facts seemed on the side of the New Democrats. Before the election was called, Collver faced two lawsuits related to his previous business career. In one case he was being sued by three medical doctors, his former business partners in Saskatoon—the Baltzan brothers—whom Collver had worked for as their financial and business manager, including as a joint owner with them of the Bessborough Hotel. The Baltzans alleged they had interest in business assets that Collver held and claimed he exclusively owned, which led Collver to launch action against his former business partners. The Baltzans countersued Collver, accusing him of poor management and taking "excessive and unconscionable fees" as their business manager. The Baltzans claimed that Collver had paid himself management fees of more than $1.8 million, while at the same time the Baltzan companies managed by Collver lost more than $1.4 million.[5] In the course of proceedings, the existence of a numbered Swiss bank account was revealed, which Collver said was intended for his daughter's French-language lessons.

A second suit in early 1978 was filed by the provincially owned Saskatchewan Government Insurance (SGI) against Buildall Construction, of which Collver had previously been a part owner and a personal guarantor of company-issued construction bonds. The Crown corporation alleged that it was owed $1.2 million by Buildall; although Collver was no longer associated with the company he remained as one its bond guarantors, and SGI wanted its money.[6]

The SGI-Buildall case unfolded in the spring of 1978 and became a dominant topic in the spring session of the legislature, with members of the PC caucus claiming it had been politically orchestrated to sully Collver's reputation. The Tories alleged that, because the issue had been raised in the Blakeney cabinet, it was all politically motivated. But Blakeney countered that it was only mentioned in cabinet by the minister responsible because the lawsuit named Collver and cabinet needed to be aware. The only direction to the minister was that SGI should act no differently than if Collver were a private citizen. "We should proceed with it down the middle, as you might say, the same as we would have proceeded had Mr. Collver not been involved," Blakeney said in the legislature.[7]

All this unfolded in the months leading to an October 1978 provincial election. It took its political toll, creating doubt in the public mind about Collver. The question became, could he be trusted? Internal public opinion research done by the Conservatives in the spring of 1978 showed the party with a lead in the popular vote.[8] For the New Democrats, having Collver and Trudeau as prime targets was the perfect combination. It became even better in the final weeks of the campaign when the Supreme Court issued its decision on the constitutional challenge to the Blakeney government's potash reserve tax that had been announced in 1974. When the court ruled the tax was unconstitutional, and also that the government would have to pay back $500 million that it had raised from its oil tax, which was also deemed unconstitutional, it created an ideal political wedge issue for the NDP. "It was the perfect script," wrote Dennis Gruending in his biography of Blakeney. "Blakeney was running against Trudeau on resources, and against Collver on trust."[9]

Another key factor that led to the unravelling of PC support was the appearance of former premier and CCF-NDP icon Tommy Douglas in the campaign. The NDP fashioned a campaign advertisement that used Douglas, the "father" of Medicare, to deliver a message that warned people about the threat that Collver and the PCs posed to publicly funded health care. "Don't let them take it away," Douglas was quoted as saying. Only a decade after the creation of a national Medicare system, based on the model implemented in Saskatchewan in 1962, any suggestion that the health care system could be put at risk touched a raw nerve with Saskatchewan people. The message resonated. Another factor that indirectly helped sow doubt about Collver on the health care issue was the lawsuit lodged against him by his former business partners. The Baltzan brothers were all well-known medical doctors in Saskatoon and although the legal action had nothing to do with health care or the medical system, the fact that doctors would be taking action against Collver helped feed the public anxiety about Collver and his motives on health care policy.

On election night, the NDP coasted to a majority victory, winning forty-four seats and 48 percent of the popular vote. The PCs ended with eighteen seats, a gain of seven but far below expectations of only a few months earlier. The Liberals, who went into the campaign with eleven seats, failed to elect a single member. Media reports tended to focus on the NDP and the Liberals. The *Calgary Herald* opened its story on the election as follows: "The NDP government of Saskatchewan Premier Allan Blakeney was returned to office Wednesday over the corpse of the provincial Liberal Party, which formed the government as recently as 1964–71."[10] In its coverage, CBC Radio noted how the Saskatchewan NDP was "swept back into office" on the heels of Progressive Conservative wins in Manitoba and Nova Scotia and, in the process, routed the Liberals. Only two provincial Liberal MLAs remained west of Ontario in the wake of the Saskatchewan election.

The CBC television segment on the election was titled "Blakeney's NDP obliterates the Saskatchewan Liberals." As reporter John Calver explained, "The NDP based its campaign on resource development, claiming government has a right to control resource development for the good of the province.

During the campaign the government was hit with two Supreme Court of Canada judgments, claiming some of its resource policies were unconstitutional. Mr. Blakeney immediately blamed the Trudeau government, claiming it was trying to take over provincial jurisdiction of resources."[11] For his part, Collver summed up the result simply. "The people of Saskatchewan chose to continue with more government, and bigger government, and that, after all, is our system; that, after all, is the people's right," the PC leader said.[12]

But there was also an ominous subtext to the result for the NDP. The party's campaign to discredit Collver had been highly effective. By undermining public trust in the Conservatives' leader, it halted and reversed the momentum the PCs had been building as the Liberal vote was evaporating. Just how much comfort the New Democrats could take from the result was uncertain. It was obvious in the wake of the election that Collver had proven to be a liability for the party and that the PCs would have to search for a new leader.

With the political landscape consolidated into what was clearly a two-party system, if the PCs were to find a leader who was a fresh face, with none of the baggage that Collver brought to the party, the dynamic in the next campaign would be far different. It would be even more challenging if the next leader of the Conservatives came with a streak of rural populism that had been absent in Saskatchewan politics since the days of Tommy Douglas.

CHAPTER 9

1980

The Second Coming

T HE BALLROOM OF THE CHÂTEAU LAURIER HOTEL IN Ottawa was packed on the night of February 18. A beaming Pierre Trudeau looked down at the crowd from the podium waiting for the cheering to subside. "Well, welcome to the 1980s," Trudeau said, triggering an even louder and longer outburst of roars from the throng of Liberals.[1] The excitement and jubilation in federal Liberal ranks was hardly surprising.

Less than a year earlier, Trudeau was planning his departure from politics. In the vernacular of politics, he was a "dead man walking." His Liberal government had been defeated 273 days earlier in 1979 after eleven years in power, with Joe Clark and the Progressive Conservatives winning a minority. Trudeau announced soon after that he would be stepping down as leader. But then fate intervened. It arrived in the form of the defeat of the Clark government's first budget, which triggered the February 1980 election. Lazarus-like, Trudeau was able to rise and lead the Liberals back not only to power but to a majority government. The political resurrection of Trudeau only added to his mystique.

The pivotal issue in the defeated budget had been the Conservatives' proposal to impose an 18-cents-a-gallon tax on gasoline as part of a deficit-reduction plan. The negative public reaction was enough for the Liberals to win thirty-three more seats than they did in the 1979 election and reclaim government. But it was a government with a mandate that was exclusively based in central and Atlantic Canada—the Liberals won no seats in Saskatchewan, Alberta, or British Columbia, none in the Northwest Territories or Yukon, and only two in Manitoba. The political cleavage along regional lines in Canada could not have been more stark or ominous.

"In Canada, this decade will be full of problems and equally full of opportunity," Trudeau said to his supporters. "We must remind ourselves on the night of this general election that Canada has been, that Canada is, and that Canada will remain more than the sum of its parts. The province of Quebec has understood for a long time one can be a citizen of Canada and yet be proud at the same time to be loyal members of the province. One single Canada." Recognizing that the Liberals were shut out in western Canada, Trudeau noted that "about one voter in four voted for our party" in those provinces. He promised his government would be a "government for every part of the country" but, first and foremost, the country needed to be put ahead of the regions. Trudeau ended his speech with a quote from poet Robert Frost: "I have promises to keep, and miles to go before I sleep." They were prophetic words.[2]

The election result proved to be a crucial moment in Canada's history. Trudeau's return would shape events in the coming weeks, months, and years in ways that are felt to this day and will echo into the future for years to come.

Trudeau's victory came three months before the planned Quebec referendum in May on what Premier René Lévesque and the Parti Québécois (PQ) government termed "sovereignty-association"—in other words, separation and statehood for Quebec, with an undefined and to-be-negotiated association with the rest of Canada. For Trudeau, who had long been a powerful voice of federalism against the Quebec separatists, his return to power as prime minister set the stage for the ultimate conflict with Lévesque and the secessionists. It is interesting to note that Lévesque, who had been elected in 1976, had avoided calling the referendum while Trudeau was in power, knowing what a powerful voice for federalism Trudeau was in Quebec. What happened was that shortly after Clark had won power federally, Lévesque made his move and announced the May 1980 referendum date, never expecting that Trudeau would rise from the dead to become PM again. In the process, Trudeau and the Liberals swept Quebec in the February election, winning seventy-four of the province's seventy-five seats, allowing Trudeau to lay claim to the argument that his mandate included overwhelming support from Quebec.

In the background of all this was a rhetorical artifact from the 1968 federal election that had originally brought Trudeau to power. In that election, Trudeau's campaign was based on the promise of a "just society." An essential ingredient in Trudeau's vision was for Canada to finally erase the vestiges of its colonial status. It would become a truly independent country by patriating the *British North America Act* from the British Parliament and creating Canada's own, free-standing constitution with a *Charter of Rights and Freedoms*. Attempts with the provinces dating back more than a decade to advance the constitution patriation agenda had failed to make any significant progress. A federal-provincial agreement in June 1971, the so-called Victoria Charter, was unable to gain the approval of provincial legislatures. As the 1970s unfolded, the constitutional issue was pushed aside by the jurisdictional struggle over resources. However, with the election of the PQ in Quebec in 1976, national unity and the need for constitutional reform took on greater urgency.

The other intensely regional issue at the time that remained unresolved was energy policy. What had started with the OPEC oil crisis in 1973 returned with another oil price shock in 1979, triggered by the Iranian revolution and a decline in oil output that led to a doubling in oil prices, to an unheard-of level of almost $40 a barrel by early 1980.[3]

In retrospect, it is impossible not to recognize the significance of these events in the wake of the 1980 election and the Trudeau agenda that was about to unfold. They would each have momentous political and economic repercussions in Saskatchewan. Over a two-year period, they would further consume the Blakeney government during a period of economic recession and punishing interest rates in a way that helped alter the course of the province's economic and political history. The depth of challenges facing the nation was not lost on Blakeney. Four days before the Quebec referendum, he sent a letter warning Trudeau that the unresolved federal-provincial issue over resources was fuelling western alienation and stirring regional nationalisms.[4]

The May 20, 1980, referendum transfixed Canada, and for good reason. The unity of the nation was on the line as Quebecers voted on whether they wanted their provincial government to pursue sovereignty-association with Canada. The federalist campaign, led by Trudeau, proved successful, as the sovereignty-association option was defeated by a 60 percent to 40 percent margin. During the campaign, Trudeau had pledged constitutional reform if Quebec voters turned down the separatist option. A key moment was Trudeau's speech to an overflow crowd on May 14 in the Paul Sauvé Arena in Montreal. He said that constitutional reform would begin the day after a "no" vote and that he would never, as prime minister, negotiate sovereignty-association on behalf of Canada with Quebec. It was a moment of stark rhetoric that exposed the depth of the political emotion in Canada as Trudeau mocked the whole notion of sovereignty-association.

"In this question, there is sovereignty and there is everything else," Trudeau said. "Everything else is a new agreement. It is equality of nations. It is at the same time economic association. It is a common currency. It is change through another referendum. It is a mandate to negotiate. And we know very well what they are doing, these hucksters of the YES vote. They are trying to appeal to everyone who would say YES to a new agreement. Yes to equality of nations. Yes at the same time to association. Yes at the same time to a common currency. Yes to a second referendum. Yes to a simple mandate to negotiate."

He scoffed too at the assertion by Lévesque that the whole world was watching to see if Quebec "would come of age." Trudeau rejected the idea at a time when "the whole world is interdependent, when Europe is trying to seek some kind of political union, these people in Quebec and Canada want to split it up, they want to take it away from our children, they want to break it down? No! That's our answer."[5]

In the House of Commons the day after the referendum, Trudeau said his government would immediately begin the process of patriation and reform of the Constitution. He viewed the outcome of the referendum as Quebecers expressing "massive support for change within the federal framework." At the same time, Trudeau set out his preconditions for constitutional change, which included a clarification of federal and provincial powers and entrenchment in the constitution of a charter of fundamental rights and freedoms.[6]

Immediately, Trudeau dispatched his justice minister, Jean Chrétien, to tour the provinces and outline the federal objectives for constitutional reform to each of the premiers. Shortly after, the Continuing Committee of Ministers on the Constitution (CCMC)—which had been formed in 1978 to work toward finding areas of agreement on the agenda for constitutional talks—was restarted. Saskatchewan attorney general Roy Romanow, who had been the provincial co-chair during the 1978–79 round of talks, assumed the same position in 1980, with Chrétien the federal co-chair as the CCMC began its post–Quebec referendum work. Before long the travelling duo of Chrétien and Romanow, given their respective Quebecois and Ukrainian heritage, became known colloquially as "the Toque and the Uke Show." The scale of the issues and challenges was daunting, as the process sought to deal with not only a charter of fundamental rights and freedoms but the economic powers of the federal and provincial governments as part of the economic union and the management of resources, including the offshore and fisheries. For his part, consistent with his notion of national will, Trudeau wanted a commitment to the maintenance of Canada's economic union.[7]

For both the Saskatchewan and Alberta governments, whose economies were built upon natural resource extraction, the stakes were enormously high. In its previous incarnation, the Trudeau government had made clear its intent when it came to natural resources. It wanted a greater share of the economic rent as part of defending the national interest, and Canadian consumers protected from the effects of rising resource prices, particularly related to oil. Although the work of the CCMC was carried out in private sessions, its role was public and attracted continuing media attention. With Romanow a key figure in the ongoing process, and with the critical nature of the high-profile resource issues that for years had tested federal-provincial relations, the Saskatchewan government became recognized as an important player in the constitutional process. Yet, as significant as the constitutional issue was for governments, many in the public regarded the constitutional talks as arcane and far removed from their personal priorities.[8]

The process formally started with a meeting between Trudeau and the premiers on June 9, 1980, in Ottawa. Three days before the meeting, Trudeau sent the premiers a statement of principles that he believed should guide the new round of constitutional negotiations in the wake of the Quebec referendum, including to "reaffirm the official status of French and English languages... and the diversity of cultures" in Canada. Also, according to Trudeau's directive, the new constitution would "enshrine our fundamental freedoms" and would "define the authority of Parliament and the legislative assemblies." For their part, the provinces had a long list of their own demands. These included Newfoundland's authority over the offshore, the Atlantic provinces' focus on equalization and regional development, Ontario's concern about Saskatchewan and Alberta's determination to solidify their jurisdiction over resources, and BC wanting a Senate based on five distinct regions in Canada, with BC being one of them. All of these ingredients created a recipe for failure.

That failure came when the First Ministers' Conference of September 1980 ended in acrimony. There was no agreement on the key issues of minority French-English language rights, control of natural resources, or an amending formula for what would be the new constitution. Emerging from the meeting was the so-called Gang of Eight provinces that opposed Trudeau's positions on those three key items and others, including a charter of rights. Saskatchewan was a member of the Gang. So too was Lévesque, who, according to American academic Donald Nuechterlein, sought only to oppose Trudeau so as to further the tension between his province and the rest of Canada.[9]

Stymied by the need for federal-provincial unanimity to make constitutional change, Trudeau decided the federal government would act unilaterally. It would go directly to the British Parliament and ask for the *BNA Act* to be patriated to the Canadian Parliament. In a televised address to the nation on October 2, Trudeau dramatically raised the stakes. "We assumed that it was possible in a system of diverse governments for all to agree in all respects on everything....In accepting that the only agreement could be unanimous agreement, we took that ideal of unanimity and made it a tyrant," he said. The argument was that unanimity meant each provincial premier had a veto, and it became a weapon for regional or provincial advantage at the expense of the good of the nation. "So we achieved the good of none, least of all did we achieve the good of all, the common good," Trudeau declared.[10]

The move by Trudeau triggered a deepening federal-provincial crisis that shifted to the Supreme Court, with Saskatchewan leading a provincial challenge to the federal unilateral action. The decision came eleven months later, when the Supreme Court ruled that legally the federal government could act unilaterally, but that doing so would be a breach of constitutional convention.

If the escalating tensions over constitutional change between Ottawa and the provinces were not enough, then the well was further poisoned on October 28, 1980, with the federal government's budget delivered by Allan MacEachen, the minister of finance and deputy prime minister. A central feature of the budget was the announcement of the government's National Energy Program. The vague language of the budget speech sounded almost soothing in its definition of the NEP: "An energy policy which continues protection for Canadians against violent shocks of OPEC oil price increases, promotes the most economic use of energy and substitution off-oil, and encourages development of new energy supply sources."[11] The details were not so anodyne.

The NEP included a "blended oil price regime," which meant a domestic price well below world oil price levels; a petroleum gas revenue tax (PGRT) of 8 percent; a petroleum compensation charge designed to cover the cost of subsidizing imported oil imports; a Canadianization levy to finance purchases of multinational oil companies; and an increase from 10 percent to 24 percent of the federal share of petroleum production income. There would be small, staged increases in the domestic price, and the amount would always be lower than the world price. The artificially created domestic oil price would protect Canadian consumers, the large majority of whom lived in Ontario and Quebec, from having to pay the full world price for imported oil. The benefit to consumers would be paid for by the oil-producing provinces, primarily Alberta and, to a lesser extent, Saskatchewan. With the NDP, the fight over control of natural resources, and oil in particular, that had been raging since 1973 entered a whole new dimension of controversy and regional division. The after-effects linger over the federation to this day.

Leading the outrage against the actions of the federal government was Peter Lougheed. The Alberta premier linked both the constitutional agenda of Ottawa and its NEP as evidence of a strategy of division that would "produce disunity and bitterness in Canada at a time crucial in our history." The day after the federal budget, Lougheed went on province-wide television to announce his government's retaliation. It included a reduction in oil production by increments of 15 percent in each of three, six, and nine months. At the same time, he assured Canadians that if going forward there was any issue with supply in the rest of Canada, he would rescind the order.[12]

For Lougheed the federal government was engaged in a takeover of resources that constitutionally belonged to the provinces. In a February 1981 speech he said,

> It is not an overstatement to say that the basic objective of the federal energy proposal of October 28th, 1980, is an attempt to take over the resource ownership rights of this province and others in due course. The taxing and pricing powers of the federal government have been used in a clearly discriminatory way primarily directed at two million Albertans and to a lesser extent at citizens in British Columbia and Saskatchewan, unparalleled in our history. The essential word to describe these proposals is unfair. They basically change the rules of Confederation. They change the rules in terms of resource ownership rights of the provinces.[13]

For Blakeney, the NEP was a further evidence of the federal government's intent to take greater control of resources at the expense of the producing provinces. Blakeney said the federal PGRT tax on every barrel of oil and unit of natural gas production "added another swear word to vocabularies in the West—PGRT." He called the NEP "a new assault" by Ottawa, following earlier attacks in the wake of the OPEC oil crisis and the 1974 federal budget. Both he and Lougheed, he said, had lost their belief "in the good faith of the federal government's negotiating tactics."[14]

The intensity of the constitutional negotiations in 1980 and 1981 consumed much of the emotional energy and focus of the Blakeney government. In a very real way it created a political misalignment in the province, at least in the minds of many, between the needs of government and its people. On the one hand, the shape of the federation was at stake as Trudeau pursued his agenda of a "just society" by redefining federal-provincial relations and the very relationship of people to government through a charter of rights and freedoms. They were heady times for the Blakeney government, which was intimately involved in the statecraft of constitutional negotiations and the drama that unfolded.

But on the other hand, there was something else going on for average Saskatchewan people—something far more prosaic, but also far more important to their day-to-day lives. They were not so engrossed in the significance of obscure constitutional matters. Instead, they were trying to make ends meet and simply pay their bills. In 1981, the interest rate on a five-year mortgage was 18.38 percent.[15] The inflation rate in October 1981 was 12.78 percent.[16] A grim reality had settled in among some that high interest rates were simply the reality and people would have to learn to live with them. It was a view expressed in December 1981 by William Mulholland, president of the Bank of Montreal. At the time, the prime lending rate of chartered banks—that is, the interest rate they charge to their best corporate clients—was 17.2 percent, while consumer loans started several points higher. "I'm seriously concerned that in a year interest rates will be higher, perhaps much higher, than current levels," Mulholland warned.[17] He went on to say that if Canada could not lower inflation, it would face a difficult choice: either go through a protracted U.S.-style recession, with a drop in interest rates at the cost of higher unemployment, or stimulate the economy and let interest rates rise to record levels again.

A few months later, on April 17, 1982—nine days before what would turn out to be a watershed election in Saskatchewan that became known as the Monday Night Massacre—Blakeney was in Ottawa to take part in national ceremonies for the official signing of the Canada *Constitution Act* by Queen Elizabeth 11. Clearly, Blakeney was proud of what was widely seen as Canada's coming of age. "Having a constitution that is wholly Canadian is an important symbol for us as Canadians and for our sense of being Canadian," he said. He went on to note that Saskatchewan, and particularly himself and Romanow, had played a significant role in the outcome. "We believe this approach, particularly our presentation to the Supreme Court and its acceptance by that court, played a crucial role that made the constitutional agreement of last November possible."[18]

The same day, new Saskatchewan Progressive Conservative leader Grant Devine was in Prince Albert saying that he wasn't certain if his promised removal of the 29 cents-a-gallon provincial gas tax could be done the day after the election. "All I know I will remove it as fast as I can get the machinery together to get it off," Devine said.[19] Meanwhile, CTV News was announcing that a poll it had commissioned on the Saskatchewan election was showing Devine and the PCs in a slight lead.

It would be many years later, in 1992, when James Carville, a political strategist for the Democrats in the presidential election that brought Bill Clinton to power, famously said politics and elections could be distilled down to four words: "It's the economy, stupid." He was to be proven right in Saskatchewan, ten years before he even said it.

CHAPTER 10

1989

Waterloo?

W HEN TRYING TO UNDERSTAND HOW AND WHY HIS-
tory unfolds the way it does, there is the inevitable urge to look
for "defining" moments. They serve as touchstones, specific
events that help validate not only the way things were but why they became
the way they are now. When it comes to politics, very often these events are
mirror opposites that reflect the ongoing ebbs and flows of a political economy, the place where state and the economy intersect. In recent Saskatchewan
history, there have been two such key moments.

The first came in 1976. That's when the Blakeney NDP government nationalized a major portion of the potash sector by creating the government-owned
Potash Corporation of Saskatchewan, which became the policy vehicle to
purchase existing privately held potash mines. If one event had the effect of
"defining" the Blakeney government in the sense of reflecting its values and
principles, it was nationalization of the potash industry.

Admittedly there were other policies—such as the Land Bank, the creation of SaskOil and the SMDC, adherence to the Crow Rate, and the orderly marketing principle of the Canadian Wheat Board—that reflected the NDP's belief in the role of government to shape the province's economy. But potash was different. The fact is, potash and politics had become deeply interwoven in the psychology of the province during the 1960s and the days of the Ross Thatcher government, which oversaw the rapid expansion of the potash industry fuelled through tax and royalty incentives that generated private investment. It was a period when Thatcher boasted that potash would do for Saskatchewan's economy what oil did for Alberta's.[1] Like many such pronouncements, this was said for political effect, not because it was necessarily accurate. To suggest that deposits of potash fertilizer would have the same value as oil—a global commodity essential to the production of energy, fuel for transportation, and the very functioning of a modern society—is exaggeration in the extreme. Energy is the lifeblood of all economies. Potash is a fertilizer. But overstatement did have the desired political result, as potash became a commodity that formed a major part of Saskatchewan's economic identity.

The NDP had come to power determined to change the relationship between potash and government. The 1976 potash nationalization initiative was completely consistent with the NDP's commitment to greater control by government of natural resource development as the means to derive greater benefits for Saskatchewan's people. It was a policy that clearly set the NDP apart ideologically from its political opponents. To put it another way, public ownership of potash was a dividing line in Saskatchewan politics. What side of the line you were on determined your partisanship.

It is only logical, then, that the other crucial moment came thirteen years later, in 1989, when the Grant Devine PC government undid what the Blakeney government had done by privatizing the Potash Corporation of Saskatchewan. Just as nationalization in the Blakeney years gave the NDP a defining political moment, so too did potash privatization for the Devine Conservatives. The significance was reflected by the fact that it triggered the longest debate in Saskatchewan's legislative history. The effects of what happened in 1989, which was the culmination of nine privatizations of major corporations that included SaskOil, SMDC, and the Prince Albert Pulp Company (Papco), became an emphatic turning point in the transformation of the economy and politics of Saskatchewan.[2] Recognizing the political and economic implication of privatization, the Devine government spent several years preparing the public environment for the sale of resource Crown corporations, with potash privatization the capstone moment.

Shortly after it was elected in 1982, the Devine government did public opinion research into the level of investment by Saskatchewan people in publicly traded equities. The Conservatives had come to power with a huge majority but did not feel confident they could win re-election given the CCF-NDP's decades of political domination in the province.[3] The findings indicated not only a low level of investment activity but, similarly, a low level of knowledge of the equities market itself. Only 6 percent of respondents identified themselves as investors, which was half the national average. More revealing, perhaps, was that of the 6 percent who considered themselves investors, two-thirds of them invested in guaranteed Canada Savings Bonds, not equities. Nonetheless, they counted themselves as "investors." So, to prepare the ground for major privatization efforts, the government believed it needed to change the way people in Saskatchewan thought about "public" investment. Instead of the sale of Crown corporations being termed "privatization," it became "public participation."

The first step was to create the Crown Investment Review Commission, led by chartered accountant Wolfgang Wolff. The commission's 1983 report grouped Saskatchewan Crowns into three categories: government service companies; monopoly utilities; and commercial Crown corporations, defined as enterprises "which pursue profits and are clearly competitive with private business in marketing their outputs." It called for less political control of the corporations, recommending that ministers no longer chair or be members of the corporations' boards of directors. The intent was to eliminate the political direction of a corporation's activities, even though it was owned by the government. The commission did not express a view on privatization, although

it said that commercial Crown corporations should "pay maximum dividends" and operate more like private corporations, using similar accounting
practices and issuing quarterly reports.[4] Decisions on whether they remained
government owned hinged on their business roles. But before any significant
privatization agenda could unfold, the Devine government needed to create a public environment that was more comfortable with, and more literate
about, the idea of government-owned corporations becoming publicly traded
enterprises. That is, it had to undo the decades of history going back to the
Douglas years, and even earlier, when public ownership became a part of
Saskatchewan's political culture.

Responding to the existing appetite for guaranteed bonds, the Devine
government issued "public participation" bonds, available to the public,
which were backed by Crown corporations, specifically, SaskPower, SaskTel,
SaskOil, and the Potash Corporation. In other words, these bonds were guaranteed by the provincial government. It was all part of a strategy to prepare
the public environment for major privatization initiatives by creating the
sense among the population that people were "investing" in Crown corporations by purchasing bonds, even though what they were acquiring was debt,
not equity.[5]

In many cases, the Crowns were well capitalized with no need to seek debt
financing. But that was not the point. The purpose was to get Saskatchewan
people comfortable with "public participation" bonds that not only carried
attractive interest rates guaranteed by the government-owned enterprises but
also created the sense of having a personal investment in the corporations.
The next step was to launch small-scale privatizations that were unlikely
to cause a public backlash, such as the sale of the Saskatchewan Computer
Utility Corporation, followed by the privatization of court reporting services,
which was done during Devine's first term in office.

At the same time, Devine used his farm background to shape his government's focus on agriculture and rural Saskatchewan. This was reflected in gov-
ernment-subsidized low-interest farm purchase and production loans as policies to replace the government-owned Saskatchewan Land Bank. Devine also

consistently pressured the federal government to provide farm "deficiency" payments and to increase drought relief programs.[6]

In its second term, with the public preconditioned to the idea of "investing" in Crown corporations through the purchase of debt issued as bonds, the Devine government quickly ramped up its privatization agenda. The NDP had made serious inroads in the 1986 election, winning twenty-five seats and cutting the PCs majority to thirteen. More significantly, the New Democrats narrowly won the popular vote, by less than a percentage point.[7] The clear NDP momentum convinced Devine and others that if they did not move aggressively on their privatization agenda in their second term, they might not get another opportunity. The strategy was signalled in November 1987 at the PCs' annual convention when Devine said that all Crown corporations, other than utilities, were on the selling block, which was quickly followed by the creation of a Department of Public Participation.[8] In rapid succession the government sold SaskOil and then SMDC, setting the stage for its signature privatization initiative, the 1989 sale of the Potash Corporation of Saskatchewan. The plan was consummated by issuing an initial public offering (IPO) for shares in PCS at a price of $18 a share. Based on that IPO, the government valued PCS at $630 million.[9]

To help advance the privatization efforts, a group of Saskatchewan businesspeople, led by Regina-based IPSCO steel company CEO Roger Phillips, formed the Institute for Saskatchewan Enterprise (ISE), a transitory advocacy group that became a voice in support of the sale of PCS. The ISE commissioned a report by Arthur Andersen and Company, an international accounting, audit, and tax management group. The analysis included a value assessment of PCS based on existing estimates of the company's value, which ranged from $500 million to $800 million to $1 billion. The report said the government's investment in PCS in 1988 dollar equivalents was $1.95 billion. While the value of the company would not be known with certainty until a share offering was made, Arthur Andersen concluded that under the three scenarios the province would lose between $950 million and $1.45 billion on its potash investment.[10]

The transformative political significance of that three-year era from 1986 to 1989 cannot be overstated. At one point at the height of the privatization debate, Devine predicted the NDP would be doomed and would never recover from what was unfolding. "This is their Alamo, their Waterloo. This is the end of the line for them," Devine said.[11] It was an intense period of partisanship framed explicitly in ideological terms in a way that the province has not seen since. Ironically, it reached its public zenith with what proved to be a failed privatization attempt.

It came when, in the midst of the potash privatization debate, the Devine government hived off the gas division of SaskPower into the new corporate entity of SaskEnergy and then moved to privatize it. The action was seen as the government going a step too far into the privatization of a core Crown corporation utility, which, for the NDP Opposition, was a line it would not allow to be crossed. The potential sale of SaskEnergy was qualitatively different from the privatization of a commercial enterprise like PCS. The NDP walked out of the legislature in protest of SaskEnergy privatization. The bells to summon members to a vote on the SaskEnergy legislation rang for seventeen calendar days. When an Angus Reid poll found that only 22 percent of respondents approved of SaskEnergy privatization while 58 percent opposed it, and a petition opposed to the privatization gathered 100,000 signatures, the government backed down.[12] Looking back on it now one can reasonably argue that the NDP's defence of SaskEnergy was the party's last stand on a major ideological issue in Saskatchewan.

What the NDP saw as a "win" in getting the government to back off SaskEnergy privatization actually helped set the stage for the passage of legislation to privatize PCS a few months later. The success in defending one Crown corporation from being sold gave the NDP something of an ideological victory, allowing it to retain its integrity and principles on public ownership. Or at least, so it thought. In fact, what it did was relieve some of the pressure over the PCS struggle, and after eighty hours of debate the government shut down further wrangling with closure and the Potash Corporation privatization legislation was passed in August 1989.[13]

The political and economic consequences of the Devine government's privatization initiatives reached far beyond Saskatchewan. As noted in *Maclean's* magazine, "In one of Canada's least likely twists, Saskatchewan, the cradle of Canadian socialism, is rapidly becoming a symbol of free enterprise....Grant Devine is selling off some of the province's largest publicly owned corporations and he has made it the dominant economic and political issue in the province."[14]

Since that time, there has been intermittent debate over the privatization of potash. Discussion has ranged from whether the government received a fair-market price for PCS to whether a government-owned PCS would have flourished financially the way it did as a publicly traded company. A few observations seem credible. One is that, judging by how the share price of a publicly traded Potash Corporation escalated after a short decline, the IPO price was undervalued. But it mattered not. In terms of politics, the Rubicon had been crossed with the privatization of the Potash Corporation. It was a body blow to the NDP because it erased a critical part of its identity that the party has been unable to reclaim.

Never has the NDP taken the position that if returned to power, it would renationalize potash, or, for that matter, launch another agenda of nationalization as it did in the 1970s, whether through expropriation of existing private assets or direct public investment in new public enterprise. The closest the NDP came to public enterprise was a 1996 public-private partnership in a potato company known as Spudco, formally the Saskatchewan Potato Utility Development Company. It ended in what bordered on farce. The government lost $28 million and faced several lawsuits as well as disputes over the construction of sheds to house the potatoes.[15] It was a far cry from the heady days of twenty years earlier when the Blakeney government took control of the potash industry in Saskatchewan and became the world's dominant player in the sector.

To appreciate the significance of the moment of potash privatization in 1989, which stands as the longest debate in the Saskatchewan Legislature, it is important to recognize the broader context beyond Saskatchewan. Other important factors put privatization in a Canadian and even global context.

The last half of the 1980s was a period when the rise of market forces and the diminution of government in the economy were very much the dominant political and economic consensus. In Canada, it was primarily reflected in the free trade federal election of 1988. The core ballot question that Canadians were asked to answer was whether to endorse the Mulroney government and its negotiated free trade agreement with the United States or to reject it by supporting John Turner and the Liberals. The debate revolved around two clashing ideas. One was market expansion to foster economic growth; the other was the loss of sovereignty and self-determination resulting from the federal government's reduced control of Canada's national economic levers.

The Canada-U.S. free trade negotiations were spawned by the Royal Commission on the Economic Union and Development Prospects for Canada. Led by former federal finance minister Donald Macdonald, it had been formed by the Trudeau government in 1982 to help map a policy pathway for greater economic growth after years of stagflation. The report was delivered in 1984 to newly elected prime minister Brian Mulroney. Its focus was on encouraging a more flexible economy and, in particular, a greater reliance on the market to shape the economy, by establishing a free trade relationship with the United States. One of the members of the Macdonald Commission and a strong proponent of free trade was Jack Messer, a former minister in the Blakeney government.

To say the free trade debate during the election of 1988 was emotionally charged would be an understatement. It was at times bitter and divisive. Take, for example, the exchange between Turner and Mulroney in the televised leaders' debate held in the midst of the campaign. Turner declared,

> The Americans can't believe their good luck. No wonder the Senate of the United States passed this deal in one day, no wonder the House of Representatives passed it in one day, no wonder President Reagan says that this is the fulfillment of the American dream. We gave away our energy. We gave away our investment. We sold out our supply management and agriculture. And we have left hundreds of thousands of workers vulnerable

because of the social programs involved, because of the minimum wages that we will have to start to compare and harmonize, because of the fact they are in vulnerable industries.

Mulroney bristled at the suggestion he was selling out Canada. "You do not have a monopoly on patriotism," Mulroney said to Turner. The Conservative leader shot back,

Let me tell you something, sir. This country is only about 120 years old, but my own father 55 years ago went himself as a labourer with hundreds of other Canadians and with their own hands, in northeastern Quebec, they built a little town, schools and churches, and they in their own way were nation-building. In the same way that the waves of immigrants from the Ukraine and Eastern Europe rolled back the prairies and in their own way, in their own time, they were nation-building because they loved Canada. I today, sir, as a Canadian believe genuinely in what I am doing. I believe it is right for Canada. I believe that in my own modest way I am nation-building because I believe this benefits Canada, and I love Canada.[16]

When Canadians had their say on November 21, 1988, the Mulroney government won a second majority, and the free trade agreement with the United States subsequently took effect January 1, 1990. The federal vote in Saskatchewan did not mirror the national outcome. Of the fourteen seats in the province, the NDP won ten seats and the PCs four. It seemed to be a clear statement that a majority of Saskatchewan people remained committed to the notion of an activist government that maintains its ability to intervene in the economy as part of a social democratic agenda. The result, however, did not deter the Devine government from its privatization agenda. They saw it as a way to neuter the NDP. By reversing what the Blakeney government had done in the 1970s, the Devine Tories believed there would be no going back when the NDP inevitably returned to power.

This was also a period of epoch changes in the world order. The Cold War paradigm of West versus East, capitalism versus communism, that had shaped the world through much of the twentieth century was ending. It was a time of "glasnost" and "perestroika" in the Soviet Union under Mikhail Gorbachev. Upon assuming power in 1985, Gorbachev had set out to reform what was a collapsing communist economic system. He proposed restructuring of the economy and greater transparency. In effect, Gorbachev reduced central control of businesses, encouraging a market-based approach where farmers and manufacturers could decide on their own what to produce, how much to produce, and what price to sell their products at. It meant that the price controls set by powerful central committees were eliminated. The next stage was to allow the emergence of a private sector, with privately owned stores, restaurants, and manufacturing enterprises. Gorbachev also looked beyond the domestic economy and recognized that foreign investment was crucial for the development of the economy. The first step was to allow foreign private investment in as part of joint ventures with Soviet business, which initially were to have majority ownership.[17]

Ironically, in July 1989, a few weeks before the privatization bill for the Potash Corporation of Saskatchewan was passed, Gorbachev was seeking an invitation to a meeting of the G7. He was asking for (in fact, imploring) the Western world to help in the Soviet Union's transition to a market-based economy. His letter to then French president François Mitterrand, who was to be the summit host, clearly stated the need for the USSR to become integrated into the global economy. Gorbachev wrote,

> Like other countries, the Soviet Union seeks to complete the task of adapting its national economy to a new structure of the international division of labor which is developing. Our *perestroika* is inseparable from the policy that aims at full and complete participation in the world economy. That orientation, which is in keeping with current political thought, is equally determined by our direct economic interest. But it is clear the rest of the world can only gain from the opening up to the world economy of a

market like that of the USSR. Of course, mutual advantage implies mutual responsibility and respect for the rights of all the participants in international economic relations.[18]

Gorbachev continued lobbying the G7 in 1991 as the Soviet Union fractured. With the Russian economy in disarray and Gorbachev's future growing more precarious by the day, he wrote to the G7 requesting $100 billion to support a Russian economic recovery. Gorbachev maintained that the fate of the dissolving Soviet Union and the economic and political change that came with the demise of communism were as important to the stability of the world as to the future of the Soviet Union itself.[19]

The fall of communism came when Margaret Thatcher was the prime minister of Great Britain. Thatcher, who had led the Conservatives to a crushing defeat of the British Labour Party a decade earlier, had been a powerful voice supporting free-market liberalism and globalization. She was a radical who challenged many characteristics of the state, including the idea of social democracy itself. At one point, in a 1988 interview, Thatcher famously spoke about individuals and governments, specifically, those who see government as being able to solve their ills. "They are casting their problems at society. And, you know, there's no such thing as society. There are individual men and women and there are families. And no government can do anything except through people, and people must look after themselves first. It is our duty to look after ourselves and then, also, to look after our neighbours," she said.[20] Her global impact could not be ignored and she was seen as a key figure in the end of the Cold War and the fall of the Soviet Union. The influence of Thatcher on the world was immense. It can be measured in the fact that she and her beliefs became an "ism," which is rarely achieved by a politician. When she died in 2013, the *Economist* magazine summed up Thatcherism as follows: "Mrs Thatcher believed that societies have to encourage and reward the risk-takers, the entrepreneurs, who alone create the wealth without which governments cannot do anything, let alone help the weak. A country can prosper only by encouraging people to save and to spend no more than they earn; profligacy (and, even worse, borrowing) were her road to perdition. The essence of Thatcherism was a strong state and a free economy."[21]

While in power, Thatcher implemented an aggressive agenda that sought to dismantle much of the British state apparatus to make way for the market. One of the primary tools she used was privatization. In 1989, as she was nearing the end of her time as prime minister, Thatcher had privatized public assets totalling $44 billion. The wave of privatizations included British Telecom, British Gas, and British Airways.[22] What emerged was an entire cottage industry of privatization advocates and experts who became privatization consultants for hire by governments that wanted to follow Thatcher's lead. So far reaching was Thatcher's influence that two such "experts" from the United Kingdom found their way to Saskatchewan to act as privatization consultants to the Devine government. Oliver Letwin and Madsen Pirie were associated with the Adam Smith Institute, a libertarian, free-market think tank in London. Letwin, a director of the privatization unit at N.M. Rothschild & Sons, was eventually elected as a Conservative member of Parliament in 1997. Their communications advice was to position privatization as a sound financial and business decision by government, not an initiative driven by ideology. The argument was that government could maintain control through the use of taxation and regulation policy levers to achieve economic and social policy objectives.

The pair had direct contact with members of the Devine government caucus, who by 1987 had been given copies of an essay by Pirie called "The Buying Out of Socialism," which was also circulated among members of the Saskatchewan public service. As well, the PC caucus got a private screening of a three-hour British documentary called *The Death of Socialism*.[23] As the potash debate was growing in intensity and global events were unfolding rapidly, Devine couldn't help but mention what was happening in the Soviet Union. It was months before the fall of the Berlin Wall, a momentous moment that signalled the disintegration of the Soviet communists' hold on eastern Europe. "If Mikhail Gorbachev was the premier of Saskatchewan, he would be way ahead of me," Devine said.[24] It was no coincidence that in January 1990 Devine travelled to Moscow as part of a six-nation visit to Europe, less than two months after the fall of the Berlin Wall. The message from the visit to the Soviet Union was that an early-stage free-enterprise, capitalist economy was emerging and it provided trade and investment opportunities for Saskatchewan business. "If ever there was an opportunity, then now is the time to be here," Devine said after meeting with Georgi Kirichenko, the Soviet deputy minister for agriculture machine and automobile building, responsible for 3,500 manufacturing enterprises that employed 2.8 million people. "He told me that he was very eager. He said he was on fire, anxious to do things."[25]

What unfolded in Saskatchewan was truly part of a global phenomenon that changed the terms of the political and economic debate. "During the 1980s and 1990, a major wave of disenchantment with state intervention swept through industrial nations," Pier Angelo Toninelli explains in the introduction to *The Rise and Fall of State-Owned Enterprise in the Western World*, a compilation of perspectives on public enterprise by academics across Europe and the United States. "The poor performance of mixed economies in the 1970s and 1980s, as well as the collapse of collectivist regimes in the early 1990s, contributed to the reappraisal of the economic role of the state in the West as well as elsewhere."[26]

Using one measurement, one could argue that the political effect of the privatization debate was that it led to the defeat of the Devine government in 1991, when the NDP, under new leader Roy Romanow, crushed the PCs, leaving them with only ten seats to the New Democrats' fifty-five. But, as is always the case in elections, there are many factors that affect voters' decisions and it is impossible to know with any certainty how big a role any one consideration played in the defeat of a government. Normally it is the accumulation of many issues and events that shapes opinions of governments and people in power. When it comes to the Devine government, there certainly were reasons other than just privatization that determined public opinion. Certainly the province's dire fiscal situation after years of annual budget deficits and mounting provincial debt during the Devine years was a key factor in the Conservative government's defeat. In just its six budgets from 1986 through 1991, the Devine government ran deficits totalling $3.6 billion. Over its nine years in office, from 1982 to 1991, the annual operating deficits totalled $5.2 billion and the net debt of the province grew from what was a net asset of $712 million in the last year of the Blakeney government to a net debt of $6 billion when the Devine government left office.[27]

In their study of elections, Richard Lau and David Redlawsk argue that determining the process by which voters decide who to support is essential in understanding how democracy itself works. They state that "there can be no more important question in political science."[28] But they also conclude that voters reach a decision on how to cast their ballot as a result of a dynamic process that includes events and the management of issues before and during election campaigns. Instead of traditional analysis of voting behaviour based on social, economic, and demographic factors, the authors study specific individuals and conclude that individual behaviour may not be reflective of individual preferences. In other words, people might vote in a manner that is contrary to their own interests.

It is a view not dissimilar to that expressed by Bryan Caplan, who studied how individuals often vote based on false beliefs. "When people vote under the influence of false beliefs that feel good, democracy consistently delivers bad policies," Caplan says. He maintains that voters often do not act rationally in their own best interests. That's because emotion, not fact, can have a powerful influence on judgment. "We habitually tune out information on subjects we don't care about...we turn off our rational faculties on subjects where we don't care about the truth."[29] In other words, there are times when it seems rational to individuals to hold irrational beliefs, particularly if the consequences to the individual are negligible or even non-existent. As a result, the emotional comfort or satisfaction from holding the belief is greater than the potential costs to the individual. The thesis, therefore, is that voters often elect politicians who share their biases, or pretend to—a proposition that seems self-evidently true in the recent rise of Donald Trump to the U.S. presidency.

There were many issues that shaped public opinion of the Devine government. Its second and final term was a period of growing budget deficits. In fact, the privatization agenda had a fiscal rationale, as the government saw the sale of Crown corporations as a source of revenue to help reduce the deficit. From the time it assumed power in 1982, the Devine government had spent $3.3 billion more than what it had taken in revenue. The fiscal mismanagement that spawned rapid growth in the public debt became a political albatross, one that was eventually handed to, and hobbled, the incoming Romanow government. The Fraser Institute, a free market–oriented think tank, suggested that the Devine government could collect $1.5 billion from the privatization efforts and use it to balance its budget.[30] But selling public assets to pay for operating costs is something that, intuitively, the average person understands is not a sustainable remedy to solving a household budget deficit. The same holds true for governments.

In its final months, the Devine government appeared to be rudderless and desperate. Ignoring the tradition of provincial elections being held every four years, it delayed calling an election until October 21, 1991, at the end of its fifth year and of the legal limits of its mandate. Rather than providing people with transparency and introduce a budget in the spring of 1991, before the start of a new fiscal year on April 1, it governed by special warrants of cabinet for more than six months. The perception that the government was adrift, faced serious fiscal trouble, and feared its date with the electorate had set into the public consciousness. In a desperate attempt to shore up its rural base, the Conservative government announced what it called "Fair Share Saskatchewan." The initiative would see the decentralization of government, with many departments and agencies to be transferred from Regina to communities across the province. Then, as the campaign was about to unfold, a dark cloud of scandal relating to misuse of PC government caucus communication allowances was beginning to form. The election-day reckoning would mark the end of a discredited and what would be exposed as a scandal-ridden government. But its political and economic legacy would live on.

To this day, Saskatchewan has never been the same.

CHAPTER 11

1993

Pain and Suffering

T HE PHONE RANG AT 3:00 A.M. A GROGGY ROY ROMANOW reached to pick up the receiver. "Hello?"

There was a brief pause. "Is this Roy Romanow?" the man's voice on the line abruptly asked. "Yes. Who is this?" Romanow replied.

"You listen to me. I've got something to tell you. I know you're planning to come to Yorkton. If you do, I've got a gun and I'm going to blow your fucking head off," the man said. Rattled by the threat, Romanow instinctively answered to disguise his fear, "Well, I'll tell you one thing. You better not miss because if you do I'm going to beat the shit out of you."

"You're the premier, you can't talk to me like that," the caller snapped.

"I just did," Romanow said, and he hung up the phone.

The threatening middle-of-the-night calls from the same man continued for the next few days. The RCMP were alerted and before long the police told Romanow not to worry; they had identified the caller and would have the man under close surveillance. Two plainclothes officers would be at the town hall meeting in Yorkton, one sitting on each side of the man who had made the threats. When Romanow got up to speak he recognized the two police members and saw an angry-looking man sitting between them. Nothing happened.[1]

Weeks later, in the summer of 1993, Romanow travelled to the town of Eston to meet with local officials. It was billed as a visit by the premier to hear concerns about his government's plans to close fifty-two rural acute care hospitals as part of broadly based health restructuring and reform. Hundreds of local and district residents turned out to confront Romanow. They lined both sides of the street shouting taunts at the premier as he walked the gauntlet to a meeting with the town's board of trade and members of the district health board.[2]

Lying on the sidewalk were two youngsters with chalk outlines around them, as if they were dead. Romanow bent over in what was to be a playful gesture and grabbed the toe of the shoe of one of the boys. "Don't you dare touch my son!" a woman shouted at Romanow. Others joined in with a chorus, shouting that he had given the town its death sentence.[3]

Welcome to the politics of Saskatchewan in the first half of the 1990s. Across rural Saskatchewan emotions were raw, anger was palpable, and it was all directed at the NDP government of Romanow. The party that for decades had built its credibility, and appeal, as the creator and defender of universal publicly funded health care had become the object of derision. It was seen to be abandoning health care across much of rural Saskatchewan.

The NDP had returned to power in November 1991—after nine years of a PC government under Premier Grant Devine—with a landslide fifty-five seats in the sixty-six-seat Saskatchewan Legislature. It won on a platform that contained few promises other than to restore sound financial management to government. Its primary commitment was to address the huge debt and deficit that had been created through the 1980s and was crippling the government. It would require rationalization in the delivery of services as part of rebalancing expenditures and revenues.

In office, from 1982 to 1991, the Devine government ran ten consecutive deficit budgets that totalled more than 5 billion dollars. The annual operating deficits reached their peak in 1986–87 at more than $1.2 billion. In the

Romanow government's first budget, facing a deficit of $852 million, the third-largest expenditure after health care and education was $517 million in interest on the provincial debt.[4] The deadweight cost just to pay interest on the debt crippled the fiscal capacity of government to act on numerous fronts.

It is worth noting that Saskatchewan was not a budget deficit outlier, although Alberta and Manitoba did not run operating deficits on the same scale as Saskatchewan. The 1980s were a decade when deficit budgets became the norm for many provinces. For example, in Alberta from 1985 to 1992 the PC government racked up annual operating deficits of $14.7 billion. The story was not dissimilar in Manitoba, which accumulated operating deficits totalling $3.7 billion from 1982 to 1992.[5]

Having said that, Saskatchewan experienced the largest change in its debt position relative to other provinces when its net debt-to-GDP ratio increased by more than 24 percentage points between 1980–81 and 1989–90. At one point, Moody's Investors Service forecast that Saskatchewan's debt-servicing costs would increase 97 percent between 1985 and 1987.[6] Many factors helped create the fiscal problems, including a 1986 fall in oil and gas prices coupled with low commodity prices for potash, uranium, and grain for much of the decade. In spite of primary surpluses (that is, an operating surplus excluding debt interest payments) later in the decade, the province's exposure to the effects of high interest rates and continued low commodity prices caused the province's debt-to-GDP ratio to continue to grow.[7]

Another factor was recurring years of drought and poor crop production that put fiscal pressure on the government to support the farm economy. Indeed, a key factor in the Devine government's re-election to a second majority term in 1986 was a $1 billion "deficiency payment" to grain farmers announced by the Mulroney government in the midst of the campaign. Word of the farm aid leaked out when a reporter in a hotel room next to the premier's on the campaign trail overheard a 5:00 a.m. phone call between federal agriculture minister John Wise and Devine. The premier was pleading to the federal minister for the assistance, saying his election fortunes depended on the Mulroney government coming to his rescue. "It just showed once more, whether it's at midnight or 5 am, that I'm defending farmers," Devine said when the payment to farmers was announced.[8] But what it also did was further embed expectations among members of the farm community that they were entitled to government support whenever farmers faced financial pressure from low prices or poor yields.

When the Romanow government took power in 1991, social democracy was under siege. The rise of globalization and trade liberalization, the economic collapse and disintegration of the Soviet Union, the growth of transnational corporations, and flows of global investments had created seismic changes in the world economy and politics. It was only a decade removed from the 1970s and the days of public ownership, marketing boards, and defensive efforts to shield Saskatchewan from events beyond the province's borders—a time that seemed almost old-fashioned in the world of the early 1990s.

Ironically, the same year the NDP returned to power in Saskatchewan, a group of academics and others who numbered themselves New Democrats issued a book called *Social Democracy without Illusions*; its subtitle was *Renewal of the Canadian Left*. The book was edited by John Richards, Larry Pratt, and Robert Cairns. A professor at Simon Fraser University, Richards was, for a time, a one-term MLA in the Blakeney government. Unhappy with the Blakeney government's lack of action in pursuing nationalization of the resource sector, Richards left the NDP caucus to sit as an independent socialist. He was defeated in the 1975 election. In 1979 he co-authored with Pratt a book entitled *Prairie Capitalism*—to this day it remains a seminal work— that looked at the role of the state and politics in the development of resources in Alberta and Saskatchewan.

The publication of *Social Democracy without Illusions* was a forerunner to the emergence of what became known as the "Third Way" movement among social democrats who sought to reconcile their socialist beliefs with the world as it existed in the 1990s. So, well before the likes of Bill Clinton in the United States, Gerhard Schröder in Germany, and Tony Blair in the United Kingdom became proponents of a "Third Way" for the left, Richards and the others had already been engaged in the debate. One of the contributors to

Social Democracy without Illusions was Blakeney, who, in his chapter, noted, "When we look at the actual policies of NDP governments, or the themes publicly stressed by NDP politicians in opposition, the emphasis has consistently been on how wealth and power are distributed rather than on how they are produced."[9] It was a telling comment that reflected the challenge facing social democrats. The book argued that social democrats in Canada needed to rethink their approach on public policies including management of the economy, the environment, collective bargaining, social programs, economic nationalism, and foreign policy. A focus on wealth redistribution rather than wealth creation had become a defining feature of the NDP that over time eroded its credibility with many. The fact that Blakeney saw it as a flaw was itself very significant.

Such was the political, fiscal, and economic climate that greeted the Romanow government when it came into office in 1991. Not only were the solutions of the 1970s passé, but the new terms of economic growth and the lack of fiscal capacity rendered the pursuit of traditional social democratic policies impossible. It was only a decade removed from the 1970s, but it felt like a lifetime had passed.

There was little doubt that the primary motivation for health care reform was the Romanow government's overarching goal of reaching a balanced budget. The first thing Romanow did, knowing the extent of the fiscal challenge he faced and the likely internal tensions it would create, was to form an initial "war cabinet" of eleven members. At its first formal meeting, the cabinet was confronted with the depth of the fiscal challenge the province faced in a presentation by Department of Finance officials. The issue was put in stark terms. The province was uncertain whether it could raise money on the New York bond markets, other than at exorbitant "junk bond" interest rates, to finance payment on its debt and cover its operating deficit. The question to be answered was simply stated: Should the government allow the IMF to implement the kind of budget solutions necessary to stabilize the province's budget situation, or should the government take the necessary action so that the province could at least control its own destiny? The choice was obvious, if unpalatable. It was up to the newly elected government to design its fiscal recovery.

An unspoken but defining feature of the Romanow government's fiscal plan was to rebalance rural versus urban spending. It was in many ways going to be an attempt to deal with deeply rooted, structural issues in the province that had been well known for decades but never tackled owing to a lack of political will by successive governments to confront reality.

The challenge had long been identified. It was set out by the Royal Commission on Agriculture and Rural Life, which from 1952 to 1957 had extensively and exhaustively explored the structural issues facing Saskatchewan. The goals of what became euphemistically called "the never-ending commission" were "to search out and organize the fullest possible set of facts relevant to Saskatchewan's complex rural economic and social conditions; [and] on the basis of these facts, to establish guides for future rural improvement."[10] Its creation was itself an acknowledgement that by the 1950s the pattern of rural life in Saskatchewan had dramatically changed from the early days of settlement, when the social and economic institutions of governance had been created. Rapid mechanization resulting from the Second World War effort and the subsequent growth in farm size were altering the fabric of rural Saskatchewan.

From March 1955 to April 1957, the commission issued fourteen reports. Its recommendations included a redefinition of the family farm "to reflect the new realities of post-war agriculture" and the amalgamation of rural municipalities into a pattern of larger county governance.[11] The first report stated that "the evidence conclusively indicates the urgent necessity of basic reorganization of rural municipal government in Saskatchewan."[12] That was in 1955.

Based on the principle of never letting a crisis go to waste, the budget challenge that the Romanow government faced thirty-six years later was seen as an opportunity to tackle the structural issues that had long been ignored. The situation was aptly described later by Janice MacKinnon, who served as the second finance minister in Romanow's government after Ed Tchorzewski had to step aside for health reasons. "The drama that unfolded in Saskatchewan between the swearing in of the Romanow war cabinet on 1.November 1991 and the budget of 18 March 1993 portrays in graphic detail what happens when governments become so beholden to credit-rating agencies that they, rather than the voters, dictate the budgets," MacKinnon writes. "The events of this period also reveal the struggle within the NDP as deficit reduction and changes associated with the global economy challenged orthodox NDP views."[13]

Adding pressure was the fact that the Devine government had not passed a budget for 1991–92. For six months it had financed government by issuing cabinet special warrants. Upon taking over as premier, Romanow faced demands to pass a budget. Prime Minister Mulroney himself called Romanow to demand that Saskatchewan get a budget through the legislature and in place. Romanow was not amused. "Did you phone Devine and demand the same of him?" Romanow snapped.[14]

To create the context and prepare the public environment for what needed to be done, within weeks of taking power Romanow appointed an independent fiscal review commission headed by accountant Don Gass to study and report back on the province's books. When it did, the Gass Commission painted a bleak picture of the province's financial situation. It determined that the province's debt was $7.5 billion, double what had been estimated by the Devine government. The annual operating deficit, according to Gass, was $975 million, not the $360 million forecast by the previous government. The province had the largest per capita debt and deficit in Canada, with the debt equalling 180 percent of the province's annual revenue.[15] "Our economy can no longer support the public sector infrastructure that we have built to serve the quality of life and standard of living we have come to expect," Gass said when his report was released in February 1992. "Our report is like a diagnosis before the treatment. It lets us know what we're up against and is the basis for further decisions before recovery."[16] As it turned out, the treatment became bitter medicine, literally and figuratively.

Next came a public consultations initiative leading to the 1993 budget that created the plan for a return to a balanced budget. The architect of the strategy was Tchorzewski. Although he had stepped down for health reasons prior to the 1993 budget that was delivered by MacKinnon, it was Tchorzewski who did the heavy lifting and deserves credit for creating the fiscal framework to overcome the deficit and debt crisis. The twenty-page paper set out the scope of the challenge by outlining how the province's debt had grown exponentially over the course of the previous ten years, how annual costs of paying interest on the debt and the resulting operating deficit, further added to the debt. "We are all in this together. Those who can help, must. Those who need protection will be protected," Tchorzewski said.[17] It was a clear signal of what was to come.

The matter of how to address the budget issue was deeply divisive within the government caucus. Internally the government was in an ideological war with itself. Some New Democrats, unhappy with a fiscally conservative agenda, saw it as nothing less than a surrender to neoliberalism. Romanow's argument was that the NDP had been elected on a mandate to eliminate the deficit and balance the budget. When the proposed 1993 budget was presented to caucus, it included deep cuts in health spending over two years that totalled 5.8 percent for hospitals, as well as the elimination of the provincial drug plan for those not on social assistance. But the budget also went far beyond cuts to health care. In included 6 percent cuts to K–12 education, cuts to funding for universities, a staggering 13 percent cut in funding to urban municipalities, and 11 percent cut to rural municipalities.[18]

The carnage of cuts led to a brief, but tense, moment of brinkmanship. Some outraged members of the NDP caucus pushed back, threatening to not support the budget, taking the position that the government would be better to simply default on the debt than impose the kind of cuts being planned. It was a naïve argument that would simply take the control of fiscal decisions out of the hands of government and give it to bond holders, who would dictate terms or simply refuse to finance the province's debt. Romanow rejected the idea. He argued that the government was elected to deal with the budget deficit and growing debt, and if the caucus was not willing to deliver on what it had promised the electorate, then the government would fall. "If this caucus will not support the wishes of the people of Saskatchewan, then I will see to it that the people of Saskatchewan have a chance to choose a government that will," Romanow said.[19] Romanow abruptly walked out of the caucus meeting and went to see Lieutenant Governor Sylvia Fedoruk, ostensibly to ask her to dissolve the legislature and call an election. Fedoruk pushed back and said Romanow needed to try harder to gain the support of his caucus. By the time Romanow returned to the legislature, the mood in caucus had mellowed. Cooler heads prevailed with the realization that not supporting the budget would result in an unwanted election.

The fiscal pressure on the provincial government from health care was partly a result of changes in health transfer payments from the federal government. Originally the federal government support for provincial health care had been on a cost-shared, matching grants basis. In effect the feds paid half the costs. In 1977 that began to change, with the creation of Established Program Financing by Ottawa, which put a cap on federal health transfers and effectively transferred more responsibility for covering the costs of health care to the provinces.

The internal tension and divisions that consumed the NDP government at the time were largely below the surface in the months leading to the 1993 budget. When the government had put the idea of health reform on the agenda, it sounded reasonable enough. It was outlined in a document titled "A Saskatchewan Vision for Health: A Framework for Change," issued by Health Minister Louise Simard in August 1992. The twenty-four-page document was based on six months of meetings "held with many groups, private individuals and health professionals to review the province's health system." The consultations had "led to a consensus about the need for comprehensive series of reforms to the current system."[20] The consensus was that health care reform should be based on a "wellness approach," an idea that had been established by the government in January 1992 when it announced the "Wellness Project" as the first step in reforming the health care system.

Reform of the health care system was going to be a critical dimension of the solution. There would be two phases to health reform: first, to reorganize and restructure the system; and second, to change the focus of health care

itself from acute care—in other words, dealing with "sickness"—to the pre-
vention of illness and a "wellness" model. In effect, the wellness concept was
as much a sociological approach to health as it was traditional medicine. "The
wellness approach is a new way of looking at the province's health system to
help us achieve the highest possible level of health in all aspects of our lives,"
the Simard paper stated. It went on to note "that our health is determined by
factors that go beyond the traditional definition of health and health care.
Factors like employment, income, education, housing, the environment and
individual lifestyle choices all play a major role in determining our health."[21]

The idea of shifting the emphasis of health care from sickness to wellness
was an uncontroversial idea. Intuitively it made sense to most people—unless,
of course, it was perceived to be coming at the expense of diminishing the
hospital-based acute care capacity of health care. The true test of good health
care for most people is the accessibility and quality of care you get when you're
sick, not the care you're not getting when you don't need it.

But there was also a "Nixon-to-China" dimension to the health reform
initiative. If any party had the credibility and public trust to truly reform
health care, it was surely the New Democrats. Just as no one doubted that
an avowed anti-communist like Nixon could be trusted to establish relations
with Communist China, no one doubted the commitment by the NDP, as the
party of Medicare, to publicly funded universal health care. To demonstrate
that the NDP government was doing the right thing, a quote from the father
of Medicare himself, Tommy Douglas, appeared as evidence in the introduction of the Simard document. "When we began to plan Medicare, we pointed
out that it would be in two phases," Douglas had said in 1982. "The first phase
would be to remove the financial barrier between those giving the service and
those receiving it. The second phase would be to reorganize and revamp the
whole delivery system—and of course, that's the big item. That's the thing we
haven't done yet."[22]

So, in other words, the Romanow government was staying true to
Douglas's words. Saskatchewan would reassert its health care credentials by
taking on a new frontier of health care. It would lead the nation by going from

a "sickness" model built around high-cost acute care to a "wellness" model that would reduce costs by providing primary health care that kept people from becoming sick. Or at least, such was the theory.

At a notional and aspirational level, no one could argue with the intent. But as is often the case when it comes to policy, a good idea is only as good as its implementation. The wellness model never did advance in any truly meaningful manner. It went off the rails early because what needed to happen first was the reorganization of the acute care health system, particularly in rural Saskatchewan where a network of small-town hospitals, built over generations, no longer reflected the assumptions or reality on which the system was originally based. Thus, the starting point in the public debate over health care reform was less about health and more about cutting costs, which inevitably led to the decision to close—or, in the government's vernacular at the time, to "convert into wellness centres"—fifty-two small community hospitals. This created a firestorm of protest across rural Saskatchewan.

The process included the elimination of local community-based hospital boards for a model of regionalization that created thirty regional health boards, which meant consolidating four hundred boards that represented hospitals, home care, long-term care, and ambulance services. Each would be funded by the province and make decisions on how to allocate resources and coordinate care in their areas. The idea of reorganization into regions had been proposed two years earlier by the Saskatchewan Commission on Directions in Health Care. Not surprisingly, Dr. Bob Murray, who had chaired the commission, called the Romanow government's health reform announcement "a great step forward."[23]

The laudatory sentiment was not widely shared by the public. Opinion against the closure of hospitals was bluntly expressed by Lorraine Didrick, a cook at the Radville Community Hospital. "I think Louise Simard should have to ride out of the Big Muddy [a rugged badlands in the area] in the back of a half-ton truck with a broken back," Didrick said.[24] In partisan political terms, the backlash in rural Saskatchewan gave the Progressive Conservatives, who had been banished to Opposition status in the election less than a year earlier, a political lifeline that allowed opponents of the NDP government to rally across rural Saskatchewan.

Souring public opinion in rural Saskatchewan further against the government was the manner in which the new system of thirty health districts was created. Originally the government had said that each of the newly created districts would make the decisions as to which hospitals would survive. But with the 1993 budget, the decisions had been made in advance by the government and imposed on the health districts. Criticized initially for pitting one community against another by having district boards decide what hospitals survive, Simard was then attacked for breaking her promise and making decisions herself. In an editorial, the *Saskatoon StarPhoenix* said the process had been "clumsily" handled. "The government promised decisions would be made by local people. It broke that promise, in almost brutal fashion, by announcing it would take acute-care money from 52 small hospitals," the newspaper said.[25] Simard couldn't help but note the hypocrisy. In response to the criticism, she said, "We've heard repeatedly over the last few months that what you're doing is passing the buck to district boards. Now that we've made tough decisions, the same people are saying 'Well why are you making these decisions? Shouldn't district boards be making these decisions?'"[26] Moreover, the anger with reform was not limited to rural Saskatchewan. As part of its deficit-reduction measures, the government announced that the nineteen-year-old Plains Health Centre in Regina would close. Ironically, the hospital had originally been built as a "base hospital" that would serve primarily the residents of southern Saskatchewan who could not get the acute care they needed at their community hospital. A large and modern teaching hospital that served many living on farms or in smaller rural communities, its closure added to the public angst.

In Saskatchewan, the health care debate has always been steeped in emotion. It has been such a defining issue in political terms that it effectively has been the third rail of politics. You address it at your own peril. And even though the NDP was widely acknowledged as the party of Medicare, that was not enough to insulate it from the anger over changing the pattern of rural health care that was considered crucial to the identity and viability of the communities affected by the reforms. Many in rural Saskatchewan saw the health reform as evidence that the NDP was dominated by urban interests.

There certainly were good financial and management reasons for cutting the acute care funding for the rural hospitals. In 1991, Saskatchewan's hospital bed ratio was 7.2 per 1,000 of population, well above the national average of 4.7 per 1,000.[27] The government determined which hospitals would close based on three factors. First, hospitals with fewer than eight beds would close. The second factor was utilization; that is, hospitals averaging fewer than eight patients daily for the past two consecutive years would lose funding. And third was the distance to the nearest alternative acute care facility. But while a minimum size, usage, and distance formula might make sense in terms of the management and proper allocation of taxpayers' dollars, it failed to grasp the emotional impact on people.

The point on emotion was made in a study of health reform in Saskatchewan by Rein Lepnurm and Marje K. Lepnurm published in the journal *Social Science & Medicine*. "Closing a hospital is a sad event. For most small communities the hospital represents accumulated memories for the elders, and economic stature for the younger residents," they wrote. "While the elderly remember the value of past services received from the hospital, younger residents value the jobs that the hospital provided, more than its real capabilities. For many small communities, having a small hospital is not only a matter of local prestige, but also economic necessity."[28] In other words, emotion, not rational argument based in fact, was the most important factor in determining the outcome and political implications of the Romanow government's health reform initiative. There was particular irony to the emotional dimension that shaped the issue, in that Romanow often said the three most important factors in politics are "emotion, emotion, and emotion."

The closure of hospitals as part of health reform was seen by many as striking at the heart of rural life in the province, a policy that was eroding the fabric of the community itself. There were deeply rooted historical reasons for the sentiment. Reaching back to 1916, farmers in Saskatchewan had been the driving force in creating a local health care system that included establishing municipal doctor plans and the creation of union hospitals by towns and villages that assessed property taxes to fund local health care. In their book on the creation of Medicare in Saskatchewan, Robin Badgley and Samuel Wolfe capture the historical significance and emotional dimension to rural health care: "The men who pioneered the prairie wheat land, living in small, separated communities, were deeply concerned about medical care, about bringing doctors to their areas and paying for their services and about providing a small hospital where they could treat patients."[29] The rural reality was that small-town hospitals were integral to the community's sense of both identity and viability. Much more than medical facilities, they were symbols that validated the community's very being. What's interesting, and consistent with the argument that emotion more than facts determined the political effects of rural hospital closures, is that there was no evidence of negative health outcomes from the loss of acute care in rural communities. An analysis of the health outcomes by five researchers at the Health Services Utilization and Research Commission in 2001 found that the hospital closures did not adversely affect rural residents' health status or even their access to in-patient hospital services. The resulting published report states, "Despite widespread fears that health status would decline, residents in these communities reported that hospital closures did not adversely affect their own health. Although some communities continue to struggle with changes to health care delivery, others appear to have adapted as a result of strong community leadership, the development of widely accepted alternative services, and local support for creating innovative solutions."[30]

It is also worth noting that a 2001 report on health care in Saskatchewan by Ken Fyke, a former deputy minister of health in the province, echoed many of the sentiments that shaped the health reform effort of almost a decade earlier. "There is no doubt that the province embarked on the right road for the right reasons in the early 1990s. The province was among the first out of the gate with many reforms subsequently embraced by others," Fyke writes. His study acknowledges that Saskatchewan's health system was fiscally unsustainable, but he argues that improved efficiency and reduced demand for services, resulting from a healthier population, could provide the necessary savings to restore a balance between resources and demand. Essentially, Fyke confirms that the policy reasons behind the hospital closures were sound.[31]

In retrospect, the true impact of the Romanow government's health reform had less to do with health and more to do with politics. As one of many factors over the last forty years that have reshaped political attitudes in rural Saskatchewan, the health reform agenda of the early 1990s played a key role. For many people, it came to represent a belief that the NDP had become a more urban-centric party, one that had abandoned and lost touch with its rural roots dating back to the days of the CCF.

But the health care agenda of that time was only a symptom of a larger plan dictated by the fiscal situation facing the government. Simply put, the Romanow government did not have the financial capacity to pursue an activist social or economic plan. It had been dealt a hand that left it with very little latitude to establish an identity other than one of fiscal probity. In and of itself, this was not inconsistent with the fiscally conservative tradition of past CCF and NDP governments, which had governed with balanced budgets. Over the forty-seven years when either the CCF or the NDP have governed Saskatchewan, there have been only three budgets with operating deficits, and they were in Romanow's first three years as premier, before his government returned itself to balanced budgets—the first government in Canada to do so. It reflected the conservative nature of Saskatchewan people, much of which is rooted in the economic and social trauma of the 1930s.

Eliminating the operating deficit was not easy. Aside from the backlash against rural health reform measures, the Romanow government had to take steps to increase revenue. These steps included a series of significant tax increases, such as raising both the corporate income and capital tax rates, applying a flat 10 percent deficit income surtax on all taxpayers, repealing the harmonization of the provincial sales tax with the federal goods and services tax, and implementing a corresponding increase in the PST from 7 to 9 percent.

One other factor often overlooked was the critical role the Romanow government played in the eventual creation of a National Child Benefit Program for Canada. Although not of similar scale or impact, one can make the case that it was not unlike the pivotal role Saskatchewan played in the development of national Medicare. In the very depths of the fiscal crisis faced in the Romanow government's early years, the decision was made to tackle the staggering reality of child poverty in the province. The extent of child poverty in Saskatchewan was expressed by one senior official intimately involved in addressing the issue: "It was so bad that some children were washing and showering themselves at gas stations because they couldn't do it at home. The hunting season was even extended so that kids could get enough to eat." What emerged was a Child Action Plan, which included a child benefit paid to low-income families. It was part of a broader strategy to address the so-called welfare wall, where members of families on social assistance would lose their health and other benefits if they left social assistance for low-wage employment. In early 1992 at a federal-provincial conference, Saskatchewan presented a scheme for a federal-provincial child benefit designed to address child poverty. The federal government at the time was open to the idea but eventually balked at a new cost-shared program when it was faced with its own massive deficit. So instead, in 1993 Saskatchewan decided to go it alone in spite of its own fiscal pressures, with the creation of a provincial child benefit. It was announced in the budget of 1994 and paved the way for the federal government to launch a national child benefit in 1997, which continues to this day.

Once his government reached a balanced budget, Romanow put in place a "balanced" approach to the allocation of surplus spending. It would be done on an equal one-third basis: a third for new investment in social programs, a third going to tax reductions, and a third allocated to paying down the debt. The federal government subsequently followed the same formula when it reached a balanced budget in 1998. Shortly before he stepped down as premier, Romanow defended his government austerity as the means to ensure government could be a positive force in society. "The reason we sacrificed so much in the early years of our administration was to ensure that we could one day rebuild the social and physical infrastructure of the province," Romanow said.[32] In reflecting on Romanow's time in office, Janice McFarland of the *Globe and Mail* paid tribute to his record, while also noting the toll it took on the NDP in rural Saskatchewan. "It's probable the full extent of his accomplishment will only become clear in hindsight. Whether it's appreciated or not, Saskatchewan narrowly dodged disaster, and Mr. Romanow deserves credit," she wrote.[33]

Having said that, it is difficult to overstate the longer-term political implications and effects of the 1993 Saskatchewan budget. For the Romanow government it became a politically defining moment. The combination of the rural hospital closures and the deep across-the-board cuts in spending and tax increases as part of a fiscal austerity agenda became a signature event for the NDP. For better or worse, the NDP had established that balancing the budget was its most important priority. It was completely consistent with the principle of balanced budgets that, prior to the Devine government, was a core governing principle for all governments. The need to avoid debt was a belief that had been deeply ingrained in Saskatchewan, one that reflected the conservative nature of the pioneers who settled the province, an attitude that was strengthened during the drought and Great Depression of the "dirty thirties."

There is no denying that the hospital closure policy became one of two dominant defining issues of the Romanow government. The other was its success in being the first province in Canada to restore a balanced budget. That fiscal milestone was significant not only for Saskatchewan but for Canada. Several years later, former prime minister Paul Martin, who was finance minister when Canada balanced its budget, said the efforts of the Romanow government in dealing with its fiscal crisis "stiffened the spine" of the federal government to do the same.[34] Years later while reflecting on his time as Saskatchewan premier, Brad Wall paid tribute to Romanow and the difficult choices his government faced in restoring the province's finances. "It was the foundation for the growth that followed," Wall said.[35]

The other legacy was political. In the June 21, 1995, provincial election, the Romanow NDP won a second majority term, but it came with signals of voter unease. The voter turnout was less than 60 percent and the NDP seat total, in a slimmed down legislature of fifty-eight members, declined by thirteen.

Having survived the bruising battle over rural health reform, the second-term Romanow government set its sights on a restructuring of rural governance. With 1,006 various rural governance bodies, the notion of amalgamation and streamlining delivery of services seemed like a perfectly reasonable idea. The idea had first been put on the public agenda in 1992 when the Association of Professional Community Planners (APCP) issued a report that said it was time to act. It noted that 701 of the province's 813 municipalities had a population under one thousand, and 177 had fewer than one hundred residents. Laurent Mougeot, APCP president, said that Saskatchewan had more municipalities than Alberta and Manitoba combined but less than a quarter of the collective population of those two provinces. "The province is eventually going to say we can't keep dealing with this many municipalities, because whenever a grant is made available, there are 813 little hands out," Mougeot said. "There's a lot of emotion attached to these communities, but we can't keep pumping money into these places. To be very blunt, a bunch of these municipalities are going to die."[36]

With its second mandate, the Romanow government signalled its intent to look at municipal restructuring. "I think our local government system has served us well, but it does need to change to respond to some fundamental and really profound changes in the world we live in," said Carol Teichrob, the minister of municipal governance, suggesting the process could be driven by shrinking tax bases for many rural municipalities.[37] Backlash was quickly evident. At the 1996 annual meeting of the Saskatchewan Association of Rural Municipalities (SARM), Romanow said his government's upcoming budget cuts would have "some impact" on how local politicians view the issue of amalgamation, but the government was not working on a hidden agenda of amalgamation. In a subsequent "bear pit" question-and-answer sessions, one SARM delegate said, "I trust this isn't a backdoor, slimy vehicle that perhaps could lead to effectively regional government?"[38]

The government enlisted University of Saskatchewan professor Joe Garcea to carry out public consultations and propose recommendations, in a process that dragged on for months. Eventually, Garcea proposed that the number of municipalities be reduced to 125. The reaction was overwhelmingly negative and the fact that a separate report, by economist Jack Stabler, came to the same conclusion did not weaken the backlash. The idea died, but further political damage to the NDP in rural Saskatchewan had been done.

Clearly, by the late 1990s the NDP government was deeply in a conflict with itself and large swaths of the public across a wide range of issues that had emerged in a rapidly changing world. These became distilled into the need to tackle long-standing systemic issues such as budget deficits, paying down debt, and restructuring to adapt Saskatchewan to the economic and social reality of the times. It mattered not that the government really had little choice. To ignore the predicament of debt would have simply made the outcome for health care and other social programs even more severe. It was a Hobson's choice. In other words, there was no choice. Still, many in rural Saskatchewan were not going to forget it.

CHAPTER 12

1995

The Perils of Progress

The challenge facing the people of Saskatchewan at this time is to acknowledge that past efforts to prevent the adjustment have failed, that continued restructuring is inevitable, and the future adjustments will occur in an austere economic environment. Within this context an approach must be chosen that will guide efforts to restructure the rural economy so that it can effectively participate in the economic and social order of the 1990s and beyond.

—Jack C. Stabler and M. Rose Olfert

HOW DO YOU DEFINE PROGRESS? IT'S A QUESTION THAT, in many ways, defies a universally accepted answer. Most agree that one dimension inherent to progress is improvement—that is, improved lives, higher standards of living, enhanced quality of life, a greater sense of community well-being. It is the belief that progress is measured in people being "better off," both economically and socially, individually and collectively. The other essential ingredient in progress is change, because without it you are captive of the status quo. Then the question becomes, how do you manage change in a way that produces the greatest good for the greatest number? In other words, change is not necessarily synonymous with progress. Which then leads to other questions: Who has the power to effect change, and who benefits from the results? Assuming there can be agreement on how to define progress and the factors that actually create it, the next question to be answered is how to achieve it. How do we balance individual liberty with collective interests? And so it goes.

Welcome to the world of politics.

In rural Saskatchewan, progress has long been something of a politically contested notion. It has been a defining feature of the partisan debate over the political economy of agriculture throughout much of the province's history. Since the 1950s, the most important statistics at the centre of the debate over the future of rural Saskatchewan have been the number and size of farms. Farms in the province reached their numeric peak in 1941 at 126,900, with an average size of 473 acres.[1] For some in the political debate over farm policy, this became a kind of benchmark against which to measure progress, both good and bad.

No one was foolish enough to say that 126,900 was the optimum number, or that change was not inevitable. But it was at least a metric that could be used as a reference point in the debate over policy and the pace and quality of change.

So for some, if the number increased, or at least did not decline, that was seen as progressive because it reflected a vibrant and resilient farm economy and society that was meeting the economic and social needs of its people. This view is partly rooted in the belief that intangibles matter when measuring progress—things like quality of life that go beyond specific economic outcomes. It's not entirely about GDP growth, which is an abstraction that, by itself, does not meaningfully measure progress. For example, we measure standard of living (SOL) with a simple formula that divides a jurisdiction's GDP by its total population. It is a crude method that fails to consider equity in terms of wealth distribution. Some argue that an index of well-being, which seeks to reflect quality of life, is a better and more accurate way to measure a society's progress than a mere economic formula for SOL. The Saskatchewan Index of Wellbeing uses eight yardsticks, including education, healthy populations, democratic engagement, and environment, among others, to determine well-being.[2]

The distribution of the benefits from a growing economy, the essence of social democracy, is as important as growth itself. When it comes to farm policy in Saskatchewan, the historical bias has tended to favour stability. Or, at least, to resist change by slowing its effects and protecting the farm community as much as possible from disruptive transformation, whether caused by external economic forces or the unpredictability of the weather. Much of public policy, regardless of the economic sector, is about two things: protecting people from change and/or helping them cope with it.

Conversely, the growth in the size of farms, and the corresponding decline in rural population, resulting in the slow deterioration of what were once vibrant farm communities, was seen as evidence of regression, not progress. It's a conservative opinion based in the belief that change is not always good and needs to be done with caution. The argument is that tradition matters because it reflects the accumulated wisdom from the trials and errors of human history, so if we are going to break from history in the name of progress, we had better do it carefully.

Another view of progress is much more accepting of change. In fact, it believes that progress can only happen through change, and the disruption itself is essential to progress. Its most stark characterization came from economist Joseph Schumpeter, who coined the paradoxical term "creative destruction" as an expression of how progress happens. There is no shortage of pithy quotations about progress and change. You can Google them. For example, Robert Kennedy is quoted as saying, "Progress is a nice word, but change is its motivator. And change has its enemies." Then there's this one from George

Bernard Shaw: "Progress is impossible without change; and those who cannot change their minds, cannot change anything."

Having said that, a defining feature of rural Saskatchewan for more than the last forty years has been change—economic, social, and political. It has occurred in a multitude of ways, resulting in a remaking of the farm economy and the pattern of rural life. Going back to the farm-size yardstick, the number of farms in Saskatchewan had declined to 34,523 by 2016, with average farm size having grown to 1,784 acres.[3] What has driven the change over the years has been rising productivity. Saskatchewan has had fewer farms, fewer people, and fewer economically viable towns, but at the same time the farm economy has produced more, largely because technology has allowed individuals to become far more productive. In effect, capital has replaced labour. In macro terms, the value of farm implements and machinery was $1.2 billion in 1969 and by 2018 had reached $16.2 billion.[4] So, while there has been what some see as a social regression and a fraying of the fabric of rural life as the rural economy has been transformed, there has also been economic growth, rising productivity, and increasing farm incomes.

There can be no denying the importance of productivity growth to an economy and society. "Productivity isn't everything, but in the long run it is almost everything," says Nobel laureate economist Paul Krugman. "A country's ability to improve its standard of living over time depends almost entirely on its ability to raise its output per worker."[5] The view that productivity is the *sine qua non* of economic growth is a principle accepted by virtually all economists. According to Robert Heilbroner, for instance, "If we are to enjoy a greater material well-being, generally speaking, we must produce more.... The production of goods and services must rise faster than population if individual well-being is to improve."[6]

But growing productivity also brings social consequences. As farm size has grown, on-farm population has diminished, and many small towns have withered and even died. Phyllis Conger puts it succinctly: "When farms get larger, towns get smaller."[7] She should know; she witnessed it up close and personal. She lived her entire life in the now tiny community of Truax, seventy kilometres southwest of Regina, which was incorporated in 1912, a year after the railway arrived. It once had more than two hundred residents. Today its population is twelve.[8] "First the schools close, then the stores close, then the railway is gone," she says. In its prime, Truax had a bank, two churches, a municipal office, two lumberyards, a butcher shop, two schools, a real estate and insurance business, two hotels, a closed-in curling and skating rink, and three grain elevators to serve farmers in the surrounding district.

The slow, relentless process of decline stretched over decades. On December 31, 1970, what had been the village of Truax became a hamlet, and by 2002 the hamlet was dissolved and it simply became part of the jurisdiction of the Elmsthorpe Rural Municipality. All that remains are six houses and a lonely, abandoned Sask Pool grain elevator that is now a heritage property. That, and recollections gathered in *Golden Memories of Truax and District*, a local history that chronicles the life of the community through the voices of its those who have lived there. The same story can be told about countless other rural Saskatchewan communities. For many, it does not sound or feel like progress.

In 1989, Southern Rails Co-operative was formed and operated a short line railway on the Avonlea subdivision that had been abandoned by CN. The line served Truax, Parry, Avonlea, Briercrest, and Tilney, connecting to Moose Jaw and the CPR mainline. But by 2004 the short line service to Truax and Parry was no longer viable and the service was terminated.[9]

It is possible to track the economic and social transformation to the rural Saskatchewan of today through the lens of several key developments. But, in one way or another, they are all linked to what for generations was considered the foundation of Saskatchewan's rural economy and way of life: the Crow's Nest Pass freight rate. Known as the Crow Rate, or simply "the Crow," it was the underpinning of the wheat economy, a fixed rate for the shipment of grain by rail that was originally set in statute in 1897, and a guarantee that land-locked Saskatchewan farmers would not be left at the mercy of railways in getting their grain to markets. It was part of a bargain made with farmers by the federal government, an offset to what at the time was a $3.3 million subsidy to Canadian Pacific to build a rail line west from southern Alberta into the coalfields of southern British Columbia. The Crow was suspended temporarily during the First World War and then reinstated in statute by the federal government in 1925.

Almost a century later, the last remnants of the Crow died. It came with the federal government repealing the *Western Grain Transportation Act* (WGTA) and replacing it with the *Canada Transportation Act*.[10] The legislation was the final step in a long, often painful, and politically perilous journey. It came in February 1995 when federal agriculture minister Ralph Goodale, on behalf of the minister of transport, began the debate by setting out four core rationales for the legislation. A key part of the context was the federal operating deficit, which had reached $42 billion. Under the WGTA Ottawa was paying the railways a "Crow benefit" that had peaked at $720 million annually in 1990, while allowing through regulation the railways to gradually raise the grain freight rates charged to farmers. Goodale said, "First, we must deal with the harsh reality of fiscal limitations and the battle against debt and deficits. Second, we must comply with the requirements of the new GATT agreement with respect to the disciplines that apply on trade distorting export subsidies. Third, we need to unlock new grain handling and transportation efficiencies, leading to a lower cost and faster system overall. Fourth, we need to foster greater agricultural diversification and a trend toward more value added processing and further processing."[11] In other words, there would no longer be any federal subsidy—the so-called Crow benefit—paid to railways for the movement of grain. The market would determine the amount farmers would be charged to ship their grain to export positions at the West Coast and Thunder Bay.

There was an undeniable irony in Goodale being the one to open the second-reading debate on the legislation. Thirteen years earlier, in 1982, he was leader of the Saskatchewan Liberal Party when the then Trudeau government made its intentions to tackle the Crow evident, which led to the enactment of the WGTA in 1983. Federal transport minister Jean-Luc Pepin, who was the architect of the policy, met in Regina on February 7 with Goodale and other members of the provincial Liberal Party, who, according to deputy minister Arthur Kroeger, "were in a state of acute distress."[12] On the brink of a provincial election, it added up to a political disaster for Goodale and the provincial Liberals as anger against the federal Liberal government grew even stronger. When the Saskatchewan election was held on April 26, 1982, the Liberal Party again failed to elect a single member and was banished once more to the political wilderness, where it remains today, barely discernible on the extreme outer fringes of provincial politics.

The active and public dismemberment of the Crow began in the early 1980s. In 1981 Pepin was tasked with reporting to the federal cabinet on what steps were necessary to "modernize" the Crow. After extensive consultations, the federal government commissioned a report in 1982 by University of Manitoba economist Clay Gilson. The core task given to Gilson was to investigate the effects of the Crow Rate not compensating railways for the cost of shipping grain and the resulting lack of investment by the rail companies in prairie rail infrastructure. The issue had been on the public agenda for years. There had been two royal commissions on the subject, the Turgeon Royal Commission of 1949–51 and the MacPherson Royal Commission of 1959–61, that assessed the magnitude of the losses incurred by the railways.[13]

There was a brief flirtation with addressing the Crow by Otto Lang in October 1974, shortly after the Trudeau government had won re-election with a majority government. As minister responsible for the Canadian Wheat Board, Lang told the Canada Grains Council he intended to propose a "bold approach" that would examine new ways for farmers to receive the benefits of the Crow Rate. He talked of a new national policy where freight rates would be based on real costs, and of a "Crow Rate fund" for producers that would allow railways to charge the full compensatory rate for the movement of grain.[14] Lang also mused about a one-time Crow buyout of up to $7 billion that would go to farmers. The ideas triggered an immediate backlash of anger, with Sask Pool members at their subsequent annual convention calling for Lang's dismissal as minister.[15] Lang had also appointed Carl Snavely, a U.S. transportation consultant and expert in railway costing, to look into the impact of the Crow. Snavely concluded the railway losses on moving grain were $174 million in 1977 and anticipated they would rise to $1 billion by 2000.[16]

At the core of the Crow debate were opposing economic and social arguments that carried huge political significance in Saskatchewan. On one side was the position that the Crow did not come close to covering the costs absorbed by the railways to move grain. As a result, there was no incentive for railways to invest in the upkeep of the prairie rail system, particularly the network of branch lines that stitched together small towns and the Saskatchewan wheat economy. The consequences were deterioration of some rail lines across rural Saskatchewan and the outright abandonment of others, which was crippling the economic viability of many small communities. For years, the federal government made annual payments to the railways to cover some of the costs and, along with provincial governments, purchased grain hopper cars to further offset costs to the railways. Specifically, between 1972 and 1986, Ottawa purchased 14,000 hopper cars, the Canadian Wheat Board 4,000, and the governments of Saskatchewan and Alberta acquired 2,000 in total.[17] Moreover, the artificially low freight rate had distortionary effects on the farm economy. It acted as a disincentive to diversify into other crops not covered by the Crow and inhibited the development of value-added processing to farm production, including the livestock industry.

The argument in favour of retaining the Crow had more to do with economic justice and the social consequences from the effects of farmers paying the full cost of grain shipments. The statutory rate was seen as a historic bargain—some called it the Magna Carta of the Prairies. It was recognition in law of the market vulnerability that faced Saskatchewan farmers, who were at the mercy of a railway duopoly in getting their product to market. A significant increase in freight costs to farmers would force many farmers to leave the land, rail branch lines would disappear, small towns would lose their economic base, and the fabric of rural life would be irreversibly harmed.

In terms of the longer-term trajectory of Saskatchewan politics, the Crow debate of the early 1980s clearly established two competing views about the future of agriculture in the province. In the election of 1982, incumbent premier Allan Blakeney and the NDP saw the Crow as the single most important ballot question. The NDP campaign was designed around "saving the Crow" and defending Saskatchewan interests against the federal Liberal government. The frame was Blakeney and the farmers versus Minister Pepin, the railways, and the Devine Conservatives.[18] Blakeney and the NDP took aim at the "Pepin Plan" to end the Crow, setting up what it believed would be the ballot issue and a rallying cry against the federal Trudeau government. In its platform the NDP said, "The Crow freight rate is not just a benefit to farmers. It is a benefit to our cities and towns and helps preserve a unique and valuable way of life in rural Saskatchewan."[19]

There was evidence to support the notion that it was a winning position to take. In a 1981 poll of its members, the Saskatchewan Wheat Pool found that only 29 percent felt railways should be allowed to charge higher grain freight rates.[20] Additionally, running against the federal government, especially after a decade of battling over control of resources, seemed to make sense. But similar polls found that 51 percent of producers in Alberta and 55 percent in Manitoba agreed the Crow should change.[21] With the Trudeau government determined to make changes, Saskatchewan and its NDP government was offside from public opinion across the Prairies. It was a huge miscalculation that was a critical factor in the long-term political and economic transformation of the province.

Recognizing the political trap, Devine and the Progressive Conservatives did not take the bait. They agreed with the NDP position to defend the benefit that farmers derived from the Crow. But Devine also took a nuanced position. It was clear that the federal government intended to compensate farmers with some kind of Crow payout. So, Devine's position was that the Crow benefit needed to be defended, so that if there was to be a change, then there needed to be a major compensation package from Ottawa. It was clearly a mixed message, but the signal Devine sent to farmers was he would defend their interests. To underscore that intent, the PC platform also promised to subsidize interest rates, which were hovering near 20 percent, down to 8.25 percent for farm loans and 13.25 percent for homeowner mortgages. It effectively defused the Crow as a campaign issue and allowed the PCs to focus on other populist measures they put on the election agenda, such as the elimination of the provincial gas tax.

There was one complicating factor for the PC leader. During his time as an agricultural economist and academic, Devine was on record saying the Crow was constraining economic growth in Saskatchewan. But it proved not enough to raise significant concerns about his campaign commitment to the Crow. In an article he co-wrote that was published in the *Canadian Journal of Agricultural Economics* in 1978, Devine argued the Crow was not in the public interest; it distorted the allocation of resources and prevented diversification of Saskatchewan agriculture.[22] The fact that those words did not come back to haunt him politically in the 1982 election was evidence of growing acceptance that the Crow Rate's days were numbered and that this reality had taken root in the psychology of Saskatchewan. Of more significance was how the NDP had misread the mood of Saskatchewan farmers and failed to grasp changing economic dynamics. It was a crucial political turning point for the province.

Two pivotal groups in the Crow debate unleashed by Pepin were the Western Agriculture Conference (WAC) and the Saskatchewan Wheat Pool. The WAC was an umbrella organization that represented a cross-section of farm organizations, including the three prairie wheat pools, the United Grain Growers, and the Manitoba Farm Bureau. The Saskatchewan Wheat Pool, with approximately seventy thousand members, was the largely uncontested voice of the farm economy in the province. It was deeply tied politically to the NDP and a powerful partisan weapon for the New Democrats to advance their farm agenda. It also published the *Western Producer*, a highly respected weekly farm newspaper that combined sound journalism with an editorial policy that was mostly aligned with the NDP. As the Crow debate intensified, the Saskatchewan Wheat Pool was seen as a bulwark for the status quo, a powerful organization that ruled rural Saskatchewan. It was a reality perhaps best captured by Blakeney himself, who once said wryly of the Pool, "Like Harvard University, they were a little aware of their own importance."[23]

But as a pan-prairie voice, the WAC had a broader constituency from which to draw credibility. When the WAC adopted a position in favour of a policy to share future increases in grain transportation, it signalled a key cleavage in farm opinion and set up a showdown with the Pool. But it never happened.

Instead, recognizing that it risked being isolated, at its annual convention in November 1980 the Saskatchewan Wheat Pool passed a motion by a wide margin of 122 to 22 endorsing the WAC position. It felt it had little choice after the Manitoba and Alberta pools, along with the United Grain Growers, had supported the WAC policy statement.

Among most economists there was little doubt the Crow had distortionary effects on the farm economy and transportation system. This became most apparent in the 1960s as Canada began selling wheat to the Soviet Union and China and the transportation and grain handling system nearly broke down under the export pressure. Paul Earl and Barry Prentice, transportation economists from the University of Manitoba, describe this in a paper entitled "Western Grain Exceptionalism: Transportation Policy Change since 1968." They point to the "willful blindness" of the defenders of the Crow Rate and the perverse effects it had on the grain handling and transportation system. They argue that retention of the Crow was "impeding modernisation of the transportation system, stifling efficiency, and undermining the grain industry's competitiveness in international markets."[24] In other words it was an impediment to progress.

"In clinging to a regulated system," Earl and Prentice claim, the industry "lagged the rest of the world in moving steadily toward a more free-enterprise economy, and away from a reliance on the public sector." To keep the system operating, governments had purchased 8,000 rail hopper cars by 1980 and spent $170 million in capital grants to rehabilitate the western rail system. "Meanwhile, the branch line subsidies continued to grow, and at the same time, railway transportation capacity overall was becoming constrained, particularly to the West Coast—a situation that threatened havoc throughout the whole economy."[25]

University of Alberta economist Ken Norrie echoed their conclusions. In the midst of the acrimonious Crow debate, Norrie wrote a 1983 article published in the journal *Canadian Public Policy* that was unambiguous in its assessment of the unfolding issue. He opened his analysis with a blunt observation: "There can surely be few issues that illustrate the inherent difficulties in instituting major economic policy reforms in Canada as well as the current Crow controversy." What made it particularly frustrating for Norrie was that, he argued, "there is virtually unanimous agreement among all concerned that the present arrangements are archaic and costly, and that unless some fairly drastic measures are taken soon the result will be a near collapse of western railway infrastructure."[26]

Looking at the Crow debate and its outcome retrospectively, there are two obvious and intertwined ways to assess its effects. One is political and the other economic.

The demise of the Crow Rate had exactly the outcomes the NDP had expected and feared. As an underpinning of the province's farm economy for generations, the end of the Crow accelerated the pace of change in rural Saskatchewan. It marked a fundamental shift from what was largely a one-crop wheat economy to one where other crops—peas, lentils, canola, flax, and mustard, to name a few—have become major components of field production. Essentially, farming in Saskatchewan became more entrepreneurial and market based. As a result, producers also became more personally engaged in their enterprise, responding to market signals across a range of crops and making decisions on what to produce and when and how to market it. With the arrival of the Internet and the digital communications revolution it unleashed, farmers now base their market decisions on immediate, real-time, transparent information.

With this has come changed political attitudes. Greatly diminished was the collectivist bias of previous decades, when smaller-scale farmers instinctively recognized the merits of forming co-operatives to increase their market power and incomes. In the post-Crow world, survival became an issue of finding the economies of scale to increase productivity. Inevitably that meant larger farms, greater capital investment that reduced labour costs, resulting in fewer farms and rural depopulation. By the late twentieth century, farmers in Saskatchewan had become the true entrepreneurial class of the province. The generation of farmers schooled in the new post-Crow era brought with them the political beliefs of independent businesspeople who responded to political messages shaped by a market economy.

In their 2002 analysis of a changing rural Saskatchewan, which followed previous studies on the same subject, Jack Stabler and Rose Olfert clearly captured the reality of a rural society and economy in transition and how policies were misaligned with reality. They wrote,

> Provincial government policies continue to support a plethora of governments and infrastructure which are too small to capture economies of scale, too fragmented to realize economies of scope and too dispersed to generate agglomeration economies. Such policies ensure that trade centre decline reaches higher into the system than what would have been the case had rationalization been pursued at an earlier date. These policies have also left rural Saskatchewan with a set of institutions and infrastructure which is obsolete, cumbersome and inefficient. The existing structure of the rural system is actually an impediment to economic development. This is a very unfortunate framework within which to enter the highly competitive world of the 21st century.[27]

Without question, the decline and fall of the Crow Rate was a crucial factor in accelerating the rural transition. But it was not the only one. Others were to follow, namely the Saskatchewan Wheat Pool and the Canadian Wheat Board, which represent their own accounts of the economic and political transformation of a province.

CHAPTER 13

1999

Coalition of the Willing

THE EXCHANGE OF VOWS SEEMED LIKE A GOOD IDEA AT
the time. Of course, looking back on it now, more than two decades
later, it's obvious that it was a colossal mistake, both tactically and
strategically for each party in the marriage. At least, it was a miscalculation
in terms of what it would mean for the ongoing political realignment of
Saskatchewan and the fortunes of the New Democratic and Liberal Parties.
You could cut the cynicism with a knife.

The result of the provincial election in September 1999 was nothing if not
deeply unsettling for the NDP. It was, as the headline on the election story in
Maclean's stated, "A shock for Romanow." The twenty-six-seat majority the
NDP had won in 1995 for its second majority had melted away. Seeking a third
mandate, the NDP won twenty-nine seats, exactly half of the fifty-eight-seat
provincial legislature. The Saskatchewan Party won twenty-five seats, and the
Liberals took four. Romanow and the New Democrats faced governing as
an unstable minority, with the Opposition Saskatchewan Party and Liberals

together holding exactly the same number of seats as the NDP. To even survive in that scenario, the NDP would have to lure someone from one of the
two other parties into the role of Speaker to retain a one-seat voting margin.
It was considered a tightrope walk too dangerous to contemplate.

Rather than trying to govern in what was effectively a deadlocked legislature, and dealing with all the trade-offs and concessions that entails, the
decision was taken quickly to form a coalition with the willing Liberals. They
would be lured into the ranks of the governing New Democrats with the
offer of senior cabinet positions in government. As Romanow explains it, the
rationale went back to something Tommy Douglas once told him. "I remember Tommy saying to me that it is so difficult for social democratic parties
to get elected that you never give up power unless you have to. We were not
going to give up power if we didn't have to," Romanow recalls.[1] This reflected
Romanow's own pragmatism where, rather than being exclusively defined by
ideology, politics is the art of the possible.

Before the final votes had even been counted, the coalition wheels were
turning. On election night when it appeared the NDP was not going to form
a majority, the outreach to the Liberals began. After talking with Romanow,
deputy premier Dwain Lingenfelter phoned the three Liberals who had been
elected—party leader Jim Melenchuk, Jack Hillson, and Ron Osika. He urged
them not to make any rash moves and asked them to commit that they would
meet with him and Romanow once the final vote tallies were confirmed. The
three Liberals agreed. A few days later the five men met at the cabinet office in
downtown Saskatoon. Romanow expected a long-drawn-out, give-and-take
discussion lasting much of the day to iron out the terms of an agreement that
would include three or four policy concessions the NDP would have to make
to the Liberals. But that is not what happened. There was no horse-trading.
After some brief ice-breaking comments from Romanow about the election,
Melenchuk made it clear he wanted to cut to the chase. He said, "What's the
deal?" Romanow asked Melenchuk what he wanted. "We want to be in cabinet," came the reply. With that they shook hands, the meeting was over, and
the political marriage effectively consummated.[2]

Eventually, the three Liberals signed on to a seventeen-clause coalition agreement, with the critical words being that the Liberals would "adhere to the position of (the NDP) government on all matters before the legislature."[3] Fairly explicit, with no need for clarification in terms of what the Liberals were signing on to. The reward was cabinet positions for Melenchuk and Hillson, and Osika was named Speaker. The reaction was instantaneous and angry.

Elwin Hermanson, leader of the Saskatchewan Party, accused the NDP of defying the wishes of the voters. "Saskatchewan people elected a minority NDP government. Today the Liberals overturned the voters' verdict and gave the NDP its majority," Hermanson said.[4] The reaction of many Liberals was far more scathing. Former Liberal leader Dave Steuart, long considered a provincial Liberal icon, was outraged. "I don't think what's his face, the fearless leader...is going to go down in history as one of the great men of principle," Steuart said. "He had a contract with the people of Saskatchewan that he was a Liberal...so I'm disgusted of course." Perhaps the most prophetic insight came from former Liberal candidate Grant Karwacki. "I think the party will struggle to maintain a separate identity and I think that is the danger of a coalition," he said, warning of a future that would become reality.[5] Then there was this from Liberal senator Herb Sparrow: "The three of them are either dumb or slow learners. They are going against the wishes of the constituents. They were voted in as Liberals and now have turned themselves over to the power of the NDP, and that does not auger well for the Liberal party, or for them as elected members. I think it's absolutely disgusting."[6]

One particularly cutting comment came from Shirley Malkowich when asked her reaction to the NDP-Liberal deal by reporters. "I'm a nurse and I voted for Jim Melenchuk because Roy Romanow gave us nurses a really bad deal, and now I feel as if I've been kind of sold out. None of us wanted to vote for the NDP after what they did to us, and now Jim has joined up with them," Malkowich said.[7]

More important than the raw emotions of the moment, which were to be expected, was the context of the times. The Saskatchewan Party had been formed only two years earlier with an eight-member caucus made up of what were four PC and four Liberal MLAs. It came in the wake of a 1995 election when the Liberals had won eleven seats but were seen as having fallen well short of expectations. Leading up to that election, the Liberals clearly appeared to have momentum and were expected to supplant the Conservatives. It didn't happen.

One reason the Liberals failed to achieve a major breakthrough in 1995 was, in part, collusion between the NDP and Progressive Conservative Party. With polls indicating a surge by Lynda Haverstock and the Liberals, it was in the NDP's interest to do whatever it could to help shore up support for the PCs. Going into the election the PCs held ten seats, essentially the remnants of the former Devine government. Fearing the PC vote would collapse and add to the Liberals' momentum, the NDP not only shared its internal polling with the Conservatives to help them focus their efforts but also delayed the election date to give the PCs more time to get organized for the campaign. It was enough to help the PCs hang on to five seats and 18 percent of the popular vote.[8]

The subsequent internal strife in Liberal ranks over a disappointing result led to the forced resignation of Haverstock and an inability of the party under Melenchuk, a political neophyte, to assert itself as a viable alternative to the NDP. The ground was set for the creation of a new political vehicle, the Saskatchewan Party, which emerged out of the ashes of the PC Party and disillusioned Liberals. With eight MLAs it immediately became the official opposition in 1997, adding another seat in a later by-election.

Ridden with the scandal of multiple fraud charges relating to the misuse of caucus communications allowance spending during the second term of the Devine government, the PC Party brand was deeply tarnished in Saskatchewan. The public outrage was on full display in 1994 when the first round of charges against former Tory MLAs and staff were laid by the RCMP. The party's fate had become apparent in a 1996 by-election, when days before the vote former North Battleford MLA Michael Hopfner was convicted of fraud relating to the use of PC caucus funds. "The polling we were doing and the response we were getting at the doors and on the telephone changed rather dramatically from one of an open mind, to simply dismissing the

Conservative party," PC leader Bill Boyd said at the time.[9] Then, in January 1997 the final seal was put to the party's fate when former deputy premier Eric Berntson and five other MLAs and staffers were charged.

Other political forces also played into the creation of the Saskatchewan Party. Preston Manning and the Reform Party were on the rise in federal politics at the time, fuelled largely by western populism and alienation from the political hegemony of central Canada in federal politics. There was a deeply anti-elitist strain to Reform's emergence, most evident in Manning's leadership in opposition to the Charlottetown constitutional accord, which was supported by the prime minister and all the premiers. Manning's campaign resonated with grassroots Canadians and led to the defeat of the accord in a national referendum. In the wake of the razor-thin victory by the federalist side in the 1995 Quebec referendum on "sovereignty-association," Manning again tapped into the populist impulse of the West. He called for a reformed federation, beginning with an unequivocal federal stance relating to any future Quebec referendums. He said that the terms must be a "clear majority on a clear question." It was a position subsequently taken by the Supreme Court in a constitutional reference on Quebec succession. By 1997 Manning had become leader of the official opposition in Ottawa and there was speculation about the Reform Party branching off into provincial politics by creating a provincial wing in Saskatchewan. The formation of the Saskatchewan Party was, at least in part, a defensive measure to stymie the entry of the Reform Party into provincial politics.

The dynamics of the moment are explained by historian Raymond Blake. The Saskatchewan Party, he says, emerged from "a sense of frustration among the opposition elements in Saskatchewan politics," as well as "frustration and anger" that was growing across rural Saskatchewan. "The difficulties experienced in agricultural communities, combined with reductions in provincial services, sent the message to rural Saskatchewan that it was unimportant, a theme that held considerable resonance in the West and had played a key role in the formation of the Progressive Party in the 1920s. With the demise of the Progressive Conservatives in the 1991 election, both the PCs and Liberals had become little more than fringe parties," Blake argues.[10] In an August 1997 editorial, the *Saskatoon StarPhoenix* captured the sense that the formation of the new party was injecting a jolt of electricity into Saskatchewan politics: "Perhaps the biggest thing the Saskatchewan party has in its favour is momentum. Members are bristling with confidence. They are driven by the excitement of the challenge and are approaching it with missionary zeal."[11]

If there was any doubt that political realignment was taking hold, the reality was evident in the 1999 election results. Although it won four fewer seats than the NDP, the Saskatchewan Party won a larger share of the popular vote: 39.61 percent versus 38.73 percent for the NDP. The Liberals won just over 20 percent of the vote, and the NDP had assumed a majority of that Liberal vote would migrate to the NDP because of the coalition. But it was a faulty assumption. The rapid ascension of the Saskatchewan Party was unlike anything that had taken place before in the province. It eclipsed what happened with the newly created CCF in the 1930s, for example. In the provincial election of 1938— the second election since the CCF's formation in 1932 and the creation of the Regina Manifesto—the CCF won ten seats in the Saskatchewan Legislature.[12]

What also emerged in the 1999 election was the striking dominance of the Saskatchewan Party in rural Saskatchewan. All of the twenty-five Saskatchewan Party seats came from rural constituencies, towns, and villages.[13] It was a reflection of the long-term transformation of the NDP into an almost exclusively urban-based party, with the weakening of its prairie populist roots. It began decades earlier with the departure of Douglas and its formal alliance with the organized labour movement. With populism reliant on the ability of a politician to inspire emotion and a sense of connection with the "average" person, the inability of the NDP to maintain its appeal on the farms and in the small towns of Saskatchewan at the level of leadership has been a key reason for its decline. It was evident in the line of leadership succession. From the inspiration of Douglas, the NDP went to Woodrow Lloyd, a schoolteacher who lacked the charisma of his predecessor. Allan Blakeney was regarded as an intelligent technocrat, but also someone who was never fully comfortable in the small towns or on the farms of rural Saskatchewan. Roy

Romanow was an eloquent orator and extremely strong debater with a sharp mind, but a city lawyer who could never fully connect to rural Saskatchewan. Moreover, when Romanow took power he was handcuffed by a debt crisis that severely limited available policy options.

Coupled with the rural backlash to the Romanow government's closure of fifty-two rural hospitals as part of a fiscal agenda to eliminate the provincial deficit, the NDP's fate in rural Saskatchewan was sealed. It was not that Elwin Hermanson, the first leader of the Saskatchewan Party, was seen as a populist. He was not. Nor was he endowed with what might be considered the charisma of a leader with a magnetic personality. But he was seen as authentic, which is arguably the single most important quality in a politician. "Hermanson was talking to these (rural) people in a language they understood. He is one of them in a way that Romanow clearly is not," is how political scientist John Courtney put it in the wake of the 1999 election.[14]

Canada has limited experience with coalition governments, unlike multi-party states in Europe where coalitions are often the path to forming government. The evidence in Europe indicates that coalitions are often damaging to the junior partner. A 2019 study published in the *Journal of Politics* found that smaller party coalition partners suffer dramatic electoral losses, with junior partners losing an average of 17 percent of the vote in the next election, compared with senior partners. "Joining a multiparty cabinet as a junior party considerably hurts a party's future electoral prospects as junior partners cannot enact much of what they promised before the election since they cannot sufficiently differentiate themselves from their larger coalition partner," the report states.[15] Based on what unfolded in Saskatchewan's experiment with coalition government, the evidence of how damaging it is to the partners is even more stark. The Liberals effectively disappeared after serving as a useful tool to keep the NDP in power and staving off its inevitable decline from government.

All of this made the coalition idea doomed from the moment of inception. There can be a certain logic to coalition governments when they are on the right side of history. They can make sense to voters if seen as faithful to the political transition under way. In other words, when a party is on the rise and another in decline, the grouping of the ascendant party with a smaller party to further the political transformation to dislodge the incumbent party can make some inherent sense. You might say it is seen as being on the right side of history. In 1999, however, it was just the opposite. The two-term NDP government was recognized as clinging to power in an attempt to resist the unfolding political trend by creating a coalition with a weak and disintegrating third party. The result was that both the NDP and Liberals were seen as either oblivious or resistant to what was actually going on in terms of unfolding political events in the province. Not surprisingly, the coalition was the last gasp of the Saskatchewan Liberal Party, which has existed in name but not in terms of any functioning political identity or reality ever since.

There will be those who argue that the subsequent election in 2003 disproved the argument that the coalition poisoned the political ground for the NDP. After all, in that election under new leader Lorne Calvert, who took over from Romanow as both leader and premier in 2001, the NDP was re-elected with a slim, two-seat majority. That election consolidated the political landscape between the NDP and the Saskatchewan Party as the only two combatants. It is a reality that remains to this day, albeit with the Saskatchewan Party firmly established as the natural governing party and the NDP a remnant of what it once was and represented.

But the 2003 election outcome was more a mirage than a substantive manifestation of a political duopoly between equals. Rather, it was the NDP's last stand. One could say it was also a brief moment when the NDP reached into its past to claim part of its former identity in order to rescue itself from the tides of political change.

In the run-up to the election of that year, public opinion polls were showing the Saskatchewan Party poised to take power. One poll in April 2003 by Sigma Analytics, several months prior to the campaign, had the Saskatchewan Party seven points ahead of the NDP, reflecting growing support after a poll months earlier had the Saskatchewan Party holding a 2 percentage point lead.[16]

But the momentum quickly changed in the early days of the campaign when Saskatchewan Party leader Hermanson was asked about his party's position on the possible sale of Crown corporations, specifically, SaskTel, SaskPower, SGI, or SaskEnergy, which were seen as core utilities. He replied, "We'll listen. We're not going to slam the door if Bell [Canada Enterprises] came and said 'you know, we want to put a couple of billion dollars into Saskatchewan. We want to do some things together with SaskTel.'" Hermanson added, "You'd be crazy not to open the door and listen." He went on to accuse the NDP of taking an ideological position that was thirty years out of date. "Other provinces are passing us by, other industries are growing all around us and there you have the NDP saying we can't even talk about Crowns."[17]

The NDP seized on the issue. "I'm here to say we're not selling SaskTel. Period. Full stop," said Eric Cline, the finance minister at the time. "We're not selling SGI period. Full stop. We're not selling SaskPower, SaskEnergy."[18] The sudden re-emergence of debate over the fate of Crown corporations was a flashback to the 1980s when the Devine government went on its aggressive privatization agenda. It had been a time when the Romanow-led NDP Opposition drew a line in the sand when it came to the privatization of SaskEnergy. It came in the midst of the ongoing debate over the privatization of the Potash Corporation. But SaskEnergy was qualitatively and politically different. It was not a commercial Crown but a public utility, and the PC government, unlike what it had done with Potash, had made no sound business case for its privatization and thus was seen as purely driven by ideology. The legislature had ground to a halt when the NDP walked out in protest, a tactic that eventually forced the Devine government to abandon its plans.

Asserting its position in defence of the few remaining core Crown corporations, the Calvert NDP tapped into public anxiety about the loss of what were publicly owned utilities, not commercial Crown corporations. In the public's mind there was a qualitative difference between the two, and this had a dramatic effect on public opinion. A poll a week before the vote found the NDP with a 2 percentage point lead. "It confirms what I have been feeling since the campaign began, that there is a momentum, that a number of folks were coming back," Calvert said.[19] The significance of the Crown corporation issue on those polled was dramatically evident. Asked to choose between "keeping

Crown utilities publicly owned" and "selling one or more of the Crown utilities," 84.7 percent of respondents chose keeping the utilities publicly owned.
When asked which party would do the best job of "handling Crown utilities,"
58 percent said the NDP and 30 percent the Saskatchewan Party.

The controversy over Hermanson's considering the sale of utility Crown
corporations was also reflected in views about the leaders. Calvert was considered the best choice for premier by 44.5 percent of those polled, with
Hermanson the choice of 29 percent. Almost half, or 49.4 percent, said they
"would not want to see Hermanson as premier," while 29.9 percent said they
would not want Calvert as premier.[20] A leader who runs behind his or her
party in public opinion is inevitably doomed, as was Hermanson.

It was a razor-thin two-seat majority—Calvert and the NDP had dodged
a bullet that many believed had the NDP's name on it. But what mattered in
2003 was the final count. It gave the Calvert government four years to govern without shouldering the burden of debt and deficit that had weighted
down the Romanow government in the past. The province had reached a
balanced budget by 1995, being the first government in Canada to do so,
and in his second term Romanow began the slow process of reinvestment
in social programs and modest tax reductions. The other footnote to the
2003 election was that it marked the first time in the province's history
that each of the two original parties in Saskatchewan—the Liberals and
Conservatives—failed to elect a single MLA. Clearly the decades-long political realignment had taken hold.

The timing of Calvert taking over as premier in 2001 and his election win
in 2003 coincided with a period of strong growth in resource prices. During
the period from 1992 to 2000, annual resource revenues to the province in
constant dollars averaged $576 million. In the years 2000 to 2007, the annual
average flow to provincial coffers from resource revenues was more than $1.3
billion.[21] In its final full fiscal year in office, the Calvert government collected
$1.7 billion in resources revenues. The healthy budgetary situation allowed the
Calvert government during its years in office to reduce the province's total
debt by 7 percent while increasing spending by 35 percent.[22]

Another key factor during the Calvert years was changes to the treatment of potash development in the province. In 2002, the NDP government announced a six-year incentive program to stimulate base mineral exploration and development. Then in 2005, at the midpoint in its mandate, the NDP government made changes to potash royalty and investment policy that would have major impacts in terms of investment for years to come. It included a ten-year royalty holiday on new production, as well as an allowance of 120 percent related to exploration and development on investment greater than a threshold of 90 percent of a 2002 investment base.[23]

The changes ignited a period of massive potash investment that stretched more than a decade and was a major factor in driving the province's growth. But it was also a two-edged sword. It would bring fiscal implications that created huge swings, both positive and negative, in provincial revenues resulting in significant operating deficits. It also resulted in a potash tax and royalty system that tax experts Jack Mintz and Duanjie Chen deemed confusing and inefficient. "The convoluted nature of Saskatchewan's regime benefits no one—not producers, investors or the provincial government, which is left without any revenue certainty from its most significant natural resource," Mintz and Chen wrote. In terms of the negative fiscal implications for the province, they noted that a rebound in potash prices from their collapse in 2009 led to "excessive tax allowances resulting in the province incurring three years of tax revenue losses from its potash production tax."[24]

One can certainly debate the Mintz-Chen assertion that no one benefited from the potash tax and royalty regime. Judging by the massive investment that flowed into new potash production, the companies felt that even given the complex and inefficient nature of the complete regime, the corporate benefits of the royalty holiday and the 120 percent investment allowance outweighed the disadvantages.

NDP finance minister Pat Atkinson couldn't help but express optimism in June 2007 when the final public accounts for 2006–07 were released. They showed an operating surplus of $293 million. The budget itself included $240 million in corporate tax cuts over three years, a clear attempt by the NDP to

position itself as a centrist government. "Revenues were higher than anticipated, and this reflects the strength of our robust economy," Atkinson said.
"After years of prudent fiscal policy and sound financial management, our
government is once again in a position to invest in the future of the people
of our province and ensure that our citizens benefit from a fiscal surplus. We
have reduced business and provincial sales taxes, and we have also reduced
total government debt by $861 million over the last three years. I'm extremely
pleased to report that our current debt to GDP ratio, an important factor for
all credit rating agencies, is at its lowest level in 20 years."[25] It was a far cry
from sixteen years earlier when the Romanow government was handed a poisoned chalice.

An election was looming in what was a polarized, two-party political environment. After the second-longest serving NDP government, the political
cycle was turning. The inevitable mood for change, which is any incumbent
government's worst fear, was settling into the psychology of the province. The
fact that the economy was strong and growing, that the province's fiscal situation had been rescued by Romanow—whose government began reinvesting in
social programs after reaching a balanced budget, a direction continued and
even accelerated by the Calvert government—seemed not to matter. The NDP
presence in rural Saskatchewan, which years earlier had been a source of the
party's political supremacy in large swaths of the province, had largely evapo-
rated. Over the preceding twenty years it had steadily fallen out of step with
the emergence of a new rural Saskatchewan economy and society.

Moreover, the Saskatchewan Party had a new, young, energetic leader
named Brad Wall. Wall's style had a fresh flavour; he was an engaging orator
who knew how to connect with his audiences, both rural and urban, unlike
any Saskatchewan leader since the days of Douglas. Populist politics at the
leadership level was unmistakably a factor once again in Saskatchewan.

There was another important aspect to Wall as leader. He had been
a political assistant in the Devine government and had witnessed up close
both the strengths and weaknesses, the successes and failures, of those years.
In particular, Wall also remembered the brief moment in 2003 when the

importance of public ownership became a defining issue in the outcome of an election that denied Hermanson and the Saskatchewan Party the reins of government. One cannot help but think of the oft-recited quote by philosopher George Santayana, who said that "those who cannot learn from history are doomed to repeat it." It was a lesson that Brad Wall had learned well and was never to forget.

CHAPTER 14

2007

Hope versus Fear

SUCCESSFUL AND ENDURING POLITICIANS ARE DREAM WEAV-
ers. They are able to capture the moment in a way that often transcends
politics. In effect, they rise above partisanship and appeal to something
much more fundamental. What they do is identify an emotion everyone can
share and make it the essence of their political message. In a very real sense,
they depoliticize the moment for political purposes. It is the ability to capture
people's imaginations and emotions, to make them believe in some common
unifying sentiment, and it is the essence of populism's appeal.

People will argue over who was Saskatchewan's greatest political orator and
populist. It is difficult to judge because it is inherently subjective. Invariably,
people's opinions will be shaped by their political biases and perceptions
seen through the lens of different eras. The most obvious filter is history and
how political oratory has evolved over the decades. By today's standards, the
style and language of a speech delivered by a politician fifty years or more ago
sounds stilted and often formal. But one thing that has remained consistent

over the years is that, in person, an effective politician can have a positive impact on how people feel. To put it another way, they can change a room.

One objective measure by which to judge a politician is longevity. The longer a politician is successful in an electoral sense is a reflection of their ability to motivate people. The evidence is there for all to see in total votes. Based on that metric, Tommy Douglas clearly deserves to be considered one of Saskatchewan's most gifted orators. He won five successive majority governments from 1944 to 1960, which remains the longest tenure of any Saskatchewan premier. But another measure can be the size of electoral victories. It is one thing to win and another to win with overwhelming majorities. By that yardstick, Brad Wall stands alone. Three majority governments, each one larger than the one before and, in the process, relegating the opposition to the political margins, give Wall a unique political stature. Winning a third-term majority government is often very difficult. Winning it by a landslide is virtually unheard of.

If Wall and Douglas are in a category of their own in terms of oratorical ability, it is worth noting they also shared a common style. Both had a religious and colloquial dimension to their communication skills. There was a cadence to their speech that delivers messages in short, compact thoughts that people quickly absorb. They were skilled at identifying shared human ideas or beliefs that went beyond partisan politics. Each was a powerful proponent of the Saskatchewan myth. For Douglas it was the "New Jerusalem"; for Wall, the "Saskatchewan Promise."

Religion was more foundational and overt in Douglas's messaging. As a Baptist minister he espoused the politics of Christianity and the social gospel. He often used quotes from the Book of Revelations as a means to describe the kind of society he wished to build in Saskatchewan. Wall was more subtle in his use of religion but no less effective. His family belongs to the Mennonite Brethren, which is a reformist part of the Mennonite faith. Originating from central Europe, many of German extraction, Mennonites are anabaptists (that is, practising adult baptism) who subscribe to the central tenets of separation of church and state, nonviolence, the centrality of Jesus and scripture to their daily lives, and the wise discernment of community.[1]

Growing up in Swift Current, Wall attended the Pentecostal Southside Church of God, where he was greatly influenced by a pastor named Bob Reesor, whom Wall calls the most inspirational speaker he has ever heard. To this day, Wall speaks of the inspiration he receives from the classic gospel song "Leaning on the Everlasting Arms." Although religion played a big role in Wall's upbringing and shaped his world view, he seldom made use of overt religious references or imagery. But he did often speak in terms of shared values that many would identify with religious roots. It was a powerful blend. During much of his eleven years in government, Wall consistently ranked as the most popular premier in Canada, which reflected his ability to connect with people and their emotions.[2]

But Wall also had another advantage that others who came before did not have. He had the benefit of being a dream weaver during a time of instant and ubiquitous communications. He was a communicator in an age when the power of communications shaped public perceptions like never before. There were literally no limits to the number of people who could hear a single message or to the rapidity with which it could be delivered over multiple digital communication channels. No politician in Canada seemed as comfortable and adept in the communications environment of the day. Combine Wall's oratorical skills with multiple media platforms and his ability to distill his message into terms that appeal to people's instincts of commonly shared values, and the effect was powerful.

Perhaps the clearest and most compelling example of Wall's ability to reduce politics to emotion that transcends politics came on November 7, 2007, the night of his election as premier, in Swift Current. The venue was the Palliser arena, named after John Palliser, the man sent by the British government in 1857 on an expedition to explore the prairie West and report on its suitability to support agriculture settlement. Palliser concluded that the southwest of what was to become Saskatchewan was a "more or less arid desert" unsuitable for crops. Swift Current, Wall's hometown, is a city in the middle of the Palliser Triangle, a region that many people 150 years earlier believed was unfit for human habitation. The election-night event was the perfect combination of time and place.

Wall framed his victory speech that night around the theme of hope and fear. It was not a unique approach for a political speech—others have used it, including the likes of Martin Luther King Jr. and Nelson Mandela—but it created the right mood for the moment. Wall took what was an intensely partisan event and turned it into an exploration of the spirit described as the essence of the Saskatchewan myth. In fewer than three minutes he delivered a political message that was less about politics and more about the unifying thread that binds people together regardless of their political beliefs. The fact that his message was distilled into a false binary choice that did not truly reflect the political divide did not matter. The partisan subtext was there, subjugated to the universal theme of hope. This is what he said:

> There are some who said that if this election came down to hope and fear, that we would be on the wrong side of the equation. That fear is stronger. That fear beats hope. They were wrong, because this is Saskatchewan. And in Saskatchewan, hope beats fear. That is our history.
>
> This is a province carved out of dirt, rock and bush by people who had both hope, and faced fear. And they came anyway, because hope beats fear.
>
> Every time a farmer seeds in the spring, every time a farmer plants a crop there is hope and there is fear. And he plants the crop anyway, because hope beats fear. Every time someone starts a business in this province there's hope and there's fear. But they do it anyway in Saskatchewan because hope beats fear. Whenever you start a new career, whenever you decide to start a family there's hope and there's fear. But hope beats fear.
>
> Today in Saskatchewan, we're on the verge of greatness, on the verge of an economic breakthrough, a chance to convert momentum into lasting prosperity. We're on the verge of Saskatchewan taking its rightful place as the vanguard of this country, leading the West and leading Canada.... This is not some land of meek and timid souls...this is Saskatchewan, a province of amazing potential, full of confident, self-assured yet humble people ready to step boldly into that bright future. No longer willing to settle for mediocrity....If someone calls you and asks who won the election

in Saskatchewan, tell them that hope won this election, because tonight in the province of Saskatchewan hope beat fear.[3]

The use of hope is fundamental to politics and certainly nothing new. Reduced to its essence, politics is about hope—hope for, and belief in, a better future. Politicians are merchants of hope; some are simply better than others at expressing it in terms people can grasp. One of the best was Barack Obama. Not only did he write a book entitled *The Audacity of Hope*, but he built his presidential campaign around the idea of hope for what he termed "a more perfect union" in the United States. Obama's most recent book, *A Promised Land*, is a personal reflection on his belief, and hope, that America can live up to its ideals and its aspiration to be a promised land. Saskatchewan was itself a so-called promised land for immigrants who came from Europe and elsewhere to settle in the hope of creating a new and better life.

The notion of a new, more self-assured Saskatchewan, one that was finally going to reach its potential, was a consistent underlying theme to the Wall government. The proof would come in the measurable terms of growth—economic growth, population growth, and employment growth. There was certainly nothing unique in that approach. All governments use growth as a proxy for its performance. A quarter century earlier, the Devine government came to power using the same "so much more we can be" rhetoric. To build on the growth message as central to its approach, the Wall government would later introduce its Saskatchewan Plan for Growth. In keeping with Saskatchewan's historical fixation on population as a metric for success, the executive summary of the report presenting the plan opens with this sentence: "The Saskatchewan Plan for Growth sets out the Government of Saskatchewan's vision for a province of 1.2 million people by 2020."[4]

The Wall government was also very fortunate—one might even say lucky. It took power at an extremely opportune time, handed a solid foundation that had been secured by the two previous NDP governments. First, the Romanow New Democrats demonstrated what is seldom seen in politics: a government willing to do the right thing in spite of what are certain to be harmful political implications. It did the heavy lifting. The fiscal decisions taken in those early years of the 1990s provided the necessary footing for progress in the future. But it came at great cost to the NDP, especially in rural Saskatchewan. When the Calvert government took over ten years later, it was handed a surplus budget of $461 million.[5] This allowed for reinvestment and tax measures that helped to stimulate the economy.

For two years before the Wall government was elected, there was impressive evidence of significant economic growth in Saskatchewan. One measure among many was total personal income, which grew by $2.8 billion to $31.6 billion in 2007—the largest one-year increase in the province's history.[6] The economic analysis for 2007 went on to note,

> Saskatchewan's nominal GDP increased at an annual rate of 10.9 percent in 2007. Strong market demand and the accompanying increase in commodity prices boosted the value of exports last year. Grain exports rose 39.8 percent while potash exports increased by 38.4 percent. The value of crude oil exports also edged higher. Alongside these, total corporate profits before taxes advanced at an annual rate of 22.4 percent, a solid pickup from the more modest 9.4 percent increase in profits in 2006. Corporate profits reached $12.5 billion in 2007, nearly three times its level in 2001.[7]

The most important economic variables were global prices for natural resources. For each of Saskatchewan's three key natural resources—oil, potash, and uranium—demand and prices were rising in 2007. The value for oil year over year grew by $500 million, from $7.8 billion to 8.3 billion in 2007; potash climbed from $2.2 billion to $3.1 billion; and uranium rose from $639 million to $1.1 billion in 2007. Of course, the growth in value of natural resources was determined by world demand and had little or nothing to do with Government of Saskatchewan policies, but a strengthening economy always reflected positively on government, whether deservedly or not.

Growth was also evident in terms of population. In 2007 Saskatchewan saw the first signs of population growth from in-migration. The province's total population grew year over year from 987,500 in 2006 to 996,900 in 2007, edging close to the one million mark. As recently as 2001 Saskatchewan's population had surpassed the million mark, a level that also had been exceeded in the 1980s, before again dipping below a million. By 2007 it was back on the cusp of one million—long the psychological benchmark in terms of how the province saw itself—with a population of 999,700.[8] Coupled with improving economic conditions in its final three years, the Calvert NDP government recorded budgetary surpluses of $383 million, $400 million, and $293 million, respectively. In the 2007–08 fiscal year, the majority of which was governed by the NDP before the November 2007 handoff to the Wall government, the surplus was $641 million.[9]

Clearly, then, Wall and the Saskatchewan Party government were taking power at a favourable political moment in the province's economic cycle. The party had used the encouraging economic statistics to argue in the 2007 election campaign that it was best placed to ensure continued economic growth. The new premier conceded that his government had inherited a growing economy from the NDP. In the first legislative session following the election, Wall said his government's priority was to "ensure that this province's current boom, now of over one million people, translates into long-term prosperity."[10] The question was how it would manage its good fortune and use it to political advantage. This was, after all, a province that had gone through decades of the wrenching ups and downs of a resource-based economy that is at the mercy of global economic forces far beyond its borders. The imprint of the Depression and drought of the 1930s remained deeply engrained in Saskatchewan's collective memory. For generations these events formed a fear of debt and living beyond our means. And a more recent event had served as a reminder of just how quickly Saskatchewan could lose control of its financial destiny.

It was in the 1980s, when private enterprise and privatization shaped public policy decisions, that government allowed public finances to become a huge economic drag. Some of the senior members of cabinet in the Saskatchewan Party government, including Wall himself, were political aides in the Devine government of those years, and they came to power in 2007 with the same economic instincts. But they had also seen up close how expectations generated by politicians who are seduced by their own rhetoric can lead to poor policy choices. The question was, would they be better economic and fiscal managers? Surely the lessons of recent history would not be lost on this new government.

With Wall's ability to instill hope in the electorate, a new sentiment was emerging at a pivotal time when the economy was on the rise. It took the form of a public psychology that sought to break free from the old paradigm—in which caution was the guiding principle—to a new, more optimistic, hopeful outlook. This would be a government where attitudes mattered. Public expectations would be aligned to Saskatchewan's potential. You had to believe that growth could become consistent, providing the resources required for a better standard of living and quality of life, along with balanced budgets. It was not an either-or choice. You could have both: enjoy more of everything and live within your means. It was to be a new Saskatchewan. The language might have changed, but it echoed Grant Devine's exhortation of "there's so much more we can be" from two decades earlier.

An important moment came early. In 2008, during the Wall government's first full year in power, a resource revenue financial windfall occurred. Both potash and oil prices skyrocketed. The most stunning rise was in potash. The value of Saskatchewan potash sales in 2008 surged to $7.4 billion, a one-year increase of almost 140 percent from the 2007 total of $3.1 billion.[11] While not as stunning a rise, the average price for oil in 2008 was US$109.25, up 37 percent from the previous year.[12] Coincidentally, the Canadian dollar was also showing amazing strength against the U.S. dollar during this period. In fact, on November 7, 2007, the day Wall and the Saskatchewan Party won a majority government, the Canadian dollar peaked at US$1.10 and traded approximately at parity for the first half of 2008.[13] The value of the dollar reflected the importance and value of Canada's natural resource sector as the foundation for its economic growth and the nation's standard of living.

The most critical factor in terms of Saskatchewan's political economy was the spectacular rise in 2008 of the price of potash, an escalation driven by growing global demand. If there is one natural resource in Saskatchewan that

symbolizes the promise of a much greater future and destiny for the province, it is potash. Although it might not equal oil and gas in terms of revenue-
generating potential, potash is far more important to the validation of the
Saskatchewan myth. The simple fact is that Saskatchewan is the global leader
in terms of potash production and reserves. Symbolically, if not financially,
potash is to Saskatchewan the equivalent of oil to Alberta.

Couple the deeply embedded belief that potash is a proxy for the province's
stature with what happened in 2008–09 and the effect on policy decisions is
not surprising. Unbelievably, the price for a tonne of potash reached $1,100 in
Canadian dollars in March 2009. In November 2007, when the Wall government took power, the price had been $225.

Many factors drove the mind-spinning potash price rise. The key factor
was China, and to a lesser degree India. With a rapidly growing middle class,
the Chinese government recognized that to maintain its political stability it
needed to increase food production to feed its population of more than 1.3
billion. As such, the country is the world's largest consumer of potash. China
did produce and even export phosphates for a time, including five million
tonnes of potash annually;[14] while both are used for fertilizer, phosphate and
potash have different roles in crop growth and thus are not interchangeable.

Although less acknowledged, another important reason for the potash
price spike occurred in the American Midwest. A rapidly growing biofuels
market was emerging, as the United States put in place rich incentives for
production of ethanol as part of an emphasis on cleaner-burning energy.
With corn a feedstock for ethanol, the demand for greater corn production increased the U.S. demand for Saskatchewan potash, which is the most
important fertilizer for corn acreage. Concurrent to all this was massive new
investment in brownfield expansion of potash production, in large measure
a result of the ten-year royalty holiday on new production that the Calvert
government had put in place. The potash investment became a major factor in
driving economic growth throughout the first term of the Wall government.

At the same time, oil prices and production were rising. Consider this: in
July 2008 the price for Western Canada Select heavy crude reached an unheard

of US$115 a barrel. In January 2008 it was $50 a barrel.[15] For comparison purposes, the average 2020 price was approximately US$20 a barrel. Granted, the 2008 price was a momentary spike—the oil price had fallen rapidly by the end of the year as a recession triggered by the financial crisis began to grip the U.S. economy. But this, in turn, was also a temporary price collapse. In 2010 oil prices began to rise again, and the mere fact that prices had reached the level they did in 2008 created an expectation that high prices would become the norm once the recession ended and the U.S. economy recovered.

Ironically, and paradoxically, the 2009 recession itself helped to create a false sense of economic resilience in Saskatchewan. It was not that the province's economy escaped unscathed; in fact, Saskatchewan's GDP for the year dropped by 4.8 percent, while the Canadian economy only dipped by 2.9 percent. But Saskatchewan's employment numbers were resilient, with the number employed growing by 8,000 in 2009.[16] It was an economic slowdown that had nothing to do with underlying weaknesses in the Saskatchewan economy but was a function of a corrupt and ill-regulated U.S. financial system. Canada was side-swiped by the meltdown of the banking and housing sector in the United States, as demand for Canadian exports fell. Fortunately, the recession was contained to 2009 and although the United States had a long, painful road to recovery, Canada was able to escape relatively quickly and with a minimum of damage. In large part, Canada's recovery was due to the stimulative deficit spending by the then Harper government in Ottawa, combined with a low-interest-rate monetary policy.

During this strange period of mini–boom and bust a couple of important things happened in Saskatchewan, and both of them had significant long-term budget implications. The first was a decision in the fall of 2008 to announce, out of the budget cycle, a significant income tax cut for the province. Labelled by the Wall government as the largest single-year tax cut in the province's history, the centrepiece was a $4,000 increase in the basic personal exemption and the spousal exemption to $12,945, making it the second highest in Canada. The package also included a $2,000 per child increase in the Child Tax Credit. The tax measures were retroactive for 2008. "This fall, Premier Wall announced this historic tax cut as one key component of our government's plan to share in the benefits of our growing economy with Saskatchewan people," Finance Minister Rod Gantefoer explained. "This important piece of legislation we have passed today benefits every income tax filer in Saskatchewan."[17] With revenues flowing in from the resource sector, it seemed like an opportune time to deliver a major and extremely popular personal tax cut. It even seemed to make fiscal policy sense. It was as if the government believed the revenue windfall was the new normal. Even with the tax cut, the government still recorded a massive surplus of $2.9 billion for the fiscal year 2008–09.[18]

The optimism remained palpable even in March 2009 as the global financial crisis was gripping the U.S. economy and spilling over into Canada. Gantefoer expressed the upbeat mood well in his budget summary. "At a time when other areas of Canada and indeed the world are experiencing economic crises, we are forecasting economic growth," he said. "While others are shutting down factories and cutting their workforce, we are looking for workers and showing an increase in employment. Where others are lamenting lack of opportunity and are mulling greener pastures, we have experienced 10 consecutive quarters of population growth. And while others are forecasting deficit budgets, Saskatchewan is tabling a balanced budget and forecasting surpluses for the next three years."[19] Amazing how isolated Saskatchewan appeared to be from the rest of the world. The good times had finally arrived—or so it seemed.

The second thing that happened was that reality abruptly intervened. It came as yet another stark reminder of Saskatchewan's economic vulnerability to global market demand for its natural resources. With the 2009 recession came the return of sanity to global potash markets. In the wake of the financial crisis, potash sales volumes plummeted to 3.7 million tonnes, a decline of more than 62 percent.[20] The potash price of more than $1,000 a tonne was simply not sustainable and led to buyers backing out of the market. The bottom-line negative impact from 2008–09 to 2009–10 on potash revenues for Saskatchewan totalled almost $1.6 billion. From $1.4 billion in revenues one year, the government actually had to refund potash companies $184 million the next. This represented a repayment for higher-than-estimated potash royalty and taxes paid by potash companies in 2008. The fiscal bottom line was that the Wall government went from a $2.9 billion surplus in 2008–09, its first full year in office, to a deficit of $409 million in its second.[21]

But if nothing else, being whipsawed by potash markets underscored Saskatchewan's global stature as the dominant producer. The policy occupation with the potash industry in Saskatchewan has been a trait of all governments since the 1960s. The decision by the Calvert government in 2005 to implement the ten-year royalty holiday on new production, which in effect was an exemption from the profits tax on new production, coupled with accelerated capital depreciation of 120 percent on actual capital invested, was like a drug for the potash sector.[22] Not surprisingly, the changes were extremely popular with the industry.

There was no denying the stimulative effects of the potash tax and royalty changes that reached well into the future. Frankly, it was remarkable. The increase in mining investment—with the vast majority going into potash—began in 2005 with $730 million invested, a 73 percent increase over the year previous. The escalation then began to accelerate rapidly, rising to more than $1 billion in 2006 and reaching approximately $2 billion in each of 2008 and 2009; growing to $2.5 billion in 2010, $3 billion in 2011, and $4.4 billion in 2012; and peaking at more than $5 billion in 2013. Then, with the inevitable decline, the figure had dropped to $1.5 billion by 2018.[23]

Years later, in a policy brief for the Johnson Shoyama Graduate School of Public Policy, former Saskatchewan Finance Department senior economist Jim Marshall called for a long overdue recalibration of potash royalty policy:

> By allowing a 120 per cent allowance, companies receive a significant incentive to invest through a faster allowance on the first 100 per cent of their investment and, in addition, are entitled to an incentive in being able to claim an additional 20 per cent against their income....Also of concern is the exemption from profit taxes on production levels in excess of the 2001–2002 levels for existing producers and the similar exemption provided on some of the production of new mines. These two exemptions,

based on a point in time in the past, could provide a perpetual exemption if the industry grows to new production levels and could undermine the tax base in future years.[24]

Growth, whether in the economy or the population, became the dominant theme in the Wall government's narrative. It was all in support of the underlying political message that the election of the Saskatchewan Party had allowed the province to leave behind a century of meagre growth, particularly in comparison with Alberta. The subtext was that socialist policies of previous CCF and NDP governments had stunted the province's development. With a far more diverse natural resource base than Alberta of oil, potash, and uranium, as well as a multi-crop and highly productive, increasingly entrepreneurial agriculture economy, meant that Saskatchewan had the natural economic assets to support a growing economy.

A critical social and economic dimension to the first term of the Wall government was immigration policy. Its genesis, ironically, was during a candidates' debate in the 2003 election. On the stage at the University of Saskatchewan were Wall, the NDP's Eric Cline, and Liberal candidate Rob Norris. At one point, Wall and Cline got into an exchange over which party was best positioned to encourage expansion of the oil sector and the natural resource sector generally in the province. Norris intervened by noting that while the other two parties were having "the same old" debate about developing Saskatchewan's natural resources, the most important natural resource "is sitting in front of us," referring to the young students in the audience.[25]

The remark did not go unnoticed by Wall, who later recruited Norris to leave the Liberals and run for the Saskatchewan Party in the 2007 election. Norris was elected in a Saskatoon seat, and upon taking power Wall appointed him minister of advanced education, employment, labour, and immigration. Work had begun on developing a more aggressive immigration policy in the early years of the Calvert government. It was anchored in a 2003 study by former NDP MLA Pat Lorje entitled *Open Up Saskatchewan!* Lorje noted that Saskatchewan needed to significantly increase its immigration efforts. With its aging population, higher levels of immigration were essential. "This is an urgent issue. It is time for compelling public policy and action. The population stagnation in Saskatchewan won't fix itself without significant intervention. It's time to be pro-active," Lorje wrote.[26] She noted that Manitoba was far more focused, aggressive, and successful than Saskatchewan in attracting immigrants. Under the terms of the Saskatchewan Immigrant Nominee Program (SINP), the province was allowed to nominate candidates to the federal government for permanent residence in one of three primary categories: international skilled workers, experience relevant to the province's needs, and business immigration, each containing several subcategories for various types of immigrant candidates. In 1998, under the SINP, the province had nominated only one person, even though the program allowed for two hundred.

Some modest progress was made by the Calvert government, including a 2005 agreement with the federal government that established the framework for the joint management of immigration to the province. But immigration did not take on a central public policy role in government until Wall took office. In his first year in office, the SINP was ramped up from 300 applicants to 3,000. A strategy was rolled out in 2009 that was built around ongoing explicit targets. For 2009–10 the target was set at 3,400 nominees, which, when family members were included, was forecast to total 10,000 people.

With Saskatchewan traditionally getting 1 percent or less of total international immigration to Canada, the numbers and proportion relative to the national total began to rise rapidly. In 2009, a total of 6,890 people immigrated to Saskatchewan, or 2.7 percent of the national total. In 2010 the number increased to 7,625, again 2.7 percent of the national number, and in 2011 the number was 8,955, representing 3.6 percent of Canada's total immigrants for the year.[27] From 2011 to 2016, a total of 47,935 immigrants came to the province, raising the total number of immigrants to 4.5 percent of Saskatchewan's population from what had been 2.1 percent in 2001.[28]

The implications and effects of more robust immigration were both economic and political. Immigration is key to driving and sustaining economic growth, and traditionally new Canadians tend to identify politically with the government that assisted their settlement. The SINP is such that new Canadians have early contact with the provincial government in terms of job and business opportunities, which provides a basis for them to develop a partisan allegiance—in this case, with the Saskatchewan Party.

Growth became the overarching narrative for the Wall government. Its Plan for Growth set out specific and ambitious targets to reach by 2020 and beyond. The rhetoric in the document makes clear how the government saw itself in authoring the province's future.

Saskatchewan is a comeback story. Following more than a decade of population decline and an economy that lagged behind the national average, Saskatchewan now ranks among the national leaders in provincial population and economic growth....Saskatchewan will be a province of 1.2 million people by 2020. That is a foundational goal in the province's growth plan. After decades of stagnation and decline, Saskatchewan communities are growing and will continue to grow because more young people are staying in Saskatchewan, more families are moving home and more new families from across Canada and around the world are choosing Saskatchewan as the place to be.[29]

The plan also committed the government to "continue to balance the budget every year" and "cut the provincial debt in half from its 2007 level by 2017."[30] It should have been honest and promised "a return" to balanced budgets. What it didn't mention was that after recording a huge surplus of $2.9 billion in 2008–09 when potash and oil prices were at their peak, the Wall government ran three consecutive operating deficits between 2009 and 2012, of $409 million, $13 million, and $105 million, respectively.[31] But in 2012 there was reason for optimism. Resources prices were strong, the global economy was recovering from the 2009 recession, and immigration and in-migration was increasing the population.

There was even talk of creating another rainy day fund, like the Heritage Fund the province had in the 1970s during the Blakeney years when balanced budgets were the norm. The Saskatchewan Heritage Fund of that era had followed in the footsteps of the Alberta Heritage Fund created by Peter Lougheed. Both were built by capturing revenues from resources and sequestering them to be used as a shock absorber when the inevitable economic downturns arrive. Former University of Saskatchewan president Peter MacKinnon was contracted to do a study into the feasibility of a Heritage Fund and provide his recommendations. He reported in 2013. His conclusion: "This study leads to a recommendation to create a permanent Saskatchewan Futures Fund that allows for one-time resource revenues to become a lasting source of wealth, while stabilizing government use of these volatile revenues."[32]

The idea of what is essentially a government savings fund has significant political appeal. They come by different names—Heritage Funds, Future Funds, Sovereign Wealth Funds—but all seek to provide a backstop as a source for fiscal stabilization. They are most common in natural resource-based economies that must deal with the ups and downs of economies that are by their nature cyclical. The idea is that if there is a separate fund that accumulates "excess" revenue during periods of high commodity prices, then it can be drawn down to help absorb the shock to operating budgets when prices fall, as they inevitably will. Such funds are a tool for countercyclical fiscal policy, where retained financial capacity is available for use to stimulate the economy and support programs during periods of slow growth or recession.

Saving for a rainy day makes common sense, or so it would seem. But it's easier said than done. To create a rainy day fund means spending less than a government otherwise would, or could, which in the real-world of politics is a massive challenge. It requires significant diversion of annual revenues into a sequestered account, which means not funding current initiatives, whether social programs or tax cuts. The other argument against rainy day funds is that they are unnecessary. Governments can achieve fiscal stabilization through deficit budgeting, where the effects of downturns are managed through borrowing to pay for current expenses. In effect, deficit financing, like a rainy day fund, is financed—or, in other words, paid back—from income during periods of high natural resource revenues.

Not surprisingly, the MacKinnon report came and quickly went. The idea that the "new" Saskatchewan had a sightline of windfall revenues well into the future, which had been the sentiment during the first years of the Wall government, had quietly dissipated. Trouble was already brewing.

CHAPTER 15

2010

The Audacity of Nope

IT WAS NOT WHAT YOU WOULD CALL A WARM AND ENGAGING discussion. Marius Kloppers, CEO of Australia-based BHP Billiton, the world's largest mining company, had travelled to Saskatoon to meet with Premier Brad Wall and discuss BHP's bid to buy the Potash Corporation of Saskatchewan. The decision on whether the transaction would be approved was fully the jurisdiction of the Government of Canada. So, the meeting with the premier of a small Canadian province was more of a courtesy call, you might say, rather than a substantive one. Kind of like flying halfway around the world to visit the outback, or so it apparently seemed for Kloppers.

Wall didn't see it that way. After all, the people of Saskatchewan owned the potash resource that BHP wanted to exploit. It quickly became apparent in Wall's mind that Kloppers had something of a dismissive attitude toward both him and the province. Perhaps that's what happens when you're the head of a giant multinational corporation with operations around the world. You figure your time is better spent elsewhere rather than dealing with a local politician with no decision-making power over the business deal you're orchestrating. Kloppers knew the decision rested with the federal govern-ment, and BHP had hired a team of lobbyists to focus their efforts on Ottawa. He wasn't much interested in a courtesy call with someone who was not going to make the decision. "I don't think he wanted to be there meeting with me or our officials, or answering questions from us," Wall observed.[1]

The premier was not impressed. It had been almost three weeks since BHP had made a cash offer of $40 billion to purchase PCS. In the interim Kloppers's company had made no effort to contact the Government of Saskatchewan. The Potash Corp's board of directors quickly rebuffed the unsolicited bid. Less than twenty-four hours later, BHP launched a hostile bid and went directly to PCS shareholders, offering $130 a share. At the time, PCS shares were trading at approximately US$112.[2] The takeover attempt quickly escalated into a major international business story.[3] When the biggest mining company in the world is bidding to buy the world's largest potash producer, which for a time ranked as the highest-capitalized company on the Toronto Stock Exchange, it tends to get people's attention.

There was even speculation that China might get involved through one of its state-owned enterprises, either in a competitive bid for PCS or in helping the company fend off the BHP takeover. As a major importer of potash, China had a stake in ensuring it maintained some leverage in protecting its security of supply. What gave the China angle some credibility was that PCS already had a 20 percent stake in Sinofert Holdings, a Hong Kong company that mines pot-ash in China and is an agent that imports potash.[4] No such effort ever mate-rialized, but the speculation added a little more global intrigue to the story. Clearly this ranked as a major transaction with international implications.

The political stakes for Wall were obvious. Long before the BHP takeover bid there were complaints about PCS senior management having relocated to Chicago, in defiance of the PCS privatization legislation requiring that the company's head office remain in Saskatoon. The question Wall faced was how to ensure that Saskatchewan interests were protected. It was a pivotal moment with significant political and economic implications.

On the surface the issue appeared to be fairly straightforward. One widely held, publicly traded company had made a lucrative offer to buy another widely held, publicly traded company. It was the sort of stock ownership exchange that happens every day in the business world. The only thing that made it different was the scale of the financial transaction. Both companies were owned by shareholders around the world. If the owners of PCS shares want to sell their shares to someone offering a price they believe is in their interests, then surely it should be their choice. That is how the stock market works in capitalist economies.

But this transaction was different. It was about potash. In Saskatchewan, potash is the closest thing you can get to something called a "strategic" resource. With the largest and richest potash reserves in the world, and the key role it plays as a fertilizer in the global agriculture economy, Saskatchewan has significant comparative economic advantage. Just how significant? Well, consider that Saskatchewan's market dominance is such that it has its own potash cartel, called Canpotex. Just like OPEC has for oil, the Saskatchewan cartel has major influence in the global potash market. It could even have had the same acronym; instead of the Organization of the Petroleum Exporting Countries, the Saskatchewan version of OPEC could be the Organization of the Potash Exporting Companies. As a decidedly non–free market institution, Canpotex is a marketing cartel designed to keep the price of potash as high as possible through the control of production. Great for the companies. Not so great for farmers who buy the potash fertilizer. You might term it collusion to fix prices. The three members of Canpotex—the Potash Corporation, Mosaic, and Agrium—all operated in Saskatchewan. BHP Billiton indicated it was not interested in a long-term relationship with Canpotex.

Two days after receiving the letter of offer from BHP, the PCS board of directors met in Chicago to form a special committee to manage the process. Because of the great significance of the issue, the committee was one of the whole—that is, it included all twelve board members. The board mapped out six paths forward that, aside from recommending acceptance of the BHP offer, included recapitalization of the company, a strategic minority partner, organic growth, or some combination of factors. At the time, the board members felt that the board's responsibility and its decision would be guided by its fiduciary duty to act in the best interests of shareholders. To ensure that was the case, the board realized that it, not senior management, had to control the engagement with BHP. Clearly, senior executives were in potential conflict of interest because of the personal benefits and compensation they could derive should they be displaced by BHP. Being excluded from not only the process but even any details about the ongoing discussions by the board frustrated senior management, who were of the view that the deal would be decided by banks in New York and Toronto.

When it became public that Kloppers's meeting with Wall had not gone well, PCS board chair Dallas Howe felt he needed to have a conversation with the premier. Howe and board director Chris Burley, an investment banker, met with Wall, deputy premier Bill Boyd, and lawyers from the Ministry of Justice in a room at the small Swift Current airport. It became clear that Wall had an intense interest in the legal consequences of a BHP takeover and its implications for the company's presence in Saskatchewan. Sensing Wall's level of unhappiness with both the hollowing out of the PCS head office and the potential for it to disappear should BHP take ownership, Howe told Wall that "we need to renew our vows."[5] It was a reference to the obligation in legislation to keep the head office in Saskatoon, and in the following weeks PCS made a public seven-part "pledge to Saskatchewan" that included commitments to maintain "a vital corporate headquarters in Saskatchewan," to remain "committed to Canpotex," and to develop "a strong Aboriginal workforce."[6] The company's pledge became a key factor in shaping political opinion.

Over the years, Saskatchewan had gone through recurring episodes of knock-down, drag-out fights over the potash industry that had left a deep imprint on the psychology of the province. Three episodes in particular are relevant.

In the 1960s, private investment flooded into the province as the business-friendly government of Ross Thatcher offered incentives for Canadian, U.S., and European companies to develop the province's potash reserves. And flood in they did, to the point of serious market oversupply and a collapsing price. Thatcher, the free-enterpriser, intervened in the market in a major way: in 1969 he called in the heads of the companies and read the riot act in the form of imposing a system of "prorationing," where government set a floor price and dictated production levels as a way to stabilize the market. It was an action that caught the attention of U.S. authorities, who eventually pursued antitrust action against eight American companies and named Thatcher as an unindicted co-conspirator.

The next episode in potash politics came in 1976 when the NDP government of Allan Blakeney launched its agenda to nationalize more than half of the potash industry in the province. Although done through negotiation rather than expropriation, it still triggered a fierce political debate. After creating the Potash Corporation of Saskatchewan as an ownership vehicle, the first acquisition was made in 1976 when the government purchased the Duval mine for $128.5 million. Within two years PCS had purchased five more mines and controlled 40 percent of production in the province—well on its way to the goal of majority ownership of productive capacity.[7]

The subsequent chapter in the politics of potash was the privatization of PCS by the Devine government in 1989. The initiative to do an IPO to turn the Crown corporation into a publicly traded company ignited the longest debate in Saskatchewan legislative history. As noted earlier, it was a watershed moment in Saskatchewan's political and economic history, one that effectively erased the issue of non-utility public ownership from the public agenda, at least in any substantive way, whether through subsequent renationalization or significant new commercial investment with government as the majority investor.

All those periods in the potash story had given the resource iconic status in the public mind. Potash had very much become integrated into the province's identity, so anything that related in any important way to the industry would carry with it major political, as well as economic, implications. In fact, many people in Saskatchewan still believed that the province owned at least part of the Potash Corporation, even though it had been privatized two decades earlier and the Romanow NDP government had sold the province's remaining minority shares in PCS in 1994 to private investors.

Clearly, Kloppers did not grasp the political significance of what BHP was proposing in its bid to buy the Potash Corporation, as he was focused on Ottawa and the decision to be taken under the *Investment Canada Act*. But Wall did, and he knew the consequences if he did not manage the issue with Saskatchewan's interests front and centre. With an election scheduled for the following year, Wall was determined not to be perceived as selling out Saskatchewan's interests to foreign corporate interests. How this played out had the potential to be the ballot question for voters. He wanted to ensure that the management of the BHP-PCS issue would be a signature event when it came time to meet the voters and seek a second mandate.

He sought advice from others, including former premier Roy Romanow and ex–Alberta premier Peter Lougheed. Romanow told Wall to hire the best legal experts he could find so as to understand the issue and the details of the deal better than either BHP or PCS. Lougheed simply posed a question to Wall: "Who owns the resource?" When Wall answered, "The people of Saskatchewan," Lougheed replied, "You're right. Act like it, and you'll be fine."[8] It was a conversation that was key in solidifying Wall's opposition to the BHP takeover. Realizing it would be improper for the government to embed itself in the negotiating process as a go-between with BHP and PCS, two private publicly traded companies, Wall needed channels through which he could know what each of the parties was thinking so as to better judge the merits of each position. To do that he asked Don Chynoweth, a global executive, Saskatchewan native, and former federal and provincial political policy advisor, to be an interlocutor between the government and PCS. Chynoweth accepted the role on an unpaid basis. Deputy premier Bill Boyd played the same function with BHP Billiton.

Wall also hired the Conference Board of Canada to do an analysis of the pros and cons of the proposed deal. In its report, the Conference Board estimated that over ten years the province would lose $2 billion in revenue, or $200 million a year. It also said that "the acquisition would allow the company to organize its affairs in such a way as to minimize corporate taxes paid to the Province. Even if BHP were to follow the same marketing strategy as PCS's current management—which includes using Canpotex, the jointly-owned marketing and logistics arm of the Saskatchewan producers—Saskatchewan's tax yield from the potash industry would be temporarily lowered, due to the nature of the current tax and royalty regime."[9]

As well, an internal analysis and legal opinion that Wall sought from Gowling, a national Bay Street–based law firm, concluded there were two options. One was to agree. The other was to agree with conditions. Wall's response to the advice was "What about saying nope?" The thought apparently had not occurred to the law firm, ostensibly for a couple of reasons. One was that the decision was not up to Wall and the Saskatchewan government. It was exclusively a federal government decision. And second, only once previously had the federal government intervened under the *Investment Canada Act* to deny a commercial transaction. That was in 2008 in respect of the proposed acquisition by a U.S. defence company, Alliant Techsystems Inc., of the space business of MacDonald, Dettwiler & Associates Ltd., which developed and operated the Radarsat satellite program charged with defending Canada's North.[10] The deal was rejected as not being of "net benefit" to Canada. A similar net-benefit analysis was being applied to the proposed BHP-PCS transaction.

Wall realized that if the BHP deal were to go forward, he would have to protect the provincial treasury. He demanded a $1 billion payment from BHP to offset the tax advantages of the acquisition, plus hundreds of millions more in infrastructure development—a proposal BHP rejected. To increase the pressure on the Harper government to deny the sale, Wall enlisted the support of others, including premiers Jean Charest of Quebec, Ed Stelmach in Alberta, and Greg Selinger of Manitoba. Even the Opposition federal Liberal caucus in Ottawa threw its support behind Wall's opposition to the deal. "This transaction would effectively amount to the sale of the entire industry, not just a single ordinary company...that raises the stakes here to something more profound than just a normal commercial transaction," said deputy Liberal leader and Saskatchewan MP Ralph Goodale.[11]

The multi-pronged campaign by Wall was crucial in solidifying his populist image. What made it so effective politically was that he had taken a position that was counterintuitive. As a government that many labelled as right-wing conservative, Wall was behaving as a pragmatist, not an ideologue. Logically, a free enterprise–minded government would not be intervening in the transaction and would let the market and the owners of the Potash Corporation— namely the shareholders—decide if they were willing to sell their shares at the price offered by BHP. This was not the government's business.

The interventionist act by Wall set free market purists' hair on fire. It turned into a national debate, with Terence Corcoran of the *National Post* calling Saskatchewan a "banana republic." He wrote, "Did I miss the Constitutional change—the one that created the Peoples' Republic of Saskatchewan, with Brad Wall as el presidente?" It was word that Wall had asked for "BHP to pay $1 billion up front into government coffers" that set Corcoran off. "If all this is true— and there has been no government denial to date—it paints a dark picture of the political culture in Saskatchewan—and Canada," Corcoran said.[12] Joining the debate and the denunciation of Wall was University of Saskatchewan business professor Colin Boyd. He said that Corcoran was right to describe Saskatchewan as a banana republic and that Wall's stance was "bizarre and illogical."[13] Wall quickly engaged the debate with Corcoran, in a response published four days later in the *National Post*. In it, he argued that the $1 billion issue was being mischaracterized, using the words of an unnamed BHP official from an open-line radio show who apparently said, "I think that was a gross simplification of some of the things that were discussed." Wall also argued that, based on earlier examples, the promise by BHP to maintain its potash head office in Saskatchewan was doubtful at best. "Billiton's promise to maintain a global base metals headquarters in Toronto in exchange for permission to buy Rio Tinto in 2000 dissolved like prairie snow after a spring rain," Wall wrote.[14]

With the Harper government nearing its decision point, it was clear that the prime minister, an avowed free market conservative, was reluctant to step in and block the transaction. "This is a proposal for an American-controlled company to be taken over by an Australian-controlled company, and we will of course review the matter," Harper had told the House of Commons two weeks before the decision was announced. His description of the transaction signalled the prime minister's bias to let the market make its own decisions. Political considerations did not appear uppermost in Harper's mind.

Sensing the need to up the public pressure, Wall addressed the Saskatchewan Chamber of Commerce to make the case that the deal failed to meet the net-benefit test for either Canada or Saskatchewan. He recited the economic, job, fiscal, and strategic resource arguments against the takeover. "In the interests of jobs for Saskatchewan families, in the interests of our quality of life that is funded by revenues from government, in the interests of our province and country in the world, we must say no to this hostile takeover," Wall said. "And let me just say this, the answer that it is not accepted has been given in free market economies around the world....We say yes to the national interest of our country, we say yes to fulfilling the potential of our province and the nation. We say yes to controlling the resource and our future."[15]

It was clearly a pivotal moment in the politics of the province. With both a national stage and national media attention, Wall positioned himself as a populist defending the interests of Saskatchewan people against a "hostile takeover" by a distant multinational corporation with no ties to Saskatchewan. What made it even more significant was that Wall was clearly not acting out of specific ideological beliefs in the free market. His actions were pragmatic. Moreover, his language around the issue was steeped in the vernacular of economic nationalism, long the preserve of the political left in Canada. Wall talked about protecting the economic and social interests of Canada and warned of a hollowing out of the corporate sector in Canada and of becoming a "branch-plant economy." He asked, "Do we want to add PotashCorp to that list of once-proud Canadian companies that now are under foreign control?... It's our government's belief that the people of Saskatchewan deserve nothing less than a potash industry unequivocally operated and marketed for the benefit of Canada and Saskatchewan."[16]

It left the NDP Opposition not only sidelined but with no reasonable, credible, or even relevant critique of Wall's position on what was widely seen as a crucial issue. In a vain effort to insert himself and his party into the debate, NDP leader Dwain Lingenfelter outlined what was termed a seven-point plan that would give Saskatchewan more control of the takeover bid. The plan was, effectively, conceding that the deal would be approved. The NDP called for the government to demand a "golden share" that would give it veto power over other shareholders and enforce stipulations, such the corporate head office being in Saskatchewan.[17]

One other background event that had no public visibility but had political effect in both Ottawa and Regina was a private meeting between Potash Corporation board chair Dallas Howe and the Chinese ambassador to Canada. The meeting at the embassy in Ottawa was cordial, if non-substantive. It was an effort by Howe to ensure all options for the company were explored. There had been public speculation about a possible bid by China. At the meeting the ambassador said China "would not go anywhere where it is not invited."[18] Although the meeting was private, the federal government became aware the two had met, raising the troubling possibility of China taking over the company. It was a not an outcome that either the federal or provincial government would welcome.

The pivotal moment, at least in terms of what decision the minority federal government would make, came mere days before the verdict was announced. Wall's campaign to fend off the takeover of the Potash Corporation had crystallized opinion among the thirteen Conservative Saskatchewan MPs in the Harper government caucus. The group unanimously supported Wall's position that the BHP bid should be rejected by the federal government. More importantly, they said that should the government approve the takeover, they would almost certainly lose their seats in the next election, with some of the MPs even threatening to withdraw their support from the government. In effect, they put a gun to the head of the government. The potential loss of thirteen votes on a confidence motion could be enough to bring the minority government down.

The decision by the Harper government to reject the BHP Billiton takeover was issued in a terse statement by Industry Minister Tony Clement. He explained simply that the bid had failed to meet the net-benefit test of the

Investment Canada Act.[19] Although BHP was given a thirty-day window in which to make improvements to its offer that might change the federal government's calculation, nothing was forthcoming. Two and a half years later, Kloppers was asked to resign as CEO of BHP Billiton. He continued to receive his base salary of more than US$2.2 million for five months after he stepped down, plus a bonus of up to 320 percent of his salary for the 2012–13 fiscal year.[20] Meanwhile, Wall collected his premier's salary of C$159,000.

Shortly after the federal government's announcement, Wall held a press conference at the Saskatchewan Legislature. It drew a large crowd of journalists, with local, regional, and national media in attendance. Wall was obviously elated, because he knew the positive political benefits that would result for himself and the Saskatchewan Party in the coming provincial election.

"I want to especially thank minister Clement and his team," Wall said. "Most of all, I want to thank the people of Saskatchewan who were very, very, very engaged in this." He admitted that arriving at the decision to oppose the takeover had been an emotional roller coaster and he had struggled with the decision that his government had taken. Recognizing that blocking the transaction could have a negative impact on Canada's, and Saskatchewan's, global reputation as a responsible place to invest, he realized that he could not remain silent on the issue. "We are still a nation that is open...we are a free-trading country. But we have been blessed with a great amount of natural resources...and we may have to act differently in that regard. This is a very strategic resource."[21] Immediately after the news conference, Wall and members of his senior staff met in his office to celebrate. The staff presented him with a gift. He unwrapped it to see a framed plaque with the words "The Audacity of Nope."

One year later almost to the day, in November 2011, Wall and the Saskatchewan Party won its second majority mandate with a stunning 64 percent of the popular vote. The election resulted in forty-nine seats for the party in the fifty-eight-seat legislature—an increase of eleven seats, all taken from the NDP, which was reduced to nine seats and 32 percent of the vote. The NDP had become relegated to a small urban base, with seven of its seats in

Saskatoon and Regina, as well as two in the Far North. It was déjà vu all over again for the New Democrats; the nine-member caucus was the same outcome as the Monday Night Massacre almost thirty years earlier. Lingenfelter, who was defeated in his Regina constituency, announced on election night that he was stepping down as leader after two and a half futile years of trying to revitalize the NDP. It was a moment when the NDP plunged itself into what would become a non-stop crisis for survival and identity. Over the next nine years, the party would cycle through four more leaders, either acting or confirmed, vainly searching to find its political bearings.

A month after the 2011 election the Angus Reid Institute did its annual survey of Canadians to determine the most popular premier in the country. First was Wall, with 71 percent approval, 11 points ahead of his nearest rival.[22]

CHAPTER 16

2015

The Last Gasp

THE TRANSFORMATION OF THE SASKATCHEWAN FARM economy was a long, arduous, politically fraught, ironic, and often painful process. It stretched back almost fifty years, to that fateful 1969 day in Regina when Pierre Trudeau reportedly asked a crowd of angry farmers, "Why should I sell your wheat?" Deemed by many as a sacrilegious remark, it became seared into the political consciousness of the province. What makes it ironic is that whether Trudeau even said the words, at least in the context in which they have been preserved through history, is itself a subject of debate. But like most things in politics, it doesn't matter. Perception is reality. What matters is what people believe, not whether it is true or not.

It is possible to put an actual end date on the final step in the transformation. The old Saskatchewan, the one with roots in agrarian populism and protest, drew its last breath on April 15, 2015. It came when the meagre remnants of the once powerful Canadian Wheat Board—which for three years had existed as a company known simply as CWB—was sold to Global Grain

Group, a joint venture of the Saudi Agriculture and Livestock Investment Company and U.S.-based Bunge Limited. The new company was named G3 Canada Ltd. It operates now as a private-sector grain company in a North American grain trade that includes, among others, giants such as Archer Daniels Midland, Agrex Inc., Cargill, Richardson International, Viterra, and Paterson Grain.

The last gasp of the Canadian Wheat Board ended a debate that had grown in intensity over the previous three decades. As world events unfolded, trade liberalization and the market became the dominant framework for public policy. A number of crucial international factors had created the pathway to the new governing and economic paradigm; politically they were expressed in the rise of Margaret Thatcher in the United Kingdom, Ronald Reagan in the United States, Brian Mulroney in Canada, and Germany's Helmut Kohl. The period also corresponded to the demise of the Soviet Union. It was a time when globalization, the emergence of free trade, more fluid international investment flows, the decline of state-owned enterprises, and the dominance of the private sector became the political norm.

One measurement of the global transition to a more international economic environment is trade as a percentage of GDP. According to the World Bank, trade as a part of the world economy grew from 27.3 percent in 1970 to 60.4 percent in 2019.[1] For an export-oriented, trade-dependent country like Canada, not surprisingly the growth in trade has been less dramatic than it has been in terms of the global numbers. But even at that, trade as a percentage of the Canadian economy rose from 41.6 percent in 1970 to 65 percent in 2019. It actually reached 83 percent of the Canadian economy in 2000.[2]

There is also reason to believe that we have reached "peak" globalization. Even before the world economy was hobbled by the COVID-19 pandemic, there was evidence that globalization had stalled and was even beginning to recede. For the last ten years, global trade volumes have remained flat. The rise of economic nationalism in both Europe and the United States, most clearly reflected in Brexit and the election of Donald Trump, pointed to a thickening of borders and disruption of global supply chains.[3]

The effects of those global trends on Saskatchewan, a province with a major portion of its economy dependent on exports, is obviously critical. In 2017, exports of goods and services in Saskatchewan totalled $50.1 billion, of a total GDP of $79.5 billion.[4] This period of globalization and trade liberalization had profound psychological and political effects on Saskatchewan. As a province based in natural resources, agriculture, and exports, its destiny was very much tied to global markets, and the changes that unfolded internationally had inevitable consequences. The demise of the state-owned Canadian Wheat Board amounted to a final chapter in that transition.

The rise and fall of the Wheat Board very much reflects the evolution of political and economic thought in the province, which was a decades-long evolution from a collectivist to more individualistic culture. Established in 1935 in the depths of drought and the Great Depression, when protectionism dominated economic policy, the Wheat Board was an expression of farmers' desire to gain some measure of power in the international grain trade. It was based on the notion of "orderly marketing" through a single-desk seller. In 1943, by an act of Parliament, the Wheat Board was granted the monopoly for the sale of Canadian wheat and barley, which gave it significant power in terms of price. Its primary mechanism was the use of a pooling price, where farmers sold their wheat to the Wheat Board at a base price and, if necessary, received a final payment based on the average price over the course of the year if that was greater than the initial payment. In years when the price of wheat dropped, the federal government would step in to subsidize the price if it had dropped below the initial price. The need for Ottawa to backstop the price rarely arose, but it did occur in 1990–91 during a disastrous growing season when taxpayers had to make up a $670 million deficit.[5]

Other benefits of the Wheat Board were, through pooling and its economies of scale, a reduction in the transaction costs to farmers for transport, weighting, grading, and administration.[6] The Board played a key role in the grain handling system by regulating the delivery of grain to the country elevator system through the use of quotas, monitored grain markets, and coordinated delivery of grain to export ports. Although this created a stable policy environment for decades, it also meant the Board and the grain sector went through little structural transformation while global trade patterns were evolving and began changing more rapidly in the 1970s.[7]

As global opinion shifted to a more liberal trade and investment environment, attitudes also began to change as opposition to the Wheat Board's monopoly grew. In the early 1990s disapproval of the Board found its voice amongst prairie farmers who wanted to take greater individual control over the marketing of their wheat. A group calling itself "Farmers for Justice" emerged in defiance of the Wheat Board's monopoly. They directly challenged the Board by trucking their grain across the border to sell it in the United States, claiming that prices were higher south of the border. Escalating civil disobedience across the three Prairie provinces led to nine of the protesting farmers going to jail for their actions. In one case, Manitoba farmer Andy McMechan spent 155 days in jail for selling his barley in North Dakota.[8] At one point, a caravan of approximately fifty farm trucks crossed into the United States from southern Saskatchewan, loaded with grain that was sold to buyers in Plentywood, Montana.[9]

The acts of civil disobedience were clearly tinged with politics. Encouraging the farmers in their protest was the then upstart Reform Party, a right-wing populist movement fuelled by western alienation and an anti–federal government attitude. It was enough to capture the attention of media, including even the *New York Times*, which was drawn to the David and Goliath dimension of the dispute. A January 1997 report in the *Times* read as follows:

> Russell F. Barrows of Coutts, Alberta, is a third-generation grain farmer who in his 65 years never even so much as tried to reuse a postage stamp, let alone flout the law. But last April he pitched a 100-pound sack of wheat into the back of his pickup and drove across the border toward Montana. He never made it. Mr. Barrows and 13 other farmers in his group were stopped by Canadian customs agents because they did not have permits from the Wheat Board to export their own grain. It cost Mr. Barrows $4,000 Canadian in fines for a bag of wheat with a value, on a good day, of $5.[10]

Anti–Canadian Wheat Board attitudes had long been a reality in U.S. agriculture and political circles. Many American farmers, agriculture organizations, and politicians saw Ottawa's guarantee of an initial price, along with the statutory Crow Rate, as trade-distorting subsidies to western Canadian farmers. In response, Canada argued that the United States was far guiltier of agriculture subsidies that affected global markets, pointing to the multifaceted U.S. Farm Bill that made direct payments to farmers and supported a floor price for grain. In the Canada-U.S. free trade negotiations, both countries recognized the political implications of ending supports for their farmers. So instead of tackling a delicate political issue bilaterally, they committed in 1988 to addressing agriculture subsidies on a global basis, stating that "the Parties agree to work together to achieve this goal, including through multilateral trade negotiations such as the Uruguay Round."[11] The reference about the need to address the global issue of farm subsidies was aimed at the European Union's Common Agricultural Policy, a system of massive agriculture subsidies and food policies explicitly designed to "safeguard European Union farmers to make a reasonable living" and to "maintain rural areas and landscapes across the EU."[12] The result was that although the Canadian Wheat Board and the Crow Rate were spared in the Canada-U.S. free trade agreement, they ultimately could not survive the broader forces of trade liberalization that were playing out.

But the end of the Wheat Board, and of the key role it played in navigating the grain handling system for farmers, quickly brought a downside into focus. The exhilaration of "marketing freedom"—a buzzword for the Harper government and the Farmers for Justice movement—came with consequences. The 2013 harvest was a good one that, on the open market, was potentially worth between $6 billion and $9 billion. Yet, according to a special report in the *Globe and Mail*'s *Report on Business* magazine, "when it came to buying the wheat and delivering it overseas, the privatized marketing chain seemed paralyzed with incompetence." The article continued,

Overloaded elevators stopped taking delivery of wheat, and not just because of an overabundance of product—trains were unavailable. Flotillas of empty ships sat at anchor in Vancouver's English Bay with their meters running, waiting for weeks for wheat that never arrived. Cash-strapped farmers were forced to buy storage bins at $60,000 apiece to keep their crop from rotting. When farmers found an elevator that would take their grain, some got half the money they received under the Canadian Wheat Board, and were charged twice as much to ship it. So were these the long-awaited rewards of marketing freedom? Weren't these the same problems that prompted the federal government to create the Wheat Board in the first place?[13]

If the demise of the Wheat Board was the final act in transforming the Saskatchewan farm economy, the penultimate act was the death of the Saskatchewan Wheat Pool. It was a slow decline that began in the 1970s, gradually gaining speed in the 1980s and 1990s when the cash-starved Pool aggressively diversified its business investments in an effort to create revenue. The Pool's financial desperation reached its nadir when in 1996 it abandoned its co-operative structure and converted member equity into tradable shares on the Toronto Stock Exchange.

For more than seventy-five years there was arguably no more important economic and political institution in the province. Established in 1923, the Saskatchewan Wheat Pool grew to be the largest agricultural co-operative in Canada. At its peak in the 1970s, it had more than seventy thousand members. As a farmer-owned co-operative, it reflected the founding values and principles that had shaped generations of Saskatchewan farmers—specifically, how to maximize the market power of individual farmers by creating their own grain company to compete against privately owned companies. The Pool reflected their frustrations with a grain handling and marketing system controlled by private grain companies. Pooling their grain into a system of co-operatively owned country elevators that belonged to farmers themselves gave them the scale necessary to have greater control of their product.

It is virtually impossible to overstate what for decades was the Pool's political and economic influence in Saskatchewan. In terms of politics, an intimate relationship existed between the Co-operative Commonwealth Federation,

forerunner to the NDP, and the Saskatchewan Wheat Pool. Both shared collectivist principles and the belief that co-operatives provide a counterbalance
to private enterprise. At the annual Sask Pool convention in Regina—a must-
attend event for politicians, whether provincial or federal—seven hundred
or more Sask Pool delegates, elected by members in sixteen districts across
the province, gathered to debate agriculture policy. Many referred to it as a
"Farmers' Parliament."[14] More broadly, the Pool was the iconic symbol of the
co-operative movement itself, which was seen as a commercial expression of
the agrarian ideology upon which the CCF-NDP was based.

The forces that led to the end of the Pool were the same ones that were
transforming the rural economy and the politics of Saskatchewan. The rise
of trade liberalization and more porous national borders as a means to create integrated markets and escape from years of slow growth created financial challenges for co-operative enterprises. For the Pool, the new business
environment was also complicated by its own history, reflected in the aging
demographics of its members. In the 1990s, the Pool was facing a rising cash
crunch as many of its members were nearing retirement and the point when
they would be cashing in their retained member equity. It went on an aggressive, and ultimately misguided, debt-fuelled business diversification strategy
that in the 1980s and 1990s included twenty-three acquisitions, from a retail
doughnut chain to pork producers to a port in Poland. In the 1990s alone, the
Pool purchased sixteen companies, some in Europe and Mexico. In fact, the
lack of management expertise and market knowledge of the new businesses
acquired, coupled with weak board oversight, proved to be a recipe for failure.

As Murray Fulton and K.A. Lang of the University of Saskatchewan
noted in a paper published in what was then the journal of the Canadian
Agricultural Economics Society, the aggressive diversification and conversion
to a publicly traded company to raise money for the expansion failed to avert
the financial decline. They explain,

The Pool believed that in order to maintain market share and remain
competitive it had to continue diversifying its activities and modernize

its grain handling facilities. Since nearly half of the Pool's members were set to retire in the 1990s—and in doing so they would take their retained member equity with them—it was believed that a capital shortage was likely. The Pool's solution was to convert the retained member equity to tradable Class B shares, thus providing a much more long-term source of equity. In spite of maintaining this equity, as well as adding more through a 1998 share offering, the Pool's debt-to-equity ratio rose significantly. In 1985 the Pool's debt-to-equity ratio was 0.61, by 1995 it had risen to 0.72, and in 2000 the ratio was unmanageably high at 1.38.[15]

Other competitive factors were also at play in the Saskatchewan Wheat Pool's financial reckoning. A key one was the decline in commitment by its members to continue to do business with the Pool, even though they were members. The deterioration of business patronage began in the late 1970s. Fulton and Lang note that by the late 1970s, the Pool had a 67 percent market share of grain handling in Saskatchewan. Although it retained a market share in the range of 60 percent during the 1980s and into the early 1990s, its net earnings began dropping in the 1980s before plummeting in the mid-1990s. Put together, those two factors—stable market share but declining net earnings—indicate a drop in member commitment.[16] It put the Pool on a path to its ultimate demise, first with a name change to Viterra as part of becoming a publicly traded company and then finally with its purchase by Swiss-based Glencore.

Beyond the numbers, however, something else was afoot. The weakening of the Pool's core grain handling business among its own members reflected the changing business attitudes of farmers themselves. Two key factors were at play, both generational. The aging Pool members, who were schooled and operated their farms in a much more stable and regulated environment, were being replaced by a younger generation. Rural Saskatchewan was going through a profound attitudinal change when it came to the business of agriculture.

The older demographic represented a cohort only one generation removed from the trauma of the 1930s in Saskatchewan, when years of crop failure and economic depression scarred the province's psychological makeup and shaped its political outlook. In some cases they were old enough to have experienced the 1930s as children but at a minimum had the farm ethic that emerged from those years taught to them by their parents. The message from one generation to the next was to remember history and learn from it. In other words, in a business as volatile as grain farming, the hard times can and will likely return at some point, and the only way to survive is collectively through farm organizations that protect the interests of the many.

By the 1980s and 1990s, as the world rapidly began to change economically and politically, the new generation of farmers taking over the land were further removed from those founding ethics of agrarian protest, economic struggle, and populism. They became farmers in a world of open borders, free trade, the rise of the Internet, and a digitally interconnected world. Access to global markets was literally at their fingertips, through computers. Compare that to the experience of their grandparents, many of whom laboured on small farms of perhaps 160 to 320 acres, often with no telephone and with roads that made travelling any distance a challenge. Quite naturally, these two completely different worlds produced far different perspectives, each valid to the circumstances of its time.

The rise of greater individualism is often linked to the economy—specifically, that economic growth engenders greater individualism. Studies done in the United States indicate that individualism grew during periods of prosperity and dropped in recessionary times. Recessions created uncertainty in people, which created greater interdependence and less individualism.[17] It is an idea that is consistent with the generational change in rural Saskatchewan. There can be little doubt that there is far more economic stability and a higher standard of living and quality of life among farmers today than was the case sixty or seventy years ago.

The statistic most cited when explaining how farming has changed in Saskatchewan over the decades is that of farm size. It is a proxy for many things—productivity, efficiency, capital investment, cash flow, net income, and debt. You can track the change in the farm economy by following the growth of individual units and the production that has resulted. The change has been dramatic, as small, individual farm units have evolved into larger agribusiness operations. In 1961 the average farm size in Saskatchewan was 686 acres;[18] by 2016 it was 1,784 acres. Recent years have also seen rapid growth of what some describe as "factory" farms, operations on a scale of a major corporate enterprise. In 2016 there were 4,495 farms in Saskatchewan of 3,520 acres or more, almost double the number in 2001 when there were 2,785 farms of the same size. Also reflecting the growth in farm size is capital investment. Larger farms require more investment in machinery, implements, land, buildings, and livestock to operate. In 1991, total capital investment was $25.8 billion. By 2016 it had grown to $94.5 billion.[19]

Many factors, both economic and social, contributed to the growth in farm size in Saskatchewan. As globalization took hold, international investment flows accelerated and investment in farmland was among the assets investors sought out. In their study of farm ownership in the province, André Magnan and Annette Aurélie Desmarais identify the growing investor focus on land: "In recent years, farmland has taken on another set of meanings and values— as an 'alternative asset class' that appeals to investors from outside the agricultural sector. Especially since the global food price spikes of 2007–8, financial investors have touted farmland and agriculture more broadly as a new investment frontier."[20] Coupled with international reality was the decision in Saskatchewan to lift what had long been restrictions on foreign ownership of farmland. The Lorne Calvert government in 2003 relaxed the restrictions on non-Saskatchewan residents owning land, which quickly led to a controversy when the Canada Pension Plan Investment Board paid $128 million to purchase land holdings from Regina-based Assiniboia Capital Corporation.[21]

The Saskatchewan Farm Ownership Act, later renamed *The Saskatchewan Farm Security Act* (SFSA), was established in 1974 by the Blakeney government. It prohibited non-Saskatchewan residents and corporations from owning farmland in the province. Amendments made twenty-nine years later permitted non-Saskatchewan residents and Canadian corporations to purchase farmland for agriculture purposes, aligning Saskatchewan with similar legislation in other provinces. In the wake of the changes, two important new sources of outside investment capital emerged: one was recent immigrants with the means to raise financing from abroad; and the other was institutional investors, often in the form of farmland investment funds that began appearing in Saskatchewan in 2006 following the SFSA amendment.[22]

This broadening of the market of potential buyers came at a time when the demographic of farmers was such that a growing number were approaching retirement age and wanted to realize their capital that was tied up in land. As a result, two factors—land as an attractive and available investment, and willing sellers—fuelled a stunning increase in farmland values. During the ten-year period from 2010 to 2019, farmland value increased by an average annual rate of 13.62 percent. To fully appreciate the rapid growth in farm wealth, consider the four-year period from 2011 to 2014. In 2011, values increased 22.9 percent; in 2012, by 19.7 percent; in 2013, land value went up 28.5 percent; and in 2014, the increase was 18.7 percent.[23] To put the growth in farmland value into a longer-term historical perspective, consider what has happened over the last fifty years. In 1970, the average value of Saskatchewan farmland was $60 an acre; in 2019 an acre of land sold, on average, for $1,489.[24]

Clearly, the farm sector in Saskatchewan is affluent. That is not to say there aren't some farmers, particularly those with more modest operations, who aren't under the same financial pressures as other small business owners. But collectively the growth of agribusiness has seen the creation of significant pools of wealth in the rural economy. With wealth and comfortable standards of living being key factors in the rise of individualism, it is not surprising that Saskatchewan has witnessed the demise of collective institutions such as the Canadian Wheat Board and the Saskatchewan Wheat Pool.

This rise of individualism is reflected in various sociological studies. One famous and popular study is Robert Putnam's 2000 book *Bowling Alone: The Collapse and Revival of American Community*. Putnam, a political scientist, argues that the rise of individualism and the loss of social capital—in other words, human networks that bond people to get through difficult circumstances together—has weakened society. He calls bonding social capital a "superglue" that keeps society together in a way that promotes community and common values. It was that very need in Saskatchewan, particularly on the farms of the province, to band together to overcome what were seen as odds stacked against individuals that forged the collectivist culture, both politically and economically. With greater wealth and economic security, those values have been significantly eroded.

The drop in union membership over the last thirty years is also evidence of the increasingly individualistic culture. The most significant decline in Canada took place in the 1980s and 1990s, when Statistics Canada began measuring unionization through its household surveys. Beginning in that period the rate of unionization has fallen from 37.6 percent in 1981 to 28.8 percent in 2014. Reflecting perhaps a change in generational attitudes and values, the drop in the unionization rate was greatest among young workers. The rate for men decreased for every age group, but was especially pronounced among those aged twenty-five to thirty-four and those aged thirty five to forty-four. The unionization rate for young women also decreased, but to a lesser extent, mainly because the declines in the 1980s and 1990s were offset by gains in the 2000s.[25]

When considering the culture of individualism, the other factor that cannot be ignored is the effect of the Internet-based communications revolution. On the one hand, while it has created a truly interconnected global community, it has also led to social fragmentation and even isolation. The rise of social media has had the effect of narrowing people's perspectives as they design a social media world that reflects their own interests and feeds their own biases. In a study of Twitter users, the Pew Research Group found that people prefer to congregate online around like-minded individuals. Instead of seeking out and exposing themselves to new beliefs, people choose to reinforce their existing political opinions through their actions online. As the authors of the report note, "If a topic is political, it is common to see two separate, polarized crowds take shape. They form two distinct discussion groups that mostly do not interact with each other. Frequently these are recognizably liberal or conservative groups."[26] To be specific, the social media ecosystem is built on delivering more of what the user already likes.

The result is a society far removed from the community-based town hall culture that was a cornerstone of the old rural Saskatchewan. That's not to suggest some of those values do not remain today. They do and are apparent in many rural communities. But the number of those communities has also dwindled as the profile of farming in Saskatchewan has steadily evolved from small family-farm units to ever-larger and fewer farms. Now when people talk about farming, they often use the language of agribusiness to reflect that reality. The process of consolidation inexorably continues, both economically and socially, changing the economics of agriculture, the social fabric, and the priorities of individuals themselves. But what has not changed is the political dominance of rural Saskatchewan. The party that dominates on the farms and small communities by reflecting the reality of modern agriculture in rural Saskatchewan will also dominate government.

CHAPTER 17

2016

Going Global

A PERSON HAS TO ADMIT THAT THE NAME IS IMPRESSIVE. "Global transportation hub" has a certain ring to it, one that conjures up images of something really remarkable in scale and reach. After all, we're talking global. When you think of the project in those terms, you can't help but think big. It was a perfect fit for the big-thinking government of Brad Wall during its first term in office. However, by 2016 the dream was rapidly evaporating.

The idea had been around for years, dating back to the early 1990s when rail line relocation in Regina was on the minds of civic and provincial officials. But its actual genesis as something more than an idea was in 2006, when the Calvert government entered into discussions with CP Rail to relocate its downtown Regina intermodal facility to an expanded footprint just west of the city, not far from the airport. With the CP mainline facility in a new location, it seemed only logical that there were the makings of something bigger—like a transportation hub anchored by CP that would attract other distribution and production facilities, maybe even manufacturers that needed access to get their products to market. Not just any market, mind you, but the global market. Together they would create what business consultants like to call "synergies," where two plus two equals five, where rail, road, and air transportation would converge to create a seamless interchange for the production and distribution of goods and commodities. All that was needed was the word "global" and, well, you get the picture.

It was hard to imagine a time or a government that was more susceptible or seducible to the idea than the first term of the Wall government. Those were heady days. The new government wanted to think big and help create a can-do attitude in Saskatchewan. The timing was perfect. The province's economy was booming, thanks to growth that began during the previous NDP government, which had cut corporate taxes and resources royalties all while investing in social programs and balancing the budget. It was a winning formula. The Calvert government had the benefit of taking over after a decade of the previous NDP government of Roy Romanow, which in 1991 inherited a crushing government operating deficit and debt that threatened the province with insolvency. In three years the Romanow government had eliminated the province's operating deficit and slowly began paying down debt and reinvesting in programs. By the time Calvert took over as premier in 2001 the signs of economic growth were evident and quickly gained momentum.

When the Wall government was elected in November 2007 the economy was already on an upswing. From 2003 to 2007, Saskatchewan's GDP in constant dollars grew from $63.5 billion to $69.8 billion. Over that five-year period the Saskatchewan economy grew at a robust average annual rate of 4.12 percent, well above the Canadian average growth rate of 2.6 percent during the same time period.[1]

In 2008, during the first full year in office for the Wall government, the Saskatchewan economy seemed powered by jet fuel. Consider that the value of mineral sales—that is, mainly oil and gas, potash, and uranium—grew from $14.4 billion in 2007 to $23.7 billion in 2008, a staggering 65 percent increase. Leading the way was potash, which saw the value of its sales more than double year over year, from $3 billion to $7.4 billion.[2] The price of potash rose from US$200 a tonne in June 2007 to just shy of $900 a tonne by the spring of 2009.[3]

It was all an intoxicating brew that made it seem the sky was the limit, so why not a global transportation hub? What could possibly go wrong? The fact that it was in the middle of the landlocked Prairies, far from large population centres and markets, next to an airport that did not have regularly scheduled international flights—these were the kind of negative thoughts that had held Saskatchewan back for generations. But this was a new government, with new ideas, new energy, and a new attitude that would overcome such nay-sayers. To get an idea just how seized the government was with the project, consider the remarks of Wayne Elhard, the Saskatchewan Party MLA who in 2009 was chairman of the project. "I think this project could be of equal importance to the future of Saskatchewan's transportation as the coming of the railway in the 1880s," Elhard said. And so began the creation of the Global Transportation Hub (GTH).

At the sod turning for the creation of the CP intermodal terminal, Wall could not resist casting the moment in truly global terms. Picking up on Elhard's railway analogy, the premier recalled how CP had laid its tracks across Saskatchewan in 1881. "In the first decade of CP's history (in Saskatchewan), those tracks brought 900,000 settlers from around the world to Saskatchewan and the prairies of Canada," Wall said. "The CPR brought the world to Saskatchewan, and now 130 years later, the CPR is bringing Saskatchewan to the world."[4]

The first step was to get CP Rail to move its intermodal facility from downtown Regina to the GTH. With CP on-site, the idea had a measure of transportation credibility. The next critical piece was to find an "anchor" tenant, an enterprise that would instantly bring scale and stature to the GTH. Something like Loblaw.

Negotiations began in 2008 to lure Loblaw, Canada's largest food and pharmacy retailer, to establish its western Canadian distribution centre at the GTH. As one of CP's largest customers, Loblaw was a natural fit. With more than 2,400 stores across Canada, creating a network where 90 percent of Canadians are within ten kilometres of one of its outlets, Loblaw was exactly the kind of candidate to give the GTH instant credibility.[5] And the company knew it, which gave it a big advantage when the negotiations began. With the prospect of a 500,000-square-foot, $200 million facility at the GTH, and suggestions it could grow to a million square feet, the Wall government's position was to "do whatever it takes" to get a deal with Loblaw. Details of the agreement between the province and GTH were never publicly revealed, but according to one source with knowledge of the arrangement, it was the sweetest of sweetheart deals. "The expression 'giving them the farm' doesn't come close to what Loblaw got," the source says.[6]

Infused with confidence, the government launched the effort to land another really big fish. A retailer with a global footprint. Something like Home Depot, the Atlanta-based home improvement mega-giant. Home Depot was looking to establish a western Canadian distribution centre and was in negotiations with Calgary when the Saskatchewan government came calling to tell it about the GTH. It quickly became apparent, though, that getting the company to invest in the project would be easier said than done. In the fall of 2010, a decision item went to cabinet recommending that the government provide incentives so that Home Depot would locate its western Canadian Rapid Deployment Centre at the GTH. To sweeten the pot, the government was offering a five-year corporate income tax holiday and a one-time PST rebate on capital inputs as part of construction costs that would total about $7.5 million. As well, the City of Regina was kicking in a five-year 100 percent municipal tax abatement that would be worth up to $20 million to the company. Home Depot had initially been considering eight possible western Canada locations but had narrowed the bidding war down to two—Regina and Calgary. The tax concessions had reduced the gap between Regina and Calgary by 70 percent.[7] It was looking good for Saskatchewan. But in early 2011, the Home Depot board in Atlanta chose Calgary for its western Canadian Rapid Deployment Centre that would cover up to 750,000 square feet.

The failed attempt to lure Home Depot to the GTH was a significant set-back but was not considered a fatal blow at the time. Beyond the tax concessions and other incentives to attract private companies, the government itself needed to step up and do its part in creating the critical mass necessary for the GTH to be viable. It directed SaskPower and the Saskatchewan Liquor and Gaming Authority to locate facilities at the hub.

But by 2016, the GTH had gone from being a symbol of the new Saskatchewan, one with global ambitions and perceptions of itself, to being tainted with the scent of scandal and corruption. It had become enmeshed in land dealings as part of the development of the Regina bypass, a transportation infrastructure project that included the GTH as a core element of its design rational. The bypass project itself became a financial nightmare. Its original cost estimate of $400 million ballooned to more than $2 billion, or more than double than the cost of $848 million for the Coquihalla Highway in British Columbia, which stretches 543 kilometres through mountains.[8] The Regina bypass is 44.3 kilometres across prairie land.[9] The GTH and bypass projects became intimately linked through land deals that had the taint of insider knowledge used to enrich individuals with political ties to the Saskatchewan Party.

The multi-year dogged and determined work of CBC investigative reporter Geoff Leo exposed many land transactions where individuals flipped land, in one case on the same day they bought it, to make millions of dollars. The series of transactions ended with the government paying far more than its own appraised values of the land. The sequence began in 2010 when the government bought land adjacent to the GTH from the religious order Sisters of Our Lady of the Missions for $9,000 an acre and, a year later, adjacent land from McNally Enterprises for $11,000 an acre.

In 2013, Robert Tappauf, an Alberta-based land developer who rented farmland to deputy premier Bill Boyd, bought other land from the Sisters and McNally, who sold it believing the government intended to expropriate the property. Tappauf paid $45,000 an acre for eighty-seven acres of McNally land and $55,000 an acre for eleven acres from the Sisters. On the same day he bought the land, he sold it to Regina developer Anthony Marquart, who paid $71,000 an acre for the McNally land and $84,000 an acre for the Sisters' land. The same-day transaction netted Tappauf $6 million. Then, in 2014, Marquart's company sold the same land to the GTH for $103,000 an acre, for a total of $21 million. The company made $5 million. The final chapter came in March 2014 when the GTH sold fifty-eight acres it had bought from Marquart to the Ministry of Highways for $50,000 an acre, or less than half the price it paid a year earlier. Independent and separate appraisals of the land had been done for the GTH and the highways ministry in the fall of 2013. The GTH was informed that the land's appraised value was between $51,000 and $65,000 an acre, while the appraisal received by Highways was between $30,000 and $35,000 an acre.[10]

Other issues dogged the GTH, including a venture by a Chinese investor to create an 80,000-square-foot commercial mall labelled a Global Trade and Exposition Centre (GTEC). It was a business strategy tied to the government's immigration policy. The business rationale was to attract immigrant investors from China who believed they would be fast-tracked to immigrant status if they invested in the mall. At one point, on a trade mission to China in 2016, Wall took part in a Saskatchewan event that included the businessman behind the GTEC and promoted the project. In 2019 the provincial government changed its immigration rules to exclude investments in the GTEC. In explaining its decision, the government said the Saskatchewan Immigrant Nominee Program had concluded that the GTEC business model carried too much risk for entrepreneurs.[11] Shortly thereafter, Brightenview Development International, the company that created the mall, refused to pay its rent to the GTH.[12]

The failure of the GTH as a government enterprise became official in 2019. Unable to sell it as a complete package, the government contracted a private real estate company in the hopes the facility and its seven hundred acres of land could be sold in fragments. The company would also manage the hub, even though it remained in public hands until it was privatized, piece by piece. Rather than have public officials in government continue to attempt to sell the land, Don Morgan, minister responsible for the GTH, said a national real estate company would have the expertise and "exposure to a greater number of potential purchasers." During the sell-off, Morgan said, the government would work to ensure that the existing tenants, specifically CP Rail and Loblaw, were happy.[13] It was quite a humbling comedown from ten years earlier when the GTH was being heralded as the biggest thing to hit Regina since the arrival of the railroad in the 1880s.

If the rise and rapid decline of the GTH for the Wall government was an embarrassment of unrealistic expectations, what was happening in the economy during roughly the same period only added to the pain. It had become exceedingly apparent that the government had failed to manage the province's fiscal situation in a manner that recognized and accounted for the boom-and-bust cycles inherent to the Saskatchewan economy. The verdict came in a string of deficit budgets and rising provincial debt.

Actually, the warning bell had sounded back in 2013 when then provincial auditor Bonnie Lysyk issued a special report entitled *The Need to Change: Modernizing Government Budgeting and Financial Reporting in Saskatchewan*. It resulted in an "adverse opinion" when reporting on the 2012–13 Saskatchewan public accounts, the first time in the province's history that the auditor rendered such a judgment.[14] The report was scathing. According to Lysyk, the government was "keeping two sets of books," which made it virtually impossible for the public to get a clear picture of the province's financial situation. By having a general revenue fund budget and also a summary budget, Lysyk said, the government was deceiving the public as to whether it had actually achieved balanced budgets as it claimed. The auditor said that in 2010, 2011, and 2012 the government actually recorded deficits when it claimed surpluses each year. "These deficits are inconsistent with the message that Saskatchewan had been 'balancing' its budget," Lysyk said.[15] In response, the government labelled the critique a debate between accountants and claimed it was following the accounting practice of previous governments. Two years later it consolidated its reporting into a summary budget only, as Lysyk had insisted.

But in 2016, without two sets of books, there could be no hiding the fiscal facts resulting from a decline in resource revenues, in particular, a collapse in oil prices that began in the second half of 2014. In June of that year the world price for oil was hovering around US$110 a barrel. Eighteen months later, in January 2016, it was US$18 a barrel.[16] A great deal has been written about the reasons for the oil price collapse, which still hadn't recovered six years later in 2020, when the price averaged US$28 and at one point the price for Western Canada Select plummeted to US$3.50 a barrel.[17] While there are varying perspectives, consensus forms around a couple of key factors: one related to the growth in global oil production, and the other the slow recovery from the 2008 global recession that included slowing growth in China.

Much of the glut of oil on the world market was a result of the shale, light oil revolution in the United States that occurred primarily in the first decade of the twenty-first century and continued into the early 2010s. The discovery of fracking—the injection of pressurized liquids into bedrock formations to release oil and gas—as a means to access otherwise inaccessible oil revolutionized production in the United States, and also Saskatchewan. One of the richest areas is the Bakken Formation in North Dakota, which extends into southeastern Saskatchewan. Oil production from the Bakken in the province increased from 278,540 barrels a year in 2004 to more than 4.9 million in 2007.[18] Ground zero of the explosive growth in shale oil production in the United States is the Permian Basin in Texas.[19] To put this phenomenon in perspective, between 2008 and 2016 shale oil production in the United States rose from virtually nothing to 4.25 million barrels a day, representing 48 percent of total U.S. production and 5 percent of global production. To appreciate the market impact, consider that it took seven years for shale oil production in the United States to approximately equal Canada's total oil production, which took seventy years to develop.[20]

While the shale oil boom was happening, the world also experienced the 2008 financial crisis and "Great Recession." This took a heavy toll on economic growth and included a decline in demand for oil at the same time that new oil was flowing into the market from various shale formations in the

United States and Saskatchewan. What made the situation more difficult was that economic growth in China was not returning to the double-digit growth levels of before 2008.

Between 2000 and 2014, China accounted for close to 70 percent of the increase in global oil consumption. According to market analysts, what were initially strong forecasts for continued Chinese growth were followed by repeated downward revisions, which contributed to the excess oil supply response and had the effect of keeping prices artificially high. When concerns about slowing economic growth in China became fact in an oversupplied market, prices began to spiral downward, with the Brent (world) oil price hitting a low of US$29 in January of 2016. Then, when there was a correction in the domestic Chinese stock market it touched off further concerns over the sustainability of future economic growth, adding greater downward pressure on the oil price.[21]

In its analysis, the *Economist* saw the shale oil boom as a primary reason for the price collapse that began in 2014. According to the article, titled "Sheikhs v shale,"

> The main culprits are the oilmen of North Dakota and Texas. Over the past four years [since 2010], as the price hovered around $110 a barrel, they have set about extracting oil from shale formations previously considered unviable. Their manic drilling—they have completed perhaps 20,000 new wells since 2010, more than ten times Saudi Arabia's tally—has boosted America's oil production by a third, to nearly 9m barrels a day (b/d). That is just 1m b/d short of Saudi Arabia's output. The contest between the shale men and the sheikhs has tipped the world from a shortage of oil to a surplus.[22]

To appreciate just how market distorting an oil price in excess of $100 a barrel can be, consider what it means to production. According to Rystad Energy, a Norway-based independent energy research company, when the price reaches $100 a barrel, 90 percent of the world's oil can be produced with a return on capital of at least 10 percent. In terms of Canadian heavy oil production, which includes non-Bakken production in west central Saskatchewan, only 42 percent of reserves can be produced profitably when the Brent price is US$60. Of Canada's total reserves, less than 20 percent is extractable at a break-even price of US$40 per barrel.[23]

Another factor had been the belief that a natural resource "super cycle" had taken hold as part of globalization. It was fuelled by the stunning growth and modernization of China and other emerging nations, particularly India, and those in Southeast Asia where there was a rapidly growing middle class. The result was a conviction that demand for energy and other resources, including potash fertilizer to meet growing demand for food, would be so great that the oil prices in excess of US$100 would be new normal, as would a return to potash prices near $1,000 a tonne.

Beyond oil and gas, which normally represents Saskatchewan's largest single source of revenue from natural resources, the situation in terms of potash was no better. Long gone were the days of $1,000 a tonne for potash in 2008, with prices in 2015 hovering around $300. In 2013 the global potash market was upended by the announcement that Russia-based Uralkali, the largest producer of potash, was ending production restrictions and suspending a venture with a Belarusian mine. The breakup left Canpotex as the largest potash cartel, but more importantly it signalled that the $20 billion global potash market was breaking free of a duopoly that sought to keep prices high, opening the door to a freely traded potash market.

Market analysts immediately signalled the significance of the Uralkali move. "This effectively brings about a transformation of the entire potash industry, shifting it away from what has been a de facto duopoly," Matthew Korn, an analyst at Barclays Plc in New York, said in a note. "This is one of the few occasions of a market truly undergoing a sudden game-changing event, with impacts that cannot be overstated."[24] Paul Ferley, the assistant chief economist at the Royal Bank, put it in perspective for Saskatchewan: "If we assume that 90 per cent of those exports come from Saskatchewan, it would account for a more significant 17 per cent of that province's overall nominal merchandise exports."[25] In terms of the market effect, Dmitry Ryzhkov, an equity sales trader at Renaissance Capital, pointed out that "it is as if Saudi Arabia decided to leave OPEC—oil prices would fall immediately."[26] And fall they did. In 2009 the potash price was just shy of US$900 a tonne; by 2016 it was less than $300 a tonne.[27]

The impact on Saskatchewan became apparent in the wake of the 2015–16 provincial budget. When it was introduced, the budget seemed to suggest that the government believed it could somehow absorb the revenue hit from the oil price collapse and falling potash prices. It projected an operating surplus of $107 million—and it turned out to be a deficit of $675 million. But it was a budget that also recognized the economic slowdown under way and proposed capital spending of $5.8 billion over four years.

The full impact of the oil and potash price decline became most evident in the subsequent 2016–17 budget, delivered by Kevin Doherty, who took over as finance minister from Ken Krawetz, who had resigned from cabinet and as an MLA. In effect, when he was named finance minister Doherty was handed a poisoned chalice that effectively ended his leadership aspirations. The decision was made to not deliver a budget until after the April 2016 election, which Wall and the Saskatchewan Party won in another landslide, taking more than 62 percent of the popular vote and winning fifty-one seats in the sixty-one-seat legislature. Among the defeated NDP candidates was party leader Cam Broten, which plunged the New Democrats into yet another leadership cycle.

The reason the government didn't bring down a budget in the usual time period before the end of the fiscal year on March 31, which would have been in advance of the election, was obvious. The political implications of an election in the wake of what was to come in the budget could have been highly problematic. With re-election and another huge majority under his belt, Wall made the decision to leave politics—but not before the government had done a reset of the fiscal situation. Rather than turn a budget with a huge deficit and no plan to reach a balance over to his successor, Wall wanted the next budget to address the province's dire fiscal situation and map a pathway to return to a balanced budget. Such was Doherty's task. It wasn't going to be a pleasant process; in fact, it was a daunting challenge. The 2015–16 budget had projected a surplus of

$107 million[28]—which turned out to be a fantasy, with the surplus becoming a deficit of $675 million. At least, that was until a full accounting was done by the auditor in the subsequent 2015–16 public accounts. At year end the public accounts identified an actual deficit of $1.5 billion, representing a $921 million deterioration from the budget, because of a decline in revenue of $792 million and an expense increase of $137 million from the original budget.[29]

When Doherty delivered the budget in June 2016, it was built around the narrative of "Keeping Saskatchewan Strong."[30] There had been many months of preconditioning the public environment given what had happened and what was to come. The collapse of oil prices in particular, and its impact on provincial revenues, was well known. In 2015 the Saskatchewan economy had been in recession, contracting by 2.8 percent. The consensus of private sector forecasts was that the economy would grow marginally in 2016, by a meagre 0.7 percent.[31]

The revenue challenge from the fall in resource prices was clear. The 2016–17 budget forecasted a drop of $968 million in resource revenues and said the government had opted for a "manageable deficit" rather than engage in across-the-board cuts in spending. The projected deficit was $434 million. It turned out to be $1.2 billion.[32] Given the scale of the fiscal challenge, it was a far less severe approach than what fiscal conservatives might have demanded. The government increased health spending by $81 million, or 1.5 percent, to a record $5.6 billion, and education funding was up marginally to $3.7 billion.[33] There were no ideologically driven initiatives like privatization to raise money or draconian cuts to avoid a deficit. Given the economic reality, the government steered a moderate course, using the levers of public spending—deficit financing and capital investment—to support the economy. In that context, it was consistent with Wall's approach of avoiding measures that would provide a significant enough policy cleavage where the NDP could clearly differentiate itself and thus re-establish its political identity.

During his eleven years in office as premier, Wall ensured that the Saskatchewan Party government did not stray far from the pragmatic centre of Saskatchewan politics. The clearest evidence was in government spending during the Wall years: it grew from $9.3 billion in 2007–08 to $14.8 billion in

2017–18, representing a 59 percent increase. As a percentage of the economy, government grew from 14 percent in 2007 to 18.3 percent in 2018.[34] Wall's was a fiscal record that one would hardly expect from a party that believes in a smaller role for government. Over the eleven years and ten budgets during his time as premier, the province ran six deficits, including in his last three budgets that had accumulated deficits of more than $3 billion. Program expenses per capita grew from just over $9,000 to almost $12,000. As well, the net provincial debt grew from $5.9 billion to $11.3 billion.[35]

The political irony to it all is that the growth in government spending greatly limited the NDP's critique of government. There were no significant ideological ventures during the Wall government that would open the centre of the political spectrum to the NDP. When he acted on significant issues, Wall's decisions were, it could be credibly argued, driven by pragmatism rather than ideology. He consistently used the language of "Saskatchewan values" as the guiding principles of budget decisions. As a result, the only vulnerability the Wall government exposed itself to was its fiscal record of deficit budgets and rising provincial debt. The opportunity to focus its critique of the Wall government on its fiscal mismanagement was not one the NDP Opposition readily seized upon with any vigour or consistency. In one sense it was understandable, as the party wanted to represent a broader agenda than fiscal conservatism. Besides, the last time the NDP had staked its credibility on an agenda of addressing fiscal issues such as balancing the budget was in the early 1990s, and it led to difficult decisions that deeply wounded the party, especially in rural Saskatchewan.

The reality proved to be that by occupying a wide swath of the centre in Saskatchewan politics, where the significant majority of the public see themselves, Wall proved to be untouchable politically. When you add his populist image as a pragmatist, coupled with undeniable communication skills, it is clear that Wall, more than anyone, realigned Saskatchewan politics in the first two decades of the twenty-first century.

CHAPTER 18

2016

Trudeau 2.0

I T DIDN'T EXACTLY HAVE THE LUXURIOUS AND CARNAL ATMO-
sphere of the Bellagio Resort and Casino in Las Vegas. You might say it
was a more prosaic ambience, a place where you would expect to find meetings of the local Rotary Club, or attendees of a regional convention of realtors.
But in some ways, it was totally appropriate as the site of a community event
raising funds for cancer research. The Fight for a Cure, as it was called, was
staged at the Hampton Inn and Convention Centre in east Ottawa, across
the parking lot it shared with the local minor league professional baseball
team's stadium.

As unlikely and absurd as it might seem, what took place in an amateur
boxing ring that March night in 2012 would fundamentally change the tra-
jectory of Canadian politics. The three-round bout was between Patrick
Brazeau, a lean and athletic former National Chief of the Congress of
Aboriginal Peoples who, at the tender age of thirty-four, was appointed to the
Senate by Prime Minister Stephen Harper. His opponent was Justin Trudeau,

a backbench Liberal Opposition MP elected in 2008. For most Canadians at the time, Trudeau was mostly known as the well-to-do son of the late former prime minister Pierre Trudeau.

There was little in the young Trudeau's history, beyond his lineage, that drew much attention to his stature as a member of Parliament. At age forty, beyond being an MP he did not have a particularly distinguished career before politics. He earned a Bachelor of Arts degree at McGill University and later a Bachelor of Education at the University of British Columbia. Prior to being elected in a Montreal riding, he had spent several years as a high school drama teacher at a private academy in Vancouver and, before that, was briefly a snowboarding instructor and a doorman at a nightclub in the ski resort town of Whistler, British Columbia.

But things were beginning to stir in the Liberal Party. With Bob Rae as acting leader following the Liberals' electoral downward spiral and the resignation of Michael Ignatieff in 2011, a leadership convention was on the horizon. Long considered Canada's natural governing party, the Liberals were chafing over being relegated to the irrelevance of third-party status in the House of Commons. The name Trudeau was enough to attract the attention of some. But Justin Trudeau was mostly considered to be young and inexperienced. Besides, many wondered if he had the mettle of his father, who was known to have a powerful and intimidating intellect and a spine of steel to go with it. Critics saw Justin as having neither. With his long hair and sometimes goatee, he was often dismissed as something of a "pretty boy." It was not as if Trudeau himself wasn't trying to cultivate that youthful "hip" image. If he wasn't posing on the lawn in front of the Centre Block in Ottawa during noon-hour outdoor yoga sessions with hundreds of people, mostly women, he was posing for selfies with fans at Liberal events around the country.

If ever there was a set-up for Trudeau to be brought down a notch or two, or more, this boxing match was it. Forget about raising money for cancer research; for many Conservatives this was about laying some "whup-ass" on Trudeau. He was stepping into the ring to face a younger Brazeau, who not only came from a far less privileged background but had a second-degree black belt in karate. For the hardcore Conservative partisans, who harboured an intense dislike bordering on hatred for anyone named Trudeau, this was going to be a night to remember—a little bit of payback to the old man, by watching his son get thrashed. There was a carnival atmosphere in the room, bordering on electric, when the two fighters entered the ring. The now defunct right-wing Sun News TV network was all over the event, promoting it in advance and televising the fight live. "This is a one-round fight," Ezra Levant breathlessly predicted in the opening seconds as Brazeau went on the attack.

Curiously, the fight itself was Trudeau's idea. He had issued a challenge to any Conservative to step into the ring for a match as part of the charity night to raise money for cancer research. Brazeau took up the offer. There was also the added incentive that the loser would have his hair shorn off by the winner two days after the bout. With Trudeau's tresses a significant part of his image, it added to the anticipation. Trudeau himself later admitted that the pre-fight speculation was not so much around who would win but rather, "How many seconds will it take for Trudeau to land face down on the canvas?"[1]

For Trudeau, expectations could not have been lower, which is exactly what politicians need and should want. Exceeding expectations is how political careers can take flight, and Trudeau's leadership potential was launched in the ring. After an initial flurry of roundhouse rights and lefts by Brazeau in the early seconds of the first round that Trudeau mostly blocked or avoided, the tide gradually turned. Trudeau began pummelling Brazeau until the fight was stopped by the referee in the third round, with a bloodied Brazeau gasping for air and unable to defend himself against Trudeau's punches. Pretty boy no more, at that moment Trudeau as the next leader of the federal Liberal Party became inevitable.

Two years later at the leadership convention, Trudeau coasted to an easy victory with more than 80 percent of the vote on the first ballot in a six-person race. Days before the vote, the result was so obvious that the talk was about how what was about to happen did happen, even though it hadn't yet. "Trudeau and his team have spent the last eight months systematically remaking his image, from privileged gadfly and charity boxer to national leader-in-waiting," wrote Michael Den Tandt in the *Ottawa Citizen*.[2]

It was difficult to imagine a better scenario for a new leader. There was no need to unite the party behind the leader after a close and divisive race. None of the common warring camps aligned with different leadership hopefuls. It was Trudeau's party to shape as he saw fit—which is what he did, in his own image and likeness.

For millions of Canadians old enough to remember Pierre Trudeau and the Trudeaumania that swept the Liberals into a majority government in 1968, it was impossible not to wonder if the arrival of Trudeau 2.0 on the national stage was signalling a similarly seismic political shift. With the Harper government closing in on a decade in power, the inevitable mood for change was settling into the public consciousness. As a fresh face, professing an upbeat and positive message of "sunny ways" and with no record as baggage to weigh him down, Justin Trudeau was positioned to be the agent for change. Maybe former Progressive Conservative PM Brian Mulroney expressed it best: "I've known Justin since he was a child. He's young, articulate, attractive—a flawlessly bilingual young man. What's not to like with this picture? Anybody who treats Justin Trudeau with scorn or derision or underestimates him, does so at his own peril."[3]

What Trudeau accomplished as leader in the run-up to the 2015 election, and as prime minister, was to perfect image politics. He made himself a celebrity by using social and traditional media to portray himself as modern, cosmopolitan, someone to lead a generational change in federal politics. He became the centre of attention at political events, with people scrambling to take a selfie with him. A perfect example came when Trudeau, in his early months as prime minister, was to do an "impromptu" visit to the University of Regina. The plan had been for the visit to be kept low key. It would be a typical photo-op. Trudeau would arrive mid-morning and do a walkabout in the food court area of the university, shaking hands and chatting with students. But the night before, word got out on social media that Trudeau would be on campus the next morning. He was greeted by a huge mob of students. It took more than an hour to work his way through the throng, a walk that under normal circumstances would take two to three minutes. It was bedlam, with students scrambling to shake his hand and get a picture or selfie with him. It was celebrity politics on full display.[4]

This upbeat, accessible Trudeau image contrasted sharply with that of the Harper Conservatives, who were seen as tightly scripted, controlled, and overly negative. Much of their election messaging focused on Trudeau, arguing he was "just not ready," with Harper saying that "a federal election is not a popularity contest."[5] It was an odd comment, when politics, especially in an election, is very much about popularity.

Trudeau's arrival as prime minister with a majority government in November 2015 was a stunning electoral feat. The Liberals went from 36 seats to 184, a 148-seat increase, while the Harper Conservatives' share of Parliament dwindled by 60 seats and the Opposition New Democrats dropped 51 seats. But if you looked beyond the headline numbers, it was not all sweetness and light. The Trudeau victory carried with it reminders of the historic cleavages between regions in Canada. In some ways, given the scale of the Liberal electoral dominance in central and Atlantic Canada, the east-west divisions that had shaped politics in Canada for multiple generations were as evident as ever. In Saskatchewan, which was dominated by the Conservatives, the only Liberal elected was Ralph Goodale in Regina. In Alberta, other than two Liberal seats in each of Calgary and Edmonton, the rest of the province went Conservative. Outside of Winnipeg and a northern riding, Manitoba elected Conservatives.

Moreover, Trudeau was taking over at a time when storm clouds were forming. The challenge was clearly set in an *Economist* article on the election entitled "Ready or not...Justin Trudeau has proved he can campaign, but can he govern?" "It will take something more than a cheerful disposition to cope with Canada's problems," this article notes. "The commodities boom, which had shielded Canada from the worst effects of the global financial crisis, has ended, revealing economic malaise. GDP and productivity have been growing at a plodding pace, firms do not innovate enough and infrastructure is overburdened. Consumer debt and house prices are frighteningly high. Business investment and exports have yet to take over from indebted consumers as motors of economic growth."[6]

Nowhere was the challenge more apparent than in the West, particularly Alberta and Saskatchewan. Both provinces' economies were suffering the effects of a downturn in natural resources prices, with Alberta bearing the brunt of a collapse in oil prices that had begun two years earlier. With traditionally low unemployment rates relative to the national average, Alberta and Canada both shared the same unemployment rate of 7 percent in November 2015 when Trudeau took power.[7] Alberta's unemployment numbers had been climbing steadily as a result of the collapse in oil prices, with the rate up 3 percentage points from two years earlier. By June 2020, the Alberta unemployment rate had reached 15.5 percent, owing to both a much weaker oil and gas sector and the impact of COVID-19.[8] Although Saskatchewan benefits from a more diversified natural resource base, it too had been staggered by the effects of the global downturn in oil prices. Compared with Alberta, however, the unemployment situation in Saskatchewan was less grim. In October 2015, the province had an unemployment rate of 5.8 percent and, while it slowly creeped up, it was still only 6.2 percent in February 2020, in the weeks before COVID-19 hit the economy.[9]

With Trudeau's majority based primarily in Ontario, Quebec, Atlantic Canada, and the lower mainland of British Columbia, the immediate question in Saskatchewan and Alberta was, how would the new government deal with the issues faced by the two Prairie provinces?

In the background of all of this was the Trudeau legacy in the West, particularly Saskatchewan and Alberta, that reached back to the 1970s and 1980s. The battles over ownership and control of natural resources, primarily oil and gas, had left deep psychological and political scars that remained a generation later. The legal and constitutional clashes that pitted Saskatchewan and Alberta against the first Trudeau government had deepened antipathy to Ottawa in both provinces. What crystallized and hardened that sentiment was that it was not seen as a partisan fight. How could it be? The Progressive

Conservative government of Peter Lougheed in Alberta and NDP premier Allan Blakeney in Saskatchewan were allied in the same struggle against Ottawa. The tools they used to defend their provincial interests against intrusions by the Trudeau government may have differed, but both provinces were engaged in the same defence of provincial control over natural resources. It was a matter of principle, not politics. It was Pierre Trudeau who was labelled as the interloper. So, when Justin Trudeau took power in 2015—largely on a mandate that excluded the Prairie provinces—the shadow of his father loomed large over the region.

One of the first things Trudeau did upon taking office was to go to the United Nations Conference of the Parties on climate change in Paris. The new prime minister committed his government to establishing a national plan to reduce greenhouse gas (GHG) emissions as part of Canada's international commitment to address climate change. Months later, answering questions at a town hall in Calgary, Trudeau offered his opinion on the future of Alberta's oil sands. "You can't make a choice between what's good for the environment and what's good for the economy," he said. "We can't shut down the oilsands tomorrow. We need to phase them out. We need to manage the transition off of our dependence on fossil fuels. That is going to take time. And in the meantime, we have to manage that transition."[10] For comparison purposes, Alberta's energy sector is far more important to Canada's economy than Ontario's auto industry. In 2018, the energy sector in Alberta represented $76 billion of Canada's GDP, while the auto sector totalled $16 billion.[11]

Many saw Trudeau's comment as a direct attack on the province. It triggered an immediate response from Jason Kenney, who was in the midst of a campaign to become leader of the provincial Progressive Conservative Party and couldn't resist reminding people of a controversy around a vacation Trudeau had taken to the private Caribbean island home of the Aga Khan. "If we end dependence on fossil fuels," Kenney asked, "how will Justin Trudeau fly to private Caribbean islands? Planes and helicopters fuelled by pixie dust?" NDP premier Rachel Notley tried gamely to be less negative, while still defending the fossil fuel industry: "At the end of the day, this is what I know to be true: the world market for oil is not going anywhere soon. So, the job of Albertans, and the job of Canadians, is to make sure that that world market looks to the oilsands, as they should, as the first choice for where they get that product from."[12]

The Trudeau government's commitment to a national climate change strategy quickly took centre stage in its policy agenda, along with reconciliation with Indigenous Peoples in Canada. A key part of the Liberals' election platform was a focus on climate change, signalling a partnership with the provinces. "We will provide national leadership and join with the provinces and territories to take action on climate change, put a price on carbon, and reduce carbon pollution....Together, we will attend the Paris climate conference, and within 90 days formally meet to establish a pan Canadian framework for combatting climate change," the Liberal platform stated.[13]

Four months into office, the prime minister met with the premiers to establish the groundwork for a national climate change strategy. The result was the Vancouver Declaration, which included agreement on multiple commitments, most significantly those related to meeting Canada's pledge at the Paris conference to reduce its GHG emissions by 2030 to 30 percent less than 2005 levels with measures that would include "specific provincial and territorial targets and objectives." More specifically, the declaration stated that the transition to a low carbon economy would be achieved by adopting "carbon pricing mechanisms, adapted to each province's and territory's specific circumstances."[14]

What appeared to be the framework for a national consensus on climate change quickly became a struggle drawn on regional lines where Saskatchewan and Alberta felt their economies were being singled out. It had echoes of the 1970s and early 1980s.

Although this was not an attempt by Ottawa to exercise greater control over natural resources by intervening to gain a greater share of revenues, as was the case in the 1970s and '80s, it had even more ominous implications. The federal government's energy and environment policies were seen by many in Saskatchewan and Alberta as Trudeau presiding over the demise of the oil and gas industry itself as part of its climate change agenda. Another aspect reminiscent of the decades-earlier Alberta/Saskatchewan-versus-Ottawa battles that added credibility to the provinces' position was the strange bedfellows that it created. Ironically, in political terms, roles were reversed. In the first three years of the Trudeau 2.0 era, it was NDP Premier Notley in Alberta and Saskatchewan Party premier Brad Wall in Saskatchewan who were often aligned on energy issues against Ottawa. Notley became a staunch supporter of the energy sector, in particular the need for a pipeline to the West Coast to get oil sands bitumen to tidewater, which angered many climate activists. Notley was less strident and accepted the notion of a carbon price "in principle" as a way to ensure all provinces make the same effort and none is penalized economically. But Notley tied her support for a carbon price to getting the proposed Trans Mountain Pipeline built. Some were to characterize Notley's support for a carbon price as Alberta's "absolution" necessary to get the Trudeau government to support construction of the pipeline. Notley declared, "We can't be talking about the sort of (carbon) prices that got rolled out today until we get a commitment from this federal government that they're going to move on this fundamentally important economic piece that Albertans need....We need Canada to have our backs. And we need to get a pipeline."[15]

Notley was also not about to back down in her defence of the oil and gas sector in Alberta from what were seen as efforts by Ottawa through its climate change policies to undermine the sector. She wanted a new refinery built and was delaying a pledge to impose an emissions cap on the oil sands. As for the idea of other industries replacing the oil sector in Alberta, she saw it as a fantasy. "Back home we ride horses, not unicorns," Notley told an Ottawa audience.[16]

Wall shared the same view on the need for a pipeline but drew a much harder stance against the proposed national carbon price—or "carbon tax," as it was termed by opponents—contained in the Trudeau government's Pan-Canadian Framework on Clean Growth and Climate Change. When Trudeau announced plans for the national carbon price, or "tax," in the fall of 2016 it immediately became a significant political weapon for Wall and the Saskatchewan Party. The premier characterized it as a "betrayal," arguing that the imposition of a carbon tax would have disastrous effects on Saskatchewan's trade-exposed economy. The announcement of a carbon price certainly should not have come as a surprise. The idea of a national carbon price had been part of the agreement among the prime minister and premiers when they issued the Vancouver Declaration almost seven months earlier. If there was any treachery by the Trudeau government in announcing a price on carbon, it was in the interpretation of the declaration's commitments that indicated a carbon price would be adapted to each province's and territory's "specific circumstances."

Aside from being an issue that clearly and starkly pitted Wall against Trudeau, it also became a wedge issue in Saskatchewan politics. Wall took a hardline position against Ottawa's "carbon tax" in defence of the oil and gas sector, putting the NDP Opposition in a compromised position for two reasons. First, the federal NDP strongly supported the carbon tax and climate change policies, if not more aggressively than the position taken by the Trudeau government. Second, the position of Saskatchewan NDP leader Ryan Meili was at best less than categorical in defending Saskatchewan's oil and gas sector, putting the NDP at odds with many in Saskatchewan's private sector labour movement. For example, two major industrial employers in Regina are intimately linked to the oil and gas sector: Evraz Steel, which produces pipe for oil and gas pipeline projects; and the Co-op Refinery Complex, including the NewGrade Energy upgrader, which processes Saskatchewan heavy crude oil. Together, the two employ about 2,100 people.

Wall's position was easy to understand and to communicate. In terms of politics and public opinion it was effective at several levels. First, simply the term "carbon tax" had negative connotations for most people. Few welcome new taxes and this one applied to all CO_2-emitting fossil fuels, at both the production and consumption levels, so it obviously had wide application. No one would escape the impact of the tax. Second, it was designed specifically to reduce demand for oil and gas, a sector in Saskatchewan that had grown significantly in economic importance beginning in the early 2000s. It was driven by the development of shale oil production in the Bakken Formation, which includes a large swath of southeastern Saskatchewan. The Saskatchewan Bakken had grown to become one of Canada's most significant light oil plays. To put that in context, before 2005 there were fewer than 35 wells, producing 1,258 barrels of Bakken oil a day.[17] By 2012, 2,357 wells had been drilled and daily production had jumped to more than 71,000 barrels a day.[18] Third, virtually all oil produced in Saskatchewan is exported. The application of a price on carbon would competitively disadvantage Saskatchewan oil in the U.S. market, where it competes with the massive increase in shale oil production in that country, a nation without a carbon tax. Finally, the higher cost of fuel resulting from the carbon tax would disproportionately and negatively harm Saskatchewan's agriculture sector, where fuel represents a huge input cost to operations.

The federal government's response to Saskatchewan's critique of the carbon price was that the cost to individuals would be rebated to all households. As for farmers, the carbon tax paid in the purchase of fuel, whether gas or diesel, used in farm operations would also be rebated annually. The response of the farm sector was that Ottawa was not telling the whole story. The Agricultural Producers Association of Saskatchewan (APAS) noted that "farmers will still face significant cost increases on other fuel sources, like natural gas and electricity, and indirect costs like inputs and transportation." It noted that the cost of propane for grain dryers and heating fuel, electricity generation and natural gas, which are all essential to farming, would rise.[19] APAS found that, based on the initial price of $20 a tonne, the carbon tax would cost an average Saskatchewan grain farm $2 an acre in direct and indirect costs in 2019, rising to $4 per acre by 2022.[20] Of course, that amount escalates with annual increases in the carbon price, which the government announced would go up by $10 a tonne per year until 2023 and then increase by $15 a tonne annually until it reached $170 a tonne by 2030.[21]

When considered in full context, the carbon price—or tax, depending on how one wants to label it—was a defining issue that, in the hands of Wall, was a powerful weapon. It connected directly to his key political base in rural Saskatchewan. Specifically, the farm community saw it as a federal tax that unfairly affected them and singled out agriculture because of the high energy input costs that go into production. Unlike other industries, farmers are price takers and cannot pass along additional costs they face in the price for their commodity. As well, the negative impact on the oil and gas sector was self-evident and was coming at a time when the industry was trying to cope with a collapse in oil prices that had begun in 2014, which was slowly squeezing jobs out of the sector. By 2020, the number employed in oil and gas, mining, forestry, and fishing in Saskatchewan had dropped to 16,400 from 25,700 in 2015.[22]

With that as an economic backdrop, Wall could not resist putting the objective of the carbon price, as a key piece of the Trudeau government's arsenal in meeting Canada's 2030 commitment, into a global context. In an op-ed, the Saskatchewan premier wrote, "In Canada, the discussion about what we can realistically do to help the global challenges has been monopolized by a domestic carbon tax. And those who dare dissent are accused of all manner of heresy. But even if Canada were to achieve Paris targets, the resulting global emissions reductions would be an entirely irrelevant 0.51 per cent or 30 per cent of our current 1.7-per-cent share of global emissions."[23] The subtext was obvious. The climate change challenge is self-evidently a test of global will to act collectively. Whether Canada does or does not meet its GHG reduction targets will have little measurable impact on global emissions. The implicit message is that what Canada does is really of little consequence—an implication that leads to the question of whether the burden imposed on the province is justifiable, either economically or morally.

For Wall, the key political approach was to frame the issue as unfair treatment of the province and the region by the Trudeau government. In doing so, he was tapping into the populist vein of western alienation whose deep roots reached back many decades. Whether focused against a federal government or other powerful external economic and political forces, the key was to rally the population against those who were wielding power against the province's interests. In so doing, Wall helped shape Saskatchewan politics by consolidating opinion in a manner that reflected the province's history.

With history as a guide, the fact that the federal government was led by a prime minister with the name Trudeau only made it easier to once again stir the emotions of Saskatchewan as a victim.

CHAPTER 19

2018

The Project

THE BREAKFAST MEETING WOULD START OUT AT THE
swanky Calgary Golf and Country Club. At least, that was the plan.
It ended up at a nearby Phil's Pancake House. The change in venue
came when the group arrived and were about to sit down and get their discussion started, and they were politely told they would have to leave. It was
a matter of the dress code. No blue jeans were allowed at the country club,
which, in a city like Calgary, is like saying to people in Ottawa you can't wear
a suit and tie.

As it turned out, it was Brad Wall who didn't know better. He had shown
up in jeans, cowboy boots, and a sports jacket, figuring the sports jacket
would make him acceptable for a private venue. But rules are rules. So, the
group packed up and moved to Phil's a few blocks away, a place where blue
jeans are not only accepted but the preferred dress of the regular clientele. In
retrospect, given the subject of the discussion, ending up at Phil's seems somehow more appropriate.

The purpose of the meeting was two twofold: to have a free-flowing discussion about the growing sentiment of western alienation in Saskatchewan and Alberta, and to introduce Wall to a few of the more influential businesspeople in the city. It was only weeks after Wall had stepped down as premier of Saskatchewan and been replaced by Scott Moe. So, in a sense, it was Wall's coming out after his career in politics.

During his time in office, Wall established himself as a leading voice on the national stage for western concerns, particularly those related to the natural resource sector. A strong proponent of the oil and gas sector, he argued for increased pipeline capacity, opposed the federal government's imposition of a tax on carbon, and was generally seen as strong defender of western interests. While Alberta cycled through several premiers—Ed Stelmach, Alison Redford, Jim Prentice, Rachel Notley—Wall presided over Saskatchewan; he became a consistent voice for the prairie West as the others came and went. In the process he was seen to be building what looked like a political dynasty, on populist, pragmatic, centre-right, mostly free enterprise principles. He consistently ranked as the most popular premier in the country.

Wall's popularity and style got noticed in Calgary and Alberta business circles. In fact, Wall's annual fundraising dinner for the Saskatchewan Party became the biggest such political fundraiser in the country, regularly attracting more than two thousand people. It was an event that drew hundreds from Alberta who saw Wall as a voice not only for Saskatchewan but for the region. They gladly shelled out to help fill the Saskatchewan Party election war chest.

The Calgary meeting that ended up at the pancake house was a follow-up to an earlier meeting that occurred shortly before Christmas in Wall's office at the Saskatchewan Legislature. He had met with Dallas Howe and Don Chynoweth, two Calgary "movers and shakers," who had flown in to meet with the premier. Like many such influential business people in Calgary, the pair were originally from Saskatchewan and maintained close ties with the province, including as members of the Potash Corporation's board of directors.

With Wall to step down as premier in late January 2018, Howe and Chynoweth came calling to ask that he keep his post-politics options open.

They didn't want him to make any early commitments that might limit his opportunities. They had nothing firm or specific to suggest, other than the idea that they believed western Canada needed a voice. Wall listened, and he told the pair that to avoid any accusations of impropriety as premier, or conflicts of interest that could damage his reputation, he did not want to talk about what he would do or make any such decisions until after he left politics.

The Calgary breakfast in February, then, was the post-politics follow-up discussion. The Saskatchewan influence at the table was significant. Aside from Howe and Chynoweth, the small group that gathered to meet with Wall also included Kelly Ogle, president of the Canadian Global Affairs Institute who, like Howe and Chynoweth, was originally from Saskatchewan. Although he was not at the breakfast meeting, another of the founding members was Grant Fagerheim, the CEO of Calgary-based Whitecap Resources and a native of Estevan. Unlike the Regina meeting two months earlier, this was a session intended to give shape to the idea of a voice for the West, specifically Alberta and Saskatchewan, in the national debate. Wall was intrigued with the idea and saw it potentially as a way to remain relevant. But he also set down an explicit condition: if he were to be involved, it must be as part of a western voice that is committed to federalism. In other words, the invitation had to be seen as a means to ensure that the interests of Alberta and Saskatchewan are understood and appreciated in the context of a united Canada. Clearly Wall recognized the inherent danger in being part of an initiative that is fuelled by anger and resentment against Ottawa and the current structure of federalism. The potential to unleash the darker forces of populism and where they might lead were self-evident.

To make their point that Wall was the logical voice, Howe presented results of a public opinion poll he'd had done in Saskatchewan and Alberta. The purpose of the research, carried out by Demetre Eliopoulos of the public opinion research firm Maru/Matchbox in Vancouver, was to determine public attitudes toward Wall as a voice for the West.[1] Four key questions provided the evidence Howe and the others needed. When asked if Wall did a good job as premier of Saskatchewan, 62 percent of all respondents said yes, and

83 percent of those who considered themselves conservatives said yes. When asked if Wall did a good job as premier standing up for western Canada, 81 percent of conservatives said yes and overall 65 percent agreed. Asked if they would be interested in what Wall has to say if he continued to speak about western issues, 72 percent said they would, including 93 percent of conservatives.[2] Wall as a political factor in Alberta was undeniable. There was even a group of well-heeled Alberta business types in 2017 who briefly pushed the rather bizarre idea that Wall should step down as premier of Saskatchewan and run for leader of the United Conservative Party of Alberta, a position that ultimately went to Jason Kenney.

If the concept was that the two provinces would act as a region so as to be better recognized in the federation, Wall said perhaps the region should be given a name. He suggested "Buffalo," which more than a century earlier had been briefly considered as the possible name for a new province. In 1904, Frederick Haultain, the premier of what was then the North-West Territories, proposed that the prairie region be united into the single province of Buffalo. "One big province would be able to do things no other province could do," Haultain argued.[3] He was likely right, which explains what came next. A year later, the decision made in Ottawa was to form two provinces—Saskatchewan and Alberta—for fear that during a time of rapid immigration and settlement Buffalo might end up with too much power as a region, offsetting the political and economic axis of Ontario and Quebec. It was a result that apparently still bugged people 115 years later.

The point is that the group quickly agreed with Wall's suggestion. And with that, the Buffalo Project was born.

When considered in the context of the West, and particularly the Prairies, the Buffalo Project idea was consistent with both the history and the political culture of the two provinces. With alienation deeply woven into the fabric of the region and a source of populist movements for more than a century, this was just another manifestation of that fact. It tapped into a current of discontent over what many in the two provinces saw as a federal government that neither understood the region nor respected what it brought to the nation itself. The two provinces had long been aligned in terms of interests, but also had significant separate political identities. The Progressive Conservative Party had dominated Alberta for generations, while Saskatchewan had been largely the domain of the NDP. But when Wall and the Saskatchewan Party came to power in 2007, that began to change in significant and dramatic ways. There was clearly an accelerated convergence of political interests between the two provinces.

In many ways the disaffection that led to the creation of the Buffalo Project had the echoes of the 1970s and early 1980s when Pierre Trudeau was prime minister and Alberta and Saskatchewan were in a decade-long struggle to defend their natural resource interests. At that time, in spite of divergent ideological perspectives, there was close alignment between the two provincial governments. As noted, Lougheed in Alberta and Blakeney in Saskatchewan shared the same views on the defence of their provinces' interests. Some of the levers they used might have varied—Lougheed saw private investment as the key to developing the resource economy, and Blakeney favoured government investment through Crown corporations—but both pursued a common objective: to maximize the benefits of resource development for the people of their province.

During those years, Lougheed and Blakeney became both close allies and friends in asserting and defending the interests of their provinces on the national stage. They were recognized as influential and even powerful voices who brought a great deal of credibility to federal-provincial relations, seen as having the stature and skills to debate and challenge Trudeau. There was no sense at the time that the interests of the region were not being heard and defended in the national debate. Moreover, federal-provincial relations dominated the national agenda in substantive and very visible ways.

The struggle over resources was very much contained within the context of the constitution, which gave the provinces ownership and control of natural resources. At the same time, Trudeau was determined to patriate the *British North America Act* from Britain and create a free-standing Canadian constitution that included his long-held ambition of a *Charter of Rights and Freedoms*.

Those two factors—patriation and control of resources—intersected in the unfolding of a high-profile constitutional debate that played out nationally with a series of federal-provincial conferences. Both Blakeney and Lougheed were recognized as forceful advocates for their provinces, but always within the boundaries of federalism and a united Canada.

Blakeney recognized that the common interests of Saskatchewan and Alberta were stronger than partisan considerations. "The government of Peter Lougheed and our government in Saskatchewan had an interesting relationship," Blakeney would later write. "We had philosophical differences and acted in our own provinces in accordance with the principles upon which we were elected. We recognized, however, that we shared many common objectives. We had a shared desire to further the interests of Western Canada in the Canadian federation."[4]

Lougheed echoed the same sentiments toward Blakeney and Saskatchewan.

> He [Blakeney] and I became great friends, because there were so many things that Alberta and Saskatchewan worked on together, including the Western Economic Opportunity Conferences and other matters. But I think what was remarkable about the Peter Lougheed–Allan Blakeney relationship was the respect we had for each other. A wide difference of political philosophy—philosophical views—but I admired so much his brilliance, his intelligence. He was always right at the very forefront of discussions at federal-provincial conferences. He was so respected by all the other premiers when he spoke. He was an exceptional man, and I was honoured to speak about him when I went to his memorial service not too long ago.[5]

Personal tributes don't get much better than that.

For many, the situation in 2018 was fundamentally different and even more threatening to the two provinces. Unlike thirty to forty years earlier when attempts by Ottawa to siphon off natural resource wealth from the region was the core issue, the challenge had become far more existential. It was coming at a time when Wall had left politics, taking with him a national reputation as a compelling defender of Saskatchewan and western interests. Specifically, at stake was not how to carve up the spoils from the oil and gas sector but the very survival of what is the backbone of the Alberta economy and often the single largest source of revenue for the Saskatchewan government. The sector was seen to be under direct threat by Ottawa. Adding to the drama was that this time it was Prime Minister Justin Trudeau who was authoring the federal strategy. Bitter memories of the earlier years were clearly shaping attitudes in Saskatchewan and Alberta with the younger Trudeau as prime minister.

The crux of the issue was the clash of two inherently conflicting interests. One was the federal government's commitment to address climate change, the centrepiece of both its environmental and economic policies, which Trudeau had made it clear in the first weeks of his first term as prime minister at the Paris climate change conference. It was there, on an international stage, that he committed Canada to a 30 percent reduction in GHG emissions from 2005 levels by 2030 and a net-zero carbon emissions economy by 2050. What followed was the government's Pan-Canadian Framework on Clean Growth and Climate Change, the introduction of an escalating price on carbon, and an admission by Trudeau that Alberta needed to transition away from its oil-based economy.

The other interest is that of the fossil fuel sector—in particular, oil and gas—which, aside from being essential to the economies of Alberta and Saskatchewan, forms a cornerstone of the national economy. Former Bank of Canada governor and deputy minister of finance David Dodge puts the importance of the oil sector, even during a time of low prices, into perspective. "In 2019, our energy sector nonetheless contributed a net $76.6 billion to the current account, largely covering net consumer imports ($55 billion) autos ($22 billion) and travel services ($11 billion)," Dodge says. "Of the energy contribution, some 80 per cent came from crude oil and bitumen. Adding natural gas brought the share above 90 per cent. Coal was third, electricity fourth. Fossil fuels and other resources held the economy aloft, particularly through the 2008–09 recession, a reality that for now remains intact and therefore we must accept even as we transition away from them. Too abrupt a move will generate painful shocks to the overall economy."[6]

The point made by Dodge raises the question of what exports will replace oil if Canada steadily reduces its production as part of meeting its GHG emission targets, leading to the eventual phase-out of the oil sands. Natural resource extraction has been the backbone of the Canadian economy throughout its history and has given Canada the standard of living and quality of life we enjoy. The value of the Canadian dollar is intimately tied to our natural resource exports, and in particular oil and gas. The more strident advocates for aggressive actions to reduce oil and gas production, some of whom even argue for ceasing production as quickly as possible, have no feasible alternatives to replace the exports because, at this point, there are none.

The challenge facing Canada is how to reconcile those two competing interests, energy and the environment, in a way that meets the nation's climate change objectives, maintains national unity, and supports an essential part of the economy that is fundamental to economic growth and the strength of the Canadian dollar. It didn't help when Trudeau effectively said that reconciliation was not in the cards, the implication being that the two are irreconcilable.

At the root of the latest strain of western alienation is the sense that the federal government believes oil sands and the oil and gas sector have no sustainable future and will have to be diminished dramatically if Canada is to meet its climate objectives. The cleavage is evident in public attitudes in Saskatchewan and Alberta. While addressing climate change is deemed important, less than 50 percent of the population in each of the two provinces believes climate change is partly or mostly a result of human activity (compared with the national average of 60 percent), and that reaching our GHG reduction targets cannot be done in a way that will not cripple their economies.[7]

The inherent challenge for Canada in tackling climate change is explained in a 2016 research paper on the regional distribution of climate change policy effects. The six authors, from the University of California, University of Montreal, Yale, and the University of Essex, note that the significant role fossil fuel energy plays in the Canadian economy makes climate action difficult. "Implementing a national climate policy would represent a large change in economic and energy policy for Canada. Consequently, Canada is in many ways a difficult case for implementing ambitious carbon pricing," they argue. "Given geographical variation in energy resources and electricity sources, policy costs and benefits will be unevenly spread across the country. Further, as a highly decentralized federal system with regionally diverse political economies, one province could threaten to block or weaken national reform efforts."[8]

To make matters more difficult, in the 2019 election when the Trudeau government was reduced to a minority, the Liberals failed to elect a single member in either Alberta or Saskatchewan. Going into the election, the Liberals held four seats in Alberta and one in Saskatchewan, belonging to Ralph Goodale, who had held the riding for more than twenty-five years. The outcome simply aggravated the existing sense of alienation, with voters' anger toward the federal government leading to the region's isolation from decision-making in Ottawa. With the loss of Goodale at the cabinet table, Saskatchewan was effectively without a voice in the inner sanctum of the federal government. But one could ask, whose fault is that? Saskatchewan and Alberta complain about the lack of representation in government, but voters in the two provinces chose not to elect any Liberals.

It is that political vacuum the Buffalo Project sought to fill. With Wall as its voice, the project considers itself a political action committee, similar to groups that raise money for political purposes in the United States. According to Bill Turnbull, one of the founding members, "We all thought that the brightest tool in the shed was ex-premier [Wall] to talk about these issues. We made overtures to him and the Buffalo Project was created. Brad's involvement early on was to help us formulate this. To pull a larger group than the founding group together in hopes to raise some money so that we could make a difference."[9] Ironically, one area where the Buffalo Project did play a role was in supporting a group of businesspeople in Regina who ran a high-profile billboard campaign against Goodale. Their key message was to "send Trudeau a message" by defeating Goodale. Recognizing that Goodale himself was well respected for his dedication to the city and province, the objective was to turn antipathy toward Trudeau into motivation not to support Goodale's re-election, rather than an outright attack on Goodale himself.

Curiously, other than a handful of speaking engagements at fundraisers in the Buffalo Project's initial months, Wall's role subsided as he became occupied by his responsibilities as an advisor with the law firm Osler, Hoskin & Harcourt LLP. Without a formal role for Wall or his continuing engagement, the Buffalo Project's public profile has also diminished, and its focus has shifted. It has effectively turned into a lobby group. In July 2020 it issued an open letter calling for a "new deal" for Alberta and Saskatchewan in Canada. The letter, signed by sixty "high-profile" people in the two provinces and seven "concerned citizen groups," cited polling by the Angus Reid Forum that "showed 75 per cent of Alberta people and 72 per cent of Saskatchewan people are dissatisfied with their province's treatment by the federal government." The poll found strikingly unified opinion among people in both provinces, with 58 percent in Alberta and 57 percent in Saskatchewan supporting a new arrangement that would increase the autonomy of their province.[10]

Those engaged in the Buffalo Project insist they are committed to national unity. Their intent is to provide a voice for people who believe Alberta and Saskatchewan need a way to have their issues heard and on the national agenda. "We're federalists. We want to find solutions within Canada, but we have to have people actively seeking out and finding solutions," says Derek Robinson, a former aide to Wall and spokesperson for the Buffalo Project. "People have extremist views and you can't dismiss the sentiment, but we want to rise above all the noise that's happening and say there's a way we can have a nation-building conversation about how Alberta and Saskatchewan can go on living the way they want to live and develop their way of life and contribute to the wealth of the nation...and they're not demonized every step of the way."[11]

But there is also a thin line between a voice for western concerns and a vehicle that grows into a populist sense of anger and alienation. They are both part of a continuum that leads to a logical end point: western separatism. In the past, the sentiment for western separatism in Alberta and Saskatchewan had been relegated to the political margins in both provinces. But to suggest it doesn't exist as an undercurrent to the public mood would be wrong. In one of its manifestations, as the Western Canada Concept (WCC), it emerged in the 1980s and elected a member to the Alberta Legislature in a 1982 by-election. For a very brief period in 1986, two former Saskatchewan PC MLAs sat as members of the WCC. There was also the aberration when former Saskatchewan PC leader Dick Collver and one other PC MLA sat briefly as members of what they called the Unionest Party, advocating that western Canada separate and join the United States. Rather than any kind of serious political position, it was mostly an attempt to take advantage of the rules at the time that that allowed two members to have party status and receive funding from the legislature. Since that time, the political expression of western independence has persisted in various right-wing forms, including the Western Independence Party of Saskatchewan and, most recently, the Buffalo Party of Saskatchewan.

It matters not that the idea of Alberta and Saskatchewan separation makes utterly no sense economically, socially, or politically. First of all, it is constitutionally impossible. There is no legal mechanism for it to happen. Canada is a confederation. Provincial boundaries do not mean the people living there own the territory or have sovereignty. The Supreme Court has ruled that a province's unilateral secession was not legal under the Constitution of Canada.[12]

But even if the legal right to separate from Canada did exist, not only would it fail to offer a solution to the perceived grievances of the region, but it would also produce a much weaker and isolated landlocked economy. For example, there would be no sudden ability to get the much-coveted oil pipeline to tidewater, which, by the way, the Trudeau government is now financing. It is also a time when world demand for oil has peaked, or soon will peak and then begin an inexorable decline. Nor would there be any federal investment in the provinces, including transfers to support health care. Imagine the trade issues that would emerge, not to mention the need to create a new currency should Canada refuse to issue its currency to the new non-Canadian state. Moreover, as was often noted in the recurring debates over Quebec secession, if Canada is divisible, then so too are the provinces themselves.

Then there is the issue of First Nations that do not want to separate from Canada and have established legal sovereignty over their treaty land and traditional territories. Based on the Royal Proclamation of 1863, the Supreme Court has determined that the federal government has a fiduciary duty to safeguard the interests of First Nations. The *Charter of Rights and Freedoms* in the Canadian *Constitution Act* explicitly recognizes and affirms "the existing aboriginal and treaty rights of the aboriginal peoples of Canada."[13]

Unfortunately, when people are motivated by anger and a sense of exclusion, being rational is often not part of the equation. That is always the danger of populism, and even though the founders of the Buffalo Project insist they are federalists and committed to a united Canada, they are playing with populist fire and know it. Part of their argument is that they are seeking to defuse the western separatist sentiment by "giving it a place to go." Playing off the populist Brexit movement in Britain, a new party calling itself Wexit emerged in various forms across the West, each advocating separation of either the four western provinces or some combination thereof. According to public opinion research done in July 2020, 35 percent of people polled in Alberta say they think separation is a "good idea" or "could live with it." In Saskatchewan, the number was 36 percent.[14] The leader of Wexit Canada (now Maverick Party) is Jay Hill, a former cabinet minister from British Columbia in the Stephen Harper government. There is little doubt that western separatists congregate on the political fringe in the four western provinces. But there is also reason to believe that they could quickly emerge as a significant force by tapping into the raw, emotion-driven instincts of many, especially in Saskatchewan and Alberta, which have spawned the most significant populist-based parties and governments in Canada.

Small, but significant, evidence of the potential for rapid growth came in the October 2020 Saskatchewan election. Three facts emerged from the results. First was the strength and dominance of the Saskatchewan Party as it coasted to a fourth term with another huge majority. Second was the feeble state of the once proud Saskatchewan New Democratic Party. It has been reduced to a small urban base with no presence or relevance in rural

Saskatchewan, where it once had deep roots and political dominance. The third salient fact might seem insignificant and inconsequential to some. It was that the newly formed Buffalo Party, which advocates that Saskatchewan people vote on independence, finished second in four ridings ahead of the NDP. The outcome marked the first time since 1938 that the NDP didn't either win or place second in every seat in the province.

The Buffalo Party of Saskatchewan was officially formed in June 2020. It emerged out of what had been the provincial Wexit Party, which advocates for western independence from Canada. The party members voted to rebrand themselves as the Buffalo Party. It was only four months before the provincial election, and the party had virtually no organization and ran only sixteen candidates—and it still managed to gain more of the popular vote province-wide than the Green Party, which ran sixty candidates, one shy of a full slate. The Buffalo Party lists as one of its five principles "that the Saskatchewan people have the right to vote for Independence. It's the people's choice to stay within or leave confederation. No matter the outcome; We should be in full control of our destiny."[15] Wade Sira, the party's former interim leader, says the Buffalo Party takes the position of "not necessarily separation, but separation if necessary."[16] He says there are lessons to be learned from what has happened in Quebec, where the rise initially of the Parti Québécois and then the Bloc Québécois has changed how Quebec is viewed in Canada. Sira argues that the West needs to assert itself in the same manner.

It is important to recognize that the Buffalo Party has no connection to the Buffalo Project. They are separate organizationally and in terms of goals and intent. But the fact they share the use of "Buffalo" in their titles is no coincidence. Both entities reflect a popular mood that exists in the two provinces, one led by the business elite and the other a grassroots political party. Most importantly, what they share is a common sentiment—specifically, that Saskatchewan and Alberta are being treated unfairly by federal policies and are disadvantaged within the current political construct of Canadian federalism. It provides for a potentially explosive environment.

In the context of the political and economic history of the two provinces, where populist sentiments have always lurked, the sentiment is neither surprising nor inconsistent with the character of the region. The question is, where will this latest manifestation of alienation lead?

CHAPTER 20

2020

Homeland No More

THERE WAS A TIME NOT THAT LONG AGO IN ALBERTA when, in certain business circles, Saskatchewan was referred to as "the old country." The implication was obvious. It reflected a belief that somehow the province had been left behind economically. The idea was deeply rooted in the province's history and the identity it formed many decades ago. The obvious subtext to the slur was political. It was that the "socialist" political traditions of Saskatchewan, compared with "free enterprise" Alberta, had affected investment and stunted economic growth. While Alberta had grown rapidly, attracting people from across Canada, nothing similar in terms of growth had happened in Saskatchewan. In fact, a major source of in-migration to Alberta was Saskatchewan. There are no firm statistics on the number of people born in Saskatchewan who moved to Alberta, but it is generally recognized that the Saskatchewan expatriate population in the province is huge.

It is not surprising that the comparison would be made. The two provinces came into existence at the same moment in Canadian history, and at the starting line of 1905 Saskatchewan was a hotbed of immigration with a larger population than Alberta. Six years later Saskatchewan's population had almost doubled, reaching 492,432, compared with 374,663 in Alberta. It was higher even than Manitoba's population of 455,614, and Manitoba was established in 1870, thirty-five years earlier than Saskatchewan and Alberta.[1] From that moment, population size became a fixation so deeply embedded in the Saskatchewan psyche that it represented the benchmark for success.

The argument that politics was a critical factor in the divergent growth paths between Saskatchewan and Alberta is a logical assumption. But whether it is true—and specifically, whether Saskatchewan's politics had a dampening effect on economic growth—is another thing.

An often-cited example came shortly after the CCF came to power in 1944, when Imperial Oil approached the government with the proposal of a long-term contract to give it exclusive rights to develop oil over a large portion of the province. When the government said no—contrary, by the way, to bureaucratic advice that an agreement would be in order, given the speculative nature of oil investment—Imperial put its exploration focus on Alberta.[2]

One of the few attempts to seriously investigate the assertion that differing political ideologies, and particularly the "socialist" traditions of Saskatchewan, primarily explain the deviating growth paths for the two provinces was done by Herbert Emery and Ronald Kneebone, two economists from the University of Calgary. Their analysis, titled "Socialists, Populists, Resources, and the Divergent Development of Alberta and Saskatchewan" and published in a 2008 issue of *Canadian Public Policy Journal*, concludes that in fact comparative natural advantage was the crucial factor. Politics had little to do with it. They acknowledge that in resource-dependent economies, government policy can play an important role in determining the pace and scale of development. But their review of policies in the two provinces over the course of many decades demonstrates little divergence in terms of tax policy and regulation.

Our analysis shows that while the rhetoric of the political leaders of the two provinces may have differed, except for a short time during an important time of their economic development, there has been little difference in the policies pursued by the governments of Alberta and Saskatchewan with respect to the development of natural resources. Any claim that institutions played a key role in explaining the difference in economic development in the two provinces must rest on an argument that differences in policy practiced during that critical period had a substantial and prolonged influence. We examine that possibility and dismiss it in favour of an argument that Alberta's early lead in manufacturing development, and the fact its mineral endowments were discovered first, are the reasons for its economic leadership. In our assessment, geography, not institutions, is responsible for the divergent outcomes of the twin provinces.[3]

To put it another way, four words dating from 1947 explain why the economic history of the prairie West unfolded the way it did: the Leduc oil discovery.

But we must not underestimate the effect of perceptions. Early CCF rhetoric created the impression of Saskatchewan as a kind of socialist "haven." When the CCF took power it was often described as the only democratically elected socialist government in North America, which seemed an entirely appropriate and accurate label. After all, in the years leading to the 1944 provincial election that brought the CCF to power, the party campaigned on the notion of "social ownership" of major industry, which was less stark than simply saying government or state ownership. Still, it was hard for people not to notice something else, called the Regina Manifesto. The party's founding document defiantly vowed that "no C.C.F. Government will rest content until it has eradicated capitalism." One has to admit it was a fairly categorical objective.

But the reality is the province only briefly flirted with what could be described as significant socialist-based endeavours. In its first term in office, from 1944 to 1948, Tommy Douglas and his CCF government embarked on an aggressive agenda of public enterprise, which led to several failed ventures and poorly considered enterprises. They included a brick manufacturing plant, a shoe factory, a leather tannery, and a box factory.[4] The Douglas government abruptly pulled back in terms of government ownership in its second term and from that point on followed a policy of private-sector-driven economic development. The government quickly learned that it lacked the capital capacity to diversify the economy as it had hoped and that private investment was the primary ingredient needed to fuel economic development.[5]

Over the years the socialist view of Saskatchewan remained and was deepened nationally when the province brought in publicly funded Medicare in 1962. It emerged again for a time in the 1970s when the Blakeney government embarked on its agenda to nationalize portions of the natural resource sector. But for all its symbolic and substantive importance, publicly funded medical care was not outside the mainstream of policy debate at the time. In fact, as far back as the First World War the concept of state-financed health insurance had been endorsed by many federal Liberals. In 1952, Douglas had urged Prime Minister Louis St. Laurent to move forward on a national Medicare plan.[6] The sticking point was always the inability to agree on a federal-provincial formula to share costs, not the actual concept of Medicare. Frustrated when no consensus could be reached on the financial framework for a national program of publicly funded universal health care, Douglas eventually decided that Saskatchewan would act alone, but not until he determined the province had the financial resources to fund a provincial Medicare scheme.

The belief in the socialist character of the province is often nurtured and magnified by those who are committed to socialist or social democratic principles. Saskatchewan became symbolically important as a means for people to defend and advance their ideological biases. But the reality is that at its core, Saskatchewan is a province deeply committed to private investment and a capitalist economy. In their study, Emery and Kneebone found that through to the mid-1960s, private investment per capita in Saskatchewan was roughly equal to that in Alberta and Ontario. "It is interesting to note that, other than during the early 1970s, Saskatchewan has generated levels of per capita private investment comparable to those in Ontario," they state.[7]

The most obvious evidence of Saskatchewan's private, free enterprise culture is its very economic foundation—agriculture. There never was a time in Saskatchewan when private ownership of farmland was ever in serious question. As Duff Spafford notes, the CCF originally labelled itself as socialist, but when the term quickly turned into a liability the party avoided it. More to the point, its initial policy of nationalization of all natural resources was considered to include farmland, with farmers to receive security of tenure. An idea that struck at the heart of Saskatchewan's rural culture, it was soon discarded in favour of a much more "motherhood" position of supporting the traditional family farm.[8] And as Lipset himself noted, "Socialism for the farmer was henceforth to mean the protection of his property by control of the rest of the economy and especially big business."[9]

The only other time the party ventured anywhere close to the idea of farmers as renters and not owners of the land they farmed was with the Saskatchewan Land Bank Commission of the 1970s. Even though it was proposed as mechanism for government to temporarily hold farmland to assist in the generational transfer of land, it became a huge political blunder and was a key factor in the defeat of the Blakeney government in 1982. In effect, the Land Bank was seen as a threat to the underpinnings of the province, to its raison d'être—private ownership of farmland. The very foundation of the province, the reason Saskatchewan became a mecca for immigration from Europe, was the offer of private property, the essence of a capitalist economy.

All of this is to suggest that the term "socialism" in Saskatchewan has most often been an overstatement of the reality. This explains the CCF-NDP's migration from the label of "socialism" to the less precise and more anodyne term "social democracy." The origins of the CCF and its rise to power were considered evidence that differentiated the province in Canada, and particularly set it apart from Alberta. But the truth is that Saskatchewan has never strayed far from the political mainstream, and when it has, it quickly returned to the centre. So, the application of a left-right ideological framework to describe the fundamental nature of Saskatchewan politics has always been somewhat overstated. It provides a convenient descriptive shorthand but overstates the ideological divide in the province, which has become evident over the last thirty years.

The clearest evidence of Saskatchewan's true character as a province that reflects the common traits of the prairie region, rather than any distinct political identity, is the rise and dominance of the Saskatchewan Party. It was on vivid display at a precise moment of leadership transition. When Brad Wall's time at the helm of the Saskatchewan Party officially ended, it did not take his successor, Scott Moe, long to set the tone for engagement with the federal government. Only minutes, to be exact.

Moe had just been declared the party's new leader and with it, premier of Saskatchewan. The new premier was not exactly a household name and obviously had big political shoes to fill. Lacking the profile, populist flair, and communication skills of Wall, Moe clearly felt the need to quickly and dramatically assert himself. So, what he did was to immediately tap into Saskatchewan's political culture of alienation by picking up the mantle of opposition to a planned federal price on carbon from Wall. A federally mandated carbon price was the centrepiece of the Justin Trudeau government's climate change policy agenda. There would be no mistaking Moe's position, intent, or determination. His would be a robust and muscular leadership that would stand up to Ottawa in defence of Saskatchewan interests. "We will not impose a carbon tax on the good people of this province," Moe vowed. "And Justin Trudeau, if you're wondering how far I will go—just watch me."[10] The line drew a roar of approval from the assembled partisans who had chosen Moe as leader on a fifth ballot in a five-person race. The irony of the words was rather explicit. Arguably they are the most memorable, in both a positive and negative sense, in the lexicon of famous Canadian political quotations. They were, of course, uttered by Pierre Trudeau during the October crisis of 1970. Their intent at the time was to make certain no one underestimated Trudeau's intention of crushing a domestic terrorist cell of militant Quebec separatists who had kidnapped and threatened to execute a Quebec cabinet minister and British trade commissioner. It was a watershed moment in Canadian history.

In one sense, it was not surprising that Moe would zero in on the carbon price, as it had been a consistent theme in his leadership campaign. The "carbon tax" had been a powerful rallying point for many conservative-minded people, particularly in rural Saskatchewan, where it is seen as something that would significantly raise costs for farmers. Moe was a rural MLA and former farm machinery salesperson—his base was key in his winning the leadership. In some ways he emerged as an unlikely leader. First elected in 2011, Moe had not been seen by many as a probable leadership candidate during his time first as minister of environment, then as minister of advanced education, and finally in another stint as environment minister. But internal party dynamics rapidly took hold. Recognizing that the rural base was the foundation for its ongoing political success, the Saskatchewan Party caucus quickly coalesced behind Moe's leadership campaign. He was surrounded by many of the twenty-one MLAs who supported his bid when he had launched his leadership campaign. The only policy position Moe stated at the time was his opposition to the carbon tax.

The carbon tax was a useful issue for further solidifying the party's rural base. It did not matter that the carbon price would not apply to agriculture diesel and gas fuels used for on-farm purposes. What mattered was that people believed it would increase their total costs, which farmers are unable to pass along to consumers. Ultimately, however, the fight with Ottawa over the carbon tax ended in defeat for the Moe government in 2021 when the Supreme Court ruled in a majority decision that the federal government's policy was constitutional.[11]

The more remarkable thing about Moe's direct challenge to Trudeau was its context and timing. Here was someone who had just been named leader and premier of a small province, and the first words out of his mouth were a direct challenge to the prime minister of the country. Reciting the phrase used by Pierre Trudeau at a time of an intense crisis in Canada guaranteed impact. No doubt for some Moe's echoing the remark for his own political purposes bordered on pomposity.

Granting even the politics of the issue, there is something bizarre about the elevation of a carbon price, or "tax," into some kind of Rubicon, never to be crossed. The fact is, the vast majority of economists say a carbon price is the most effective and fairest means to achieve a reduction in GHG emissions. Take, for example, the 3,589 economists, 4 former chairs of the U.S. Federal Reserve, 28 Nobel laureate economists, and 15 former chairs of the Council of Economic Advisers to U.S. presidents who endorse a carbon tax. In what is described as "the largest public statement of economists in history" they state, in part,

> A carbon tax offers the most cost-effective lever to reduce carbon emissions at the scale and speed that is necessary. By correcting a well-known market failure, a carbon tax will send a powerful price signal that harnesses the invisible hand of the marketplace to steer economic actors towards a low-carbon future.
>
> A carbon tax should increase every year until emissions reductions goals are met and be revenue neutral to avoid debates over the size of government. A consistently rising carbon price will encourage technological innovation and large-scale infrastructure development. It will also accelerate the diffusion of carbon-efficient goods and services.[12]

A carbon tax is also supported by an array of Canadian think tanks, advocacy groups, and even many senior oil and gas company executives. One example is the Ecofiscal Commission, which strongly endorses a price on carbon. Members of the commission's advisory board include former prime minister Paul Martin, former Quebec premier Jean Charest, former Alberta finance minister Jim Dinning, and Steve Williams, past CEO of Suncor Energy. Members of the commission itself include former TD Bank senior vice-president and chief economist Don Drummond, and Paul Boothe, a past Saskatchewan deputy of finance and federal deputy minister of environment.[13] An advisor to the Ecofiscal Commission is Reform Party founder and former leader Preston Manning.

In other words, if you believe in the principles of a market as the most effective means to allocate resources—something you would think that conservatives would normally profess—putting a price on carbon is the logical tool. As for the cost to individuals, the federal plan rebates to households an equal or greater amount than what they pay in a carbon price or tax. The rebate is based on the average of carbon tax paid in each province. So, the invisible hand of the market does its thing. People respond to price signals, change their behaviour by altering their purchases, avoid spending on things that have an embedded carbon price, and then end up being better off financially because of the carbon tax rebate they receive.

The economic case for the carbon tax to drive changes in behaviour is made in a 2018 study by five academics from four Canadian universities, including the Institute for Energy, Environment and Sustainable Communities at the University of Regina. The authors note that a "carbon tax can create a powerful incentive to reduce carbon emissions by means of conservation, substitution and innovation." But the same study also found that a carbon tax will have a negative economic impact on Saskatchewan. It concludes that in "a resource-intense economy such as Saskatchewan, where there is little opportunity for fuel switching, a carbon tax will simply result in decisions to contract economy activity, rather than adjust to it."[14]

The Saskatchewan government's position to address climate change is expressed in its Prairie Resilience plan, which it calls a "made-in-Saskatchewan" strategy. It argues that relative to other regions in Canada, the federal broadly based carbon price approach will disadvantage Saskatchewan's agricultural and oil-and-gas production economy. Instead, the provincial government proposes to require large industrial emitters to take compliance measures if they exceed a maximum allowable level of GHG emissions. Coupled with that measure will be other actions that include nature-based carbon sinks and energy efficiency goals to improve the performance of physical infrastructure.[15]

But no one should be deceived about the underlying motivation. For many in Saskatchewan, opposition to carbon pricing goes beyond simply resistance to a tax. It is far more fundamental. It reflects an underlying sentiment that questions the causes, effects, and even validity of climate change. A significant proportion of the population doubts whether climate change is truly happening and, if it is, challenges the notion that it is caused by human activity. Making it an even more difficult public policy issue is that the effects of climate change are not immediately felt by most people and increase incrementally over time. So, it's an issue that requires action now for benefits that often won't be experienced for decades but also will never be actually identifiable because the result will be the avoidance of what would have been the outcome of not acting. Both Saskatchewan and Alberta share similar levels of skepticism about climate change. In 2019, public opinion research found that 47 percent of Saskatchewan residents believed the earth was warming, and 42 percent in Alberta shared the same view. The national average of Canadians who agree that climate change is happening was 60 percent. The research also found a significant divide in opinion in both provinces between rural and urban respondents, with the rural population far less convinced the earth is warming from human activity.[16]

Shortly after becoming premier, Moe met with Kenney at the Manning Centre Networking Conference in Ottawa, an annual event that attracts conservatives from across Canada. The two talked over dinner and agreed that a united front against the Trudeau government on the carbon price issue and defence of the energy sector would be wise. "We talked at length about the need to create a coalition at the provincial level," Kenney said of his meeting with Moe. "Saskatchewan itself had been bravely taking this fight on its own and had been isolated around the premiers' table. Premier Moe was very happy to have a strong ally in our Alberta opposition."[17]

This unitary majority opinion in the two provinces became the primary political tool used by the Moe government in the lead-up to the 2019 federal election. By the time of the election, Kenney had been elected premier of Alberta and the political framework was set for engagement. In both provinces, the overriding narrative would be based on regional alienation from the federal Trudeau government. It would be characterized as a defence of the oil and gas sector from federal policies such as the carbon price and climate change policy that assumed a major reduction, if not complete phase-out, of the fossil fuel sector, with Alberta's oil sands as a specific target.

As part of a region where alienation is at the core of its political culture, Saskatchewan reverted to form.

The fact that someone named Trudeau was leader of the Liberals and prime minister merely added emotional fuel to the prairie fire of regional politics. So deeply woven is the grievance mentality, a fact often exploited for political gain, that memories reaching back to the days of Pierre Trudeau remain a powerful source of passion to marshal against Ottawa. The result can be fertile ground on which populist fervour can emerge. As is often the case when politicians appeal to emotions as a motivating force for support, facts do not really matter. In the federal election of 2019, anger in the prairie West was the result of an economic reality that had more to do with global forces than any domestic policies of the federal government. The key factor was a rapid decline in oil prices that was a function of oversupply, driven largely by the massive increase in production in the United States as a result of fracking technology. The inability to get an oil pipeline built from Alberta to tidewater in British Columbia because of legal challenges and the assertion of Indigenous rights was somehow considered the fault of the Trudeau government and its lack of support for the energy sector. It mattered not that it was the Trudeau government that had stepped in to buy the Trans Mountain Pipeline to ensure the project was completed when the proponent Kinder Morgan walked away from the project. Assuming the pipeline is constructed and operating, it will be sold to the private sector; Trudeau says his government is not interested in being in the pipeline business and became involved only to meet the export needs of the oil sector in Alberta.

Nor did it matter that when Stephen Harper was prime minister, he was unable to get his government to deliver a pipeline to tidewater. As someone from Alberta, Harper was a strong and vocal advocate for the oil and gas sector, labelling Canada an "energy superpower." There were no political consequences or outrage in the West against his Conservative government when it was unable to get the Northern Gateway pipeline project from Alberta to the northern coast of British Columbia through the regulatory and approval process. The project was eventually abandoned by Enbridge, the proponent, after $373 million was spent on the effort.[18]

The outcome of the 2019 federal election emphatically underscored the regional cleavage between Saskatchewan and Alberta and Ottawa. The Conservatives won every seat in both provinces, making it the first time in decades that the NDP and Liberals were completely erased from the electoral map.

The frame for Saskatchewan politics during the Wall government and subsequently continued by Moe was set in defence of the province's natural resource sector. It was first evident in Wall's aggressive intervention to prevent the sale of the Saskatoon-based Potash Corporation to Australia-based mining giant BHP Billiton. It then shifted, with the election of the Trudeau Liberals, to a full-throated defence of the oil and gas sector from federal climate change policies. Inherent in that posture was support for construction of pipelines that would get oil to tidewater and access to the global market. It mattered little that, for the most part, the pipelines would be carrying oil sands bitumen crude from Alberta. The point was that the heart of the oil and gas industry is found in Alberta and Saskatchewan, making the industry essential to shared economic interests of the region. The explicit narrative was that the government was defending Saskatchewan jobs and the province's economic security. It was a simple and categorical message that left little, if any, room for ambiguity.

Throughout the dispute between Saskatchewan and Ottawa over energy and climate policy, the NDP appeared at best to be a bystander, and at worse complicit with the federal Liberal agenda. The NDP attempted to take a more nuanced position in a debate that in the public mind had been cast as a binary choice between fossil fuels and climate change. Moe took to citing a quote by Ryan Meili from his days before becoming NDP leader, when Meili said that he agreed "in principle" with a carbon tax, an echo of what Wall did to define Meili before he could define himself.[19] Coupled with the carbon tax message were Saskatchewan Party ads showing Meili attending anti-pipeline rallies.

Finally, the Saskatchewan NDP was further marginalized by the fact that the federal NDP strongly supported the Trudeau government's climate change policies, including the price on carbon. Moreover, in 2017 at the NDP convention that selected Jagmeet Singh as leader, the federal party, as it had with the

Regina and Waffle manifestos, adopted yet another manifesto. This time it was the "Leap Manifesto," which calls for an end to the oil and gas industry in Canada. Again, the party was deeply divided by a manifesto largely fashioned by Toronto-based academics.

The Leap Manifesto, filled with loaded language of energy transformation away from the fossil fuel sector, was lacking what many believed was a credible path forward. Among the critics were Wall, Alberta NDP premier Rachel Notley, labour leaders, and long-time left-wing activist and Waffle Manifesto co-author James Laxer. "The document suggests that most new jobs will be created in a host of caregiving sectors. That may sound good if you live in the Annex in downtown Toronto. But what does it say to miners in Sudbury, steelworkers, autoworkers, workers in the energy sector in Alberta, and to the young on Native reserves who have been abandoned by the larger society to a marginal existence?" Laxer asks. "And what about agriculture? Leap makes it sound as though we are about to shift to local agriculture directed at local markets. Have the people who wrote this ever looked at the agricultural sector in this country?"[20]

There was little drama going into the 2020 Saskatchewan election, as public opinion research indicated that the Saskatchewan Party under Moe was on the road to another huge majority government. One poll less than two weeks before the vote had the Saskatchewan Party with an astounding 27 percentage point lead.[21] But arguably the most compelling evidence of the Saskatchewan Party's utter dominance, particularly in rural Saskatchewan, came many months earlier, mere weeks after Moe had taken over as leader. In three rural by-elections, with Wall no longer a factor and the government into the last half of its third mandate, one could reasonably think that the Saskatchewan Party might be vulnerable. Traditionally, by-elections tend to be opportunities for people to express their unhappiness with government, without actually having to defeat it. So what happened? The Saskatchewan Party won by massive margins. In Kindersley, it took 88.1 percent of the popular vote. In Wall's former riding of Swift Current the Saskatchewan Party won with 73.4 percent of the vote; in Melfort it won 78.3 percent of the vote.[22] As bizarre as it might seem, to put those results in perspective one can look to Russia. Little more than two weeks later, Vladimir Putin was re-elected to his second consecutive term, his fourth overall, as president of Russia. He won with 76.7 percent of the vote in an election where the consensus view among democratic nations was that the electoral system is corrupt and the result was baked in before Russian people voted.[23] The fact that the Saskatchewan Party can command Putin-like majorities and more in rural Saskatchewan gives a person an idea of the desperate situation facing the NDP across much of the province.

Far in the background of all this has been the absence of one critical issue. A major, and perhaps the most important, factor confronting the province is the reality of life for most Indigenous people. Their lives have been largely untransformed during the political and economic transformation of Saskatchewan. It is difficult not to realize in reflecting on the major currents that have shaped and changed the province during the past fifty years that the involvement in any truly significant way of Indigenous people has been lacking. The October 2020 election was no different. Like provincial elections before it for the last fifty years, parties paid only scant, if any, attention to the challenges facing Indigenous people. Even though the word "reconciliation" is so readily on the lips of so many Canadians, it was seldom heard in any substantive way during the campaign.

As a group Indigenous people remain marginalized and are a people apart from the mainstream. Admittedly, it is possible to identify some examples of economic and social progress for First Nations and Indigenous people. But no one should be deceived by anecdotal evidence. By most yardsticks, progress has been incremental and not substantive in any holistic or systemic way. Whether in rates of poverty, education attainment, unemployment, or health outcomes, Indigenous and First Nations people lag far behind the rest of Saskatchewan society. In all eight measurements used to assess community well-being in Saskatchewan, the story is the same—Indigenous people are left behind. According to a 2019 report by the Canadian Index of Wellbeing, entitled *How Are Residents of Saskatchewan Really Doing?*, the Indigenous population experiences the benefits of progress in well-being to a much lesser degree than the non-Indigenous population.[24]

The statistics confirm that conclusion. A few examples: in 2016, according to Statistics Canada, 36 percent of on-reserve First Nations people and 16 percent of those off reserve live in crowded homes that have more than one person per room; the comparable figure for non-Indigenous people is 3 percent. Fully a third of Indigenous people have homes in need of significant repair, with the number rising to 47 percent of those on living on First Nations reserves.[25] The situation is reflected in a wide range of statistics. Before the COVID-19 pandemic, the unemployment rate for Indigenous people in Saskatchewan was 15 percent, or more than three times the rate for non-Indigenous people. Life expectancy for Indigenous people is fifteen years less than for the non-Indigenous population, and infant mortality rates are three times higher.[26] In Saskatoon more than 60 percent of Indigenous residents fall below the low income cut-off line, which is considered the poverty level; the comparable number for the non-Indigenous population is 18 percent. Adding greater urgency to the situation faced by Indigenous people in Saskatchewan is that they represent the fastest-growing segment of the population and are projected to represent a third of the population by 2045.[27]

No challenge is greater than the need to improve the lives of an impoverished population. Admittedly, on the ground it is complicated by federal-provincial jurisdictional issues. The responsibility for on-reserve First Nations rests with the federal government, but many Indigenous people leave their reserves to find work in the cities, where provincial and municipal policies and services apply. The question is, will the need to find solutions to what for generations has been so clearly an unacceptable reality become a defining issue, and how will it influence the political and economic trajectory of the province in the years to come? True reconciliation and progress begins with a recognition that there has been a collective failure of leadership at all levels, politically and economically, among non-Indigenous and Indigenous leaders.

In his assessment of the 2020 provincial election result, long-time Saskatchewan political and policy analyst Ken Rasmussen from the Johnson

Shoyama Graduate School of Public Policy concisely sums up the reality of the political transformation that has taken place in the province.

> The 2020 provincial election resulted in the continued dominance of the Saskatchewan Party, which won a fourth consecutive majority government, further solidifying long-term changes taking place in Saskatchewan's political culture. With a solid majority of seats and over 60 percent of the popular vote, the election has provided more evidence that the old era of deeply divisive ideological-focused elections is over, and instead, what matters to voters are leadership and the perceived ability to manage the province's volatile resource economy. This is not an uncommon trend across Canada, but in Saskatchewan it is a noteworthy development. Saskatchewan has moved away from a history of polarized elections that were fought between the "socialist" NDP on the left and a changing assortment of bearers of the banner of the "free market" party. This election result confirmed that a new context has emerged involving two dominant parties that focus on who will be better able to manage the status quo.[28]

The transition has been long and, at times, painful. It has been driven by many factors and events that have reshaped not only Saskatchewan's politics and its economy but how others now see a province that once stood out as a homeland of Canadian socialism.

EPILOGUE

2021

Reckoning

I N TERMS OF THE POLITICAL AND ECONOMIC TRANSFORMA-
tion of Saskatchewan, it is difficult to know where to begin when
considering the demise of the New Democratic Party. There is no one
obvious moment or event when the party's future, or even existence, was
clearly in peril. There are always many factors, a combination of influences
and people, that lead to transformative outcomes. The same is true of the
NDP's fate. One can point to a litany of things, each with varying degrees
of significance.

The unfolding of events through the course of more than half a century
have led to the political and economic reality of Saskatchewan today. There
was the loss of the party's prairie populist roots when Tommy Douglas left
the leadership in 1961. From that point forward, the NDP was never to regain
what it had in the charisma and largely pragmatic populism of Douglas.
There have been the endless struggles between left and centrist factions, all
of which took their toll on the party, sapping its energy and shaping its

public image. Too often the NDP was seen as a crucible for pitched ideological battles, dear to the hearts of ideologues but far removed from the reality
of Saskatchewan people.

There were also the conflicts with the federal government in the 1970s
and early 1980s. At stake was control of natural resources and the details of
a Canadian constitution that would alter the power balance between elected
politicians and the courts. It was a period when the New Democrats were in
government and lost touch with the struggles of a population dealing with an
extended period of stagflation. It was a time that led to the re-emergence of
populism and the rise of the Grant Devine government.

There were the difficult, gut-wrenching decisions in government of the
1990s when the party had to manage an inherited debt-driven fiscal crisis that
forced the closure of rural hospitals, exacting a political price that is still being
paid to this day. There was the coalition with a handful of Liberals to maintain
power, which effectively created a two-party political landscape and resulted
in a binary electoral choice that the NDP had long sought to avoid, knowing that a polarized electoral environment would most likely lead to defeat.
There have been successive changes in leadership in the last fifteen years, none
of which has produced the kind of introspection and critical analysis a party
needs to regenerate itself and adapt to the reality of the world it faces.

Then there more extraneous factors—in other words, not so much what
the NDP did or did not do, but what others did. In that regard, there was
the rise of the Saskatchewan Party and the influence of Brad Wall as premier.
Some, usually with opposing ideological views, branded Wall and his government as right-wing conservatism. Some use the term "neoliberal." But in
many ways, those sorts of labels, whether "neoliberal" or "social democratic,"
have lost much of their meaning. The Wall government is a good example.

The key point is that, by many measures, Wall was a mild populist in the
practical, centrist prairie tradition. His was a government that at its core was
pragmatic and activist, far from the austere tight-fisted conservatism some
like to suggest. If anything, it was a government that at times spent with abandon. The single best measure is the size of government itself. During Wall's,

eleven-year tenure, total government spending grew by 53 percent, from $9.3 billion to $14.3 billion. As a percentage of the economy, government grew from 18.8 percent in 2007–08, reached 21 percent by 2010–11, and was at 19.6 percent of the economy by 2016–17.[1] To put that in context, Saskatchewan's GDP grew by 23 percent, from $65.9 billion in 2007 to $81.5 billion in 2019.[2]

In power, the Saskatchewan Party has presided over the accumulation of annual budget deficits and growth in the provincial debt unparalleled in the province's history. What is most damning is that it occurred during what, for the most part, was a period of strong economic growth. In recent decades it has become something of a pathology in Saskatchewan politics and governing. Free enterprise, business-oriented "conservative" governments operate with financial ineptitude, leaving their fiscal mess to be cleaned up by others, namely the New Democrats. In the case of the Saskatchewan Party, the mid-year operating deficit projection for the 2021–22 fiscal year is more than $2.7 billion. The net debt of the province had reached $16.7 billion, representing almost 20 percent of the provincial economy.[3] To put that into a governing context, the net debt of the province was $6.4 billion when the Saskatchewan Party took power from the NDP in 2007.[4]

With that kind of spending profile, the Saskatchewan Party government gave the NDP little ground of its own on which it could stand and fight on matters in a way that would create a significant political cleavage on key defining issues. That's not to say there were not issues for the NDP as the Opposition to seize, but they were always on the margins and not fundamental in the minds of most Saskatchewan people. In the meantime, Wall had the communication skills to establish himself in populist terms, not as a right-wing ideologue but rather as a leader who understood and could reflect the communitarian values of the province.

At the same time, the label "social democracy" has been rendered almost meaningless in any partisan sense. The concept of social democracy had long been embedded in Canadian government, at the federal and provincial levels. There are many ways to define the term, one of which comes from Tom Kent, the highly regarded former public servant and journalist, in a paper he wrote in 2012 for the Broadbent Institute. Kent says social democracy describes "a society where the enterprise of productive employment in a market economy is joined with active government to secure the public interest in equality of opportunities and fairness of outcomes."[5] On that basis, all governments in Canada are social democratic in some form. The role of the state in equalizing opportunity and easing the impact of the market on individuals is fundamental to governance. The only debate is about the degree to which governments engage in the pursuit of social democracy, or in other words, where they are situated on the social democratic spectrum. The Saskatchewan Party government under Wall was, for the most part, in the Canadian mainstream of social democracy.

The other external factor that arguably was the most critical in the demise of the NDP came in the 1980s, an era marked by the rise of economic liberalism globally and reflected in Saskatchewan by the privatization agenda of the Grant Devine government. The scale of the privatization of commercial government corporations, many created by the Blakeney NDP government of the 1970s, was substantial. It was clearly a seismic shift and transformative in terms of the role of the public sector in the Saskatchewan economy. But the most critical factor in terms of the unfolding politics of the province was that the privatization of those years robbed the NDP of its identity. The issue of government ownership in any significant economic sense, which had been firmly established in the Blakeney years, was removed from the political agenda of the province and has never returned in any meaningful way. What comes to mind is Devine's remark that potash privatization would be the NDP's "Waterloo." Judging by today's political and economic landscape in Saskatchewan, he was right.

Certainly, there are many other key events and factors. One has been the NDP's inability to adapt to the rapidly changing global economy of the late twentieth and early twenty-first centuries. It was as if the party was locked in a time warp, unable to recognize that, as Einstein said, to change the world we must change our thinking. In effect, the NDP seemed to be left behind by events, transformed into a voice that echoed from a different time and reality.

Then there is the endless tension in the NDP between the so-called purists and the pragmatists. It goes back to the very origins of the party and its British Fabian Society traditions, beginning with the Regina Manifesto in 1933 and including the Winnipeg Declaration of 1956 and the Waffle Manifesto of 1969. Essentially the question is whether the NDP is a "movement" or an actual political party seeking to get elected and run a government. When Roy Romanow was facing an internal revolt over the difficult budget decisions required of his government, he told his caucus, "We're not a goddamn debating society. We're a political party trying to put together a governing agenda."[6]

Today it is easy to see the NDP is a party divided into groups of anachronists, each living in an era it would like to revive. One group, circa the late 1960s, still believes the party is socialist. Others are Allan Blakeney loyalists who long for the 1970s and the return to a form of state capitalism, with Crown corporations as a means of greater public control of resources. A third cohort has its roots in 1961 and the formal alliance of organized labour with the NDP. An ever declining and aging rural faction is made up of those who long for a return to the family farm, the revival of the co-op movement, and orderly marketing. Another group, who unlike the others represent a more contemporary perspective, are single-issue minded, motivated almost exclusively by environmentalism and climate change. The party is also the captive of identity politics, a belief that who you are in terms of racial, gender, ethnic, and sexual identity dictates your priorities. The result is a party that itself is a collection of silos that spends much of its time and energy trying to reconcile the factions within, without ever producing a coherent and cohesive narrative that makes sense to the broader public.

One cannot help but be reminded of advice that the late Edward Kennedy gave in 1985 to the Democratic Party in the United States. "We must understand that there is a difference between being a party that cares about labour and being a labour party," Kennedy said. "There is a difference between being a party that cares about women and being the women's party. And we can and we must be a party that cares about minorities without becoming a minority party. We are citizens first."[7] The point is that the role of politics should be to unite people by reflecting the core values people share as citizens, not dividing society into identity groups defined by their differences.

But whatever the combination of factors, it is what it is, and the NDP in Saskatchewan is now a shadow of the party that was once deeply woven into the fabric of the province. The October 2020 election that gave the Saskatchewan Party its fourth majority, and third consecutive landslide, left the New Democrats buried in the rubble of the final result. The electoral facts were unequivocal. Today the NDP is frankly irrelevant in rural Saskatchewan—not only shut out but in four constituencies finishing third behind the Buffalo Party. Espousing a policy of provincial independence, either within the federation or through separation, the Buffalo Party was able to begin tapping into the populist vein of western alienation and has become something of a wild card as a potentially disruptive force in provincial politics. In a very real sense, the partisan cleavage in Saskatchewan reflects a defining characteristic in politics throughout much of the world. Whether it's Canada, the U.S., or many nations in Europe, the polarization that shapes politics today is more a function of geography than ideology. It is between rural and urban, often fueled by alienation and populist anger against so-called elites who are seen to dictate the acceptable terms of political debate.

The hard truth is that in the wake of the 2020 election the NDP was mired deeply in dissension and division, in turmoil over whether leader Ryan Meili, who very narrowly won his own seat, should stay as leader. What didn't help was that a few days after the election Meili fired his chief of staff and the party secretary, as if those people needed to take the fall for the long, and pitiful, decline of the NDP. As one of its members, who has been through the successive defeats, asks, "How many times do we need to eat our guts out with a spoon?"[8]

It is a good question. You would think that a meeting of the party's hundred-member provincial council two months after the election would have amounted to one of those "come-to-Jesus" moments when all is laid bare in a catharsis of emotion. But that didn't happen. In the age of the COVID-19 pandemic, it was, like all such gatherings, done virtually via Zoom. Without the emotional and interpersonal dynamics that come with people being in a room together, the result was more perfunctory than passionate. An election review committee was formed that included what some describe as the "usual suspects," such as defeated federal candidates from Ontario. The fact that in defeat the party would turn to the defeated for advice is instructive in itself. Meili said it was not a time for fault finding and that everyone needed to unite. No question-and-answer session was held with the leader. There was no serious discussion about leadership, even though for many the topic was the elephant in the virtual meeting room. The matter was left for the party's next convention many months later, buying time for emotions to subside and, no doubt, also leading many to abandon any further active role in the party. When the time came for a leadership review in October 2021, Meili mustered support from 72 percent of party members.[9] Hardly a ringing endorsement, but enough for him to soldier on, while also having to constantly look over his shoulder. But the simple fact that there is focus on the leader as a key factor in its electoral dilemma is itself instructive. It is evidence of how the party fails to grasp fully how it has become lost in the tides of history. In its feeble state, the NDP cannot afford to bleed any more members. The party's membership has been in steady and remorseless decline for years, falling from approximately 45,000 in 1991 to an estimated 5,000 to 6,000 in 2021, a number some say is inflated.

The NDP election review committee released a report in April 2021, in the wake of the last election defeat, that too was a reflection of the party's malaise and inability to recognize its vulnerabilities. Its mandate was to "focus on both the root causes of the result, and solution-based recommendations to prepare for the next election."[10] But instead of confronting the party's existential issue—that is, the practical relevance of its beliefs, priorities, and policies in the Saskatchewan of today that have pushed it to the political margins in what was its homeland—the report focused on process and tactics. It talked of the need to "reconnect with working class voters" and "squarely address the future of resource industries" as well as the necessity for the party "to be rebuilt in rural Saskatchewan."[11] But these aspirations did not come with any hint of the specifics that would make them possible.

The optimistic narrative that a few in the NDP are telling themselves, led in large measure by the leader, is that the party has solidified its position in opposition with thirteen seats, a gain of three. But the gain also included the loss of an urban seat won in a by-election. It is thin gruel for many, especially when the New Democrats were running against a Saskatchewan Party seeking an unheard of fourth mandate, and without Brad Wall as leader. The fact is that Scott Moe lacks the profile, oratorical flourish, and populist appeal of Wall. He is not, as they say, overburdened with charisma. So, if ever there appeared to be a time when the Saskatchewan Party could be vulnerable, at least to the point that the NDP could inflict serious damage by making significant inroads, it was thought to be in the post-Wall era.

There is reason to believe that the Saskatchewan Party's political stranglehold on the province is weakening. In its October 2021 survey of approval ratings for premiers, the Angus Reid Institute found that Scott Moe's approval had "plummeted" almost 20 points, from 61 to 43 percent.[12] It's not surprising, except to those in the Saskatchewan Party ranks who admit to being surprised that the premier's approval rating had not dropped even more. A subsequent Angus Reid survey in January 2022 showed that Moe's approval rating had risen insignificantly by two percentage points, well within the margin of error.[13] The result confirmed the toll the government's management of the pandemic had taken on the premier's political stature. Also, an NDP-commissioned poll in December 2021 indicated the NDP was leading in Saskatoon and Regina, but still trailing in rural Saskatchewan.

A universally acknowledged fact in Saskatchewan politics is that the most important issue on the public agenda is health care. The sentiment has deep roots that reach back to the introduction of Medicare in 1962. But it also goes well beyond the issue of public-versus-private health care to the actual day-to-day management of the system. By that measurement, the COVID-19 pandemic has exposed a political dilemma facing the Moe government: it has staked its political future on retaining the support of rural Saskatchewan, in part by maintaining a largely hands-off pandemic public health strategy.

The consequences of that strategy emerged with the fourth wave of the pandemic, driven by the Delta variant, in the late summer of 2021 and well into the fall. For the first sixteen months of the pandemic, the Moe government did as well as most governments in managing what was a challenging and complex public health situation. But then it declared victory in July 2021, mirroring the position of the Jason Kenney government of Alberta. "Let's go and enjoy a great Saskatchewan summer," Moe said.[14] Rather than risk alienating its political base and raising the potential for a populist backlash on its right, as the fourth wave rose the Moe government consistently ignored advice from medical professionals to impose strict public health mandates, vowing never to go back to another series of lockdowns. As a result, COVID infection and death rates in Saskatchewan very quickly became the highest in Canada, to the point where the health care system was, in the words of many in the system, "in a crisis."[15]

The almost laissez-faire management of the pandemic in recent months by the Moe government continued into early 2022 with the arrival of the fifth wave, driven by the highly contagious, if less severe, Omicron variant. It was a public health strategy almost entirely based on a political calculation to not anger the government's hardline, individual liberty adherents on the right, many of whom see vaccine mandates as an infringement on their "personal freedoms." They accept no personal responsibility as members of a society to act in a way that protects others. Deluded by conspiracy theories and health charlatans—mostly imported from the fringes of U.S. politics that has now become almost mainstream—for them public health orders are part of a government plot to exercise greater control over their lives.

At this stage the magnitude of the health care blunder in political terms for the Saskatchewan Party government is difficult to gauge with any certainty, particularly when the next provincial election is not due until the fall of 2024. But clearly the miscalculation was Moe's July announcement that all pandemic restrictions were being lifted. "Instead of trying to control the infection rate through government-imposed restrictions and government rules, we can now control COVID through vaccines," he said.[16] It was a categorical statement that lacked any qualification for the reimposition of public health measures should numbers warrant. The government had boxed itself in with its own words, which came back with a vengeance two months later to undermine public confidence in its management of the pandemic at a crucial time.

But the real political effect of the pandemic might be less about the actual day-to-day management of the pandemic itself. The fact is that there was no obvious playbook for governments to follow. Approaches and outcomes varied around the world, with multiple risks, variables, and impacts part of the decision making—ranging from impact on the health system, jobs and the economy, education, and mental health to the limits of public acceptance.

For the Saskatchewan Party government and frankly all governments in Canada, what the pandemic has done is expose the fragility of the health care system. If the public loses faith in the capability of the public health system to deliver, including nursing care for the elderly, then there is no one to blame other than government. Ironically, it is not impossible to imagine that just as rural health care became an Achilles heel to the former Romanow NDP government, so too could it haunt the Moe government. Finding qualified health care workers in rural Saskatchewan, whether doctors, nurses, or support staff, has become a massive problem. Faced with the additional pressures created by an aging population, the system is in a precarious condition that could quickly lead to political consequences.

But as history over the last fifty years has shown, the drivers of politics in Saskatchewan reach far beyond the parochialism of provincial politics. Much bigger forces will shape the province's political and economic future.

At the top of that list are growing concerns about the Canadian and global economies. Many respected economists—including Nouriel Roubini, who famously predicted the financial sector meltdown and recession of 2008–09—believe that the combination of rising prices, supply shocks from the disruption of global trade by the pandemic, and escalating energy costs is a recipe for a return of stagflation.[17] The suggestion of stagflation, or even a sustained period of inflation, is a contested view among economists. But it is an opinion shared by others, such as former U.S. treasury secretary and Harvard University president Larry Summers, who noted in December 2021 the U.S. Federal Reserve's recognition that inflation is not temporary.[18] Moreover, Summers also points out that periods of inflation have never ended without an economic recession. In December 2021, Canada's inflation rate, which had been dormant for many years, had risen to 4.8 percent, its highest in thirty years.[19]

Adding further uncertainty is the seriously disconcerting geopolitical volatility as 2022 began to unfold—whether China's domestic and global agenda, Russia's belligerence, rising nationalisms of Europe, or the growing risks of U.S. political instability and civil unrest. The potential of significant political upheaval in the U.S. that leads to actual civil conflict is no longer a far-fetched notion. Such a reality would create an existential challenge for Canada and destabilize the world even further.

Then there is Canada's persistently weak productivity growth and the huge federal operating deficit that leaves Ottawa with little fiscal capacity to deal with a future economic downturn. The reality is that, with interest rates expected to rise, all governments—including Saskatchewan's, which is mired in debt—face challenging times. In fact, to get a clear understanding of Canada's national fiscal situation, one has only to look at the total debt of all the provinces, which now almost equals the federal government's accumulated debt.[20]

For a party out of power, those ingredients should represent an opportunity. Still, the challenge for the NDP to resurrect itself cannot be overstated. The transformation of Saskatchewan politics has been unfolding for many years, at both the federal and provincial levels. Federally, it can be traced to the rise of the populist Reform Party of the 1990s and the Canadian Alliance of the early 2000s, which was fuelled by western alienation. Those gains were then consolidated by Stephen Harper's Conservative Party in 2006, which brought together elements of Reform, Canadian Alliance, and Progressive Conservatives. In that election, the NDP failed to elect a single MP in Saskatchewan for the first time since 1958.[21]

But perhaps the starkest evidence of the transformation came in the federal election of November 2019. It was the moment when the political convergence of Saskatchewan with Alberta became most apparent. In both provinces, the Conservatives won every seat, shutting out the NDP and toppling even long-time Liberal cabinet minister Ralph Goodale in Regina. Beyond the topline results, the most telling statistic was the size of the Conservative margin on a riding-by-riding basis. In eight of fourteen ridings the Conservative candidate won with more than 60 percent of the popular vote, in two cases with more than 80 percent. Even in the far northern riding, which has long been a Liberal or NDP stronghold and saw the closest race, the Conservatives won by a 14 percentage point margin over the NDP incumbent.[22] The result was repeated in the September 2021 federal election when every seat in Saskatchewan again went to the Conservatives.

The ultimate irony for the Saskatchewan NDP is that it has reached the point where it has to look west to Alberta, of all places, for hope. At present, the United Conservative Party (UCP) government in Alberta faces significant political headwinds from a multitude of economic, environmental, pandemic, and political factors. After uniting the provincial Progressive Conservative Party with the Wildrose Party—the two dominant parties on the right in Alberta politics—to form the UCP, Jason Kenney was able to soundly defeat the NDP government of Rachel Notley in 2019 after its one term in office.

For many, going back to a free enterprise, right-wing government in Alberta was a return to a natural political state. After all, Alberta had effectively been ruled by one party, whether Social Credit or Progressive Conservative, for more than seventy years. Many were shocked when Notley was able to take advantage of both the fragmentation among parties on the right and public anger with perceived government corruption to win in 2015. But her election as premier also sensitized people to the realization that an NDP government is not venturing far from the mainstream of Alberta priorities and governance. There is a year left until the next Alberta election, but a return to power by Notley and the NDP is no longer beyond the realm of fantasy, as it had been prior to 2015.

Nothing is forever in politics. A popular saying is that "governments aren't elected, they're defeated." When the mood for change takes root in a population, it becomes a lethal force against an incumbent government, often fed by the perception that the party in power has become arrogant and sees itself as the natural governing party. Over time, success in politics ultimately breeds a belief in a party's invincibility. Its unchallenged dominance in rural parts of the province, coupled with the NDP's weakness, has given the Saskatchewan Party a belief in its own political impregnability. If that sense enters the political bloodstream, change can happen rapidly and dramatically. Saskatchewan witnessed it before, in 1982 and again in 1991. In the early months of 2022, the risk of an infection of hubris in the Moe government was becoming obvious, if not acute. Coming in the wake of the Wall era, when a populist leader became the personification of the Saskatchewan Party, the loss of that attribute inevitably erodes the party's appeal.

The Saskatchewan Party stranglehold on the province will end; the only question is when, and by whom. Being Saskatchewan, the natural assumption has been that it would be the New Democrats, a party that for decades saw itself as the rightful owner of the title of the province's natural governing party, a notion that was shattered in 1982. But that belief is no longer necessarily valid. When considered in the long sweep of Saskatchewan history and the political culture it has created, the potential exists for someone or something to emerge that ignites the province. It's not as if the province doesn't face huge challenges.

In some ways, the unfolding global and national events of today—the pandemic, a retreat from globalization, the fear of stagflation, an unfolding energy and environment crisis, rising government debt, and regional cleavages in Canada—are not unlike the major issues that politically and economically transformed the province between the late 1960s and the turn of the twenty-first century. At the same time, the populism that was so fundamental in shaping the province, its politics, and its identity many decades ago still lurks below the surface. It remains both a potent and potentially dangerous force if not managed with care. At a time when division and alienation are themes that often dominate the politics of the prairie West, the challenge for Saskatchewan's future is to ensure that its political and economic transformation does not lose sight of its past.

Indeed, there surely are lessons to be drawn for all of Canada from the issues, events, and trends that shaped the political and economic transformation of Saskatchewan. This is a story much bigger than a province. Long seen as playing a role in shaping national politics far exceeding its status in terms of population and economy, Saskatchewan might again be at the leading edge of what unfolds politically as Canada responds to its challenges.

General Election Results since 1971

LEGEND

NDP	New Democratic Party	SKMP	Saskatchewan Marijuana Party
NGA	New Green Alliance	SP	Saskatchewan Party
PC	Progressive Conservatives	WIP	Western Independence Party

	Political Party	# of Votes	% of Votes	# of Candidates Elected
1971	NDP	248,978	55.00%	45
	Liberal	193,864	42.82%	15
	PC	9,659	2.13%	0
	Independent	189	0.04%	0
	Communist	46	0.01%	0
	Total	**452,736**	**100.00%**	**60**
1975	NDP	180,700	40.04%	39
	Liberal	142,853	31.67%	15
	PC	124,573	27.62%	7
	Independent	2,897	0.64%	0
	Total	**451,023**	**100.00%**	**61**

	Political Party	# of Votes	% of Votes	# of Candidates Elected
1978	NDP	228,791	48.12%	44
	PC	181,045	38.08%	17
	Liberal	65,498	13.78%	0
	Independent	2,897	0.64%	0
	Total	**475,415**	**100.00%**	**61**
1982	PC	289,311	54.07%	55
	NDP	201,390	37.64%	9
	Liberal	24,134	4.51%	0
	Western Canada Concept	17,487	3.26%	0
	Independent	1,607	0.30%	0
	Aboriginal Peoples Party	1,156	0.22%	0
	Total	**535,085**	**100.00%**	**64**
1986	NDP	247,683	45.20%	25
	PC	244,382	44.61%	38
	Liberal	54,739	9.99%	1
	Western Canada Concept	458	0.08%	0
	Independent	358	0.07%	0
	Alliance	237	0.04%	0
	Communist	73	0.01%	0
	Total .	**547,930**	**100.00%**	**64**
1991	NDP	275,780	51.05%	55
	PC	137,994	25.54%	10
	Liberal	125,814	23.29%	1
	Independent	592	0.11%	0
	Western Canada Concept	46	0.01%	0
	Total	**540,226**	**100.00%**	**66**

	Political Party	# of Votes	% of Votes	# of Candidates Elected
1995	NDP	193,053	47.21%	42
	Liberal	141,873	34.70%	11
	PC	73,269	17.92%	5
	Independent	712	0.17%	0
	Total	**408,907**	**100.00%**	**58**
1999	SP	160,603	39.61%	25
	NDP	157,046	38.73%	29
	Liberal	81,694	20.15%	4
	NGA	4,101	1.01%	0
	PC	1,609	0.40%	0
	Independent	422	0.10%	0
	Total	**405,475**	**100.00%**	**58**
2003	NDP	190,923	44.68%	30
	SP	168,144	39.35%	28
	Liberal	60,601	14.18%	0
	WIP	2,615	0.61%	0
	NGA	2,323	0.55%	0
	Independent	1,997	0.47%	0
	PC	681	0.16%	0
	Total	**427,284**	**100.00%**	**58**
2007	SP	230,671	50.92%	38
	NDP	168,704	37.24%	20
	Liberal	42,585	9.40%	0
	Green Party	9,128	2.01%	0
	PC	832	0.18%	0
	WIP	572	0.13%	0
	SKMP	517	0.18%	0
	Total	**453,009**	**99.99%**	**58**

	Political Party	# of Votes	% of Votes	# of Candidates Elected
2011	SP	258,598	64.25%	49
	NDP	128,673	31.97%	9
	Green Party	11,561	2.87%	0
	Liberal	2,237	0.56%	0
	PC	1,315	0.33%	0
	WIP	58	0.01%	0
	Total	**402,486**	**100.00%**	**58**
2016	SP	270,776	62.36%	51
	NDP	131,137	30.20%	10
	Liberal	15,568	3.59%	0
	Green Party	7,967	1.83%	0
	PC	5,571	1.28%	0
	Independent	1,693	0.39%	0
	WIP	318	0.07%	0
	Total	**433,030**	**99.72%**	**61**
2020	SP	269,996	60.67%	48
	NDP	140,576	31.59%	13
	Buffalo Party	11,298	2.54%	0
	Green Party	10,031	2.25%	0
	PC	8,404	1.89%	0
	Independent	1,076	0.24%	0
	Liberal	355	0.08%	0
	Total	**441,736**	**99.26%**	**61**

Source: Elections Saskatchewan

Notes

INTRODUCTION

1   Howard Leeson, introduction to *Saskatchewan Politics: Crowding the Centre* (Regina: Canadian Plains Research Center, 2009), 2.

A BEFORE AND AFTER MOMENT

1   The author was in attendance.
2   See David McGrane, John Whyte, Roy Romanow, and Russell Isinger, eds., *Back to Blakeney: Revitalizing the Democratic State* (Regina: University of Regina Press, 2019).
3   "Twentieth Provincial General Election (April 26, 1982)," Election Results, Elections SK, accessed October 21, 2021, https://www.elections.sk.ca/reports-data/election-results/1982-2/.
4   "Devine's Victory Makes History," *Saskatoon Star Phoenix*, April 27, 1982, A9.
5   The line became a constant in Devine's populist appeal for a greater Saskatchewan future.
6   Progressive Conservative Party of Saskatchewan, *Commitment*, n.d. [1982], pamphlet, Poltext, Université Laval, https://www.poltext.org/sites/poltext.org/files/plateformesV2/Saskatchewan/SK_PL_1982_PC_en.pdf.
7   Saskatchewan New Democratic Party, *We Care!*, n.d. [1982], booklet, Poltext, Université Laval, https://www.poltext.org/sites/poltext.org/files/plateformesV2/Saskatchewan/SK_PL_1982_PC_en.pdf.
8   Allan Gregg, email exchange with author, December 2020.

9   Saskatchewan NDP, *We Care!*
10   "At Last the Crow Must Go," *Maclean's*, February 22, 1982.
11   National Farmers Union, "Working for Farm Families for 40 Years" (NFU, Saskatoon, October 2009), 11–12.
12   Sheilagh M. Dunn, "The Year in Review 1982: Intergovernmental Relations in Canada" (Institute of Intergovernmental Relations, Queen's University, 1982), 159, https://www.queensu.ca/iigr/sites/webpublish.queensu.ca.iigrwww/files/files/pub/archive/yearinreview/TheYearInReview1982-Dunn.pdf.
13   Saskatchewan, Legislative Assembly, *Debates and Proceedings (Hansard)*, March 22, 1982, 751.
14   New Democratic Party of Saskatchewan, *Tested and Trusted*, n.d. [1982], booklet.
15   PC Party of Saskatchewan, *Commitment*.
16   Saskatchewan, Ministry of Finance, *Budget Speech,* 19th Leg., 4th Sess. (March 18, 1982), 56, 72.
17   "Saskatchewan Leaders' Debate 1982," n.d., CBC News, video, 1:24, https://www.cbc.ca/player/play/2685743434.
18   "Twentieth Provincial General Election."

ONWARD CHRISTIAN SOLDIERS

1   See Koen Abts and Stefan Rummens, "Populism versus Democracy," *Political Studies* 55, no. 2 (2007): 405–24.
2   Richard Allen, "The Social Gospel as the Religion of the Agrarian Revolt," in *The Prairie West: Historical Readings*, ed. R. Douglas Francis and Howard Palmer (Edmonton: Pica Press, 1985), 439.
3   M.S., "What Is Populism?," The Economist Explains, *Economist*, December 19, 2016, n.p.
4   "Neoliberal" is a term that describes free-market capitalism, deregulation, and smaller government.
5   Rogers Brubaker, "Why Populism?," *Theory and Society* 46 (2007): 358–59.
6   Brubaker, 359.
7   Goodhart, *The Road to Somewhere: The Populist Revolt and the Future of Politics* (London: Hurst, 2017).
8   "David Goodhart: Anywheres versus Somewheres," Viewsnight, *BBC Newsnight*, March 16, 2017, video, 2:16, https://www.bbc.com/news/av/uk-39293519.
9   Preston Manning, conversation with author during an organizational visit to Saskatchewan, 1987.
10   Robert Lynd, introduction to *Agrarian Socialism*, by Seymour Martin Lipset (Berkeley: University of California Press, 1967), ix.
11   Seymour Martin Lipset, *Agrarian Socialism: The Cooperative Commonwealth Federation in Saskatchewan; A Study in Political Sociology* (Berkeley: University of California Press, 1967), 3.

12   Spafford, "Notes on Re-reading Lipset's Agrarian Socialism," in Lipset's *Agrarian Socialism: A Re-examination*, ed. David E. Smith (Regina: Canadian Plains Research Center and the Saskatchewan Institute of Public Policy, 2007), 29.

13   Quoted in Ian McLeod, "Tommy Douglas," *Convivium*, October 28, 2016, https://www.convivium.ca/voices/69_tommy_douglas/.

14   Allen, "Social Gospel," 440.

15   Norman Ward, "Saskatchewan (Province)," *Canadian Encyclopedia*, November 30, 2015, last updated January 21, 2021, https://www.thecanadianencyclopedia.ca/en/article/saskatchewan.

16   Quoted in Bruce L. Guenther, "Populism, Politics and Christianity in Western Canada," *Historical Papers: Canadian Society of Church History* (2000): 99.

17   Walter Rauschenbusch, *Christianity and the Social Crisis* (New York: Macmillan, 1907), 147–48.

18   Former U.S. president Barack Obama embraced the teachings of Niebuhr.

19   Quoted in Scott Michael Pittendrigh, "The Religious Perspective of T.C. Douglas: Social Gospel Theology and Pragmatism" (M A thesis, University of Regina, 1997), 33.

20   "Tommy Douglas 1971," filmed April 24, 1971, video, 13:04, posted April 21, 2011, by Fed Vid, https://www.youtube.com/watch?v=MUwRULlgMec.

21   "Tommy Douglas 1971."

22   Craig Fox, review of *Keeping Canada British: The Ku Klux Klan in 1920s Saskatchewan*, by James Pitsula, *Labour/Le Travail* 74 (Fall 2014): 351.

23   Karen Briere, "James Gardiner," *Western Producer*, December 27, 2007, https://www.producer.com/news/james-gardiner/.

24   Quoted in Norman Ward and David Smith, *Jimmy Gardiner: Relentless Liberal* (Toronto: University of Toronto Press, 1990), 29.

25   Quoted in Ward and Smith, 90.

26   Ward and Smith, 92.

27   A re-enactment of the debate in 2008 captured the intensity of the moment in Saskatchewan history. See "James Gardiner Vs the K K K – Saskatchewan History," filmed June 28, 2008, in Lemberg, S K, video, 9:13, posted December 28, 2009, https://www.youtube.com/watch?v=7A A7LT21-N A.

28   Randy Boswell, *Province with a Heart: Celebrating 100 Years in Saskatchewan*, ed. Lynn McAuley (Toronto: CanWest, 2005), 70.

29   Conservative Party of Saskatchewan 1938 platform, in the author's possession.

30   Newman, *Renegade in Power: The Diefenbaker Years* (Toronto: McClelland & Stewart, 1973), 21, 23.

31   Joe Clark, eulogy to John Diefenbaker, August 22, 1979, Canada History – Documents, https://canadahistory.com/sections/documents/leaders/Joe_Clark/Eulogy_to_John_Diefenbaker.html.

32   "Canadian Bill of Rights," Diefenbaker Canada Centre, University of Saskatchewan, accessed September 24, 2021, https://diefenbaker.usask.ca/exhibits/online-exhibits-content/the-canadian-bill-of-rights.php.

33   Don Baron, *Canada's Great Grain Robbery: The Amazing Story of How a False Social Gospel Shackled the West and Canada* (self-pub., 1998), 16.
34   Macpherson, "Missionaries of Rural Development: The Fieldmen of the Saskatchewan Wheat Pool, 1925–1965," *Agricultural History* 60, no. 2 (1986): 75.
35   Quoted in Garry Fairbairn, *From Prairie Roots: The Remarkable Story of the Saskatchewan Wheat Pool* (Saskatoon: Western Producer Prairie Books, 1984), 24–25.
36   Quoted in Macpherson, "Missionaries of Rural Development," 76–77.
37   See Hugo Drochon, "Robert Michels, the Iron Law of Oligarchy and Dynamic Democracy," *Constellations* 27, no. 2 (2020), https://doi.org/10.1111/1467-8675.12494.
38   Leach, "The Iron Law of What Again? Conceptualizing Oligarchy across Organizational Forms," *Sociological Theory* 23, no. 3 (2005): 312.

WHAT'S IN AN ERA?

1   See John D. Wong, *Global Trade in the Nineteenth Century: The House of Houqua and the Canton System* (Cambridge: Cambridge University Press, 2016).
2   Statistics Canada, "150 Years of Immigration in Canada," Canadian Megatrends, *The Daily*, June 29, 2016, https://www150.statcan.gc.ca/n1/pub/11-630-x/11-630-x2016006-eng.htm.
3   See Lindsay Van Dyk, "Canadian Immigration Acts and Legislation," Canadian Museum of Immigration at Pier 21, accessed September 24, 2021, https://pier21.ca/research/immigration-history/canadian-immigration-acts-and-legislation.
4   Alan G. Green and David Green, "The Goals of Canada's Immigration Policy," *Canadian Journal of Urban Research* 13, no. 1 (2004): 116.
5   See "White Paper on Immigration, 1966," Canadian Museum of Immigration at Pier 21, accessed October 12, 2021, https://pier21.ca/research/immigration-history/white-paper-on-immigration-1966.
6   Quoted in John W. Berry, "Research on Multiculturalism in Canada," *International Journal of Intercultural Relations* 37, no. 6 (2013): 664.
7   Whitaker, *Canadian Immigration Policy since Confederation* (Ottawa: Canadian Historical Association, 1991), 19.
8   See Pierre Trudeau and Jacques Hébert, *Two Innocents in Red China* (Toronto: Oxford University Press, 1968).
9   Jeremy Kinsman, "Why Canada Matters to China," *iPolitics*, August 20, 2016, https://ipolitics.ca/2016/08/20/why-canada-matters-to-china.
10   "Pierre Trudeau Goes to China," CBC Television News Special, broadcast October 19, 1973, video, 5:42, https://www.cbc.ca/archives/entry/trudeau-goes-to-china.
11   Sutter, "Why Does China Matter?," *Washington Quarterly* 27, no. 1 (2003): 75–89.
12   "The Journal Examines the October Crisis, 20 Years Later," *The Journal*, CBC TV, broadcast October 4, 1990, video, 15:51, https://www.cbc.ca/archives/entry/the-journal-examines-the-october-crisis-20-years-later.

13 "Pierre Elliott Trudeau's Televised Statement on the War Measures Act," October 16, 1970, Documents in Quebec History, Marianopolis College, last modified August 23, 2000, http://faculty.marianopolis.edu/c.belanger/quebechistory/docs/october/trudeau.htm.

14 Andrew McIntosh and Celine Cooper, "October Crisis," *Canadian Encyclopedia*, August 13, 2013, last updated October 1, 2020, https://www.thecanadianencyclopedia.ca/en/article/october-crisis.

15 Pierre Trudeau, *Memoirs* (Toronto: McClelland & Stewart, 1995), 143.

16 "The October Arab-Israeli War of 1973: What Happened?," *Al Jazeera*, October 8, 2018, https://www.aljazeera.com/indepth/features/2017/10/arab-israeli-war-of-1973-what-happened-171005105247349.html.

17 "October Arab-Israeli War."

18 Michael L. Ross, "How the 1973 Oil Embargo Saved the Planet," *Foreign Affairs*, October 15, 2013, https://www.foreignaffairs.com/articles/north-america/2013-10-15/how-1973-oil-embargo-saved-planet.

19 Ross, "1973 Oil Embargo."

20 John F. Helliwell, "Comparative Macroeconomics of Stagflation," *Journal of Economic Literature* 26, no. 1 (1988): 2.

21 Helliwell.

22 Mike Moffatt, "Economic Stagflation in a Historical Context," *ThoughtCo.*, January 27, 2020, www.thoughtco.com/stagflation-in-a-historical-context-1148155.

23 D.A.L. Auld, L.N. Christofides, R. Swidinsky, and D.A. Wilton, "The Impact of the Anti-Inflation Board on Negotiated Wage Settlements," *Canadian Journal of Economics* 12, no. 2 (1979): 195–213.

24 Margaret Thatcher, "Speech to Conservative Central Council," March 15, 1986, 14–15, Margaret Thatcher Foundation, https://www.margaretthatcher.org/document/106348.

25 Andrew Gamble, "Privatization, Thatcherism and the British State," *Journal of Law and Society* 16, no. 1 (1989): 1.

26 "Canada: 1984 Parliamentary Elections," Political Database of the Americas, Georgetown University, accessed September 24, 2021, https://pdba.georgetown.edu/Elecdata/Canada/parl84.html.

27 Raymond Tatalovich and John Frendreis, "Fiscal Frugality: The Heart of Canadian Conservatism?" (paper presented at the annual meeting of the Canadian Political Science Association, Concordia University, Montreal, June 3, 2010), 13–14.

28 "The Common Agricultural Policy at a Glance," European Commission, accessed September 22, 2021, https://ec.europa.eu/info/food-farming-fisheries/key-policies/common-agricultural-policy/cap-glance_en.

29 See Tim Josling, "The Uruguay Round Agreement on Agriculture: A Forward-Looking Assessment" (paper presented at the OECD Workshop on Emerging Trade Issues in Agriculture, Paris, October 26–27, 1998).

30 Tim Josling et al., "Bringing Agriculture into the GATT: The Uruguay Round Agreement on Agriculture: An Evaluation" (Commissioned Paper No. 9, International Agriculture Trade Consortium, July 1994), iii.

31 Josling et al.

32 "GDP Growth (Annual %) – Canada," World Bank, accessed September 22, 2021, https://data.worldbank.org/indicator/NY.GDP.MKTP.KD.ZG?locations=CA.

33 "Prime Mortgage Rate History," ratehub.ca, accessed September 22, 2021, https://www.ratehub.ca/prime-mortgage-rate-history.

34 Canada, Privy Council Office, *Report of the Royal Commission on the Economic Union and Development Prospects for Canada*, vol. 1 (Ottawa: Privy Council Office, 1985), 62.

35 "How Free Trade Came to Canada: Lessons in Policy Analysis," *Policy Options*, October 1, 2007, https://policyoptions.irpp.org/magazines/free-trade-20/how-free-trade-came-to-canada-lessons-in-policy-analysis/.

36 "The GATT Years, From Havana to Marrakesh," World Trade Organization, accessed September 22, 2021, https://www.wto.org/english/.

37 Canada, Department of Finance, "Fiscal Reference Tables – October 2010," table 46.

38 Livio Di Matteo, "The Path to Fiscal Crisis: Canada's Federal Government, 1970 to 1995," in *The Budget That Changed Canada: Essays on the 25th Anniversary of the 1995 Budget*, ed. William Watson and Jason Clemens (Vancouver: Fraser Institute, February 2020), 7.

39 OECD, *OECD Economic Surveys: Canada, 1988* (Paris: OECD, 1988), 43.

40 OECD, *OECD Economic Surveys: Canada, 1993* (Paris: OECD, 1993), 108.

41 National Angus Reid, Southam News Poll, cited in Seth Klein, "Good Sense versus Common Sense: Canada's Debt Debate and Competing Hegemonic Projects" (MA thesis, Simon Fraser University, 1996), 115.

42 Canada, Department of Finance, *Budget Plan*, tabled in the House of Commons February 27, 1995 (Ottawa: Department of Supply and Services, 1995), 6.

1969: "WHY SHOULD I SELL YOUR WHEAT?"

1 Saskatchewan Bureau of Statistics, *Saskatchewan Economic Review* (1975), no. 29 (Regina, October 1975), 12.

2 Saskatchewan Bureau of Statistics, *Economic Review 2018*, no. 72 (Regina, August 2019), 11.

3 See William M. Miner, "The Rise and Fall of Canadian Wheat Board" (CAED Fellows Paper, 2015-2, [2015]).

4 "Trudeau Turns Wrath on Insulting Signs," *Regina Leader-Post*, July 17, 1969, 1.

5 *Manitoba Co-operator*, October 12, 2017.

6 Stuart A. Thiesson, "Saskatchewan Farmers Union," *Encyclopedia of Saskatchewan*, accessed September 22, 2021, https://esask.uregina.ca/entry/saskatchewan_farmers_union.jsp.

7   See Darren A. Swanson and Henry David Venema, "Analysis of the Crow Rate in Prairie Canada: A Cautionary Tale" (Adaptive Policy Case Study, IISD-TERI-IDRC, International Institute for Sustainable Development, Canada, n.d.).

8   Kenneth H. Norrie, "Not Much to Crow About: A Primer on the Statutory Grain Freight Rate Issue," *Canadian Public Policy* 9, no. 4 (1983): 435.

9   See Dale Eisler, *False Expectations: Politics and the Pursuit of the Saskatchewan Myth* (Regina: Canadian Plains Research Center, 2006); and André Magnan, "Canadian Wheat Board: Rise and Fall of a Prairie Giant," *A Country by Consent*, accessed October 21, 2021, http://www.canadahistoryproject.ca/1930s/1930s-13-cwb.html.

10 John Courtney, "Lipset, de Tocqueville, Radical Group Formation, and the Fate of Socialism in Saskatchewan," in Smith, *Lipset's Agrarian Socialism*, 22.

11 Saskatchewan Treasury Department, *Saskatchewan Economic Review* (1971), no. 25 (Regina, [1971]), 11.

12 "Full Text: The CCF's Regina Manifesto," *Canadian Dimension*, May 7, 2018, https://canadiandimension.com/articles/view/the-regina-manifesto-1933-co-operative-commonwealth-federation-programme-fu.

13 Quoted in Stefan Christoff, "Recounting and Reflecting on Saskatchewan's Co-operative History," *Rabble.ca*, May 22, 2014, https://rabble.ca/news/2014/05/recounting-and-reflecting-on-saskatchewans-co-operative-history.

14 "Farmer-Labor Party: Organizational History," Marxists Internet Archive, accessed September 26, 2021, https://www.marxists.org/history/usa/eam/flp/farmerlaborparty.html.

15 "Summary of North Dakota History—Nonpartisan League," State Historical Society of North Dakota, accessed September 22, 2021, https://www.history.nd.gov/ndhistory/npl.html.

16 Statistics Canada, "Estimated Areas, Yield, Production, Average Farm Price and Total Farm Value of Principal Field Crops, in Metric and Imperial Units," Table 32-10-0359-01, released September 14, 2021, https://www150.statcan.gc.ca/t1/tbl1/en/cv.action?pid=3210035901#timeframe.

17 Saskatchewan Treasury Department, *Saskatchewan Economic Review* (1971), 14.

18 Ron Friesen, "Wheat Growers' Group Formed to Protest CWB," *Manitoba Co-operator*, January 14, 2010, https://www.manitobacooperator.ca/news-opinion/news/wheat-growers-group-formed-to-protest-cwb/.

19 "'Operation LIFT' to Lower Wheat Surplus," *Manitoba Co-operator*, March 21, 2018, https://www.manitobacooperator.ca/country-crossroads/our-history/our-history-1970-operation-lift-to-lower-wheat-surplus/.

20 "Most Sask Farmers Survived Tough Year," *Regina Leader-Post*, January 2, 1971, 2.

21 Saskatchewan Treasury Department, *Saskatchewan Economic Review* (1971), 11.

22 Marilyn Florence, *Changing the Voice of the Prairie Wheat Grower: A History of the Palliser Wheat Growers Association and the Western Canadian Wheat Growers Association* (Alberta: PWGA and WCWGA, [1995?]), 1–4.

23 Gerald Friesen, *The Canadian Prairies: A History* (Toronto: University of Toronto Press, 1987), 255.

24 See David Jarvis, "British Conservatism and Class Politics in the 1920s," *English Historical Review* 111, no. 440 (1996): 59–84.

25 Nelson Wiseman, "The Pattern of Prairie Politics," *Queen's Quarterly* 88, no. 2 (1981): 301.

26 Wiseman, 300.

1971: A NEW DEAL

1   See James M. Pitsula, *As One Who Serves: The Making of the University of Regina* (Montreal and Kingston: McGill-Queen's University Press, 2006).

2   Duncan Cameron, "The NDP and the Waffle: 50 Years Later Survival Takes On a New Meaning," *Rabble.ca*, June 11, 2019, https://rabble.ca/columnists/2019/06/ndp-and-waffle-50-years-later-survival-takes-new-meaning.

3   "Reflections on the NDP at 50," *New Socialist*, June 18, 2011, http://newsocialist.org/reflections-on-the-ndp-at-50/.

4   David G. Blocker, "'To Waffle to the Left': The Waffle, the New Democratic Party, and Canada's New Left during the Long Sixties" (PhD diss., University of Western Ontario, 2019), 28.

5   Dennis Gruending, *Promises to Keep: A Political Biography of Allan Blakeney* (Saskatoon: Western Producer Prairie Books, 1990), 77.

6   Gruending, 77.

7   Gruending, 78.

8   "Banking Land in Saskatchewan," *CBC News*, CBC TV, broadcast March 25, 1972, video, 2:43, https://www.cbc.ca/archives/entry/banking-land-in-saskatchewan.

9   "Banking Land in Saskatchewan."

10 One exception was Thatcher's aggressive intervention in the potash industry with the imposition of prorationing in 1969.

11 Blocker, "'To Waffle to the Left.'"

12 See Eleanor Glor, ed., "Is Innovation a Question of Will or Circumstance? An Exploration of the Innovation Process through the Lens of the Blakeney Government in Saskatchewan, 1971–82," special issue, *The Innovation Journal* 5, no. 2 (2000) : art. 1g.

13 Saskatchewan, Executive Council, Planning and Research, *Saskatchewan Economic Review* (1972), no. 26 (Regina, 1972), 17.

14 Eleanor Glor, ed., "Determinism: Innovation as Emergent," in "Is Innovation a Question of Will or Circumstance?," special issue, *The Innovation Journal* 5, no. 2 (2000): art. 1f10.

15 "Wheat Prices—40 Year Historical Chart," Macrotrends, accessed September 22, 2021, https://www.macrotrends.net/2534/wheat-prices-historical-chart-data.

16 Statistics Canada, "Production, Imports, Exports and Domestic Disappearance of Wheat, Canada, 1868 to 1974 (Thousands of Bushels)," Series M301-309, Excel

spreadsheet, accessed October 25, 2021, https://www150.statcan.gc.ca/n1/pub/11-516-x/sectionm/M301_309-eng.csv.

17 See Agriculture and Agri-Food Canada, *Canadian Agriculture in the Seventies: Report of the Federal Task Force on Agriculture* (Ottawa: Agriculture and Agri-Food Canada, December 1969).

18 "1971 Saskatchewan Election," *Sunday Morning*, CBC Radio, broadcast June 1971, audio, 11:14, https://www.cbc.ca/player/play/1822825614.

19 "NDP by Landslide," *Saskatoon StarPhoenix*, June 24, 1971, 1.

1974: A FEDERAL INVASION

1 Ray Warden, "Where NDP Leaders Went Wrong in Parliament," *Intercontinental Press*, June 17, 1974.

2 "Liberal Minority Government Defeated in '74," CBC Television News Special, broadcast May 8, 1974, video, 19:08, https://www.cbc.ca/archives/entry/liberal-minority-government-defeated-in-74.

3 Government of Canada, *Budget Speech*, delivered May 6, 1974, by John N. Turner (Ottawa: Department of Finance, 1974), 9–10, https://www.budget.gc.ca/pdfarch/1974-MA-sd-eng.pdf.

4 Government of Canada, *Budget Speech*, delivered November 18, 1974, by John N. Turner (Ottawa: Department of Finance, 1974), 11, https://www.budget.gc.ca/pdfarch/1974-NO-sd-eng.pdf.

5 Government of Saskatchewan, Speech from the Throne, 17th Leg., 5th Sess. (November 28, 1974).

6 Peter Tyerman, "Pricing of Alberta's Oil," *Alberta Law Review* 14 (1976): 427.

7 "Canada to Increase Tax on Oil Shipped to U.S. by 375%," *New York Times*, November 2, 1973, 13.

8 Robert W. Sexty, "The Saskatchewan Oil and Gas Corporation" (Case Study 1.89, Institute of Public Administration of Canada, 1981), 7.

9 Quoted in Rowland J. Harrison, "Natural Resources and the Constitution: Some Recent Developments and Their Implications for the Future Regulation of the Resources Industries," *Alberta Law Review* 18, no. 1 (1980): 4.

10 Arne Paus Jenssen, "Resource Taxation and the Supreme Court of Canada: The Cigol Case," *Canadian Public Policy* 5, no. 1 (1979): 45–58.

11 *Canadian Industrial Gas & Oil Ltd. v. Government of Saskatchewan et al.,* [1978] 2 SCR 545, https://scc-csc.lexum.com/scc-csc/scc-csc/en/item/6080/index.do.

12 William Ready, "The Saskatchewan Potash Prorationing Scheme," *Alberta Law Review* 9, no. 3 (1971): 592–97.

13 Quoted in John Burton, *Potash: An Inside Account of Saskatchewan's Pink Gold* (Regina: University of Regina Press, 2014), 45.

14 See Burton for a detailed history of the issue.

15   See *Central Canada Potash Co. Ltd. et al. v. Government of Saskatchewan*, [1979] 1
      SCR 42, https://scc-csc.lexum.com/scc-csc/scc-csc/en/item/2639/index.do.
16   S.I. Bushnell, "The Control of Natural Resources through the Trade and
      Commerce Power and Proprietary Rights," *Canadian Public Policy* 6, no. 2
      (1980): 314.
17   Anderson, "Mining Taxation and Royalties in Saskatchewan," in *Mining Law
      in Canada*, ed. Richard H. Bartlett (Saskatoon: Law Society of Saskatchewan,
      1984), 215.
18   Allan Blakeney, *An Honourable Calling: Political Memoirs* (Toronto: University of
      Toronto Press, 2008), 149.
19   Burton, *Potash*, 74.
20   Barry Wilson, *The Politics of Defeat: The Decline of the Liberal Party in
      Saskatchewan* (Saskatoon: Western Producer Prairie Books, 1980), 87.
21   Wilson, 75.
22   Dick Spencer, *Singing the Blues: The Conservatives in Saskatchewan* (Regina:
      Canadian Plains Research Center, 2007), 142.

1975: A NEW YEAR'S EVE PARTY

1   "The Waffle Manifesto: For an Independent Socialist Canada (1969)," Socialist
      History Project, accessed September 22, 2021, http://www.socialisthistory.ca/
      Docs/Waffle/WaffleManifesto.htm.
2   The author was in attendance.
3   Barnett and McPhail, "An Examination of the Relationship of United States
      Television and Canadian Identity," *International Journal of Intercultural Relations*
      4, no. 2 (1980): 221.
4   See Neil Bissoondath, *Selling Illusions: The Cult of Multiculturalism in Canada*
      (Toronto: Penguin, 1994).
5   Barnett and McPhail, "Examination," 228–29.
6   Stuart H. Surlin and Barry Berlin, "TV, Values, and Culture in U.S.-Canadian
      Borderland Cities: A Shared Perspective," *Canadian Journal of Communication* 16,
      no. 3 (1991): 431–39.
7   Quoted in Pip Wedge, "U.S. Programs: Their Role in Canadian Television,"
      History of Canadian Broadcasting, Canadian Communications Foundation,
      accessed September 22, 2021, https://www.broadcasting-history.ca/in-depth/
      us-programs-their-role-canadian-television.
8   Bonnie Wagner, "We Proudly Begin Our Broadcast Day: Saskatchewan and
      the Arrival of Television, 1954–1969" (MA thesis, University of Saskatchewan,
      2004), 115.
9   Simon Claus, "Canadian Broadcasting Policy at Issue: From Marconi to Netflix,"
      Canadian Radio-television and Telecommunications Commission, last modified
      November 14, 2017, https://crtc.gc.ca/eng/acrtc/prx/2017claus.htm.

10   Seymour Martin Lipset, *Continental Divide: The Values and Institutions of the United States and Canada* (New York: Routledge, 1990).

11   Metta Spencer, review of *Continental Divide: The Values and Institutions of the United States and Canada*, by Seymour Martin Lipset, *Theory and Society* 21, no. 4 (1992): 610–18.

12   Lipset, *Continental Divide*, 221.

13   Lipset, 214.

14   "Justin Trudeau's Promise to Take 25,000 Syrian Refugees This Year 'Problematic,'" *CBC News*, October 28, 2015, https://www.cbc.ca/news/politics/ trudeau-syria-refugees-settlement-groups-1.3291959.

15   Statistics Canada, "Summary Table: Time Spent Watching Television by Persons Aged 2 Years and Over, Share by Origin and Type of Programme and Origin of Station, Canada, Fall 2001," accessed September 27, 2021, https://www150.statcan. gc.ca/n1/pub/87f0006x/4068230-eng.htm.

16   Joshua Macht, "Running Out of TIME: The Slow, Sad Demise of a Great American Magazine," *The Atlantic*, April 5, 2013, https://www.theatlantic.com/ business/archive/2013/04/running-out-of-time-the-slow-sad-demise-of-a-great-american-magazine/274713/.

17   Canada, Privy Council, *Report of the Royal Commission on Publications* (Ottawa: Queen's Printer, May 1961), 94.

18   Williams Borders, "Canada Is Seeking to Reduce U.S. Cultural Influence," *New York Times*, January 11, 1975, 2.

19   Quoted in Borders, 2.

1976: THE POLITICS OF IDENTITY

1   "Saskatchewan Will Not Yield to Doctors, Premier Asserts," *New York Times*, July 8, 1962, 37.

2   "Saskatchewan Doctors Firm as Strike Continues," *New York Times*, July 15, 1962, 26.

3   Government of Saskatchewan, Speech from the Throne, 18th Leg., 1st Sess. (November 12, 1975).

4   "Saskatchewan's History of Potash, Politics and Profit ([reprinted from] Regina Leaderpost—September 28, 2013)," Republic of Mining, September 30, 2012, https://republicofmining.com/2013/09/30/saskatchewans-history-of-potash-politics-and-profit-regina-leaderpost-september-28-2013/.

5   Carl E. Beigie and Alfred Hero Jr., eds., *Natural Resources in U.S.-Canadian Relations*, vol. 2, *Patterns and Trends in Resource Supplies and Policies* (New York: Routledge, 1980).

6   "Canadians Score U.S. Tie of Saskatchewan to Potash Price Fixing," *New York Times*, August 31, 1976.

7   Robert Trumbell, "Potash Debate in Canada Heightens," *New York Times*, September 21, 1976, 62.

8   Quoted in Trumbell.

9   Saskatchewan, Legislative Assembly, *Debates and Proceedings (Hansard)*, November 27, 1975, 487–88.

10   Saskatchewan, Legislative Assembly, Budget Debate, in *Debates and Proceedings (Hansard)*, March 10, 1972, 516.

11   Saskatchewan, Legislative Assembly, *Debates and Proceedings (Hansard)*, November 27, 1975, 466.

12   Saskatchewan, Legislative Assembly, *Hansard*, November 27, 1975, 469.

13   Dennis Gruending, *Promises to Keep: A Political Biography of Allan Blakeney* (Saskatoon: Western Producer Prairie Books, 1990), 149.

14   J.C. Herbert Emery and Ronald D. Kneebone, "Socialists, Populists, Resources, and the Divergent Development of Alberta and Saskatchewan," *Canadian Public Policy* 34, no. 4 (2008): 427.

15   Emily Eaton and David Gray-Donald, "Socializing and Decolonizing Saskatchewan's Oil," *Briarpatch*, April 30, 2018.

16   Gruending, *Promises to Keep*, 152.

17   Roy Romanow, "The Justification and Evolution of Crown Corporations in Saskatchewan," Law Society of Saskatchewan, 1985, in author's possession.

18   Erik Lizee, "Rhetoric and Reality: Albertans and Their Oil Industry under Peter Lougheed" (MA thesis, University of Alberta, 2010), 49.

19   John Richards and Larry Pratt, *Prairie Capitalism: Power and Influence in the New West* (Toronto: McClelland & Stewart, 1979), 216–17.

20   Lizee, "Rhetoric and Reality."

1978: SELLING FURNITURE

1   Richard Collver, interview by the author, May 1986.

2   "Seventeenth Provincial General Election (June 23, 1971)," Election Results, Elections SK, accessed September 23, 2021, https://www.elections.sk.ca/reports-data/election-results/1971-2.

3   Collver interview.

4   Quoted in Dennis Gruending, *Promises to Keep: A Political Biography of Allan Blakeney* (Saskatoon: Western Producer Prairie Books, 1990), 172.

5   "Collver Named in Counter Claim," *Regina Leader-Post*, October 5, 1976, 3.

6   "Collver Files Defence, Counter-Claim in SGI Lawsuit," *Saskatoon StarPhoenix*, June 27, 1978, 3.

7   Saskatchewan, Legislative Assembly, *Debates and Proceedings (Hansard)*, May 11, 1978, 2658.

8   Gary Lane, interview by the author, September 7, 2020.

9   Gruending, *Promises to Keep*, 174–75.

10   "Blakeney Wins," *Calgary Herald*, October 21, 1978, A9.

11   "Blakeney's NDP Obliterates the Sask. Liberals in '78," *Sunday Morning*, CBC

Radio, broadcast October 22, 1978, audio, 4:07, https://www.cbc.ca/archives/
entry/saskatchewan-elections-blakeneys-ndp-obliterates-the-liberals-in-78.

12 "Blakeney's NDP."

1980: THE SECOND COMING

1 "When Pierre Trudeau Became PM for a Second Time in 1980,"
CBC Archives, February 18, 2019, https://www.cbc.ca/archives/
when-pierre-trudeau-became-pm-for-a-second-time-in-1980-1.5002218.

2 "'Welcome to the 1980s': Pierre Trudeau Back as Prime Minister," CBC Archives,
filmed February 18, 1980, video, 18:02, https://www.cbc.ca/player/play/
2677422713.

3 Laurel Graefe, "Oil Shock of 1978–79," Federal Reserve History, November 22,
2013, https://www.federalreservehistory.org/essays/oil_shock_of_1978_79.

4 Roy Romanow, John Whyte, and Howard Leeson, Canada...Notwithstanding:
The Making of the Constitution, 1976–1982 (Toronto: Carswell/Methuen,
1984), 63.

5 "Trudeau PQ Referendum," filmed May 14, 1980, video, 2:07, posted August 21,
2012, by Fed Vid, https://www.youtube.com/watch?v=hoqf3h1wQKQ.

6 Romanow, Whyte, and Leeson, Canada...Notwithstanding, 61.

7 Romanow, Whyte, and Leeson, 64.

8 See Christopher Page, "Opinion Research and Constitutional Renewal, 1980–1,"
in The Roles of Public Opinion Research in Canadian Government (Toronto:
University of Toronto Press, 2006), 80–103.

9 Donald Nuechterlein, "The Demise of Canada's Confederation," Political Science
Quarterly 96, no. 2 (1981): 226.

10 Nuechterlein, 226.

11 Government of Canada, Budget Speech, delivered October 28, 1980, by Allan J.
MacEachen (Ottawa: Department of Finance, 1980), 4, https://www.budget.gc.ca/
pdfarch/1980-plan-eng.pdf.

12 "Lougheed Retaliates against Trudeau for NEP," Sunday Morning, CBC Radio,
broadcast November 2, 1980, audio, 2:27, https://www.cbc.ca/archives/entry/
lougheed-retaliates-against-trudeau-for-nep.

13 Peter Lougheed, speech to Calgary Chamber of Commerce, February 13, 1981.

14 Allan Blakeney, An Honourable Calling: Political Memoirs (Toronto: University of
Toronto Press, 2008).

15 Statistics Canada, "Interest Rates and Exchange Rates," Table 7 in Canadian
Economic Observer: Historical Statistical Supplement, 2010–2011, Catalogue no.
11-210-X (Ottawa: Minister of Industry, July 2011), https://www150.statcan.gc.ca/
n1/pub/11-210-x/2010000/t098-eng.htm.

16 "1981 CPI and Inflation Rate for Canada," Inflation Canada, accessed September
23, 2021, www.inflationcalculator.ca/1981-cpi-inflation-canada.

17   "Banker Says Interest Rates Could Rise Substantially," *Regina Leader-Post*,
      December 18, 1981, C11.
18   "Premier Lauds Canadian Constitution," *Regina Leader-Post*, April 19, 1982, A11.
19   "Gas Tax Would End Soon," *Regina Leader-Post*, April 19, 1982, A4.

1989: WATERLOO?

1   See Dale Eisler, *Rumours of Glory: Saskatchewan & the Thatcher Years* (Edmonton:
      Hurtig, 1987).
2   Several other, smaller Crowns were privatized as well, including Sask Minerals,
      Saskatchewan Government Printing, and Saskatchewan Fur Marketing Company,
      among others.
3   Gary Lane, interview by the author, September 7, 2020.
4   "Overhaul Urged for Crown Corporations," *Regina Leader-Post*, January 11, 1983, 1.
5   Lane interview.
6   James M. Pitsula, "Grant Devine," in *Saskatchewan Premiers of the Twentieth
      Century*, ed. Gordon L. Barnhart (Regina: Canadian Plains Research Center,
      2004), 337.
7   "Twenty-First Provincial General Election (October 20, 1986)," Election Results,
      Elections SK, accessed October 24, 2021, https://www.elections.sk.ca/reports-data/
      election-results/1986-2/.
8   Pitsula, "Grant Devine," 332.
9   John W. Warnock, *Exploiting Saskatchewan Potash: Who Benefits?* (Regina:
      Canadian Centre for Policy Alternatives, January 2011), 17.
10   "The Potash Investment," *Regina Leader-Post*, July 28, 1989, 18.
11   Quoted in Bill Waiser, *Saskatchewan: A New History* (Calgary: Fifth House, 2005),
      451.
12   James M. Pitsula and Ken Rasmussen, *Privatizing a Province: The New Right in
      Saskatchewan* (Vancouver: New Star Books, 1990), 195–96.
13   Pitsula and Rasmussen, 197.
14   "Privatizing the Symbols," *Maclean's*, March 6, 1989, 28–29.
15   Karen Briere, "Sask. Admits Spudco Error," *Western Producer*, February 27, 2003,
      https://www.producer.com/2003/02/sask-admits-spudco-error.
16   Quoted in Dennis Gruending, "John Turner, Brian Mulroney Debate Free Trade,
      Oct. 1988," Great Canadian Speeches, accessed September 23, 2021, https://
      greatcanadianspeeches.ca/2019/09/18/john-turner-brian-mulroney-debate-free-
      trade-oct-1988/.
17   See William Taubman, *Gorbachev: His Life and Times* (New York: W.W. Norton,
      2017).
18   "Text of the Letter Sent by Mikhail Gorbachev to the President of France" (July
      15, 1989), G7 Research Group, University of Toronto, accessed September 23, 2021,
      http://www.g8.utoronto.ca/summit/1989paris/letter_english.html.

19   "Gorbachev Pleads for $100 Billion in Aid from the West," *New York Times*, May
      13, 1991, 1.

20   "Margaret Thatcher: A Life in Quotes," *Guardian*, April 8, 2013, https://www.
      theguardian.com/politics/2013/apr/08/margaret-thatcher-quotes.

21   "No Ordinary Politician," *Economist*, April 13, 2013, https://www.economist.com/
      briefing/2013/04/13/no-ordinary-politician.

22   Pitsula, "Grant Devine," 331.

23   Pitsula, 331.

24   "Romanow Slams Privatization Plan," *Regina Leader-Post*, March 9, 1989, A 4.

25   "Devine Is Eager to Help," *Regina Leader-Post*, January 5, 1990, A 2.

26   Pier Angelo Toninelli, ed., *The Rise and Fall of State-Owed Enterprise in the
      Western World* (Cambridge: Cambridge University Press, 2000), 4.

27   R B C Economics, Canadian and Provincial Fiscal Tables.

28   Lau and Redlawsk, *How Voters Decide: Information Processing in Election
      Campaigns* (New York: Cambridge University Press, 2006), 3.

29   Bryan Caplan, *The Myth of the Rational Voter: Why Democracies Choose Bad
      Policies* (Princeton: Princeton University Press, 2007), 2.

30   "Privatizing the Symbols," 29.

1993: PAIN AND SUFFERING

1   Roy Romanow, interview by the author, October 13, 2020.

2   "Premier Promises Hospital Review," *Saskatoon StarPhoenix*, July 23, 1993, 3.

3   Romanow interview.

4   Saskatchewan, Treasury Department, *Public Accounts, 1991–92: Main Financial
      Statements*, vol. 1 (Regina, 1992), 11. See also Saskatchewan, "Securing Our Future:
      Budget Address," Regina, March 1993, 77; Ronald Kneebone and Margarita
      Wilkins, "Canadian Provincial Government Budget Data, 1980/81 to 2013/14,"
      Canadian Public Policy 42, no. 1 (2016): 12.

5   Saskatchewan, Treasury Department, *Public Accounts, 1991–92*, 11, 13.

6   "N D P Fuels Skepticism about Farm Funds," *Regina Leader-Post*, October 7,
      1986, 5.

7   Ronald Kneebone, "Deficits and Debts in Canada: Some Lessons from Recent
      History," *Canadian Public Policy* 20, no. 2 (1994): 157.

8   "Premier Pleased Farm Aid Will Be New Money," *Regina Leader-Post*, October 8,
      1986, 4.

9   Blakeney, "The Social Democratic Challenge," in *Social Democracy without
      Illusions: Renewal of the Canadian Left*, ed. John Richards, Larry Pratt and Robert
      Cairns (Toronto: McClelland & Stewart, 1991), 46.

10   Saskatchewan, Royal Commission on Agriculture and Rural Life, *Report No. 1:
      The Scope and Character of the Investigation* (Regina: Queen's Printer, 1955), 9.

11   Waiser, *Saskatchewan*, 369.

12   Saskatchewan, Royal Commission on Agriculture and Rural Life, *Report No. 4: Rural Roads and Local Government* (Regina: Queen's Printer, 1955), 264.

13   Janice MacKinnon, *Minding the Public Purse: The Fiscal Crisis, Political Trade-Offs, and Canada's Future* (Montreal and Kingston: McGill-Queen's University Press, 2003), 98.

14   Romanow interview.

15   Gregory Marchildon, "Roy Romanow," in *Saskatchewan Premiers of the Twentieth Century*, ed. Gordon L. Barnhart (Regina: Canadian Plains Research Center, 2004), 369–70.

16   "Sask. Debt $7.53 Billion," *Saskatoon StarPhoenix*, February 19, 1992, 1.

17   Government of Saskatchewan, Department of Finance, "Charting the Course to Financial Freedom" (1993–94 pre-budget consultations, Regina, 1992), 2.

18   "Deficit Tamer?," *Regina Leader-Post*, March 18, 1993, 1.

19   Marchildon, "Roy Romanow," 372.

20   Saskatchewan, Ministry of Health, "A Saskatchewan Vision for Health: A Framework for Change," August 1992, 9.

21   Saskatchewan, Ministry of Health, 10.

22   Quoted in Gregory P. Marchildon, "Regionalization and Health Services Restructuring in Saskatchewan," in *Health Services Restructuring in Canada: New Evidence and New Directions*, ed. Charles M. Beach (Montreal and Kingston: McGill-Queen's University Press, 2006), 33.

23   "Health Care Plans Gain Support," *Regina Leader-Post*, August 18, 1992, 1.

24   "Anger Mounts against Health Reform," *Regina Leader-Post*, September 30, 1993, 3.

25   "Simply Listen," editorial, *Regina Leader-Post*, September 4, 1993, 4.

26   "Backlash Warnings Sounded," *Regina Leader-Post*, April 15, 1993, 36.

27   R.G. Beck, "Comments on Chapter 9: The Effects of Institutional Changes on Health Care Reform," in *A Government Reinvented: A Study of Alberta's Deficit Elimination Program*, ed. C.J. Bruce, R.D. Kneebone, and K.J. McKenzie (Toronto: Oxford University Press, Toronto, 1997), 328–29.

28   Lepnurm and Lepnurm, "The Closure of Rural Hospitals in Saskatchewan: Method or Madness?," *Social Science & Medicine* 52, no. 11 (2001): 1702–3.

29   Badgley and Wolfe, *Doctors' Strike: Medical Care and Conflict in Saskatchewan* (Toronto: Macmillan of Canada, 1967), 7.

30   Liyan Liu, Joanne Hader, Bonnie Brossart, Robin White, and Steven Lewis, "Impact of Rural Hospital Closures in Saskatchewan, Canada," *Social Science & Medicine* 52, no. 12 (2001): 1793.

31   Kenneth J. Fyke, *Caring for Medicare, Sustaining a Quality System*, report of the Saskatchewan Commission on Medicare (Regina: Government of Saskatchewan, April 2001).

32   Janet McFarland, "Unyielding Fiscal Policies Are Romanow's Greatest Legacy," Report on Business, *Globe and Mail*, September 28, 2000, https://www.theglobeandmail.com/report-on-business/unyielding-fiscal-policies-are-romanows-greatest-legacy/article770096/.

33   McFarland.

34   Paul Martin, conversation with the author, April 8, 2021.

35   Brad Wall, interview by the author, January 21, 2021.

36   "Planners Urge Amalgamation of Municipalities," *Regina Leader-Post*, March 3, 1992, 4.

37   "Amalgamation Linked to Taxes," *Regina Leader-Post*, February 23, 1996, 1.

38   "NDP Doesn't Sway SARM," *Regina Leader-Post*, May 14, 1996, 1.

1995: THE PERILS OF PROGRESS

1   Saskatchewan, Economic Advisory and Planning Board, *Saskatchewan Economic Review* (1962), no. 16 (Regina, March 1962), 13.

2   See B. Smale, *How Are Residents of Saskatchewan Really Doing?*, report by the Canadian Index of Wellbeing prepared for Heritage Saskatchewan and the Community Initiatives Fund (Waterloo, ON: Canadian Index of Wellbeing and the University of Waterloo, 2019).

3   Saskatchewan Bureau of Statistics, *Economic Review* 2018, no. 72 (Regina, August 2019), 23.

4   Saskatchewan Treasury Department, *Saskatchewan Economic Review* (1971), no. 25 (Regina, [1971]), 11; Saskatchewan Bureau of Statistics, *Economic Review 2019*, no. 73 (Regina, March 2021), 23.

5   See Paul Krugman, *The Age of Diminished Expectations*, 3rd ed. (Cambridge, MA: MIT Press, 1997), 11.

6   Robert L. Heilbroner, *The Making of Economic Society* (Englewood Cliffs, NJ: Prentice-Hall, 1968), 85.

7   Phyllis Conger, interview by the author, March 11, 2021.

8   Wikipedia, s.v. "Truax, Saskatchewan," last modified January 27, 2021, https://en.wikipedia.org/wiki/Truax,_Saskatchewan.

9   "It Only Takes 4 People to Run This Shortline," *Branchline*, November–December 2019, 6.

10   S. Pratte, "Western Canadian Grain Transportation and the Maximum Revenue Entitlement: Process, Design Considerations and Final Implementation" (paper presented at "Canadian Transportation: 150 Years of Progress," the annual conference of the Canadian Transportation Research Forum, Winnipeg, May 28–31, 2017), https://trid.trb.org/view/1537244.

11   "Ralph Goodale," Open Parliament, accessed September 23, 2021, https://openparliament.ca/politicians/ralph-goodale/?page=433.

12   Arthur Kroeger, *Retiring the Crow Rate: A Narrative of Political Management* (Edmonton: University of Alberta Press, 2009), 84.

13   Mary-Jane Bennett, "As the Crow Flies: Transportation Policy in Saskatchewan and the Crow's Nest Pass Agreement" (Policy Series no. 191, Frontier Centre for Public Policy, Winnipeg, February 2017), 11.

14   Paul D. Earl and Barry E. Prentice, "Western Grain Exceptionalism:
       Transportation Policy Change since 1968" (unpublished paper, Canadian
       Transportation Research Forum, n.d. [2016]), https://ctrf.ca/wp-content/
       uploads/2016/05/CTRF2016EarlPrenticeAgricultureTransportation.pdf.
15   Kroeger, *Retiring the Crow Rate*, 15.
16   Bennett, "As the Crow Flies."
17   Bennett.
18   Dennis Gruending, *Promises to Keep: A Political Biography of Allan Blakeney*
       (Saskatoon: Western Producer Prairie Books, 1990), 213.
19   Saskatchewan New Democratic Party, *We Care!*, n.d. [1982], 28.
20   Saskatchewan Wheat Pool, *Saskatchewan Wheat Pool 1982 Annual Report*
       ([Saskatoon]: Modern Press, January 1983).
21   Kroeger, *Retiring the Crow Rate*, 102.
22   Suren(dra) Kulshreshtha and D.G. Devine, "Historical Perspective and
       Propositions on the Crowsnest Pass Freight Rate Agreement," *Canadian Journal of
       Agricultural Economics* 26, no. 2, (1978): 72–83.
23   Quoted in Kroeger, *Retiring the Crow Rate*, 27.
24   Earl and Prentice, "Western Grain Exceptionalism," 1.
25   Earl and Prentice, 4.
26   Kenneth H. Norrie, "Not Much to Crow About: A Primer on the Statutory Grain
       Freight Rate Issue," *Canadian Public Policy* 9, no. 4 (1983): 434.
27   Jack C. Stabler and M. Rose Olfert, *Saskatchewan's Communities in the 21st
       Century: From Places to Regions* (Regina: Canadian Plains Research Center,
       2002), 64.

1999: COALITION OF THE WILLING

1   Roy Romanow, interview by the author, October 13, 2020.
2   Dwain Lingenfelter, interview by the author, November 4, 2020.
3   "Coalition Government," *Saskatoon StarPhoenix*, October 1, 1999, 1.
4   "Coalition Government," 1.
5   "Coalition Government," 2.
6   "Coalition Government to Rule for First Time in 70 Years," *Regina Leader-Post*,
       October 1, 1999, 1.
7   "Coalition Government to Rule," 1.
8   Tom Steve, interview by the author, March 10, 2021.
9   Quoted in Mark Wyatt, "Tory Party Died a Slow Death," *Regina Leader-Post*,
       August 15, 1997, 14.
10   Raymond Blake, "The Saskatchewan Party and the Politics of Branding," in
       Saskatchewan Politics: Crowding the Centre, ed. Howard Leeson (Regina:
       University of Regina Press, 2009), 169.
11   "Leadership Crucial in New Party," *Saskatoon StarPhoenix*, August 14, 1997, 4.

12 George Hoffman, "Co-operative Commonwealth Federation," *Encyclopedia of Saskatchewan*, accessed September 23,·2021, https://esask.uregina.ca/entry/ co-operative_commonwealth_federation_ccf.jsp.

13 Elections Saskatchewan, "Statement of Votes, Twenty-Fourth Provincial General Election (September 16, 1999)," vol. 1, https://cdn.elections.sk.ca/reports/1999%20 Statement-of-Votes-24th%20GE.pdf.

14 Quoted in Brian Bergman, "A Shock for Romanow," *Maclean's*, September 27, 1999, 33.

15 Heike Klüver and Jae-Jae Spoon, "Helping or Hurting? How Governing as a Junior Coalition Partner Influences Electoral Outcomes," *Journal of Politics* 82, no. 4 (2020): 1231–42.

16 Sigma Analytics, poll results in the author's possession.

17 "NDP 30 Years Out of Date," *Saskatoon StarPhoenix*, October 11, 2003, 8.

18 "NDP 30 Years."

19 "Election a Dead Heat," *Saskatoon StarPhoenix*, October 25, 2003, 1.

20 Sigma Analytics poll.

21 Computed from David McGrane, "Which Third Way? A Comparison of the Romanow and Calvert NDP Governments from 1991 to 2007," in Leeson, *Saskatchewan Politics*, 154, table 2.

22 McGrane, 155.

23 "Cline Last NDP Link with Business," *Saskatoon StarPhoenix*, April 14, 2005, A2.

24 Duanjie Chen and Jack Mintz, "Potash Taxation: How Canada's Regime Is Neither Efficient nor Competitive from an International Perspective," *School of Public Policy Research Papers* 8, no. 1 (2015), https://www.policyschool.ca/ wp-content/uploads/2016/03/Potash-Taxation-Chen-Mintz.pdf.

25 "Business-Tax Cuts, Training Cash among Budget Highlights," *CBC News*, April 6, 2006, https://www.cbc.ca/news/canada/saskatchewan/business-tax-cuts-training-cash-among-budget-highlights-1.575450.

2007: HOPE VERSUS FEAR

1 "MB History," Canadian Conference of Mennonite Brethren Churches, accessed September 23, 2021, https://www.mennonitebrethren.ca/about-ccmbc/our-history/. These beliefs were common among the original immigrant settlers to Saskatchewan.

2 "Brad Wall Still Most Popular Premier in Canada: Angus Reid Survey," *CBC News*, December 19, 2017, https://www.cbc.ca/news/canada/saskatchewan/ brad-wall-still-most-popular-premier-in-canada-angus-reid-poll-1.4446147.

3 "Hope Beats Fear," filmed November 7, 2007, video, 3:47, posted October 26, 2010, by Saskatchewan Party, https://www.youtube.com/watch?v=11fDhQDQcsc.

4 Government of Saskatchewan, *Saskatchewan Plan for Growth: Vision 2020 and Beyond* (Regina, n.d. [2012]), 4.

5   Canada, Department of Finance, "Fiscal Reference Tables, 2020," table 25.

6   Saskatchewan Bureau of Statistics, *Economic Review 2007*, no. 61 (Regina, June 2008), 2.

7   Saskatchewan Bureau of Statistics, *Economic Review 2007*, 3

8   Saskatchewan Bureau of Statistics, *Economic Review 2008*, no. 62 (Regina, June 2009), 2.

9   Government of Saskatchewan, *Public Accounts, 2007–08*, vol. 1, Main Financial Statements (Regina, 2008), 12.

10   Saskatchewan, Legislative Assembly, *Debates and Proceedings (Hansard)*, December 19, 2007, 167.

11   Saskatchewan Bureau of Statistics, *Economic Review 2008*, 2.

12   "Historical Crude Oil Prices (Table)," InflationData, accessed September 23, 2021, https://inflationdata.com/articles/inflation-adjusted-prices/historical-crude-oil-prices-table/.

13   "Brief History of the Canadian Dollar," Connor, Clark & Lunn Financial Group, accessed September 23, 2021, https://www.cclgroup.com/docs/default-source/en/en-strategic-exchange/brief-history-of-the-canadian-dollar.pdf?sfvrsn=ecc82fc8_4.

14   Melissa Pistilli, "10 Top Potash Countries by Production," Investing News Network, August 31, 2021, https://investingnews.com/daily/resource-investing/agriculture-investing/potash-investing/top-potash-countries-by-production/.

15   "Western Canadian Select Historical Pricing," *Oil Sands Magazine*, December 12, 2014. https://www.oilsandsmagazine.com/news/2014/12/12/western-canadian-select-historical-pricing.

16   Saskatchewan Bureau of Statistics, *Economic Review 2014*, no. 68 (Regina, 2015), 2.

17   Government of Saskatchewan, "Saskatchewan Legislature Passes Historic Tax Reductions," news release, December 3, 2008, https://www.saskatchewan.ca/government/news-and-media/2008/december/03/saskatchewan-legislature-passes-historic-tax-reductions.

18   Canada, Department of Finance, "Fiscal Reference Tables, 2020," table 25.

19   Rod Gantefoer, "Minister's Message," in *Saskatchewan Provincial Budget 2009–10*, Budget Summary, Saskatchewan Ministry of Finance, March 18, 2009.

20   Saskatchewan Bureau of Statistics, *Economic Review 2010*, no. 64 (Regina, June 2011), 3.

21   Government of Saskatchewan, *Public Accounts, 2009–10*, vol. 1, Main Financial Statements (Regina, 2010), 82.

22   John W. Warnock, "Natural Resources and Government Revenue: Recent Trends in Saskatchewan" (Canadian Centre for Policy Alternatives, Ottawa, June 16, 2005), 29.

23   Statistics Canada, "Flows and Stocks of Fixed Non-Residential Capital, by Industry and Type of Asset, Canada, Provinces and Territories (x 1,000,000)," Table: 36-10-0096-01 (formerly CANSIM 031-0005), released November 19, 2020.

24 Jim Marshall, "Saskatchewan Potash Taxes and Royalties: Is It Time for a Review?," *Policy Brief,* Johnson Shoyama Graduate School of Public Policy, January 21, 2019.

25 Rob Norris, interview by the author, January 18, 2021.

26 Pat Lorje, *Open Up Saskatchewan! A Report on International Immigration and Inter-Provincial In-Migration Initiatives to Increase the Population of the Province of Saskatchewan* (Regina: Government of Saskatchewan, Legislative Secretary, 2003), 5.

27 Saskatchewan, Ministry of the Economy, "Saskatchewan Statistical Immigration Report, 2009 to 2011," n.d., 8.

28 Statistics Canada, "Province of Saskatchewan," *Focus on Geography Series, 2016 Census,* https://www12.statcan.gc.ca/census-recensement/2016/as-sa/fogs-spg/ Facts-pr-eng.cfm?LANG=Eng&GK=PR&GC=47&TOPIC=7.

29 Government of Saskatchewan, *Saskatchewan Plan for Growth,* 6.

30 Government of Saskatchewan, 5.

31 Canada, Department of Finance, "Fiscal Reference Tables, 2020," table 25.

32 Peter MacKinnon, *A Futures Fund for Saskatchewan: A Report to Premier Brad Wall on the Saskatchewan Heritage Initiative.* Regina: Government of Saskatchewan, 2013.

2010: THE AUDACITY OF NOPE

1 "I Don't Think He Wanted to Be There Meeting with Me," *Regina Leader-Post,* November 14, 2020, B10.

2 "Potash Corporation of Saskatchewan (NY:)," FinancialContent, accessed September 23, 2021, https://markets.financialcontent.com/stocks/quote/historical? Year=2010&Range=1&Symbol=321%3A697749&Month=8.

3 Graeme Wearden and Eloise Veljovic, "BHP Billiton Mounts Hostile Bid for Potash Corporation," *Guardian,* August 18, 2010, https://www.theguardian.com/ business/2010/aug/18/bhpbilliton-hostile-bid-potash-corp.

4 Ian Austen, "BHP Makes Hostile Bid for Potash Corp.," *New York Times,* August 19, 2010, https://www.nytimes.com/2010/08/19/business/global/19potash.html.

5 Dallas Howe, conversation with the author, January 20, 2021.

6 Government of Saskatchewan, "Premier Welcomes 'Pledge to Saskatchewan' from PotashCorp," news release, February 14, 2011, https://www.saskatchewan.ca/ government/news-and-media/2011/february/14/premier-welcomes-pledge-to-saskatchewan-from-potashcorp.

7 John Burton, *Potash: An Inside Account of Saskatchewan's Pink Gold* (Regina: University of Regina Press, 2014), 108–9.

8 Brad Wall, interview by the author, January 21, 2021.

9 Michael Grant, Michael Burt, and Lin Ai, *Saskatchewan in the Spotlight: Acquisition of Potash Corporation of Saskatchewan Inc.—Risks and Opportunities* (Ottawa: Conference Board of Canada, October 1, 2010), ii.

10   "Investment Canada Act FAQ," Stikeman Elliott LLP, October 31, 2016, https://
     www.stikeman.com/en-ca/kh/guides/FAQ-Investment-Canada-Act.

11   "BHP's Potash Bid Falling on Deaf Ears," *Montreal Gazette*, October 21, 2010, 30.

12   Terence Corcoran, "Saskatchewan as Banana Republic," *National Post*, October 22,
     2010, 1.

13   "The Potash Debate: Off the Wall," *Financial Post*, October 26, 2010, 15.

14   "Why Potash Is Different," *National Post*, October 26, 2010, A20.

15   "Premier Brad Wall's Speech on Potash Part 1 of 3," filmed October 21, 2010,
     video, 9:45, posted October 21, 2010, by Brad Wall, https://www.youtube.com/
     watch?v=omkVuTuNqRA.

16   Erin Weir, "Getting Over Brad's Wall of Potash," Progressive Economics
     Forum, October 25, 2010, http://www.progressive-economics.ca/2010/10/25/
     wall-of-potash.

17   "Lingenfelter Unveils Plan for Potash," *Regina Leader-Post*, October 13, 2010, D2.

18   Dallas Howe, conversation with the author, January 20, 2021.

19   "BHP's PotashCorp Bid Rejected for Now," CBC News, November 3, 2010, https://
     www.cbc.ca/news/business/bhp-s-potashcorp-bid-rejected-for-now-1.868381.

20   Alex Heber, "Kloppers' Retirement Package Revealed," *Australian Mining*,
     April 18, 2013, https://www.australianmining.com.au/news/kloppers-retirement-
     package-revealed/.

21   Quoted in "Wall Thanks Clement for Potash Decision," CBC News,
     November 3, 2021, https://www.cbc.ca/news/canada/saskatchewan/
     wall-thanks-clement-for-potash-decision-1.947457.

22   "Wall Best, Charest Worst as Canadians Rank Their Premiers," Angus
     Reid Institute, accessed September 23, 2021, http://angusreid.org/
     wall-best-charest-worst-as-canadians-rank-their-premiers/.

2015: THE LAST GASP

1   "Trade (% of GDP)," World Bank, accessed September 23, 2021, https://data.
     worldbank.org/indicator/NE.TRD.GNFS.ZS.

2   "Trade (% of GDP)—Canada," World Bank, accessed September 23, 2021, https://
     data.worldbank.org/indicator/NE.TRD.GNFS.ZS?locations=CA.

3   Kevin Lynch, "Have We Hit 'Peak Globalization'?," *Policy Brief*, Johnson
     Shoyama Graduate School of Public Policy, September 2019, https://www.
     schoolofpublicpolicy.sk.ca/documents/research/policy-briefs/jsgs-policybriefs-
     peak-globalization.pdf.

4   Saskatchewan, Bureau of Statistics, "Saskatchewan Provincial Economic Accounts,"
     Ministry of Finance, February 2019.

5   Jonathan Tremblay, "The Canadian Wheat Board: The Past, Present and Future
     of Western Grain," Canadian Sailings, April 2, 2012, https://canadiansailings.ca/
     the-canadian-wheat-board-the-past-present-and-future-of-western-grain.

6   Stéfanie Proulx, "The Rise and Fall of the Canadian Wheat Board: A Historical Institutional Analysis" (research paper, Public and International Affairs, University of Ottawa, July 2012).

7   Albert Boaitey, "Grain Marketing Deregulation: A Case Study of the Canadian and Australian Wheat Boards," *Journal of Public Affairs* 13, no. 3 (2013): 282–87.

8   "Border Protest Will Be Smaller," *Regina Leader-Post*, June 14, 1997, 15.

9   "Protest Convoy Formed by Farmers," *Saskatoon StarPhoenix*, October 21, 1995, 72.

10   "On Canada's Prairie, a Farmers' Rebellion Flares," *New York Times*, January 3, 1997, A 4.

11   Government of Canada, *The Canada-U.S. Free Trade Agreement* (1987), 79, art. 701(1), https://www.international.gc.ca/trade-commerce/assets/pdfs/agreements-accords/cusfta-e.pdf.

12   "The Common Agricultural Policy at a Glance," European Commission, accessed September 22, 2021, https://ec.europa.eu/info/food-farming-fisheries/key-policies/common-agricultural-policy/cap-glance_en.

13   "Why So Many Farmers Miss the Wheat Board," Report on Business, *Globe and Mail*, November 27, 2014.

14   Ian MacPherson, "Missionaries of Rural Development: The Fieldmen of the Saskatchewan Wheat Pool, 1925–1965," *Agricultural History* 60, no. 2 (1986): 77.

15   Murray Fulton and K.A. Lang, "Member Commitment and the Market and Financial Performance of the Saskatchewan Wheat Pool," *CAFRI: Current Agriculture, Food and Resource Issues*, no. 5 (2004): 241.

16   Fulton and Lang, 239.

17   Emily C. Bianchi, "American Individualism Rises and Falls with the Economy: Cross-Temporal Evidence That Individualism Declines When the Economy Falters," *Journal of Personality and Social Psychology* 111, no. 4 (2016): 567–84.

18   Saskatchewan Treasury Department, *Saskatchewan Economic Review* (1971), no. 25 (Regina, [1971]), 11.

19   Saskatchewan Bureau of Statistics, *Economic Review 2016*, no. 70 (Regina, July 2017), table 30.

20   André Magnan and Annette Aurélie Desmarais, *Who Is Buying the Farm? Farmland Investment Patterns in Saskatchewan, 2003–14* (Regina: Canadian Centre for Policy Alternatives, March 2017), 3.

21   Magnan and Desmarais, 3.

22   Chad Lawley, "Ownership Restrictions and Farmland Values: Evidence from the 2003 Saskatchewan Farm Security Act Amendment," *American Journal of Agricultural Economics* 100, no. 1 (2018): 312.

23   Farm Credit Canada, 2019 *FCC Farmland Values Report* (Regina: Farm Credit Canada, April 2020), 11.

24   Statistics Canada, "Value per Acre of Farm Land and Buildings at July 1," Table: 32-10-0047-01 (formerly CANSIM 002-0003), released May 26, 2021.

25   Statistics Canada, "Unionization Rates Falling," Canadian Megatrends, *The Daily*, May 17, 2018, https://www150.statcan.gc.ca/n1/pub/11-630-x/11-630-x2015005-eng.htm.

26   Marc A. Smith, Lee Rainie, Ben Shneiderman, and Itai Himelboim, "Mapping Twitter Topic Networks: From Polarized Crowds to Community Clusters," Pew Research Center, February 20, 2014, https://www.pewresearch.org/internet/2014/02/20/mapping-twitter-topic-networks-from-polarized-crowds-to-community-clusters/.

2016: GOING GLOBAL

1   Saskatchewan Bureau of Statistics, "Saskatchewan Provincial Economic Accounts," Ministry of Finance, February 2021, 63; Statistics Canada, "Data Source for Chart 9.1 Gross Domestic Product and Final Domestic Demand," last modified October 7, 2016, https://www150.statcan.gc.ca/n1/pub/11-402-x/2010000/chap/econo/c-g/desc/desc01-eng.htm.

2   Saskatchewan Bureau of Statistics, *Economic Review 2010*, no. 64 (Regina, June 2011), 2.

3   Frederic Jenny, "Price Instability and Competition Law: The Case of the Potash Cartel" (presentation at OECD Global Forum on Competition, Paris, February 16–17, 2012), https://www.oecd.org/competition/globalforum/49737333.pdf.

4   "Canadian Pacific Railway Sod Turning," filmed June 10, 2011, video, 6:27, posted June 13, 2011, by Brad Wall, https://www.youtube.com/watch?v=G-pLRTYka9E.

5   "Canada's Food and Pharmacy Leader," Loblaw website, accessed September 23, 2021, https://www.loblaw.ca/en/who-we-are.

6   Based on a conversation by the author with a knowledgeable, anonymous source.

7   Government of Saskatchewan, Cabinet Decision Item, November 10, 2010, copy in the author's possession.

8   "History," Highway Robbery website, accessed September 23, 2021, https://highwayrobbery.org/pages/history.

9   Wikipedia, s.v. "Regina Bypass," last modified October 18, 2021, https://en.wikipedia.org/wiki/Regina_Bypass. See also Regina Bypass Project website, accessed September 23, 2021, https://www.reginabypass.ca.

10   Geoff Leo, "Businessmen Made Millions on Regina Land That Wound Up in Taxpayers' Hands," CBC News, February 3, 2016, https://www.cbc.ca/news/canada/saskatchewan/businessmen-millions-regina-land-bill-boyd-1.3420479.

11   Geoff Leo, "Brightenview Asks Sask. Government to Reverse Ban on Megamall Immigration Applications," CBC News, December 12, 2019, https://www.cbc.ca/news/canada/saskatchewan/brightenview-asks-sask-government-to-reverse-ban-on-megamall-immigration-applications-1.5394578.

12   Arthur White-Crummey, "NDP Blasts 'Immigration Scam at the GTH' after Ministry Drops Mega-Mall from Program," *Regina Leader-Post*, November 12,

2019, https://leaderpost.com/news/saskatchewan/ndp-blasts-immigration-scam-at-the-gth-after-ministry-drops-mega-mall-from-program.

13 Geoff Leo, "Government to Ask Private Realtors to Sell Off GTH Piece by Piece," CBC News, January 4, 2019, https://www.cbc.ca/news/canada/saskatchewan/saskatchewan-gth-1.4966213.

14 Government of Saskatchewan, *Public Accounts, 2012–13*, vol. 1, Main Financial Statements (Regina, [2013]), 50.

15 Provincial Auditor of Saskatchewan, "2013 Special Report: Provincial Auditor: The Need to Change—One Budget, One Set of Financial Statement Results Only," news release, April 30, 2013, https://auditor.sk.ca/news/news-releases/item?id=12.

16 Reinhard Ellwanger, Benjamin Sawatzky, and Konrad Zmitrowicz, "Factors behind the 2014 Oil Price Decline," *Bank of Canada Review*, Autumn 2017.

17 "Average Monthly Western Canadian Select (WCS) Crude Oil Price from January 2020 to July 2021," Statista, accessed September 23, 2021, https://www.statista.com/statistics/729770/western-canadian-select-monthly-crude-oil-price/; "Oil Prices," Government of Alberta, accessed September 23, 2021, https://economicdashboard.alberta.ca/OilPrice.

18 Jerry Langton, "Bakken Formation: Will It Fuel Canada's Oil Industry?," CBC News, June 27, 2008, https://www.cbc.ca/news/business/bakken-formation-will-it-fuel-canada-s-oil-industry-1.761789.

19 "Saudi America," *Economist*, February 15, 2014, https://www.economist.com/united-states/2014/02/14/saudi-america.

20 IHS Energy, "The Two Pillars: The Increasingly Integrated US-Canadian Oil Trade," special report, June 2016, 5; Faouzi Aloulou, Jesse Esparza, and Naser Ameen, "Permian Basin Oil Production and Resource Assessments Continue to Increase," *Today in Energy*, US Energy Information Administration, April 26, 2017, https://www.eia.gov/todayinenergy/detail.php?id=30952.

21 See Ellwanger, Sawatzky, and Zmitrowicz, "Factors."

22 "Sheikhs v Shale," *Economist*, December 4, 2014, https://www.economist.com/leaders/2014/12/04/sheikhs-v-shale.

23 "Oil Giants Want to Own Only the Cheapest, Cleanest Hydrocarbons," *Economist*, July 18, 2020, 51.

24 "Potash's $20 Billion Market Transformed by Uralkali," *Bloomberg News*, July 31, 2013.

25 Quoted in Michael Babad, "Potash Hit Could Cut Saskatchewan Economic Growth in Half, Economists Say," *Globe and Mail*, July 30, 2013.

26 Quoted in Polina Devitt and Natalia Shurmina, "Potash Sector Rocked as Russia's Uralkali Quits Cartel," Reuters, July 30, 2013.

27 "Potash Facts," Natural Resources Canada, accessed September 23, 2021, https://www.nrcan.gc.ca/our-natural-resources/minerals-mining/minerals-metals-facts/potash-facts/20521.

28 Ken Krawetz, "Minister's Message," in *Saskatchewan Provincial Budget 2015–16*, Saskatchewan Ministry of Finance, March 18, 2015.

29   Government of Saskatchewan, *Public Accounts, 2015–16*, vol. 1, Main Financial
     Statements (Regina, 2016), 7.

30   Government of Saskatchewan, "2016–17 Budget Will Keep Saskatchewan Strong
     through Challenging Year," news release, June 1, 2016, https://www.saskatchewan.
     ca/government/news-and-media/2016/june/01/budget-finance-main.

31   Conference Board of Canada, "Saskatchewan Economy to See Little Growth
     in 2016," Cision, March 8, 2016, https://www.newswire.ca/news-releases/
     saskatchewan-economy-to-see-little-growth-in-2016-571382591.html.

32   Canada, Department of Finance, "Fiscal Reference Tables, 2020," table 25.

33   Government of Saskatchewan, "2016–17 Budget Will Keep Saskatchewan Strong."

34   "Gross Domestic Product of Saskatchewan, Canada from 2000 to 2019," Statista,
     accessed September 23, 2021, https://www.statista.com/statistics/577554/
     gdp-of-saskatchewan-canada/.

35   RBC Economics, Provincial Fiscal Tables.

2016: TRUDEAU 2.0

1   "Justin Trudeau Knows How to Throw a Punch," *Daily Telegraph*, March 12, 2017,
     https://www.dailytelegraph.com.au/lifestyle/stellar/how-justin-trudeau-punched-
     out-a-black-belt-in-a-charity-boxing-match/news-story/f83fad0e75845503ce903b82
     467df69c.

2   Michael Den Tandt, "Now It Gets Tough for Trudeau," *Ottawa Citizen*, April 8,
     2013, A3.

3   "Brian Mulroney on Justin Trudeau: 'What's Not to Like?,'" CTV News, April 8,
     2013, https://www.ctvnews.ca/politics/brian-mulroney-on-justin-trudeau-what's-
     not-to-like-1.1229406.

4   The author was at the event.

5   Mireille Lalancette, "Justin Trudeau and the Play of Celebrity in the 2015 Federal
     Election Campaign," *Celebrity Studies* 11, no. 2 (2020): 158.

6   "Ready or Not...," *Economist*, October 24, 2015, https://www.economist.com/
     the-americas/2015/10/24/ready-or-not.

7   Statistics Canada, "Labour Force Survey, January 2016," *The Daily*, February 5,
     2016, chart 3, https://www150.statcan.gc.ca/n1/daily-quotidien/160205/cg-a003-
     eng.htm.

8   "Economic Dashboard," Government of Alberta, accessed September 23, 2021,
     https://economicdashboard.alberta.ca/.

9   "Unemployment Rate," Saskatchewan's Dashboard, Government of
     Saskatchewan, accessed September 23, 2021, https://dashboard.saskatchewan.ca/
     business-economy/employment-labour-market/unemployment-rate.

10   Kyle Muzyka, "Trudeau's 'Phase Out' Oilsands Comments Spark Outrage
     in Alberta," CBC News, January 13, 2017, https://www.cbc.ca/news/canada/
     edmonton/justin-trudeau-oilsands-phase-out-1.3934701.

11 "Energy and the Economy," Natural Resources Canada, last modified October 6, 2020, https://www.nrcan.gc.ca/science-data/data-analysis/energy-data-analysis/energy-facts/energy-and-economy/20062; Brendan A. Sweeney, *Canada's Automotive Industry: A Decade in Review* (London, ON: Trillium Network for Advanced Manufacturing, May 2020).

12 Muzyka, "Trudeau's 'Phase Out' Oilsands Comments."

13 Liberal Party of Canada, *Real Change: A New Plan for a Strong Middle Class*, Liberal Party Platform (Ottawa, 2015), 39.

14 "Vancouver Declaration on Clean Growth and Climate Change" (First Ministers' Meeting, Vancouver, BC, March 3, 2016), n.p.

15 James Wood, "Notley Says No Support for Liberal Carbon Price without Pipeline Progress," *Calgary Herald*, October 3, 2016, https://calgaryherald.com/news/politics/notley-says-no-support-for-liberal-carbon-price-without-pipeline-progress.

16 "Justin Trudeau's Climate Plans Are Stuck in Alberta's Tar Sands," *Economist*, December 15, 2018, https://www.economist.com/the-americas/2018/12/15/justin-trudeaus-climate-plans-are-stuck-in-albertas-tar-sands.

17 L.K. Kreis and A. Costa, "Hydrocarbon Potential of the Bakken and Torquay Formations, Southeastern Saskatchewan," in *Summary of Investigations 2005*, vol. 1 (Regina: Saskatchewan Geological Survey, 2005).

18 Wikipedia, s.v. "Bakken Formation," last modified July 5, 2021, https://en.wikipedia.org/wiki/Bakken_Formation.

19 Propane for farm use was later exempted from the carbon price.

20 Agricultural Producers Association of Saskatchewan, "Backgrounder: Preliminary Costs of the Federal Carbon Backstop on Saskatchewan Agriculture," n.d., accessed September 23, 2021, https://apas.ca/pub/documents/Advocacy%20and%20Resources/Land%20and%20Environment/Climate%20Change%20and%20Carbon%20Pricing/APAS%20Carbon%20Costing%20Backgrounder%20Final%20version.pdf.

21 John Paul Tasker, "Ottawa to Hike Federal Carbon Tax to $170 a Tonne by 2030," CBC News, December 11, 2020, https://www.cbc.ca/news/politics/carbon-tax-hike-new-climate-plan-1.5837709.

22 Saskatchewan labour force statistics from July 2016 and May 2020 are from Statistics Canada, "Labour Force Characteristics by Province, Monthly, Seasonally Adjusted," Table 14-10-0287-03, released October 3, 2021, https://www150.statcan.gc.ca/t1/tbl1/en/tv.action?pid=1410028703.

23 Brad Wall, "Canada Could Impact Emissions Were Ottawa Not So Obsessed with Carbon Taxes," *Financial Post*, January 18, 2019, https://financialpost.com/opinion/brad-wall-canada-could-impact-emissions-were-ottawa-not-so-obsessed-with-carbon-taxes.

2018: THE PROJECT

1   Eliopoulos is now senior vice president and managing director of public affairs
     with the Angus Reid Group.

2   Dallas Howe, email communication with the author, January 30, 2021.

3   Bill Waiser, *Saskatchewan: A New History* (Calgary: Fifth House, 2005), 5–6.

4   Allan Blakeney, "Federalism and Democracy," *Constitutional Forum* 5, no. 1
     (1994): 1.

5   Peter Lougheed, "A Conversation with Peter Lougheed," *Policy Options*, June 1,
     2012, https://policyoptions.irpp.org/magazines/the-best-premier-of-the-last-40-
     years/a-conversation-with-peter-lougheed/.

6   David Dodge, "Two Mountains to Climb: Canada's Twin Deficits and How to
     Scale Them," *Public Policy Forum*, September 14, 2020.

7   Kerri Breen, "New Map Shows Which Parts of Canada Lag on Believing in
     Climate Change," Global News, November 24, 2019, https://globalnews.ca/
     news/6207280/map-climate-change-canada/.

8   Matto Mildenberger, Peter Howe, Erick Lachapelle, Leah Stokes, Jennifer
     Marlon, and Timothy Gravelle, "The Distribution of Climate Change Public
     Opinion in Canada," *PLOS One*, August 3, 2016, https://doi.org/10.1371/journal.
     pone.0159774.

9   Adam Hunter, "Brad Wall Helped Create Right-of-Centre Buffalo Project and
     Grab Investors," CBC News, January 22, 2019, https://www.cbc.ca/news/canada/
     saskatchewan/brad-wall-buffalo-project-1.4987354.

10   Buffalo Project, "Open Letter Calls for Immediate and Accelerated Action on
     New Deal for Alberta and Saskatchewan," news release, July 14, 2020, https://
     buffaloproject.ca/2020/07/open-letter-calls-for-immediate-and-accelerated-action-
     on-new-deal-for-alberta-and-saskatchewan/.

11   Dene Moore, "The Buffalo Project: Behind the Powerful Cabal Working on a New
     Deal for the West," *National Post*, November 20, 2019.

12   Peter Bowal and Mackenzie Bowal, "Provinces Leaving Canada Part 1: The
     Quebec Secession Case," *Law Now*, January 7, 2020, https://www.lawnow.org/
     provinces-leaving-canada-part-i-the-quebec-secession-case/.

13   Kent McNeil, "Fiduciary Obligations and Aboriginal Peoples," in *The Law of
     Trusts: A Contextual Approach* (Toronto: Emond Montgomery, 2000), https://
     digitalcommons.osgoode.yorku.ca/cgi/viewcontent.cgi?article=1187&context=
     scholarly_works.

14   Bruce Anderson and David Coletto, "Most Think Wexit Is a Terrible Idea, but
     the Concept Could Divide Conservatives," Abacus Data, July 4, 2020, https://
     abacusdata.ca/wexit-polling-divide-conservatives/.

15   "Our Mission/Values," Buffalo Party of Saskatchewan, accessed September 23,
     2021, https://www.buffalopartybpsk.ca/our_mission_values.

16   Wade Sira, phone conversation with the author, January 20, 2021.

2020: HOMELAND NO MORE

1   Bill Waiser, *Saskatchewan: A New History* (Calgary: Fifth House, 2005), 59.

2   John Richards and Larry Pratt, *Prairie Capitalism: Power and Influence in the New West* (Toronto: McClelland & Stewart, 1979), 134.

3   J.C. Herbert Emery and Ronald D. Kneebone, "Socialists, Populists, Resources, and the Divergent Development of Alberta and Saskatchewan," *Canadian Public Policy* 34, no. 4 (2008): 421.

4   Richards and Pratt, *Prairie Capitalism*, 112.

5   Richards and Pratt, 133–34.

6   Thomas H. McLeod and Ian McLeod, *Tommy Douglas: The Road to Jerusalem* (Edmonton: Hurtig, 1987), 195.

7   Emery and Kneebone, "Socialists," 429.

8   Spafford, "Notes on Re-reading Lipset's Agrarian Socialism," in *Lipset's Agrarian Socialism: A Re-examination*, ed. David E. Smith (Regina: Canadian Plains Research Center and the Saskatchewan Institute of Public Policy, 2007), 29.

9   Seymour Martin Lipset, *Agrarian Socialism: The Cooperative Commonwealth Federation in Saskatchewan; A Study in Political Sociology* (Berkeley: University of California Press, 1967), 141.

10   Quoted in Bill Graveland, "'Just Watch Me': Saskatchewan's New Premier Warns Trudeau on Carbon Tax," BNN Bloomberg, January 29, 2018, https://www.bnnbloomberg.ca/just-watch-me-saskatchewan-s-new-premier-warns-trudeau-on-carbon-tax-1.981366.

11   Supreme Court of Canada, "References re *Greenhouse Gas Pollution Pricing Act*," Case in Brief, last modified March 25, 2021, https://www.scc-csc.ca/case-dossier/cb/2021/38663-38781-39116-eng.aspx.

12   "Economists' Statement on Carbon Dividends," *Wall Street Journal*, January 17, 2019, available on Climate Leadership Council website, accessed October 12, 2021, https://clcouncil.org/economists-statement/.

13   "The People behind the Commission," Canada's Ecofiscal Commission, accessed October 12, 2021, https://ecofiscal.ca/the-commission/the-people-behind-the-commission/.

14   Lirong Liu, Charley Z. Huang, Guohe Huang, Brian Baetz, and Scott M. Pittendrigh, "How a Carbon Tax Will Affect an Emission-Intensive Economy: A Case Study of the Province of Saskatchewan, Canada," *Energy* 159 (2018): 825.

15   Government of Saskatchewan, *Prairie Resilience: A Made-in-Saskatchewan Climate Change Strategy* (Regina, December 2017), https://publications.saskatchewan.ca/api/v1/products/88202/formats/104890/download.

16   Kerri Breen, "New Map Shows Which Parts of Canada Lag on Believing in Climate Change," Global News, November 24, 2019, https://globalnews.ca/news/6207280/map-climate-change-canada/.

17   Paul Wells, "A Carbon Tax? Just Try Them," *Maclean's*, November 7, 2018, https://www.macleans.ca/politics/ottawa/a-carbon-tax-just-try-them/.

18   "Enbridge Gets $14.7M Federal Refund over Northern Gateway Pipeline Project," CBC News, December 27, 2018, https://www.cbc.ca/news/canada/calgary/enbridge-federal-refund-northern-gateway-oil-pipeline-project-1.4959946.

19   "Moe Promises Rebate on SaskPower Bills," *Regina Leader-Post*, October 2, 2020, A3.

20   James Laxer, "Why Leap Isn't a Manifesto for the People," *Maclean's*, April 13, 2016, https://www.macleans.ca/politics/why-leap-isnt-a-manifesto-for-the-people.

21   "Saskatchewan Election: Voters Lean Heavily toward Re-electing Sask Party, Disenchanted by Lack of Third Option," Angus Reid Institute, October 15, 2020, http://angusreid.org/saskatchewan-election-2020/.

22   "Election Results," Elections SK, accessed October 13, 2021, https://www.elections.sk.ca/reports-data/election-results/.

23   Andrew Roth, "Vladimir Putin Secures Record Win in Russian Presidential Election," *Guardian*, March 19, 2018, https://www.theguardian.com/world/2018/mar/19/vladimir-putin-secures-record-win-in-russian-presidential-election.

24   B. Smale, *How Are Residents of Saskatchewan Really Doing?*, report by the Canadian Index of Wellbeing prepared for Heritage Saskatchewan and the Community Initiatives Fund (Waterloo, ON: Canadian Index of Wellbeing and the University of Waterloo, 2019), 8.

25   Statistics Canada, "Aboriginal Peoples: Fact Sheet for Saskatchewan," released March 14, 2016, https://www150.statcan.gc.ca/n1/pub/89-656-x/89-656-x2016009-eng.htm.

26   Jason Bird, "Indigenous Issues and Governance Inclusion," in *The Saskatchewan Election: A 2020 Perspective* (Regina: Johnson Shoyama Graduate School of Public Policy, 2020), 25.

27   Blair Stonechild, "Indigenous Peoples of Saskatchewan," *Indigenous Saskatchewan Encyclopedia*, accessed October 12, 2021, https://teaching.usask.ca/indigenoussk/import/indigenous_peoplesof_saskatchewan.php.

28   Ken Rasmussen, "The 2020 Saskatchewan Election in Context," in *The Saskatchewan Election: A 2020 Perspective* (Regina: Johnson Shoyama Graduate School of Public Policy, 2020), 3.

2021: RECKONING

1   Canada, Department of Finance, "Fiscal Reference Tables, 2020," table 25.

2   "Gross Domestic Product of Saskatchewan, Canada from 2000 to 2020," Statista, accessed October 13, 2021, https://www.statista.com/statistics/577554/gdp-of-saskatchewan-canada/.

3   Government of Saskatchewan, Ministry of Finance, "2021–21 Mid-Year Report" (Regina, 2021), 3.

4   Government of Saskatchewan, Public Accounts, 2006–07, vol. 1, Main Financial Statements (Regina, 2007), 13.

5   Tom Kent, "The Social Democracy of Canadian Federalism," *Policy Options*,
    February 1, 2012, https://policyoptions.irpp.org/magazines/sustainable-energy/
    the-social-democracy-of-canadian-federalism/. In other words, what is described as
    a mixed economy.

6   Roy Romanow, conversation with the author, December 23, 2020.

7   Quoted in Mark Lilla, *The Once and Future Liberal: After Identity Politics* (New
    York: HarperCollins, 2017), epigraph.

8   NDP member, personal communication with the author, January 22, 2021.

9   Arthur White-Crummey, "Sask. NDP Leader Ryan Meili Survives Leadership
    Review Vote with 72%," *Regina Leader-Post*, October 3, 2021, https://leaderpost.
    com/news/saskatchewan/sask-ndp-leader-ryan-meili-survives-leadership-review-
    vote-with-72.

10 Gerry Scott, Judy Bradley, Modeste McKenzie, Craig M. Scott, and Brian
    Topp, "Saskatchewan 2024: Making Change Happen; New Democratic Party of
    Saskatchewan Election Review Panel Report," April 2021, 3.

11 Scott et al., 44–46.

12 "Premiers' Performance: Leader Approval Plummets in Most Provinces; Moe,
    Higgs Suffer Dramatic Slides," Angus Reid Institute, October 13, 2021, https://
    angusreid.org/premiers-approval-october-2021/

13 Angus Reid Institute, "Premiers' Performance: Ford Continues to Fall in Approval,
    Houston Rides High on Strength of COVID-19 Handling," January 17, 2022.
    https://angusreid.org/premiers-performance-january-2022/.

14 "Premier Thanks Saskatchewan Residents for Doing Their Part," *Regina Leader-
    Post*, July 12, 2021.

15 Alexandra Mae Jones, "Saskatchewan and COVID-19: How Did Its Fourth Wave
    Death Rate Become the Highest in Canada?," CTVNews.ca, October 13, 2021,
    https://www.ctvnews.ca/health/coronavirus/saskatchewan-and-covid-19-how-
    did-its-fourth-wave-death-rate-become-the-highest-in-canada-1.5622372; David
    Lao, "'We're in a Crisis': Top Saskatchewan Doctor Says COVID-19 Surge Won't
    End Soon," Global News, October 3, 2021, https://globalnews.ca/news/8239012/
    saskatchewan-west-block-covid-crisis/.

16 Kelly Skjerven, "Saskatchewan Lifts All Remaining COVID-19 Public Health
    Restrictions," Global News, July 11, 2021, https://globalnews.ca/news/8018372/
    sask-covid-19-restrictions-lift/.

17 Nouriel Roubini, "The Stagflation Threat Is Real," Project Syndicate, August 30,
    2021, https://www.project-syndicate.org/commentary/mild-stagflation-is-here-and-
    could-persist-or-deepen-by-nouriel-roubini-2021-08.

18 Federal Reserve Board, "Federal Reserve Issues FOMC Statement," Press
    Release, Dec 15, 2021. https://www.federalreserve.gov/newsevents/pressreleases/
    monetary20211215a.htm

19 Kevin Carmichael, "Inflation Climbs to Highest in More than 30 Years,
    Raising Odds of Rate Hike Next Week," *Financial Post*, Jan 19, 2022. https://

      financialpost.com/news/economy/inflation-hits-highest-level-since-1991?utm_
      source=Sailthru&utm_medium=email&utm_campaign=National.

20   Louis Levesque, Intelligence Memo, C.D. Howe Institute, June 28, 2021. https://
      www.cdhowe.org/intelligence-memos/louis-l%C3%A9vesque-%E2%80%93-
      provincial-debt-levels-i-historic-heights-pre-pandemic.

21   Wikipedia, s.v. "2006 Canadian Federal Election," last modified September 23,
      2021, https://en.wikipedia.org/wiki/2006_Canadian_federal_election.

22   Wikipedia, s.v., "Results of the 2019 Canadian Federal Election by
      Riding," last modified September 30, 2021, https://en.wikipedia.org/wiki/
      Results_of_the_2019_Canadian_federal_election_by_riding.

Selected Bibliography

JOURNAL ARTICLES/CHAPTERS IN BOOKS

Abts, Koen, and Stefan Rummens. "Populism versus Democracy." *Political Studies* 55, no. 2 (2007): 405–24.

Allen, Richard. "The Social Gospel as the Religion of the Agrarian Revolt." In *The Prairie West: Historical Readings*, edited by R. Douglas Francis and Howard Palmer, 439. Edmonton: Pica Press, 1985.

Anderson, David L. "Mining Taxation and Royalties in Saskatchewan." In *Mining Law in Canada*, edited by Richard H. Bartlett, 215. Saskatoon: Law Society of Saskatchewan, 1984.

Auld, D.A.L., L.N. Christofides, R. Swidinsky, and D.A. Wilton. "The Impact of the Anti-Inflation Board on Negotiated Wage Settlements." *Canadian Journal of Economics* 12, no. 2 (1979): 195–213.

Barnett, George A., and Thomas L. McPhail. "An Examination of the Relationship of United States Television and Canadian Identity." *International Journal of Intercultural Relations* 4, no. 2 (1980): 221.

Beck, R.G. "Comments on Chapter 9: The Effects of Institutional Changes on Health Care Reform." In *A Government Reinvented: A Study of Alberta's Deficit Elimination Program*, edited by C.J. Bruce, R.D. Kneebone, and K.J. McKenzie, 328–29. Toronto: Oxford University Press, Toronto, 1997.

Berry, John W. "Research on Multiculturalism in Canada." *International Journal of Intercultural Relations* 37, no. 6 (2013): 664.

Bianchi, Emily C. "American Individualism Rises and Falls with the Economy: Cross-Temporal Evidence That Individualism Declines When the Economy Falters." *Journal of Personality and Social Psychology* 111, no. 4 (2016): 567–84.

Blake, Raymond. "The Saskatchewan Party and the Politics of Branding." In
    Saskatchewan Politics: Crowding the Centre, edited by Howard Leeson, 169. Regina:
    Canada Plains Research Center, 2009.
Blakeney, Allan. "Federalism and Democracy." *Constitutional Forum* 5, no. 1 (1994): 1.
——. "The Social Democratic Challenge." In *Social Democracy without Illusions:
    Renewal of the Canadian Left*, edited by John Richards, Larry Pratt, and Robert
    Cairns, 46. Toronto: McClelland & Stewart, 1991.
Blocker, David G. "'To Waffle to the Left': The Waffle, the New Democratic Party, and
    Canada's New Left during the Long Sixties." PhD diss., University of Western
    Ontario, 2019.
Boaitey, Albert. "Grain Marketing Deregulation: A Case Study of the Canadian and
    Australian Wheat Boards." *Journal of Public Affairs* 13, no. 3 (2013): 282–87.
Brubaker, Rogers. "Why Populism?" *Theory and Society* 46 (2007): 358–59.
Bushnell, S.I. "The Control of Natural Resources through the Trade and Commerce
    Power and Proprietary Rights." *Canadian Public Policy* 6, no. 2 (1980): 314.
Chen, Duanjie, and Jack Mintz. "Potash Taxation: How Canada's Regime Is Neither
    Efficient nor Competitive from an International Perspective." *School of Public
    Policy Research Papers* 8, no. 1 (2015), https://www.policyschool.ca/wp-content/
    uploads/2016/03/Potash-Taxation-Chen-Mintz.pdf.
Courtney, John. "Lipset, de Tocqueville, Radical Group Formation, and the Fate of
    Socialism in Saskatchewan." In *Lipset's Agrarian Socialism: A Re-examination*,
    edited by David E. Smith, 22. Regina: Canadian Plains Research Center and the
    Saskatchewan Institute of Public Policy, 2007.
Di Matteo, Livio. "The Path to Fiscal Crisis: Canada's Federal Government, 1970 to
    1995." In *The Budget That Changed Canada: Essays on the 25th Anniversary of the
    1995 Budget*, edited by William Watson and Jason Clemens, 7. Vancouver: Fraser
    Institute, February 2020.
Dodge, David. "Two Mountains to Climb: Canada's Twin Deficits and How to Scale
    Them." *Public Policy Forum*, September 14, 2020.
Drochon, Hugo. "Robert Michels, the Iron Law of Oligarchy and Dynamic
    Democracy." *Constellations* 27, no. 2 (2020), https://doi.org/10.1111/1467-8675.
    12494.
Emery, J.C. Herbert, and Ronald D. Kneebone. "Socialists, Populists, Resources, and
    the Divergent Development of Alberta and Saskatchewan." *Canadian Public Policy*
    34, no. 4 (2008): 427.
Fox, Craig. Review of *Keeping Canada British: The Ku Klux Klan in 1920s Saskatchewan*,
    by James Pitsula. *Labour/Le Travail* 74 (Fall 2014): 351.
Fulton, Murray, and K.A. Lang. "Member Commitment and the Market and Financial
    Performance of the Saskatchewan Wheat Pool." *CAFRI: Current Agriculture, Food
    and Resource Issues*, no. 5 (2004): 241.
Gamble, Andrew. "Privatization, Thatcherism and the British State." *Journal of Law
    and Society* 16, no. 1 (1989): 1.

Glor, Eleanor, ed. "Determinism: Innovation as Emergent." In "Is Innovation a Question of Will or Circumstance?" Special issue, *The Innovation Journal* 5, no. 2 (2000): art. 1f10.

———, ed. "Is Innovation a Question of Will or Circumstance? An Exploration of the Innovation Process through the Lens of the Blakeney Government in Saskatchewan, 1971–82." Special issue, *The Innovation Journal* 5, no. 2 (2000) : art. 1g.

Green, Alan G., and David Green, "The Goals of Canada's Immigration Policy." *Canadian Journal of Urban Research* 13, no. 1 (2004): 116.

Guenther, Bruce L. "Populism, Politics and Christianity in Western Canada." *Historical Papers: Canadian Society of Church History* (2000): 99.

Harrison, Rowland J. "Natural Resources and the Constitution: Some Recent Developments and Their Implications for the Future Regulation of the Resources Industries." *Alberta Law Review* 18, no. 1 (1980): 4.

Helliwell, John F. "Comparative Macroeconomics of Stagflation." *Journal of Economic Literature* 26, no. 1 (1988): 2.

Jarvis, David. "British Conservatism and Class Politics in the 1920s." *English Historical Review* 111, no. 440 (1996): 59–84.

Klein, Seth. "Good Sense versus Common Sense: Canada's Debt Debate and Competing Hegemonic Projects." M A thesis, Simon Fraser University, 1996.

Klüver, Heike, and Jae-Jae Spoon, "Helping or Hurting? How Governing as a Junior Coalition Partner Influences Electoral Outcomes." *Journal of Politics* 82, no. 4 (2020): 1231–42.

Kneebone, Ronald. "Deficits and Debts in Canada: Some Lessons from Recent History." *Canadian Public Policy* 20, no. 2 (1994): 157.

Kneebone, Ronald, and Margarita Wilkins. "Canadian Provincial Government Budget Data, 1980/81 to 2013/14." *Canadian Public Policy* 42, no. 1 (2016): 12

Kreis, L.K., and A. Costa. "Hydrocarbon Potential of the Bakken and Torquay Formations, Southeastern Saskatchewan." In *Summary of Investigations 2005*, vol. 1. Regina: Saskatchewan Geological Survey, 2005.

Kulshreshtha, Suren(dra), and D.G. Devine. "Historical Perspective and Propositions on the Crowsnest Pass Freight Rate Agreement." *Canadian Journal of Agricultural Economics* 26, no. 2 (1978): 72–83.

Lalancette, Mireille. "Justin Trudeau and the Play of Celebrity in the 2015 Federal Election Campaign." *Celebrity Studies* 11, no. 2 (2020): 158.

Lawley, Chad. "Ownership Restrictions and Farmland Values: Evidence from the 2003 Saskatchewan Farm Security Act Amendment." *American Journal of Agricultural Economics* 100, no. 1 (2018): 312.

Leach, Darcy K. "The Iron Law of *What* Again? Conceptualizing Oligarchy across Organizational Forms." *Sociological Theory* 23, no. 3 (2005): 312.

Leeson, Howard. Introduction to *Saskatchewan Politics: Crowding the Centre*, 2. Regina: Canadian Plains Research Center, 2009.

Lepnurm, Rein, and Marje K. Lepnurm. "The Closure of Rural Hospitals in
    Saskatchewan: Method or Madness?" *Social Science & Medicine* 52, no. 11 (2001):
    1702–3.
Liu, Lirong, Charley Z. Huang, Guohe Huang, Brian Baetz, and Scott M. Pittendrigh.
    "How a Carbon Tax Will Affect an Emission-Intensive Economy: A Case Study of
    the Province of Saskatchewan, Canada." *Energy* 159 (2018): 825.
Liu, Liyan, Joanne Hader, Bonnie Brossart, Robin White, and Steven Lewis. "Impact of
    Rural Hospital Closures in Saskatchewan, Canada." *Social Science & Medicine* 52,
    no. 12 (2001): 1793.
Lizee, Erik. "Rhetoric and Reality: Albertans and Their Oil Industry under Peter
    Lougheed." MA thesis, University of Alberta, 2010.
Lynch, Kevin. "Have We Hit 'Peak Globalization'?" *Policy Brief,* Johnson
    Shoyama Graduate School of Public Policy, September 2019, https://www.
    schoolofpublicpolicy.sk.ca/documents/research/policy-briefs/jsgs-policybriefs-
    peak-globalization.pdf.
Lynd, Robert. Introduction to *Agrarian Socialism*, by Seymour Martin Lipset, ix.
    Berkeley: University of California Press, 1967.
Macpherson, Ian. "Missionaries of Rural Development: The Fieldmen of the
    Saskatchewan Wheat Pool, 1925–1965." *Agricultural History* 60, no. 2 (1986): 75.
Marchildon, Gregory P. "Regionalization and Health Services Restructuring in
    Saskatchewan." In *Health Services Restructuring in Canada: New Evidence and
    New Directions*, edited by Charles M. Beach, 33. Montreal and Kingston: McGill-
    Queen's University Press, 2006.
———. "Roy Romanow." In *Saskatchewan Premiers of the Twentieth Century*, edited
    by Gordon L. Barnhart, 369–70. Regina: Canadian Plains Research Center,
    2004.
Marshall, Jim. "Saskatchewan Potash Taxes and Royalties: Is It Time for a Review?"
    Policy Brief, Johnson Shoyama Graduate School of Public Policy, January 21, 2019.
McGrane, David. "Which Third Way? A Comparison of the Romanow and Calvert
    NDP Governments from 1991 to 2007." In *Saskatchewan Politics: Crowding the
    Centre*, edited by Howard Leeson, 154, table 2. Regina: Canada Plains Research
    Center, 2009.
McNeil, Kent. "Fiduciary Obligations and Aboriginal Peoples." In *The Law of Trusts: A
    Contextual Approach*, edited by Jeffrey Bruce Berryman, Mark R. Gillen, and Faye
    Woodman. Toronto: Emond Montgomery, 2000.
Mildenberger, Matto, Peter Howe, Erick Lachapelle, Leah Stokes, Jennifer Marlon,
    and Timothy Gravelle. "The Distribution of Climate Change Public Opinion in
    Canada." *PLOS One*, August 3, 2016, https://doi.org/10.1371/journal.pone.0159774.
Norrie, Kenneth H. "Not Much to Crow About: A Primer on the Statutory Grain
    Freight Rate Issue." *Canadian Public Policy* 9, no. 4 (1983): 435.
Nuechterlein, Donald. "The Demise of Canada's Confederation." *Political Science
    Quarterly* 96, no. 2 (1981): 226.

Page, Christopher. "Opinion Research and Constitutional Renewal, 1980–1." In *The Roles of Public Opinion Research in Canadian Government*, 80–103. Toronto: University of Toronto Press, 2006.

Paus Jenssen, Arne. "Resource Taxation and the Supreme Court of Canada: The Cigol Case." *Canadian Public Policy* 5, no. 1 (1979): 45–58.

Pitsula, James M. "Grant Devine." In *Saskatchewan Premiers of the Twentieth Century*, edited by Gordon L. Barnhart, 337. Regina: Canadian Plains Research Center, 2004.

Pittendrigh, Scott Michael. "The Religious Perspective of T.C. Douglas: Social Gospel Theology and Pragmatism." MA thesis, University of Regina, 1997.

Rasmussen, Ken. "The 2020 Saskatchewan Election in Context." In *The Saskatchewan Election: A 2020 Perspective*, 3. Regina: Johnson Shoyama Graduate School of Public Policy, 2020.

Ready, William. "The Saskatchewan Potash Prorationing Scheme." *Alberta Law Review* 9, no. 3 (1971): 592–97.

Romanow, Roy. "The Justification and Evolution of Crown Corporations in Saskatchewan." Law Society of Saskatchewan, 1985.

Spafford, Duff. "Notes on Re-reading Lipset's *Agrarian Socialism*." In *Lipset's Agrarian Socialism: A Re-examination*, edited by David E. Smith, 29. Regina: Canadian Plains Research Center and the Saskatchewan Institute of Public Policy, 2007.

Spencer, Metta. Review of *Continental Divide: The Values and Institutions of the United States and Canada*, by Seymour Martin Lipset. *Theory and Society* 21, no. 4 (1992): 610–18.

Surlin, Stuart H., and Barry Berlin. "TV, Values, and Culture in U.S.-Canadian Borderland Cities: A Shared Perspective." *Canadian Journal of Communication* 16, no. 3 (1991): 431–39.

Sutter, Robert. "Why Does China Matter?" *Washington Quarterly* 27, no. 1 (2003): 75–89.

Tyerman, Peter. "Pricing of Alberta's Oil." *Alberta Law Review* 14 (1976): 427.

Wagner, Bonnie. "We Proudly Begin Our Broadcast Day: Saskatchewan and the Arrival of Television, 1954–1969." MA thesis, University of Saskatchewan, 2004.

Warnock, John W. "Natural Resources and Government Revenue: Recent Trends in Saskatchewan." *Canadian Centre for Policy Alternatives*, June 16, 2005: 29.

Wiseman, Nelson. "The Pattern of Prairie Politics." *Queen's Quarterly* 88, no. 2 (1981): 301.

BOOKS

Badgley, Robin F., and Samuel Wolfe. *Doctors' Strike: Medical Care and Conflict in Saskatchewan*. Toronto: Macmillan of Canada, 1967.

Baron, Don. *Canada's Great Grain Robbery: The Amazing Story of How a False Social Gospel Shackled the West and Canada*. Self-published, 1998.

Beigie, Carl E., and Alfred Hero Jr., eds. *Natural Resources in U.S.-Canadian Relations*, vol. 2, *Patterns and Trends in Resource Supplies and Policies*. New York: Routledge, 1980.

Bissoondath, Neil. *Selling Illusions: The Cult of Multiculturalism in Canada*. Toronto: Penguin, 1994.

Blakeney, Allan. *An Honourable Calling: Political Memoirs*. Toronto: University of Toronto Press, 2008.

Boswell, Randy. *Province with a Heart: Celebrating 100 Years in Saskatchewan*, edited by Lynn McAuley. Toronto: CanWest, 2005.

Burton, John. *Potash: An Inside Account of Saskatchewan's Pink Gold*. Regina: University of Regina Press, 2014.

Caplan, Bryan. *The Myth of the Rational Voter: Why Democracies Choose Bad Policies*. Princeton: Princeton University Press, 2007.

Eisler, Dale. *False Expectations: Politics and the Pursuit of the Saskatchewan Myth*. Regina: Canadian Plains Research Center, 2006.

———. *Rumours of Glory: Saskatchewan & the Thatcher Years*. Edmonton: Hurtig, 1987.

Fairbairn, Garry. *From Prairie Roots: The Remarkable Story of the Saskatchewan Wheat Pool*. Saskatoon: Western Producer Prairie Books, 1984.

Friesen, Gerald. *The Canadian Prairies: A History*. Toronto: University of Toronto Press, 1987.

Goodhart, David. *The Road to Somewhere: The Populist Revolt and the Future of Politics*. London: Hurst, 2017.

Gruending, Dennis. *Promises to Keep: A Political Biography of Allan Blakeney*. Saskatoon: Western Producer Prairie Books, 1990.

Heilbroner, Robert L. *The Making of Economic Society*. Englewood Cliffs, NJ: Prentice-Hall, 1968.

Kroeger, Arthur. *Retiring the Crow Rate: A Narrative of Political Management*. Edmonton: University of Alberta Press, 2009.

Krugman, Paul. *The Age of Diminished Expectations*. 3rd ed. Cambridge, MA: MIT Press, 1997.

Lau, Richard R., and David P. Redlawsk. *How Voters Decide: Information Processing in Election Campaigns*. New York: Cambridge University Press, 2006.

Lilla, Mark. *The Once and Future Liberal: After Identity Politics*. New York: HarperCollins, 2017.

Lipset, Seymour Martin. *Agrarian Socialism: The Cooperative Commonwealth Federation in Saskatchewan; A Study in Political Sociology*. Berkeley: University of California Press, 1967.

———. *Continental Divide: The Values and Institutions of the United States and Canada*. New York: Routledge, 1990.

MacKinnon, Janice. *Minding the Public Purse: The Fiscal Crisis, Political Trade-Offs, and Canada's Future*. Montreal and Kingston: McGill-Queen's University Press, 2003.

McGrane, David, John Whyte, Roy Romanow, and Russell Isinger, eds. *Back to Blakeney: Revitalizing the Democratic State*. Regina: University of Regina Press, 2019.

McLeod, Thomas H., and Ian McLeod. *Tommy Douglas: The Road to Jerusalem.* Edmonton: Hurtig, 1987.

Newman, Peter C. *Renegade in Power: The Diefenbaker Years.* Toronto: McClelland & Stewart, 1973.

Pitsula, James M. *As One Who Serves: The Making of the University of Regina.* Montreal and Kingston: McGill-Queen's University Press, 2006.

Pitsula, James M., and Ken Rasmussen. *Privatizing a Province: The New Right in Saskatchewan.* Vancouver: New Star Books, 1990.

Rauschenbusch, Walter. *Christianity and the Social Crisis.* New York: Macmillan, 1907.

Richards, John, and Larry Pratt. *Prairie Capitalism: Power and Influence in the New West.* Toronto: McClelland & Stewart, 1979.

Romanow, Roy, John Whyte, and Howard Leeson, *Canada...Notwithstanding: The Making of the Constitution, 1976–1982.* Toronto: Carswell/Methuen, 1984.

Spencer, Dick. *Singing the Blues: The Conservatives in Saskatchewan.* Regina: Canadian Plains Research Center, 2007.

Stabler, Jack C., and M. Rose Olfert. *Saskatchewan's Communities in the 21st Century: From Places to Regions.* Regina: Canadian Plains Research Center, 2002.

Taubman, William. *Gorbachev: His Life and Times.* New York: W.W. Norton, 2017.

Toninelli, Pier Angelo, ed. *The Rise and Fall of State-Owed Enterprise in the Western World.* Cambridge: Cambridge University Press, 2000.

Trudeau, Pierre. *Memoirs.* Toronto: McClelland & Stewart, 1995.

Trudeau, Pierre, and Jacques Hébert. *Two Innocents in Red China.* Toronto: Oxford University Press, 1968.

Waiser, Bill. *Saskatchewan: A New History.* Calgary: Fifth House, 2005.

Ward, Norman, and David Smith. *Jimmy Gardiner: Relentless Liberal.* Toronto: University of Toronto Press, 1990.

Whitaker, Reg. *Canadian Immigration Policy since Confederation.* Ottawa: Canadian Historical Association, 1991.

Wilson, Barry. *The Politics of Defeat: The Decline of the Liberal Party in Saskatchewan.* Saskatoon: Western Producer Prairie Books, 1980.

Wong, John D. *Global Trade in the Nineteenth Century: The House of Houqua and the Canton System.* Cambridge: Cambridge University Press, 2016.

GOVERNMENT AND LEGAL DOCUMENTS

Agriculture and Agri-Food Canada. *Canadian Agriculture in the Seventies: Report of the Federal Task Force on Agriculture.* Ottawa: Agriculture and Agri-Food Canada, December 1969.

Canadian Industrial Gas & Oil Ltd. v. Government of Saskatchewan et al., [1978] 2 SCR 545.

Central Canada Potash Co. Ltd. et al. v. Government of Saskatchewan, [1979] 1 SCR 42.

Conference Board of Canada. "Saskatchewan Economy to See Little Growth in 2016." Cision, March 8, 2016.

Ellwanger, Reinhard, Benjamin Sawatzky, and Konrad Zmitrowicz. "Factors behind the 2014 Oil Price Decline." Bank of Canada Review, 2017.

Fyke, Kenneth J. *Caring for Medicare, Sustaining a Quality System*. Report of the Saskatchewan Commission on Medicare. Regina: Government of Saskatchewan, April 2001.

Gantefoer, Rod. "Minister's Message." In *Saskatchewan Provincial Budget 2009–10, Budget Summary*, Saskatchewan Ministry of Finance, March 18, 2009.

Government of Alberta. "Economic Dashboard." Accessed September 23, 2021.

Government of Canada. *Budget Speech, Delivered by Allan J. MacEachen*. Ottawa: Department of Finance, October 28, 1980.

———. *Budget Speech, Delivered by John N. Turner*. Ottawa: Department of Finance, May 6, 1974.

———. *Budget Speech, Delivered by John N. Turner*. Ottawa: Department of Finance, November 18, 1974.

———. *The Canada-U.S. Free Trade Agreement* (1987), 79, art. 701(1), https://www.international.gc.ca/trade-commerce/assets/pdfs/agreements-accords/cusfta-e.pdf.

———. Department of Finance. Budget Plan, tabled in the House of Commons February 27, 1995. Ottawa: Department of Supply and Services, 1995.

———. Department of Finance. "Fiscal Reference Tables, 2020," table 25.

———. Privy Council. *Report of the Royal Commission on Publications*. Ottawa: Queen's Printer, May 1961.

———. Privy Council Office. *Report of the Royal Commission on the Economic Union and Development Prospects for Canada*, vol. 1. Ottawa: Privy Council Office, 1985.

Government of Saskatchewan. "2016–17 Budget Will Keep Saskatchewan Strong through Challenging Year." news release, June 1, 2016, https://www.saskatchewan.ca/government/news-and-media/2016/june/01/budget-finance-main.

———. Bureau of Statistics. *Saskatchewan Economic Review 1971*, no. 25. Regina: Ministry of Finance, 1971.

———. Bureau of Statistics. *Saskatchewan Economic Review 1975*, no. 29. Regina: Ministry of Finance, October 1975.

———. Bureau of Statistics. *Saskatchewan Economic Review 2007*, no. 61. Regina: Ministry of Finance, June 2008.

———. Bureau of Statistics. *Saskatchewan Economic Review 2008*, no. 62. Regina: Ministry of Finance, June 2009.

———. Bureau of Statistics. *Saskatchewan Economic Review 2010*, no. 64. Regina: Ministry of Finance, June 2011.

———. Bureau of Statistics. *Saskatchewan Economic Review 2014*, no. 68. Regina: Ministry of Finance, July 2015.

———. Bureau of Statistics. *Saskatchewan Economic Review 2016*, no. 70. Regina: Ministry of Finance, July 2017.

———. Bureau of Statistics. *Saskatchewan Economic Review 2018*, no. 72. Regina: Ministry of Finance, August 2019.

———. Bureau of Statistics. *Saskatchewan Economic Review 2019*, no. 73. Regina: Ministry of Finance, March 2021.

———. Bureau of Statistics. "Saskatchewan Provincial Economic Accounts." Ministry of Finance, February 2019.

———. Bureau of Statistics. "Saskatchewan Provincial Economic Accounts." Regina: Ministry of Finance, February 2021.

———. Cabinet Decision Item, November 10, 2010.

———. Department of Finance. "Charting the Course to Financial Freedom" (1993–94 pre-budget consultations, Regina, 1992), 2.

———. Economic Advisory and Planning Board. *Saskatchewan Economic Review 1962*, no. 16. Regina: Ministry of Finance, March 1962.

———. Executive Council, Planning and Research. *Saskatchewan Economic Review 1972*, no. 26. Regina: Ministry of Finance, 1972.

———. Legislative Assembly, Budget Debate, In *Debates and Proceedings (Hansard)*, March 10, 1972.

———. Legislative Assembly, In *Debates and Proceedings (Hansard)*, November 27, 1975.

———. Legislative Assembly, In *Debates and Proceedings (Hansard)*, May 11, 1978.

———. Legislative Assembly, In *Debates and Proceedings (Hansard)*, March 22, 1982.

———. Legislative Assembly, In *Debates and Proceedings (Hansard)*, December 19, 2007.

———. Ministry of the Economy, "Saskatchewan Statistical Immigration Report, 2009 to 2011." n.d.

———. Ministry of Finance, "2021–21 Mid-Year Report." Regina, 2021.

———. Ministry of Health, "A Saskatchewan Vision for Health: A Framework for Change." August 1992.

———. "Prairie Resilience: A Made-in-Saskatchewan Climate Change Strategy." Regina, December 2017, https://publications.saskatchewan.ca/api/v1/products/88202/formats/104890/download.

———. "Premier Welcomes 'Pledge to Saskatchewan' from PotashCorp," news release, February 14, 2011, https://www.saskatchewan.ca/government/news-and-media/2011/february/14/premier-welcomes-pledge-to-saskatchewan-from-potashcorp.

———. Public Accounts, 2006–07, vol. 1, Main Financial Statements. Regina, 2007.

———. Public Accounts, 2007–08, vol. 1, Main Financial Statements. Regina, 2008.

———. Public Accounts, 2009–10, vol. 1, Main Financial Statements. Regina, 2010.

———. Public Accounts, 2012–13, vol. 1, Main Financial Statements. Regina, [2013].

———. Public Accounts, 2015–16, vol. 1, Main Financial Statements. Regina, 2016.

———. Royal Commission on Agriculture and Rural Life, *Report No. 1: The Scope and Character of the Investigation*. Regina: Queen's Printer, 1955.

———. Royal Commission on Agriculture and Rural Life, *Report No. 4: Rural Roads and Local Government*. Regina: Queen's Printer, 1955.

———. "Saskatchewan Legislature Passes Historic Tax Reductions," news release, December 3, 2008, https://www.saskatchewan.ca/government/news-and-media/2008/december/03/saskatchewan-legislature-passes-historic-tax-reductions.

———. *Saskatchewan Plan for Growth: Vision 2020 and Beyond*. Regina, n.d. [2012].

———. "Securing Our Future: Budget Address." Regina, March 1993.

———. "Speech from the Throne," In *Debates and Proceedings* (*Hansard*), 18th Leg, 1st Sess (November 12, 1975).

———. "Speech from the Throne." In *Debates and Proceedings* (*Hansard*), 17th Leg, 5th Sess (November 28, 1974).

———. Treasury Department. *Public Accounts, 1991–92: Main Financial Statements*, vol. 1. Regina, 1992.

———. "Unemployment Rate." Accessed September 23, 2021, https://dashboard. saskatchewan.ca/business-economy/employment-labour-market/ unemployment-rate.

Grant, Michael, Michael Burt, and Lin Ai. *Saskatchewan in the Spotlight: Acquisition of Potash Corporation of Saskatchewan Inc.—Risks and Opportunities*. Ottawa: Conference Board of Canada, October 1, 2010.

Krawetz, Ken. "Minister's Message." In *Saskatchewan Provincial Budget 2015–16*. Saskatchewan Ministry of Finance, March 18, 2015.

MacKinnon, Peter. *A Futures Fund for Saskatchewan: A Report to Premier Brad Wall on the Saskatchewan Heritage Initiative*. Regina: Government of Saskatchewan, 2013.

National Resources Canada. "Energy and the Economy." Last modified October 6, 2020, https://www.nrcan.gc.ca/science-data/data-analysis/energy-data-analysis/ energy-facts/energy-and-economy/20062.

Sexty, Robert W. "The Saskatchewan Oil and Gas Corporation." Case Study 1.89, Institute of Public Administration of Canada, 1981.

Statistics Canada. "Aboriginal Peoples: Fact Sheet for Saskatchewan." Released March 14, 2016, https://www150.statcan.gc.ca/n1/pub/89-656-x/89-656-x2016009-eng.htm.

———. "Data Source for Chart 9.1 Gross Domestic Product and Final Domestic Demand." Last modified October 7, 2016, https://www150.statcan.gc.ca/n1/ pub/11-402-x/2010000/chap/econo/c-g/desc/desc01-eng.htm.

———. "Flows and Stocks of Fixed Non-Residential Capital, by Industry and Type of Asset, Canada, Provinces and Territories (x 1,000,000)." Table: 36-10-0096-01 (formerly CANSIM 031-0005), released November 19, 2020.

———. "Interest Rates and Exchange Rates." Table 7 in *Canadian Economic Observer: Historical Statistical Supplement, 2010–2011*, Catalogue no. 11-210-X. Ottawa: Minister of Industry, July 2011, https://www150.statcan.gc.ca/n1/pub/11- 210-x/2010000/t098-eng.htm.

———. "Production, Imports, Exports and Domestic Disappearance of Wheat, Canada, 1868 to 1974 (Thousands of Bushels)." Series M301-309, Excel spreadsheet, accessed October 25, 2021, https://www150.statcan.gc.ca/n1/pub/11-516-x/sectionm/ M301_309-eng.csv.

———. "Province of Saskatchewan." Focus on Geography Series, 2016 Census, https:// www12.statcan.gc.ca/census-recensement/2016/as-sa/fogs-spg/Facts-pr-eng.cfm?L ANG=Eng&GK=PR&GC=47&TOPIC=7.

———. Saskatchewan labour force statistics from July 2016 and May 2020 are from Statistics Canada. "Labour Force Characteristics by Province, Monthly, Seasonally Adjusted," Table 14-10-0287-03, released October 3, 2021, https://www150.statcan.gc.ca/t1/tbl1/en/tv.action?pid=1410028703.

———. "Summary Table: Time Spent Watching Television by Persons Aged 2 Years and Over, Share by Origin and Type of Programme and Origin of Station , Canada, Fall 2001." Accessed September 27, 2021, https://www150.statcan.gc.ca/n1/pub/87f0006x/4068230-eng.htm.

———. "Unionization Rates Falling." Canadian Megatrends, The Daily, May 17, 2018, https://www150.statcan.gc.ca/n1/pub/11-630-x/11-630-x2015005-eng.htm.

———. "Value per Acre of Farm Land and Buildings at July 1." Table: 32-10-0047-01 (formerly CANSIM 002-0003), released May 26, 2021.

Supreme Court of Canada. "References re Greenhouse Gas Pollution Pricing Act." Case in Brief, last modified March 25, 2021, https://www.scc-csc.ca/case-dossier/cb/2021/38663-38781-39116-eng.aspx

MISCELLANEOUS: BROCHURES, PAMPHLETS, REPORTS, AND PAPERS PRESENTED AT MEETINGS

Bennett, Mary-Jane. "As the Crow Flies: Transportation Policy in Saskatchewan and the Crow's Nest Pass Agreement." Policy Series no. 191, Frontier Centre for Public Policy, Winnipeg, February 2017.

Dunn, Sheilagh M. "The Year in Review 1982: Intergovernmental Relations in Canada." Institute of Intergovernmental Relations, Queen's University, 1982, https://www.queensu.ca/iigr/sites/webpublish.queensu.ca.iigrwww/files/files/pub/archive/yearinreview/TheYearInReview1982-Dunn.pdf.

Farm Credit Canada. 2019 FCC Farmland Values Report. Regina: Farm Credit Canada, April 2020.

Jenny, Frederic. "Price Instability and Competition Law: The Case of the Potash Cartel." Presentation at OECD Global Forum on Competition, Paris, February 16–17, 2012, https://www.oecd.org/competition/globalforum/49737333.pdf.

Josling, Tim. "The Uruguay Round Agreement on Agriculture: A Forward-Looking Assessment." Paper presented at the OECD Workshop on Emerging Trade Issues in Agriculture, Paris, October 26–27, 1998.

Lorje, Pat. Open Up Saskatchewan! A Report on International Immigration and Inter-Provincial In-Migration Initiatives to Increase the Population of the Province of Saskatchewan. Regina: Government of Saskatchewan, Legislative Secretary, 2003.

Magnan, André, and Annette Aurélie Desmarais. Who Is Buying the Farm? Farmland Investment Patterns in Saskatchewan, 2003–14. Regina: Canadian Centre for Policy Alternatives, March 2017.

Marshall, Jim. "Saskatchewan Potash Taxes and Royalties: Is It Time for a Review?" Policy Brief, Johnson Shoyama Graduate School of Public Policy, January 21, 2019.

Miner, William M. "The Rise and Fall of Canadian Wheat Board." CAED Fellows
    Paper, 2015-2.
National Farmers Union. "Working for Farm Families for 40 Years." NFU, Saskatoon,
    October 2009.
Pratte, S. "Western Canadian Grain Transportation and the Maximum Revenue
    Entitlement: Process, Design Considerations and Final Implementation." Paper
    presented at "Canadian Transportation: 150 Years of Progress," the annual
    conference of the Canadian Transportation Research Forum, Winnipeg, May
    28–31, 2017, https://trid.trb.org/view/1537244.
Proulx, Stéfanie. "The Rise and Fall of the Canadian Wheat Board: A Historical
    Institutional Analysis." Research paper, Public and International Affairs,
    University of Ottawa, July 2012.
RBC Economics. *Canadian and Provincial Fiscal Tables.* November 16, 2021. http://
    www.rbc.com/economics/economic-reports/pdf/canadian-fiscal/prov_fiscal.pdf.
Saskatchewan Wheat Pool. *Saskatchewan Wheat Pool 1982 Annual Report.* Saskatoon,
    SK: Modern Press, 1983.
Scott, Gerry, Judy Bradley, Modeste McKenzie, Craig M. Scott, and Brian Topp.
    "Saskatchewan 2024: Making Change Happen; New Democratic Party of
    Saskatchewan Election Review Panel Report." New Democratic Party, April 2021.
Smale, B. *How Are Residents of Saskatchewan Really Doing?* A Report by Canadian
    Index of Wellbeing prepared for Heritage Saskatchewan and the Community
    Initiatives Fund. Waterloo, ON: Canadian Index of Wellbeing and the University
    of Waterloo, 2019.
Smith, Marc A., Lee Rainie, Ben Shneiderman, and Itai Himelboim. "Mapping Twitter
    Topic Networks: From Polarized Crowds to Community Clusters." Pew Research
    Center, February 20, 2014.
Swanson, Darren A., and Henry David Venema. "Analysis of the Crow Rate in Prairie
    Canada: A Cautionary Tale." Adaptive Policy Case Study, IISD-TERI-IDRC,
    International Institute for Sustainable Development, Canada, n.d.
Sweeney, Brendan A. *Canada's Automotive Industry: A Decade in Review.* London, ON:
    Trillium Network for Advanced Manufacturing, 2020.
Tatalovich, Raymond, and John Frendreis. "Fiscal Frugality: The Heart of Canadian
    Conservatism?" Paper presented at the annual meeting of the Canadian Political
    Science Association, Concordia University, Montreal, June 3, 2010.
Warnock, John W. *Exploiting Saskatchewan Potash: Who Benefits?* Regina: Canadian
    Centre for Policy Alternatives, 2011.

Index

Dale Eisler is a senior policy fellow at the Johnson Shoyama Graduate School of Public Policy, and *From Left to Right* is his fourth book. He is a former assistant deputy minister with the Government of Canada and Consul General for Canada in the United States. Prior to his career in government, he was a journalist in Saskatchewan and Alberta. Eisler is the author of two previous books on Saskatchewan politics, *False Expectations: Politics and the Pursuit of the Saskatchewan Myth* and *Rumours of Glory: Saskatchewan & the Thatcher Years*. He is also the author of the historical novel *Anton: A Young Boy, His Friend & the Russian Revolution*, which is the basis for the feature movie *Anton*, filmed on location in Ukraine and released in 2019.

Author Photo: University of Regina Photographic Services